LONGITUDES

AND

ATTITUDES

Exploring the World Before and After September 11

———

THOMAS FRIEDMAN

PENGUIN BOOKS

PENGUIN BOOKS

Published by the Penguin Group
Penguin Books Ltd, 80 Strand, London WC2R 0RL, England
Penguin Putnam Inc., 375 Hudson Street, New York, New York 10014, USA
Penguin Books Australia Ltd, 250 Camberwell Road, Camberwell, Victoria 3124, Australia
Penguin Books Canada Ltd, 10 Alcorn Avenue, Toronto, Ontario, Canada M4V 3B2
Penguin Books India (P) Ltd, 11 Community Centre, Panchsheel Park, New Delhi – 110 017, India
Penguin Books (NZ) Ltd, Cnr Rosedale and Airborne Roads,Albany, Auckland, New Zealand
Penguin Books (South Africa) (Pty) Ltd, 24 Sturdee Avenue, Rosebank 2196, South Africa

Penguin Books Ltd, Registered Offices: 80 Strand, London WC2R 0RL, England

www.penguin.com

First published in the United States of America by Farrar, Straus and Giroux 2002
First published in Great Britain by Penguin Books 2003
1

Copyright © Thomas L. Friedman, 2002, 2003
All rights reserved

The columns on which much of this book is based originally appeared in *The New York Times*, and to the extent that they are reprinted here they are reprinted with permission. *The New York Times* owns the copyright in the columns that were published in *The New York Times* newspaper. Inquiries concerning permission to reprint any column or portion thereof should be directed to the New York Times Company, News Services Division, Rights and Permissions, Ninth Floor, 229 West 43rd Street, New York, NY 10036

Grateful acknowledgement is made for permission to reprint material from the following: Excerpt from "Mending Wall" by Robert Frost from *The Poetry of Robert Frost*, edited by Edward Connery Lathem. Copyright © 1915, 1923, 1969 by Henry Holt and Co., copyright © 1958 by Robert Frost, copyright © 1967 Lesley Frost Ballantine. Reprinted by permission of Henry Holt and Company, LLC

Printed in England by Clays Ltd, St Ives plc

PENGUIN BOOKS

LONGITUDES AND ATTITUDES

Thomas Friedman has won the Pulitzer Prize three times for his work at *The New York Times*, where he is Foreign Affairs Columnist. He is the author of two bestselling books: *From Beirut to Jerusalem*, winner of the National Book Award for non-fiction and still considered the definitive work on the Middle East, and *The Lexus and the Olive Tree: Understanding Globalization*. He lives in Bethesda, Maryland, with his family.

To my girls,
Orly and Natalie Friedman

CONTENTS

———•———

Introduction to the Penguin Edition   ix

Introduction: A Word Album   xi

Prologue: The Super-Story   3

COLUMNS
Before: December 15, 2000–September 11, 2001   7
After: September 13, 2001–July 3, 2002   31

DIARY
Travels in a World Without Walls:
    September 11, 2001–July 3, 2002   319

Acknowledgments   397

INTRODUCTION TO THE
PENGUIN EDITION

I am thrilled that there is a British edition of *Longitudes and Attitudes*, but no doubt some in the vast English-speaking market stretching from London to Sydney will ask why they should read a book about the events of September 11, 2001? The short answer is that this event has so fundamentally transformed America and its relations with the rest of the world that it will either directly or indirectly impact every corner of the globe. Without understanding the traumatic impact 9/11 had on the American psyche, it will be impossible for non-Americans to make sense of Washington's behavior after 9/11. We are a different country, and in many ways this book is an American's travel guide to how different his country has become since 9/11 and the impact that this is having on his family, his nation, his nation's friends and his nation's enemies.

In some ways, the argument presented in this book is gloriously simple: 9/11 was the beginning of World War III. World War II was a war fought against Fascist totalitarianism. The Cold War was fought against Communist totalitarianism. World War III is a war being fought between open societies everywhere against religious totalitarians. America was simply the first target, but every open society is a potential target and every open society is being affected by the course of this war – in simple ways, such as heightened security measures everywhere, and in profound ways as a spillover from America's direct assault on the breeding grounds of this religious totalitarianism in the Middle East and Afghanistan.

In this World War III, the world is again divided in two, but the division is not between East and West, North or South, or even free and unfree. No, the new bipolar system is divided between the World of Order and the World of Disorder. The World of Order is built on five pillars – the U.S., the European Union, Russia, India and China, along with all the smaller powers around them. The World of Disorder is comprised of failed states (such as Liberia), rogue states (Iraq and

North Korea), messy states – states that are too big to fail but too messy to work (Pakistan, Colombia, Indonesia, many Arab and African states) and finally the terrorist and Mafia networks that feed off the World of Disorder.

There has always been a World of Disorder, but what makes it more dangerous today is that in a networked universe, with widely diffused technologies, open borders and a highly integrated global financial and Internet system, very small groups of people can amass huge amounts of power to disrupt the World of Order. Individuals can become super-empowered, and in some ways 9/11 was the first major battle between a superpower and a small band of super-empowered angry men from the World of Disorder.

The job of the five pillars of the World of Order is to work together, both bilaterally and through institutions like NATO and the UN, to help stabilize the World of Disorder, lift countries from it into the World Order, and coordinate police and military strategies to limit the ability of super-empowered angry people to disrupt the World of Order.

The columns and diary that make up this book catalogue the evolution of this new struggle – from small stories about my daughter's school, to interviews with the leader of Saudi Arabia, to analyses of how Gulf War II evolved. All the time, what I am trying to both explain and understand is how this huge event of 9/11 is transforming America – its agenda, priorities and anxieties – and how this transformed America is affecting everyone else.

In that sense, this is not an American book. It is a book by an American columnist (one who got his graduate degree from a British university, Oxford) about the biggest earthquake in his life and how he charted the aftershocks around the globe.

March 2003

INTRODUCTION: A WORD ALBUM

Long before the events of September 11, 2001, I always said that being the foreign affairs columnist for *The New York Times* was the best job in the world—the most fun you could have legally that I knew of. You got to be a tourist with an attitude, and they paid you for it. My basic view has not changed since 9/11, but I am not sure I would call the job "fun" since then. I think "compelling" would probably be a better description. It has been enormously compelling to have the freedom to explore, and write about, the biggest single news story in my life.

From the beginning, two concerns really drove my reporting. The first was a desire to fully comprehend who the nineteen suicide hijackers who burst into our lives on 9/11 were, and what motivated them to do what they did, and what motivated large parts of the Arab and Muslim worlds to give them passive support. It seemed to me that if we, as a nation, could not satisfactorily answer that big question—*Who were they?*—we would never begin to be safe again, and would never be able to take appropriate steps to protect ourselves from the next 9/11. The other issue that motivated me was a desire to better understand, and express, who we are—we, America. I tried to explore the attributes we have as a country—attributes that helped get us through this crisis but also helped explain why we were the targets of others' anger and envy.

This book is the product of my own personal journey of exploration. It has three parts. Part One consists of a prologue and eleven columns written before 9/11; I hope these analyses will help readers better understand the context of 9/11 and why I approached it the way I did. Part Two consists of virtually all my columns from September 13, 2001, to April 20, 2003. The columns are presented in chronological order as they appeared in *The New York Times*. Those written from abroad carry the dateline of the city I was in; those written from the United States bear no dateline. Part Three consists of the diary I kept during the raw, tumultuous months immediately after 9/11, as I journeyed around the Arab and Muslim worlds. Because as a columnist I write only twice a week, and only 740 words each time, I collect much more material, and have many more stimulating encounters, than I am able to fit into the columns. After 9/11, I began collecting some of these into a kind of diary that might give readers a sense of what was going on around me as I was writing the first year of post-9/11 columns, and why and how I developed some of the opinions that went into them. If the columns are my weekly dots, then the diary is my attempt to connect the dots.

Just a brief word about being a columnist. The only person who sees my two columns each week before they show up in the newspaper is a copy editor who edits them for grammar and spelling, but does not have any say about what opinion I adopt or where I go. In that sense, I am completely home alone. I decide where to travel and when. And I have total editorial freedom to take whatever stance I want on an issue. As I said, it's a great job! I have been the foreign affairs columnist since January 1995, and since then I have never had a conversation with the Publisher of *The New York Times* about any opinion I've adopted—before or after any column I've written. No one sent me to Afghanistan or Pakistan, Israel or Indonesia—they were all impulse visits based on my sense of where the larger story was at the time and what questions I thought needed answering or reflecting upon. I have total freedom, and an almost unlimited budget, to explore.

I've gone through several phases as a columnist. I started by focusing a lot on global economics, then on the whole phenomenon of globalization, then on NATO, the Middle East, China, and environmentalism. The events of 9/11 were particularly compelling for me because they brought together my two strongest interests—globalization and the Middle East. In the first year after 9/11, as the columns indicate, my focus was on the wider Muslim world and the Israeli-Palestinian conflict. In the second year after 9/11, I tended to focus on many of these same issues, in adddition to the whole global debate about the war with Iraq and then the war itself.

As a columnist, I want readers to have one of four reactions to my columns—any one will do. One reaction is for them to read a column and say: "I didn't know that." Sometimes it's fun to try to be a teacher. Another reaction is for them to read a column and say: "You know, I never looked at it that way before." It's also satisfying to give people a different perspective on events. Still another reaction—my favorite, really, as a columnist—is for them to read a column and declare: "You said *exactly* what I feel, but I didn't quite know how to express it." And, finally, another appropriate reaction is for them to read my column and say: "I hate you and everything you stand for." A column is defined as much by the people who hate it as by those who love it. I want to challenge, to provoke, and, at times, to get some of my readers angry. I am not looking to do it by provoking just to provoke. I am looking to do it by being very clear about what I feel. If I were afraid to do that, I would not be doing my job. I hope all the columns in this book fall into one of these four categories.

This collection and diary are not meant to be a comprehensive history or study of 9/11 or the U.S. invasion of Iraq, and all the factors that went into them. That is a task for historians. My hope is that this diary and these columns might provide them with some raw material—one reporter's journey in the world after 9/11, a journey that stretched from Jerusalem to Ground Zero, from Umm Qasr in southern Iraq to the Madrassahs of Pakistan, and from Cairo to the Muslim neighborhoods of Belgium. My hope is that this collection and diary will constitute a "word album" for the September 11 experience. There are many photo albums that people will collect to remind themselves, their children, or their grandchildren what it was like to experience 9/11. These columns and this diary are an attempt to capture and preserve in words, rather than pictures, some of those same emotions.

And now, on to the album.

LONGITUDES AND ATTITUDES

PROLOGUE: THE SUPER-STORY

I am a big believer in the idea of the super-story, the notion that we all carry around with us a big lens, a big framework, through which we look at the world, order events, and decide what is important and what is not. The events of 9/11 did not happen in a vacuum. They happened in the context of a new international system—a system that cannot explain everything but *can* explain and connect more things in more places on more days than anything else. That new international system is called globalization. It came together in the late 1980s and replaced the previous international system, the cold war system, which had reigned since the end of World War II. This new system is the lens, the super-story, through which I viewed the events of 9/11.

I define globalization as the inexorable integration of markets, transportation systems, and communication systems to a degree never witnessed before—in a way that is enabling corporations, countries, and individuals to reach around the world farther, faster, deeper, and cheaper than ever before, and in a way that is enabling the world to reach into corporations, countries, and individuals farther, faster, deeper, and cheaper than ever before.

Several important features of this globalization system differ from those of the cold war system in ways that are quite relevant for understanding the events of 9/11. I examined them in detail in my previous book, *The Lexus and the Olive Tree*, and want to simply highlight them here.

The cold war system was characterized by one overarching feature— and that was *division*. That world was a divided-up, chopped-up place, and whether you were a country or a company, your threats and opportunities in the cold war system tended to grow out of who you were divided from. Appropriately, this cold war system was symbolized by a single word—*wall*, the Berlin Wall.

The globalization system is different. It also has one overarching feature—and that is *integration*. The world has become an increasingly interwoven place, and today, whether you are a company or a country, your threats and opportunities increasingly derive from who you are connected to. This globalization system is also characterized by a single word—*web*, the World Wide Web. So in the broadest sense we have gone from an international system built around division and walls to a system increasingly built around integration and webs. In the cold war we reached for the hot line, which was a symbol that we were all divided but at least two people were in charge—the leaders of the United States and the Soviet Union. In the globalization system we reach for the Internet, which is a symbol that we are all connected and nobody is quite in charge.

Everyone in the world is directly or indirectly affected by this new system, but not everyone benefits from it, not by a long shot, which is why the more it becomes diffused, the more it also produces a backlash by people who feel overwhelmed by it, homogenized by it, or unable to keep pace with its demands.

The other key difference between the cold war system and the globalization system is how power is structured within them. The cold war system was built primarily around nation-states. You acted on the world in that system through your state. The cold war was a drama of states confronting states, balancing states, and aligning with states. And, as a system, the cold war was balanced at the center by two superstates, two superpowers: the United States and the Soviet Union.

The globalization system, by contrast, is built around three balances, which overlap and affect one another. The first is the traditional balance of power between nation-states. In the globalization system, the United States is now the sole and dominant superpower and all other nations are subordinate to it to one degree or another. The shifting balance of power between the United States and other states, or simply between other states, still very much matters for the stability of this system. And it can still explain a lot of the news you read on the front page of the paper, whether it is the news of China balancing Russia, Iran balancing Iraq, or India confronting Pakistan.

The second important power balance in the globalization system is between nation-states and global markets. These global markets are made up of millions of investors moving money around the world with the click of a mouse. I call them the Electronic Herd, and this herd gathers in key global financial centers—such as Wall Street, Hong Kong, London, and Frankfurt—which I call the Supermarkets. The attitudes and actions of the Electronic Herd and the Supermarkets can have a huge impact on nation-states today, even to the point of triggering the downfall of governments. Who ousted Suharto in Indonesia in 1998? It wasn't another state, it was the Supermarkets, by withdrawing their support for, and confidence in, the Indonesian economy. You also will not understand the front page of the newspaper today unless you bring the Supermarkets into your analysis. Because the United States can destroy you by dropping bombs, but the Supermarkets can destroy you by downgrading your bonds. In other words, the United States is the dominant player in maintaining the globalization game board, but it is hardly alone in influencing the moves on that game board.

The third balance that you have to pay attention to—the one that is really the newest of all and the most relevant to the events of 9/11—is the balance between individuals and nation-states. Because globalization has brought down many of the walls that limited the movement and reach of people, and because it has simultaneously wired the world into networks, it gives more power to *individuals* to influence both markets and nation-states than at any other time in history. Whether by enabling people to use the Internet to communicate instantly at almost no cost over vast distances, or by enabling them to use the Web to transfer money or obtain weapons designs that normally would have been controlled by states, or by enabling them to go into a hardware store now and buy a five-hundred-dollar global positioning device, connected to a satellite, that can direct a hijacked airplane—globalization can be an incredible force-multiplier for individuals. Individuals can increasingly act on the world stage directly, unmediated by a state.

So you have today not only a superpower, not only Supermarkets, but also what I call "super-empowered individuals." Some of these super-empowered individuals are quite angry, some of them quite wonderful—but all of them are now able to act much more directly and much more powerfully on the world stage.

Osama bin Laden declared war on the United States in the late 1990s. After he organized the bombing of two American embassies in Africa, the U.S. Air Force retaliated with a cruise missile attack on his bases in Afghanistan as though he were another nation-state. Think about that: on one day in 1998, the United States fired 75 cruise missiles at bin Laden. The United States fired 75 cruise missiles, at $1 million apiece, at a person! That was the first battle in history between a superpower and a super-empowered angry man. September 11 was just the second such battle.

Jody Williams won the Nobel Peace Prize in 1997 for helping to build an international coalition to bring about a treaty outlawing land mines. Although nearly 120 governments endorsed the treaty, it was opposed by Russia, China, and the United States. When Jody Williams was asked, "How did you do that? How did you organize one thousand different citizens' groups and nongovernmental organizations on five continents to forge a treaty that was opposed by the major powers?" she had a very brief answer: "E-mail." Jody Williams used e-mail and the networked world to super-empower herself.

Nation-states, and the American superpower in particular, are still hugely important today, but so too now are Supermarkets and super-empowered individuals. You will never understand the globalization system, or the front page of the morning paper—or 9/11—unless you see each as a complex interaction between all three of these actors: states bumping up against states, states bumping up against Supermarkets, and Supermarkets and states bumping up against super-empowered individuals—many of whom, unfortunately, are super-empowered angry men.

COLUMNS

———✦———

Before:

December 15, 2000–September 11, 2001

MEDAL OF HONOR

When Al Gore was in Vietnam he never saw much combat. Through-out his presidential campaign, though, he insisted he wanted to "fight" for every American. Well, Wednesday night, in his concession speech, Mr. Gore took a bullet for the country.

The shot was fired at the heart of the nation by the five conservative justices of the U.S. Supreme Court, with their politically inspired ruling that installed George W. Bush as President. The five justices essentially said that it was more important that Florida meet its self-imposed dead-line of December 12 for choosing a slate of electors than for the Florida Supreme Court to try to come up with a fair and uniform way to ensure that every possible vote in Florida was counted—and still meet the real federal deadline, for the nationwide Electoral College vote on Decem-ber 18. The five conservative justices essentially ruled that the sanctity of dates, even meaningless ones, mattered more than the sanctity of votes, even meaningful ones.

The Rehnquist Court now has its legacy: "In calendars we trust."

You don't need an inside source to realize that the five conservative justices were acting as the last in a team of Republican Party elders who helped drag Governor Bush across the finish line. You just needed to read the withering dissents of Justices Breyer, Ginsburg, Souter, and Stevens, who told the country exactly what their five colleagues were up to—acting without legal principle or logic and thereby inflicting a wound, said Justice Breyer, "that may harm not just the Court, but the nation."

Or, as the Harvard moral philosopher Michael Sandel put it: "Not only did the Court fail to produce any compelling argument of principle to justify its ruling. But, on top of that, the conservative majority contra-dicted its long-held insistence on protecting states' rights against federal interference. That's why this ruling looks more like partisanship than principle. And that's why many will conclude that the five conservative justices voted twice for President—once in November and once in December."

Which brings us back to Mr. Gore and his concession speech. It was the equivalent of taking a bullet for the country, because the rule of law is most reinforced when—even though it may have been imposed wrongly or with bias—the recipient of the judgment accepts it, and the system behind it, as final and legitimate. Only in that way—only when we reaffirm our fidelity to the legal system, even though it rules against us—can the system endure, improve, and learn from its mistakes. And that was exactly what Mr. Gore understood, bowing out with grace because, as he put it, "this is America, and we put country before party."

If Chinese or Russian spies are looking for the most valuable secret they can steal in Washington, here's a free tip: Steal Al Gore's speech. For in a few brief pages it contains the real secret to America's sauce.

That secret is not Wall Street, and it's not Silicon Valley, it's not the Air Force and it's not the Navy, it's not the free press and it's not the free market—it is the enduring rule of law and the institutions that underlie them all, and that allow each to flourish no matter who is in power.

One can only hope that Mr. Bush also understands that the ultimate strength of America and the impact it has on the world does not come from all the military systems he plans to expand (though they too are important), or from Intel's latest microchip. It comes from this remarkable system of laws and institutions we have inherited—a system, they say, that was designed by geniuses so it could be run by idiots.

Mr. Bush will soon discover that preserving this system is critical not only for America, it is critical for the world. America today is the Michael Jordan of geopolitics. Many envy the institutions and economy that ensure our dominance; others deeply resent us for the same. But all are watching our example—and all understand, at some level, that the stability of the world today rests on the ability of our system and economy to endure.

Al Gore reinforced that system by his graceful concession; Mr. Bush will have to reinforce it by his presidency. Now that the campaign is over and the system has determined the winner, no one should root for his failure. Because, as Al Gore would say, "this is America," and it's the only one we've got.

December 15, 2000

MY FAVORITE TEACHER

Last Sunday's *New York Times Magazine* published its annual review of people who died last year who left a particular mark on the world. I am sure all readers have their own such list. I certainly do. Indeed, someone who made the most important difference in my life died last year — my high school journalism teacher, Hattie M. Steinberg.

I grew up in a small suburb of Minneapolis, and Hattie was the legendary journalism teacher at St. Louis Park High School, Room 313. I took her Intro to Journalism course in tenth grade, back in 1969, and have never needed, or taken, another course in journalism since. She was that good.

Hattie was a woman who believed that the secret for success in life was getting the fundamentals right.

And boy, she pounded the fundamentals of journalism into her students — not simply how to write a lead or accurately transcribe a quote, but, more important, how to comport yourself in a professional way and to always do quality work. To this day, when I forget to wear a tie on assignment, I think of Hattie scolding me. I once interviewed an ad exec for our high school paper who used a four-letter word. We debated whether to run it. Hattie ruled yes. That ad man almost lost his job when it appeared. She wanted to teach us about consequences.

Hattie was the toughest teacher I ever had. After you took her journalism course in tenth grade, you tried out for the paper, *The Echo*, which she supervised. Competition was fierce. In eleventh grade, I didn't quite come up to her writing standards, so she made me business manager, selling ads to the local pizza parlors.

That year, though, she let me write one story. It was about an Israeli general who had been a hero in the Six-Day War, who was giving a lecture at the University of Minnesota. I covered his lecture and interviewed him briefly. His name was Ariel Sharon. First story I ever got published.

Those of us on the paper, and the yearbook that she also supervised, lived in Hattie's classroom. We hung out there before and after school. Now, you have to understand, Hattie was a single woman, nearing sixty at the time, and this was the 1960s. She was the polar opposite of "cool," but we hung around her classroom like it was a malt shop and she was Wolfman Jack. None of us could have articulated it then, but it was because we enjoyed being harangued by her, disciplined by her, and taught by her. She was a woman of clarity in an age of uncertainty.

We remained friends for thirty years, and she followed, bragged about, and critiqued every twist in my career. After she died, her friends sent me a pile of my stories that she had saved over the years. Indeed, her students were her family—only closer. Judy Harrington, one of Hattie's former students, remarked about other friends who were on Hattie's newspapers and yearbooks: "We all graduated forty-one years ago; and yet nearly each day in our lives something comes up—some mental image, some admonition, that makes us think of Hattie."

Judy also told the story of one of Hattie's last birthday parties, when one man said he had to leave early to take his daughter somewhere. "Sit down," said Hattie. "You're not leaving yet. She can just be a little late."

That was my teacher! I sit up straight just thinkin' about her.

Among the fundamentals Hattie introduced me to was *The New York Times*. Every morning it was delivered to Room 313. I had never seen it before then. Real journalists, she taught us, start their day by reading the *Times* and columnists like Anthony Lewis and James Reston.

I have been thinking about Hattie a lot this year, not just because she died on July 31, but because the lessons she imparted to us seem so relevant now. We've just gone through this huge dot.com-Internet-globalization bubble—during which a lot of smart people got carried away and forgot the fundamentals of how you build a profitable company, a lasting portfolio, a nation-state, or a thriving student. It turns out that the real secret of success in the information age is what it always was: fundamentals—reading, writing, and arithmetic; church, synagogue, and mosque; the rule of law and good governance.

The Internet can make you smarter, but it can't make you smart. It can extend your reach, but it will never tell you what to say at a PTA meeting. These fundamentals cannot be downloaded. You can only upload them, the old-fashioned way, one by one, in places like Room 313 at St. Louis Park High. I only regret that I didn't write this column when the woman who taught me all that was still alive.

January 9, 2001

CLINTON'S LAST MEMO

———

To: The Arab Street
From: President Bill Clinton

Dear ladies and gentlemen, over the last few years I've often written your leaders, but now that my term is ending I've decided my last letter should be to you, the Arab masses, the Arab street, who have paid such a high price for this ongoing conflict.

I'm going to be blunt. I've done all I could to build a fair, realistic pathway out of the Arab-Israeli conflict for both you and the Israelis, but if you want to continue fighting it out and avoiding a deal that gives you 95 percent of what you want, well, there's nothing more I can do.

But there is something I can say, and it's this: What troubles me most about the mood on the Arab street today is the hostility I detect there to modernization, globalization, democratization, and the information revolution. What you do with the Israelis is up to you now, but what you do with your own societies is going to affect the stability of the whole Middle East.

Where other countries are focused on developing world-class competitive industries, you are still focused on protecting your uncompetitive ones. Where others are aggressively trading with the world, you barely trade with each other. Where others are freeing their presses, you are still controlling yours. Where other world leaders are building their legitimacy by pushing education, most of yours are still building their legitimacy by pushing a religious conflict. Where others are seeking foreign investors in order to create jobs for their young people, you are driving off foreign investors with unfriendly bureaucracies and pursuit of a conflict that scares everyone away from your region. In an age when others are making microchips, you are making potato chips.

I would have thought that this reality would be a hotly debated subject among your elites, and I know some have raised it. But for the most part your intellectuals, pundits, and parliamentarians, rather than fostering an honest debate, prefer to make excuses. When I ask Arab leaders why South Korea had roughly the same per capita income in the early 1950s as Syria or Egypt, and now South Korea is a highly developed country and Syria and Egypt are still developing, the answer I get is that the Arab states had to fight wars. Well, South Korea had a struggle with North Korea for decades. Another excuse I get is that the Arab states had population problems. Well, so does China, and it's been growing at 10 percent per year.

Your intellectuals seem more interested in protecting their perks by coming up with excuses for the weakness of their regimes than in fostering an honest debate.

I realize that the issue of Israel and who rules over the Muslim holy places in Jerusalem touches the soul of the Arab street. I would not think of asking you to give up on controlling your religious sites. But I would urge you to consider asking more than one question. Who rules Al-Aksa Mosque is critical for the dignity of every Arab and Palestinian Muslim in the modern world. But what sort of education you offer your kids, what sort of economy you build, and what sort of rule of law you establish will also determine your dignity and standing in the modern world. You should be concerned with answering the old questions, but you have to recognize that they are not the only questions.

There has to be a balance. A society that forgets its roots will never be stable. But a society that is preoccupied with its roots, and is asking the question only of who owns which root, will never grow into the world or bear fruit. Your intellectuals don't care. They eat the fruit no matter what. They are protected by the regimes while they keep you living only by the old questions and the old role models. In doing so, they ensure that you never reach your full potential.

I understand you get frustrated with America. But when you follow the Arab elites into supporting Saddam Hussein, I don't understand. Forget about us; think about this man and what he has done to his neighbors, the poison gas he has used on his own people, the generation of Iraqis he has destroyed. Is this a role model? Is this the sort of Arab leader you want for your own societies?

I hope not. I hope one day soon I will see an intifada not only for an independent Palestine but for Arab education, for an Arab free press, for Arab legality, for Arab democracy. An Arab street that can ask only one question will, in the end, not be a very nice place to raise your kids.

Sincerely,
Bill Clinton

January 12, 2001

POWELL'S PERSPECTIVE

Secretary of State–designate Colin Powell has his Senate confirmation hearing this week. I doubt Mr. Powell will say much about specific policies. What I'd listen for is whether he offers a big-picture view of the world, as we really don't know what his views are since he left Army service in 1993.

One way to think about Mr. Powell is this: He spent thirty-five years of his life with America Onduty, as a military officer. But for the past two years he's been associated with America Online, as a member of the AOL corporate board. So which perspective will Mr. Powell bring to his job as Secretary of State—the perspective he gleaned with America Onduty during the cold war or the perspective he gleaned with America Online in the post–cold war?

These are two different perspectives: America Onduty tends to see the world as being built around walls and America Online tends to see the world as being built around webs.

That is, America Onduty believes that U.S. foreign policy has been, and continues to be, about defending, erecting, and bringing down walls. That means building walls of containment around enemies or rivals, from North Korea to Iraq to China. It means being largely indifferent to what goes on behind the walls of countries as long as they are not bothering us—e.g., not really caring how Russia's internal reform plays out—and it means working to bring down the last few walls of Communism around North Korea and Cuba.

America Online, by contrast, sees America at the center of an increasingly integrated global web—a web of trade, telecommunications, finance, and environment. For America Online, U.S. foreign policy is about protecting that web from those who would disrupt it, strengthening that web, and expanding it to others—because, after all, America is now the biggest beneficiary of that web, since American products, technologies, values, ideas, movies, and foods are the most widely distributed through it.

One way you preserve that web is by being prepared to defend it from those who would disrupt it, such as Saddam Hussein. Another way is by being ready to promote the expansion of free trade, to join with others in protecting the global environment, or to help with bailouts when key strands of the web—such as Mexico or Thailand—are threatened with financial crises that could infect the whole network. Still another way is by putting a higher priority on working with Russia to solve web problems that endanger us both—such as nuclear or missile proliferation—rather than by expanding NATO's wall to Russia's border, thus making cooperation with Moscow impossible.

The wall people, the America Onduty people, love the movie *A Few Good Men*, particularly the closing scene where Jack Nicholson, the tough marine colonel, sneers at Tom Cruise, the navy lawyer who has Mr. Nicholson on trial for the death of a weak U.S. soldier on a U.S. base in Cuba during the cold war.

Mr. Nicholson says: "Son, we live in a world that has walls, and those walls have to be guarded by men with guns. Who's gonna do it? You? . . . Deep down, in places you don't talk about at parties, you want me on that wall. You need me on that wall."

The web people, the America Online people, love the movie *You've Got Mail*, because they know that in today's more integrated world we can, and do, get mail from all kinds of strangers that can suddenly change our lives. When Russia has a financial crisis now, we've got mail. When a networked world enables small terrorist groups to become super-empowered so they can blow up a U.S. destroyer in Yemen with a dinghy, we've got mail. When two Filipino computer hackers put their "Love Bug" virus on the World Wide Web and melt down ten million computers and $10 billion in data in twenty-four hours, we've got mail.

For the America Onduty people, the world is divided between friends and enemies. For the America Online people, it is divided between members and nonmembers of the network. The America Onduty people focus on who's on America's terrorism list. The America Online people focus on who's on America's buddy list.

Yes, these are caricatures. But there's something to them. They reflect two different ways of looking at the world. So which lens is Mr. Powell wearing—the one he developed with America Onduty, or with America Online?

January 16, 2001

CYBER-SERFDOM

The Davos World Economic Forum is always useful for gauging global trends. In recent years much of the buzz at Davos was about what technology will do for us. This year, more and more, the buzz has been about what technology is doing to us. If Davos is any indicator, there is a backlash brewing against the proliferation of technology in our lives.

When participants arrived at Davos this year, they were given yet another gadget to communicate with other participants—a Compaq pocket PC. As I fumbled around trying to figure out how mine worked, and interfaced with the complex Davos e-mail system that you access with a badge, the *Washington Post* columnist Richard Cohen, who was trying to do the same, said to me: "I have so many devices now to make my life easier that I need someone just to carry them all around for me."

Then there was the panel about the twenty-first-century corporation, during which participants described this age of digital Darwinism in chilling terms: The key to winning in business today is adapt or die, get wired or get killed, work twenty-four hours a day from everywhere or be left behind. Finally, during the question time, Howard Stringer, chairman of Sony America, stood up and said: "Doesn't anyone here think this sounds like a vision of hell? While we are all competing or dying, when will there be time for sex or music or books? Stop the world, I want to get off."

To be sure, this is a developed-world problem. In much of Africa you don't see executives walking around, as you do in Europe, with so many beepers, phones, and pagers clipped onto their belts that they look like telephone repairmen. But with the cost of this technology rapidly decreasing, it will spread faster than you think. And so will the social stresses associated with it. Apropos of such a future, I heard a lot of new phrases this week: "device creep," "Machines don't serve us, we serve them," and "My identity is now less important than the data that is stored about me." Have a nice day.

My favorite, though, was that we now live in an age of what a Microsoft researcher, Linda Stone, called continuous partial attention. I love that phrase. It means that while you are answering your e-mail and talking to your kid, your cell phone rings and you have a conversation. You are now involved in a continuous flow of interactions in which you can only partially concentrate on each.

"If being fulfilled is about committing yourself to someone else, or some experience, that requires a level of sustained attention," said Ms. Stone. And that is what we are losing the skills for, because we are constantly scanning the world for opportunities and we are constantly in fear of missing something better. That has become incredibly spiritually depleting.

I am struck by how many people call my office, ask if I'm in, and, if I'm not, immediately ask to be connected to my cell phone or pager. (I carry neither.) You're never out anymore. The assumption now is that you're always in. Out is over. Now you are always in. And when you are always in, you are always on. And when you are always on, what are you most like? A computer server.

They say these devices will eventually be invisible, but for now they feel in your face. And here's the scary part: It's just the beginning. By 2005 we will see a convergence of wireless technology, fiber optics, software applications, and next-generation Internet switches, IP version 6, that will permit anything with electricity to have a Web address and run off the Internet—from your bedroom lights to your toaster to your pacemaker (which will report your heart rate directly to your doctor). This Evernet will allow us all to be on-line all the time from everywhere. People will boast: "I have twenty-five Web addresses in my house; how many do you have? My wired refrigerator automatically reorders milk. How about yours?"

The problem is that human beings simply are not designed to be like computer servers. For one thing, they are designed to sleep eight hours a night. So there is a big misfit brewing here. I still can't program my VCR; how am I going to program my toaster? As Jeffrey Garten, dean of the Yale School of Management and author of a smart new book that deals with some of these themes, *The Mind of the C.E.O.*, said: "Maybe it's not time for us to adapt or die, but for the technology to adapt or die."

January 30, 2001

SHARON, ARAFAT, AND MAO

So I'm at the Davos World Economic Forum two weeks ago, and Shimon Peres walks by. One of the reporters with him asks me if I'm going to hear Mr. Peres and Yasir Arafat address the one thousand global investors and ministers attending Davos. No, I tell him, I have a strict rule, I'm only interested in what Mr. Arafat says to his own people in Arabic. Too bad, says the reporter, because the fix is in. Mr. Peres is going to extend an olive branch to Mr. Arafat, Mr. Arafat is going to do the same back, and the whole lovefest will get beamed back to Israel to boost the peace process and Ehud Barak's reelection. Good, I'll catch it on TV, I said.

Well, Mr. Peres did extend the olive branch, as planned, but Mr. Arafat torched it. Reading in Arabic from a prepared text, Mr. Arafat denounced Israel for its "fascist military aggression" and "colonialist armed expansionism," and its policies of "murder, persecution, assassination, destruction, and devastation."

Mr. Arafat's performance at Davos was a seminal event, and is critical for understanding Ariel Sharon's landslide election. What was Mr. Arafat saying by this speech, with Mr. Peres sitting by his side? First, he was saying that there is no difference between Mr. Barak and Mr. Sharon. Because giving such a speech on the eve of the Israeli election, in the wake of an eleventh-hour Barak bid to conclude a final deal with the Palestinians in Taba, made Mr. Barak's far-reaching offer to Mr. Arafat look silly. Moreover, Mr. Arafat was saying that there is no difference between Mr. Peres and Mr. Sharon, because giving such a speech just after the warm words of Mr. Peres made Mr. Peres look like a dupe, as all the Israeli papers reported. Finally, at a time when Palestinians are starving for work, Mr. Arafat's subliminal message to the global investors was: Stay away.

That's why the press is asking exactly the wrong question about the Sharon election. They're asking, Who is Ariel Sharon? The real question is, Who is Yasir Arafat? The press keeps asking: Will Mr. Sharon become another Charles de Gaulle, the hard-line general who pulled the French army out of Algeria? Or will he be Richard Nixon, the anti-

Communist who made peace with Communist China? Such questions totally miss the point.

Why? Because Israel just had its de Gaulle. His name was Ehud Barak. Mr. Barak was Israel's most decorated soldier. He abstained in the cabinet vote over the Oslo II peace accords. But once in office he changed 180 degrees. He offered Mr. Arafat 94 percent of the West Bank for a Palestinian state, plus territorial compensation for most of the other 6 percent, plus half of Jerusalem, plus restitution and resettlement in Palestine for Palestinian refugees. And Mr. Arafat not only said no to all this, but described Israel as "fascist" as Mr. Barak struggled for reelection. It would be as though de Gaulle had offered to withdraw from Algeria and the Algerians said: "Thank you. You're a fascist. Of course we'll take all of Algeria, but we won't stop this conflict until we get Bordeaux, Marseilles, and Nice as well."

If the Palestinians don't care who Ariel Sharon is, why should we? If Mr. Arafat wanted an Israeli leader who would not force him to make big decisions, which he is incapable of making, why should we ask whether Mr. Sharon is going to be de Gaulle and make him a big offer? What good is it for Israel to have a Nixon if the Palestinians have no Mao?

The Oslo peace process was about a test. It was about testing whether Israel had a Palestinian partner for a secure and final peace. It was a test that Israel could afford, it was a test that the vast majority of Israelis wanted, and it was a test that Mr. Barak courageously took to the limits of the Israeli political consensus—and beyond. Mr. Arafat squandered that opportunity. Eventually Palestinians will ask for a makeup exam. And eventually Israelis may want to give it to them, if they again see a chance to get this conflict over with. But who knows what violence and pain will be inflicted in the meantime?

All we know is that for now, the Oslo test is over. That is what a vast majority of Israelis said in this election. So stop asking whether Mr. Sharon will become de Gaulle. That is not why Israelis elected him.

They elected him to be Patton. They elected Mr. Sharon because they know exactly who he is, and because seven years of Oslo have taught them exactly who Yasir Arafat is.

February 8, 2001

HYPE AND ANTI-HYPE

The Gartner Group consultants have developed a useful concept to describe the hype around new technologies, which they call the "hype cycle." As a new technology—like the Internet—is triggered, the hype curve soars upward until it reaches a peak of inflated expectations. Then it sinks almost straight down into a trough of disillusionment as the less successful players drop out. And finally it climbs steadily upward again to a new stable plateau as clear winners emerge and the new technology is absorbed, integrated, and made profitable by people and industries that understand it.

According to the hype curve, where we are now with the Internet is in the trough—where all those who didn't really understand it or who are disillusioned by their dot.com investments pronounce it all a bubble. This trough, though, can be as misleading as the hype cycle's peak. If you think that just because Pets.com didn't make it the Internet is over, then you're not paying attention.

The real Internet wars are just beginning, and they aren't going to be between Amazon.com and eToys.com. The real Internet wars happen when all the old-line companies with real assets, real size, and real business models fully absorb the Internet—including e-commerce, e-inventory, e-bookkeeping, e-training, e-customer management—into their traditional businesses and start to take each other on with meaner, leaner companies.

The real Internet wars happen when Goliaths like Target, Kmart, and Wal-Mart, or GM, Toyota, and Ford, or Dell and Compaq, fully absorb the Internet to speed up, lighten up, and globalize every aspect of their businesses. And the real Internet wars also happen when the NGOs, human rights groups, conservationists, and other activists become fully Internet-enabled and use its power to challenge big companies and to force transparency on big governments.

As Jeffrey Garten writes in his new book, *The Mind of the C.E.O.*, "The big question is whether today's C.E.O.'s have the savvy and the stamina to defeat the dot.coms, which is the first leg of the race, and then run this second, more difficult and much longer race against their peers—or whether it will take their successors to do it."

The measure of what's happening with the Internet today is not Buy.com or the Nasdaq. It's what is happening in China, where Internet deployment is moving so fast that Chinese will be the most popular language on the Web by 2007; in India, where AOL just announced a $100 million investment; and in Europe, where the net economy is expected to grow twentyfold by 2004.

"People talked about the Internet as a business revolution; it actually constitutes more of a business evolution," argues Orit Gadiesh, the chairman of Bain & Company consultants. "Revolution is when the nature or distribution of power shifts. But what is happening now is that the traditional holders of assets are absorbing the Internet and leveraging it as a tool. The Internet is, though, an instrument of social revolution. It has put power in different people's hands and connected people who have never been connected before."

Because the Internet build-out is proceeding apace, the next generation could trigger a business revolution as well. "Internet II," about four years away, will combine broadband, wireless, and IPv6 Internet switches, which will enable everything with electricity to have its own Web address that will make it intelligent. So your refrigerator will be able to talk to your grocery store over the Web, or your company's cash registers directly to your manufacturer's assembly line. "Internet II is a smarter Internet that will allow us to have many more devices connected and controlled, and to be informed about those devices," says Bill Nuti, the president of Cisco Europe.

As this Internet build-out continues, says Joel Cawley, the director of business strategy for IBM, it will enable businesses, individuals, and activists to tap into a much broader and more powerful base of creativity and innovation with a much lighter touch. "So," he adds, "smaller and smaller units will become more and more empowered and bigger and bigger units will become more and more decentralized. None of us knows how this will play out, but we do know it will impact the hierarchy of power in, and between, institutions, governments, and activists. And the new rules for these interactions are just beginning to be evolved."

February 23, 2001

CODE RED

So I came home the other night, and one of my daughters was doing her homework and asked me to remind her which were the good guys: the North Koreans or South Koreans? That triggered a dinner table discussion of the cold war and the Cuban missile crisis. I explained that I vividly remember listening to the radio during the Cuba crisis and that our school had regular drills where we had to hide in the basement during a simulated nuclear attack.

Oh, my daughters said to me, we have those kinds of drills too. When I asked them to explain, it quickly became apparent that the threat they were practicing for was not a nuclear attack, and not just a bad storm, but an attack by an armed student or intruder shooting up their public schools. We have "code red" and "code blue," my daughters, ages twelve and fifteen, said. Code blue means all students must remain in their classroom or go immediately there. Code red means a total lockdown—all students must remain in their classroom or rush to the nearest classroom. Teachers must lock their classroom doors, move students into the safest corner, keep them silent, and cover the window of their classroom door with paper so no gunman can see if students are inside.

There you have it: My kids aren't quite sure whether North Korea or South Korea is on our side, but they know the difference between code red and code blue. I grew up terrified of another superpower with a nuclear missile. They grow up terrified of a super-empowered angry person with an automatic weapon. I knew the threat to my life came from Moscow. They have no idea which student might be carrying a gun or a knife.

Which brings me to the latest news: What is it that we and the Russians are actually spying on each other about? This whole espionage affair seems straight out of *Mad* magazine's "Spy vs. Spy" cartoon. The Russians are spying on us to try to find out why we are spying on them. I mean, be honest, is there anything about the Russians today you want to know?

Their navy is rusting in port. Their latest nuclear submarine is resting on the bottom of the ocean. We know they're selling weapons to Iran and Iraq, because they told us. And their current political system, unlike

Communism, is not exactly exportable—unless you think corruption, chaos, and KGB rule amount to an ideology. Khrushchev threatened to bury us. Putin threatens to corrupt us.

I was friendly with one of the Russian diplomats who was sent home for spying. He was very smart, very likable, and never asked me for anything except to pick up the bill for lunch. He spent most of our meetings complaining about how stupid his government was. Maybe it was all an act, but it was sure delivered with enthusiasm.

Which brings me back to my daughters' schools. While what threatened me when I was their age—the Soviet Union—is different from what threatens them—a troubled student—they have one big feature in common: they have no simple cures. When authority is lost at the state level, or at the home level, it's not easy to recover. Such nations, and such families, become ungovernable, and threaten us by their weakness, not their strength. Children or countries without a sense of direction, but with easy access to weapons, are dangerous.

How you pull a country like Russia away from becoming an angry, failed state, acting out on the world stage, and make it a responsible member of the world community has no easy formula. And how you pull a lost young person away from becoming an angry assassin and make him instead a responsible member of the local community has no easy formula.

Kids now grow up in diverse and fractured homes, and dealing with the most disturbed ones requires multiple approaches. Head Start alone, or midnight basketball alone, or more testing alone, won't do it. So it is with countries. How a country like Russia builds the rule of law, an honest civil service, and the habits of a modern democratic society is so much more complex a task than simply importing textbooks, holding elections, or bringing Russia into the G-7.

Which brings me back to my dinner table. About the only thing we do know for sure is where the cure has to start. It has to start in the home, the basic building block for any community or country. Nothing good will happen in your statehouse, or in your schoolhouse, if it does not start, and is not sustained, in your own house.

March 30, 2001

THEY HATE US! THEY NEED US!

Reading about all the anti-Americanism President Bush has encountered on his trip to Europe, I was reminded of the 1970s Randy Newman song "Political Science." In its main verse he wryly laments that no matter how much we do for the world, nobody likes us. What to do about it? Newman proposes we just nuke the whole rest of the world—allies and all—so we'll be left without any complainers: "Drop the big one and see what happens."

Mr. Newman's ditty is a reminder that anti-Americanism didn't start with George Dubya. The key question is whether there is anything new in today's anti-Americanism and whether it has any strategic consequences.

Actually, there are a couple of things new. You can taste it in Greece. In his upcoming book *Unholy Alliance: Greece and Milošević's Serbia*, the Greek journalist Takis Michas explains that during the cold war anti-Americanism in Greece and Europe tended to be driven by the left and focused on "what America did"—and how it wasn't living up to its own ideals when it backed dictators in Greece and elsewhere.

Today's version of anti-Americanism in Europe is more focused on "what America is," says Mr. Michas, and it brings together the far left, the far right, and the Orthodox Church. The old left hates America for its free-market capitalism, the death penalty, and globalization. The far right hates it for promoting its multiculturalism in the Balkans, which threatens Greek nationalism. And the Orthodox Archbishop hates America for enticing Greek youths away from their heritage and religion.

Fine: so now the Europeans don't like us for who we are. Does it matter? Is it producing an alliance of countries against America that threatens our vital interests? That's the real question.

Not yet, says the German foreign policy analyst Josef Joffe, in a smart essay in the journal *The National Interest* titled "Who's Afraid of Mr. Big?" Mr. Joffe argues that one reason no alliance has formed against America yet is that, while resentment of America is rife, particularly among European elites, the attraction of America—its culture, universities, movies, food, clothing, and technologies—is just as strong, and today no power in the world can balance it. For every European elitist who resents America for what it is, there are ten Euro-kids who want what America is. "America is both menace and seducer, both monster and model," says Mr. Joffe.

While America's soft power can't be balanced—there's no Disney World in Moscow, no Harvard in Beijing—America's hard power doesn't need to be balanced. "Why is there no real ganging up against the United States?" asks Mr. Joffe. "[Because] America annoys and antagonizes, but it does not conquer. He who does not conquer does not provoke counteralliances and war." Mr. Joffe refers to today's European anti-Americanism as "neo-ganging up"—noisy but not serious.

Another reason we have not provoked an alliance against us is that America continues to be willing to provide "public goods" to the global system, says Mr. Joffe. Public goods are things that everyone can benefit from—keeping the sea-lanes open, stabilizing the free-trade system, or beating back bad guys in Iraq. This gives lesser powers an incentive to cooperate with us even as they criticize us; otherwise who else would uphold global security and financial stability?

This is hugely important. History teaches that periods of relative peace occur when you have a benign power that is ready to provide public services to maintain an orderly global system—even if it means paying a disproportionate share of the costs.

That's why the greatest danger today is not European anti-Americanism, but American anti-Americanism. The greatest danger is if America is no longer ready to play America—the benign superpower that pays a disproportionate price to maintain the system of which it's the biggest beneficiary. This could happen because Congress becomes too cheap or stupid, or because our economy becomes too enfeebled, or because we have an administration dominated by people unwilling to put any limits on U.S. behavior, from energy consumption to missile defense. That sort of America, if taken to extremes, could nullify our attractiveness and generate an alliance against us. Surely the Bushies know that—don't they?

June 15, 2001

A MEMO FROM OSAMA

To: All field operatives
From: Osama bin Laden

My men: This is a great day! Did you see what we accomplished last week? We drove the U.S. armed forces out of three Arab countries by just threatening to hit them. I had some of our boys discuss an attack against the U.S. over cell phones, the CIA picked it up, and look what happened: the FBI team in Yemen, which was investigating our destruction of the U.S.S. *Cole* in Aden harbor, just packed up and left—even though the State Department was begging them to stay. See ya. Then, after we made a few more phone calls, hundreds of U.S. marines—marines!—who were conducting a joint exercise with the Jordanian Army cut short their operation, got back on their amphibious vessels, and fled Jordan on Saturday. See ya. Then all the U.S. warships in Bahrain, which is the headquarters of the U.S. Fifth Fleet, were so scared of being hit by us they evacuated Bahrain's harbor and sailed out into the Persian Gulf. Boys, there is a military term for all this; it's called a "retreat." Allahu Akbar! God is Great!

This is a superpower? The Americans turned tail as soon as they picked up a few threats from us. The U.S. press barely reported it; the White House press didn't even ask the President about it. But trust me, everyone out here noticed it. It told them many things: The Americans are afraid of sustaining even one casualty to their soldiers; they don't trust their own intelligence or weak Arab allies to protect them; and they have no military answer for our threat.

I love America. The Bush people want to spend $100 billion on a missile defense shield to deal with a threat that doesn't yet exist, and they run away from the threat that already exists. They think we rogues are going to attack them with an intercontinental ballistic missile with a return address on it. Are they kidding? Am I wearing a sign that says STU-PID on it? We'll hit them the way the Iranians blew up the U.S. base at Al Khobar, in Saudi Arabia. We'll use layers of local operatives who can't be traced to any country. Look at the indictment the U.S. courts just passed down for the Al Khobar bombing. They named fourteen people, and they hinted that Iranian agents had coordinated them all, but they had no proof, so they could never pin it on Iran, so they could never retaliate against Iran.

The people who had the proof were the Saudis, but they refused to turn it over to the FBI. Why? Because the Saudis never trusted the Americans to retaliate properly. They figured the U.S. would launch a few cruise missiles at Iran and then run—leaving the Saudis to face Iran alone. Which reminds me, the Russians have hinted that if the U.S. builds a missile defense system against Russia's wishes, the Russians will just sell more missiles to Iraq, Iran, or China to overwhelm the system. The fools at the Bush Pentagon say the Russians would never do that because the missiles would also threaten them. Oh, yeah? The Russians don't believe in missile shields. They believe in classic deterrence. When the Chechens blew up a few apartment blocks in Moscow with human missiles, the Russians blew up Chechnya. Remember when four Russian diplomats were kidnapped in Beirut in 1985? The Russians retaliated by kidnapping a member of the kidnappers' group, chopping off one of his body parts, and sending it back in the mail. Presto! The Russians were released. This isn't Norway out here.

That's why we'd never mess with the Russians. But the great thing is that Donald Rumsfeld is so obsessed with getting his missile-shield toy, he's been telling everyone that deterrence doesn't work anymore against people like us. So they need a missile shield instead. And Bush just repeats it. I love it, because we are not going to attack America's strength at home, we are going to attack soft U.S. targets abroad through shadows. So I hope the Americans invest all their defense budget in a Star Wars shield that will have no effect on us, but will divert them from the real means and the real deterrence that could hurt us.

Yo, Rummy, who needs missiles? We just drove the FBI, the Marines, and the U.S. Navy out of the Middle East with a few threats whispered over Nokia cell phones! So who's the dummy, Rummy?

God is Great. America is stupid. Revolution until victory.

Osama@Jihadonline [JOL]

June 26, 2001

WALLS

———◆———

As I was preparing to leave for this trip the other day, my teenage daughter asked me where I was going. "Israel," I said.

"Why do you have to go there?" she asked, with a worried frown.

Hmm, I thought. I've been visiting Israel since my youth, but my daughter—who was born in Jerusalem while I was there as the *Times* bureau chief—now thinks it's Kosovo.

Think how corrosive this will be for Israel and world Jewry, if this cycle of Palestinian suicide bombs and Israeli retaliations continues. A hard core of Orthodox Jews and Middle East nuts like myself will continue to visit Israel, but no matter how many solidarity marches they hold in New York, the next generation of American Jews will not share an intimate connection with the Jewish state.

I relate this story because it's one of the many "mini-partitions" that have been set off by Intifada II and the collapse of Oslo. What's happening is that the big diplomacy is totally stuck. Israel, the PLO, the Bush team, and the Arabs lack either the power, the will, or the way to separate, with a grand partition, into a Jewish state and a Palestinian state.

In fact, the status quo is politically quite tolerable for both the Palestinian leader, Yasir Arafat, and Israel's prime minister, Ariel Sharon. For the moment, each is riding high in the polls, and neither has to confront his hard-line base and say the game is up. The status quo is also tolerable for President Bush, because as long as there is no peace process he doesn't have to pressure Israel to compromise, which is the last thing he wants to do, since it would inevitably force a clash with U.S. Jews, whose votes and donations he needs to protect his GOP majority in the House.

But while the leaders are unable to forge the big partition, and can tolerate the status quo, the people increasingly can't. So what's happening on the ground is a million little personal partitions. People all over Israel are building their own walls to separate themselves from danger. "Everyone is now their own minister of defense," said an Israeli colleague.

West Bank settlers are isolated from friends in Israel because they are afraid to take responsibility for inviting anyone to visit their settlements for fear they will be shot on the roads. Israeli parents refuse to let their kids go to malls, cinemas, or discos that might be targets of suicide bombers. "First I decide which movie theater I think will be the safest, then I check which movie is playing," an Israeli mother told me.

You drive north to the Jerusalem suburb of Psagot, which overlooks Ramallah, and you find that the houses with the best view of the Ramallah hills now have an anti-sniper concrete wall in front of them and sandbags on the windows. You drive south, between the Jerusalem suburb of Gilo and the Arab village of Beit Jala, and there is another long concrete wall blocking snipers from hitting Gilo, but also sealing in Gilo. There are Hebrew posters all over this wall that read THE NEW MIDDLE EAST. Some Israeli coffee shops now have security guards at the door to deter suicide bombers.

I was driving with an Israeli journalist to Har Gilo, an Israeli settlement south of Jerusalem, when we came to an Israeli checkpoint at a fork in the road; one branch went to Jerusalem and the other to the Arab village of Vallaje. When we accidentally turned down the branch to the Arab village, an Israeli soldier angrily waved us back: "Do you want to get lynched?" he exclaimed. Think about this: Vallaje is an Arab village that is actually part of Israel-annexed East Jerusalem. But while it is officially part of Jerusalem, no Jew can go there anymore. There's a wall.

The building of Israeli settlements all over the West Bank has made the big partition, or even unilateral separation, extremely difficult. And Mr. Arafat's mendacity has made it even harder. But living with Palestinian suicide bombers and Israeli retaliations has become unbearable for Israelis, and Palestinians, so people are just building a wall, or carrying one around in their heads—partitioning themselves wherever they can. Israelis wall themselves into their homes and wall the Palestinians off their roads, and the Palestinians go to Durban and try to wall the Israelis off from the world.

There are so many walls going up around here you can't tell anymore: Who is jailing whom?

September 11, 2001

COLUMNS

———◆———

After:

September 13, 2001–July 3, 2002

WORLD WAR III

As I restlessly lay awake early yesterday, with CNN on my TV and dawn breaking over the holy places of Jerusalem, my ear somehow latched onto a statement made by the U.S. transportation secretary, Norman Mineta, about the new precautions that would be put in place at U.S. airports in the wake of Tuesday's unspeakable terrorist attacks: There will be no more curbside check-in, he said.

I suddenly imagined a group of terrorists somewhere here in the Middle East, sipping coffee, also watching CNN, and laughing hysterically: "Hey boss, did you hear that? We just blew up Wall Street and the Pentagon and their response is no more curbside check-in?"

I don't mean to criticize Mr. Mineta. He is doing what he can. And I have absolutely no doubt that the Bush team, when it identifies the perpetrators, will make them pay dearly. Yet there was something so absurdly futile and American about the curbside ban that I couldn't help but wonder: Does my country really understand that this is World War III? And if this attack was the Pearl Harbor of World War III, it means there is a long, long war ahead.

And this Third World War does not pit us against another superpower. It pits us—the world's only superpower and quintessential symbol of liberal, free-market Western values—against all the super-empowered angry men and women out there. Many of these super-empowered angry people hail from failing states in the Muslim and third world. They do not share our values; they resent America's influence over their lives, politics, and children, not to mention our support for Israel; and they often blame America for the failure of their societies to master modernity.

What makes them super-empowered, though, is their genius at using the networked world, the Internet and the very high technology they hate, to attack us. Think about it: They turned our most advanced civilian planes into human-directed, precision-guided cruise missiles—a diabolical melding of their fanaticism and our technology. Jihad On-line. And think of what they hit: *the World Trade Center*, the beacon of American-led capitalism that both tempts and repels them, and the Pentagon, the embodiment of American military superiority.

And think about what places in Israel the Palestinian suicide bombers have targeted most. "They never hit synagogues or settlements or Israeli religious zealots," said the *Ha'aretz* columnist Ari Shavit. "They hit the Sbarro pizza parlor, the Netanya shopping mall. The Dolphinarium disco. They hit the yuppie Israel, not the yeshiva Israel."

So what is required to fight a war against such people in such a world? To start with, we as Americans will never be able to penetrate such small groups, often based on family ties, who live in places such as Afghanistan, Pakistan, or Lebanon's wild Bekaa Valley. The only people who can penetrate these shadowy and ever-mutating groups, and deter them, are their own societies. And even they can't do it consistently. So give the CIA a break.

Israeli officials will tell you that the only time they have had real quiet and real control over the suicide bombers and radical Palestinian groups, such as Hamas and Islamic Jihad, is when Yasir Arafat and his Palestinian Authority tracked them, jailed them, or deterred them.

So then the question becomes, What does it take for us to get the societies that host terrorist groups to truly act against them?

First, we have to prove that we are serious, and that we understand that many of these terrorists hate our existence, not just our policies. In June I wrote a column about the fact that a few cell-phone threats from Osama bin Laden had prompted President Bush to withdraw the FBI from Yemen, a U.S. Marine contingent from Jordan, and the U.S. Fifth Fleet from its home base in the Persian Gulf. This U.S. retreat was noticed all over the region, but it did not merit a headline in any major U.S. paper. That must have encouraged the terrorists. Forget about our civilians, we didn't even want to risk our soldiers to face their threats.

The people who planned Tuesday's bombings combined world-class evil with world-class genius to devastating effect. And unless we are ready to put our best minds to work combating them—the World War III Manhattan Project—in an equally daring, unconventional, and unremitting fashion, we're in trouble. Because while this may have been the first major battle of World War III, it may be the last one that involves only conventional nonnuclear weapons.

Second, we have been allowing a double game to go on with our Middle East allies for years, and that has to stop. A country like Syria has to decide: Does it want a Hezbollah embassy in Damascus or an American one? If it wants a U.S. embassy, then it cannot play host to a rogue's gallery of terrorist groups.

Does that mean the United States must ignore Palestinian concerns and Muslim economic grievances? No. Many in this part of the world crave the best of America, and we cannot forget that we are their ray of hope. But apropos of the Palestinians, the United States put on the table at Camp David a plan that would have gotten Yasir Arafat much of what he now claims to be fighting for. That U.S. plan may not be sufficient for Palestinians, but to say that the justifiable response to it is suicide terrorism is utterly sick.

Third, we need to have a serious and respectful dialogue with the Muslim world and its political leaders about why many of its people are falling behind. The fact is, no region in the world, including sub-Saharan Africa, has fewer freely elected governments than the Arab-Muslim world, which has none. Why? Egypt went through a whole period of self-criticism after the 1967 war, which produced a stronger country. Why is such self-criticism not tolerated today by any Arab leader?

Where are the Muslim leaders who will tell their sons to resist the Israelis—but not to kill themselves or innocent noncombatants? No matter how bad, your life is sacred. Surely Islam, a grand religion that never perpetrated the sort of Holocaust against the Jews in its midst that Europe did, is being distorted when it is treated as a guidebook for suicide bombing. How is it that not a single Muslim leader will say that?

These are some of the issues we will have to address as we fight World War III. It will be a long war against a brilliant and motivated foe. When I remarked to an Israeli military official what an amazing technological feat it was for the terrorists to hijack the planes and then fly them directly into the most vulnerable spot in each building, he pooh-poohed me.

"It's not that difficult to learn how to fly a plane once it's up in the air," he said. "And remember, they never had to learn how to land."

No, they didn't. They only had to destroy. We, by contrast, have to fight in a way that is effective without destroying the very open society we are trying to protect. We have to fight hard and land safely. We have to fight the terrorists as if there were no rules, and preserve our open society as if there were no terrorists. It won't be easy. It will require our best strategies, our most creative diplomats, and our bravest soldiers. Semper Fi.

September 13, 2001

SMOKING OR NONSMOKING?

JERUSALEM

If this attack on America by an extensive terrorist cell is the equivalent of World War III, it's not too early to begin thinking about what could be its long-term geopolitical consequences. Just as World Wars I and II produced new orders and divisions, so too might this war. What might it look like?

Israel's foreign minister, Shimon Peres, offers the following possibility: Several decades ago, he notes, they discovered that smoking causes cancer. Soon after that, people started to demand smoking and non-smoking sections. "Well, terrorism is the cancer of our age," says Mr. Peres. "For the past decade, a lot of countries wanted to deny that, or make excuses for why they could go on dealing with terrorists. But after what's happened in New York and Washington, now everyone knows. This is a cancer. It's a danger to us all. So every country must now decide whether it wants to be a smoking or nonsmoking country, a country that supports terrorism or one that doesn't."

Mr. Peres is on to something—this sort of division *is* going to emerge—but we must be very, very careful about how it is done, and whom we, the United States, assign to the smoking and nonsmoking worlds.

As Mr. Peres himself notes, this is not a clash of civilizations—the Muslim world versus the Christian, Hindu, Buddhist, and Jewish worlds. The real clash today is actually not between civilizations, but within them—between those Muslims, Christians, Hindus, Buddhists, and Jews with a modern and progressive outlook and those with a medieval one. We make a great mistake if we simply write off the Muslim world and fail to understand how many Muslims feel themselves trapped in failing states and look to America as a model and inspiration.

"President Lincoln said of the South after the Civil War: 'Remember, they pray to the same God,'" remarked the Middle East analyst Stephen P. Cohen. "The same is true of many, many Muslims. We must fight those among them who pray only to the God of Hate, but we do not want to go to war with Islam, with all the millions of Muslims who pray to the same God we do."

The terrorists who hit the United States this week are people who pray to the God of Hate. Their terrorism is not aimed at reversing any specific U.S. policy. Indeed, they made no demands. Their terrorism is driven by pure hatred and nihilism, and its targets are the institutions that undergird America's way of life, from our markets to our military.

These terrorists must be rooted out and destroyed. But that must be done in a way that doesn't make us Osama bin Laden's chief recruiter. Because these Muslim terrorists did not just want to kill Americans.

That is not the totality of their mission. These people think strategically. They also want to trigger the sort of massive U.S. retaliation that makes no distinction between them and other Muslims. That would be their ultimate victory—because they *do* see the world as a clash of civilizations, and they want every Muslim to see it that way as well and to join their jihad.

Americans were really only able to defeat Big Tobacco when whistle-blowers within the tobacco industry went public and took on their own industry, and their own bosses, as peddlers of cancer.

Similarly, the only chance to really defeat these nihilistic terrorists is not just by bombing them. That is necessary, but not sufficient, because another generation will sprout up behind them. Only their own religious communities and societies can really restrain and delegitimize them. And that will happen only when the Muslim majority recognizes that what the Osama bin Ladens are leading to is the destruction and denigration of their own religion and societies.

This civil war within Islam, between the modernists and the medievalists, has actually been going on for years—particularly in Egypt, Algeria, Saudi Arabia, Jordan, and Pakistan. We need to strengthen the good guys in this civil war. And that requires a social, political, and economic strategy as sophisticated, and generous, as our military one.

To not retaliate ferociously for this attack on our people is only to invite a worse attack tomorrow and an endless war with terrorists. But to retaliate in a way that doesn't distinguish between those who pray to a God of Hate and those who pray to the same God we do is to invite an endless war between civilizations—a war that will land us all in the smoking section.

September 14, 2001

THE BIG TERRIBLE

AMMAN, JORDAN

By a quirk of fate I have been in Jordan for much of the World Trade Center crisis. Sitting here, I've been struck by the number of e-mails that have reached me from friends around the Arab-Muslim world—from Kuwait and Cairo, from Lebanon and Turkey—all just wanting to say how upset they were with what happened and checking if the family was OK. In their own way, they each echoed what a secretary in Jordan tried to say to me in the most eloquent broken English—that this terrorist attack was "the big terrible."

I relate this not to suggest that my friends around the Middle East reflect all public opinion out here. They do not. One need only visit some of the most popular Arabic Web sites and chat rooms to see that public opinion in the Arab world is split about 50-50—between those appalled by the bombing and those applauding it. The harshest e-mails, Arab techies tell me, come from Islamists in Saudi Arabia and the Gulf, home to some of the hijackers.

No, I relate this simply to say that America still has many admirers in this part of the world. For all that Middle Easterners get enraged with America, many of them value it, envy it, and want their kids there.

They envy the sense of ownership that Americans have over their own government; they envy its naïve optimism, its celebration of individual freedom, and its abiding faith that the past won't always bury the future. For a brief, terrifying moment last week, people out here got a glimpse of what the world could be like without America, and many did not like it. America is not something external to them; people carry around pieces of it in ways often not articulated.

Why does all this matter? Because we need the help of the moderate Arab states to fight this war. And for now, most of these Arab leaders are ready to cooperate with us—because enough of their publics are tilted our way. But the moderate Arab leaders are praying that the United States will proceed carefully and surgically, because they know that public opinion here, even after all the American deaths, is by no means solidly pro-American.

On Sunday I interviewed Jordan's King Abdullah, one of America's real friends. He had three wise messages: We can win if you Americans don't forget who you are, if you don't forget who your friends are, and if we work together. "The terrorists are trying to break down the fabric of the United States," said the Jordanian monarch. "They want to break down what America stands for. The terrorists actually want to provoke attacks on Arabs or Muslims in the United States, because if the American communities start going after each other, if we see America fragment, then you destroy that special thing that America stands for. That's what the terrorists want—they want to be able to turn to your friends here and say, 'Look, this is all a myth.'

"That is why you have to be very careful when you respond—make sure you respond in a way that punishes the real perpetrators, that brings justice, not revenge, because otherwise you will be going against your own ideals, and that is what the terrorists want most."

At the same time, U.S. strategy can't just be about punishing the bad guys. It also has to be about helping the good guys. Jordan is a country with a decent government and an economy that—despite the Intifada— grew 3.9 percent last year, thanks largely to a free-market approach with an emphasis on software, technology, and textile development that is drawing U.S. investors. That's a lot of jobs. (Jordan is also the first Arab country to sign a free trade agreement with the United States, but ratification has been foolishly held up by the Senate.) In short, Jordan is becoming a good Arab model for how to do things right. We have a fundamental interest in this model succeeding, for all its neighbors to see. Terrorists thrive in failing, stagnant, weak states with illegitimate regimes—not countries on the rise.

Which brings up the king's last point: "The bad guys work together, but we don't. The terrorist groups are a global organization. They know how to cooperate and stay focused on their military objectives. We have not. Some people didn't want to share intelligence. [Some] said, 'Islamic terrorism is not my problem,' and looked the other way. We can defeat them, but only if we learn to cooperate globally as effectively as they do."

September 18, 2001

HAMA RULES

In February 1982 the secular Syrian government of President Hafez al-Assad faced a mortal threat from Islamist extremists, who sought to topple the Assad regime. How did it respond? President Assad identified the rebellion as emanating from Syria's fourth-largest city—Hama—and he literally leveled it, pounding the fundamentalist neighborhoods with artillery for days. Once the guns fell silent, he plowed up the rubble and bulldozed it flat, into vast parking lots. Amnesty International estimated that 10,000 to 25,000 Syrians, mostly civilians, were killed in the merciless crackdown. Syria has not had a Muslim extremist problem since.

I visited Hama a few months after it was leveled. The regime actually wanted Syrians to go see it, to contemplate Hama's silence and to reflect on its meaning. I wrote afterward, "The whole town looked as though a tornado had swept back and forth over it for a week—but this was not the work of Mother Nature."

This was "Hama Rules"—the real rules of Middle East politics—and Hama Rules are no rules at all. I tell this story not to suggest this should be America's approach. We can't go around leveling cities. We need to be much more focused, selective, and smart in uprooting the terrorists.

No, I tell this story because it's important that we understand that Syria, Egypt, Algeria, and Tunisia have all faced Islamist threats and crushed them without mercy or Miranda rights. Part of the problem America now faces is actually the fallout from these crackdowns. Three things happened:

First, once the fundamentalists were crushed by the Arab states, they fled to the last wild, uncontrolled places in the region—Lebanon's Bekaa Valley and Afghanistan—or to the freedom of America and Europe.

Second, some Arab regimes, most of which are corrupt dictatorships afraid of their own people, made a devil's pact with the fundamentalists. They allowed the Islamists' domestic supporters to continue raising money, ostensibly for Muslim welfare groups, and to funnel it to the Osama bin Ladens—on the condition that the Islamist extremists not attack these regimes. The Saudis in particular struck that bargain.

Third, these Arab regimes, feeling defensive about their Islamist crackdowns, allowed their own press and intellectuals total freedom to attack America and Israel, as a way of deflecting criticism from themselves.

As a result, a generation of Muslims and Arabs have been raised on such distorted views of America that despite the fact that America gives Egypt $2 billion a year, despite the fact that America fought for the freedom of Muslims in Kuwait, Bosnia, and Kosovo, and despite the fact that Bill Clinton met with Yasir Arafat more than with any other foreign leader, America has been vilified as the biggest enemy of Islam. And that is one reason that many people in the Arab-Muslim world today have either applauded the attack on America or will tell you—with a straight face—that it was all a CIA-Mossad plot to embarrass the Muslim world.

We need the moderate Arab states as our partners—but we don't need only their intelligence. We need them to be intelligent. I don't expect them to order their press to say nice things about America or Israel. They are entitled to their views on both, and both at times deserve criticism. But what they have never encouraged at all is for anyone to consistently present an alternative, positive view of America—even though they were sending their kids here to be educated. Anyone who did would be immediately branded a CIA agent.

And while the Arab states have crushed their Islamist terrorists, they have never confronted them ideologically and delegitimized their behavior as un-Islamic. Arab and Muslim Americans are not part of this problem. But they could be an important part of the solution by engaging in the debate back in the Arab world, and presenting another vision of America.

So America's standing in the Arab-Muslim world is now very low—partly because we have not told our story well, partly because of policies we have adopted, and partly because inept, barely legitimate Arab leaders have deliberately deflected domestic criticism of themselves onto us. The result: we must now fight a war against terrorists who are crazy and evil but who, it grieves me to say, reflect the mood in their home countries more than we might think.

September 21, 2001

TERRORISM GAME THEORY

When I lived in Beirut in the early 1980s—the era when suicide bombing was born—I had a Lebanese friend, Diala, who used to quip that whenever she traveled on an airplane she carried a bomb in her luggage, because the odds against two people carrying a bomb on the same plane were so much higher.

Diala's was one of a million mind games Lebanese played in order to survive in a city where suicide bombings and exploding cars became part of the background noise of daily life. My favorite quote from those days was from the Beirut hostess who turned to us at a dinner party one evening and asked casually: "Would you like to eat now, or wait for the cease-fire?"

I never expected that I or my neighbors would ever have to play such mind games in America. I certainly understand why Americans are scared. I understand why at a parent-teacher meeting at my daughter's junior high school last week, there was unanimous support for postponing the eighth-grade class's trip to New York, scheduled in two weeks. I understand that this particular act of terrorism we just experienced is something so much more frightening than what Beirutis had to deal with.

How so? It is hard to trust anything after such an attack, because trust is based on a certain presumptive morality, a sense that certain actions are simply outside the bounds of human behavior or imagination. That nineteen people would take over four civilian airliners and then steer three of them into buildings loaded with thousands of innocent people was, I confess, outside the boundary of my imagination. The World Trade Center is not the place where our intelligence agencies failed. It is the place where our imaginations failed.

What we know of these terrorists is that they were evil, educated, and suicidal. That is a combination I have never seen before in a large group of people. People who are evil and educated don't tend to be suicidal (they get other people to kill themselves). People who are evil and suicidal don't tend to be educated.

Naturally, when our imaginations fail us in such a shocking way, there is a tendency to push out the boundaries so far that we see threats everywhere and become paralyzed. We must not. I took my family to the Baltimore Orioles baseball game last Friday night, and as we drove into the parking lot we were handed a slip of paper with "security precautions"—new restrictions about things you could not take into the ballpark anymore. When I get on a plane at the airport, frankly, you can X-ray me until I glow in the dark, but I hope we are not headed for a day where we permanently do the same at ball games and concerts.

Believe me, I'm not naïve about these threats. But I'm still hoping that what we're dealing with here is a relatively small number of terrorists, and possibly a crazy state or two—which, over time, can be combated and contained without totally shackling ourselves.

Beirutis had it right: There is no such thing as perfect security in today's world. All rational precautions need to be taken. But once you take them, then you basically have to decide: Am I going to sit home and hide in the basement forever, or am I, like my friend Diala, going to play whatever mind game it takes, or none at all, and just go on with my life?

My mentor in such things is my late departed friend George Beaver, a crazy Englishman who played golf—as a man in his eighties—almost every day of the Lebanese civil war at the Beirut Golf and Country Club. (I confess that I joined him on some days.) When I would say to him, "You know, George, it's crazy to play golf under such conditions," he always had the best answer: "I know I am crazy to do it, but I would be even crazier if I didn't."

Unable to actually imprison us, these terrorists want us to imprison ourselves. Sorry, but no way. It breaks my heart to think about the people who lost loved ones on September 11, but I will not let it break my spirit.

I went to the ball game Friday night, took in Dvorak's *New World* Symphony at the Kennedy Center Saturday, took my girls out to breakfast in Washington Sunday morning, and then flew to the University of Michigan. Heck, I even went out yesterday and bought some stock. What a great country.

I wonder what Osama bin Laden did in his cave in Afghanistan yesterday?

September 25, 2001

TALK LATER

The day after the World Trade Center bombings, an Egyptian TV show called and asked me to explain the impact on Americans. I scanned my brain for an analogy and finally said: Imagine how Egyptians would feel if three suicide bombers rammed airplanes into the Pyramids, with thousands of people inside. The World Trade Towers were our Pyramids, built with glass and steel rather than stones, but Pyramids to American enterprise and free markets, and someone has destroyed them.

I'm still not sure the world fully appreciates what this has meant to Americans. We are not fighting for Kosovo, and we are not fighting for Bosnia, Somalia, or Kuwait. *We are fighting for our country.* And Americans will fight for their country and they will die for their country.

The big question is how we fight this war to deliver to Americans what they want—which is not revenge, but justice and security. It requires a new attitude toward the battle and new strategy on the battlefield.

What attitude? We need to be really focused, really serious, and just a little bit crazy. I don't mean we should indiscriminately kill people, especially innocent Afghans. I mean that the terrorists and their supporters need to know that from here forward we will do whatever it takes to defend our way of life—and then some. From here forward, it's the bad guys who need to be afraid every waking moment. The more frightened our enemies are today, the fewer we will have to fight tomorrow.

As for the new strategy, if our first priority is to destroy the Osama bin Laden network in Afghanistan, then we need to understand that it takes a homegrown network to destroy a homegrown network. Let me put it another way: If Osama bin Laden were hiding in the jungles of Colombia instead of Afghanistan, whose help would we enlist to find him? U.S. Army Special Forces? The Colombian army? I don't think so.

Actually, we would enlist the drug cartels. They have the three attributes we need: They know how to operate as a covert network and how to root out a competing network, such as Mr. bin Laden's. They can be bought and know how to buy others. And they understand that when we say we want someone "dead or alive," we mean "dead or dead."

The Cali cartel doesn't operate in Afghanistan. But the Russian mafia sure does, as do various Afghan factions, drug rings, and Pakistani secret agents. They all have their local, homegrown networks, and it is through such networks that the Afghan part of this war on terrorism will be fought. "The best news I've heard all week was that Vladimir Putin is serious about joining the coalition," said Moises Naim, editor of the journal *Foreign Policy.* "This sort of character can really help now."

Moises is right. Something tells me Mr. Putin, the Russian president and former KGB spymaster, has the phone number of the guy in the Russian mafia who knows the guy in the Afghan cartels who knows the guy who knows the guy who knows where Mr. bin Laden is hiding. It is going to be that kind of war: an aboveground army you fight with tanks and generals, an underground network you fight with moles and exterminators.

In fighting this kind of war, President Bush and his advisers would do themselves a huge favor by not talking so much. They are already starting to contradict themselves and get tied up in knots. Be like the terrorists: let your actions speak. It is much more unnerving to the enemy.

For everything there is a season. There will be a season later on for talking. There will be a season for dealing with other states that have supported terrorism. And there will be a season for promoting Arab-Israeli peace or economic development. But right now—right now is the season of hunting down people who want to destroy our country. War alone may not solve this problem, but neither will social work. And one thing a focused, covert war will do is create a level of deterrence that has not existed up to now. Every state has to know that after September 11, harboring anti-U.S. terrorists will be lethal.

To drive that point home, though, people have to see that we are focused, serious, and ready to use whatever tactics will make the terrorists feel bad, not make us feel good. As the Lebanese militia leader Bashir Gemayel once said about the Middle East—before he himself was assassinated—"This is not Norway here, and it is not Denmark."

September 28, 2001

EASTERN MIDDLE SCHOOL

I recently attended meet-the-teacher night at Eastern Middle School, my daughter Natalie's school in Silver Spring, Maryland. The evening began with the principal noting that Eastern, a public school in suburban Washington, had forty different nationalities among its students. Before the teachers were introduced, the school's choir and orchestra, a Noah's Ark of black, Hispanic, Asian, and white kids, led everyone in "God Bless America." There was something about the way those kids sang together, and the earnest, if not always melodious, way the school orchestra pounded out the National Anthem, that was both moving and soothing. As I took in the scene, it occurred to me how much the Islamist terrorists who just hit America do not understand about America.

Their constant refrain is that America is a country with wealth and power but "no values." The Islamist terrorists think our wealth and power are unrelated to anything in the soul of this country—that we are basically a godless nation, indeed the enemies of God. And if you are an enemy of God, you deserve to die. These terrorists believe that wealth and power can be achieved only by giving up your values, because they look at places such as Saudi Arabia and see that many of the wealthy and powerful there lead lives disconnected from their faith.

Of course, what this view of America completely misses is that American power and wealth flow directly from a deep spiritual source—a spirit of respect for the individual, a spirit of tolerance for differences of faith or politics, a respect for freedom of thought as the necessary foundation for all creativity, and a spirit of unity that encompasses all kinds of differences. Only a society with a deep spiritual energy, which welcomes immigrants and worships freedom, could constantly renew itself and its sources of power and wealth.

Which is why the terrorists can hijack Boeing planes, but in the spiritless, monolithic societies they want to build, they could never produce them. The terrorists can exploit the U.S.-made Internet, but in their suffocated world of one God, one truth, one way, one leader, they could never invent it.

Lord knows, ours is hardly a perfect country. Many times we have deviated from the American spirit or applied it selfishly. But it is because we come back to this spirit more times than not, in more communities than not, that our country remains both strong and renewable.

Why can't we convey that? In part, we're to blame. President Bush denigrated Washington during his campaign and repeated the selfish mantra about the surplus that "it's your money—not the government's money." How thankful we are today that we have a Washington, D.C., with its strong institutions—FEMA, the FAA, the FBI, and armed forces—not to mention a surplus to help manage our way out of this crisis.

In part we don't talk about these issues so we don't embarrass our autocratic allies in the Middle East. But this negative view of America as a nation that achieved wealth and power without any spiritual values is also deliberately nurtured by governments and groups in the Middle East. It is a way of explaining away their own failures to deliver a better life for their own people: The Americans are powerful only because they stole from us or from others—not because of anything intrinsically spiritual or humane in their society.

A society that will dig until it has found every body in the World Trade Center rubble—because at some level it believes every individual is created in the image of God—a society that raises $600 million for the victims in two weeks, is a godless, spiritless place? Guess again.

These terrorists so misread America. They think our strength lies only in the World Trade Center and the Pentagon—the twin pillars of our wealth and power—and if they can just knock them down we'll start to fold: as if we, like them, have only one truth, one power center.

Actually, our strength lies in the slightly dilapidated gym of Eastern Middle School on parent-teacher night, and in thousands of such schools across the land. That is where you'll find the spirit that built the Twin Towers and can build them over again anytime we please.

So in these troubled times, if you want to feel reassured about how strong this country is or what we're fighting to preserve, just attend a PTA meeting. It's all there, hiding in plain sight.

October 2, 2001

YES, BUT WHAT?

Judging from the foreign press, the most popular world reaction to the terrorist attacks on America has not been outright condemnation, but rather: "Yes, but . . ." Yes, this was terrible, but somehow America deserved it or is responsible for the anger behind it.

One can only be amazed at the ease with which some people abroad and at campus teach-ins now tell us what motivated the terrorists. Guess what? The terrorists didn't leave an explanatory note. Because their deed was their note: We want to destroy America, starting with its military and financial centers. Which part of that sentence don't people understand?

Have you ever seen Osama bin Laden say "I just want to see a smaller Israel in its pre-1967 borders" or "I have no problem with America, it just needs to have a lower cultural and military profile in the Muslim world"? These terrorists aren't out for a new kind of coexistence with us. They are out for our nonexistence.

None of this seems to have seeped into the "Yes, but . . ." crowd, whose most prominent "Yes, but" states: This terrorist act would never have happened if America hadn't been so supportive of Israel. My response is, "Yes, but . . . but . . ."

Yes, there is no question, America's support of Israel—even when Israel builds greedy, provocative settlements in the heart of the Gaza Strip—has produced understandable Muslim anger. But the argument doesn't end there. America has also taken the lead role in trying to reverse this situation. We know the September 11 attack was being planned a year ago—exactly when President Clinton was proposing to Yasir Arafat a Palestinian state on roughly 95 percent of the West Bank and East Jerusalem—with the Israeli settlers uprooted from all but 5 percent. In other words, this terrorism was being planned *because America was trying to build Israeli-Palestinian coexistence*, not because it wasn't.

Ah, say the "Yes, but" folks, but Arab public opinion has been inflamed by the Arab TV images of Israel suppressing the Palestinian uprising. Yes, at times Israel has used excessive force, and one can understand how that looks to Arab eyes, but Israel has also been responding to Palestinian suicide attacks on Israeli pizza parlors and discos—which isn't highlighted on Arab TV.

Moreover, this uprising by the Palestinians was not their only recourse. There was an active U.S.-sponsored diplomatic track, with a deal on the table, which may not have been fully acceptable to Palestinians but was certainly worth building upon and hardly justified suicide-bombing Israeli civilians. The Arab media and leaders now talk as though the Clinton proposal for a Palestinian state never happened. But it did.

The second "Yes, but" is that the terrorists reflect a protest over Muslim poverty. Yes, poverty can breed desperate people. However, most of the hijackers were middle-class Saudis or Egyptians.

Is it America's fault that the richest ruling family in the world, the Saudis, have citizens who are poor and frustrated? Is it America's fault that Korea had the same per capita income in the 1950s as many Arab states but Korea has managed its development so much better since that it now dwarfs all Arab economies? Afghanistan is run by a medieval Taliban theocracy that bans women from working or going to school. How could such a place not be poor? And who was the biggest protector of that backward Taliban society? Osama bin Laden and his men.

There is something wrong with Saudi Arabia's citing U.S. support for Israel as the root cause for this Islamist terror—when many Saudi men were among the hijackers, when the Saudi regime has tolerated the harsh Islamist movements that provided ideological guidance for these young men, when Saudi Arabia was the biggest funder of the Taliban, when the Saudi ruling family has alienated some of its most devout subjects to a degree that produced Islamist militancy, and when the Saudi regime—as *The Economist* just noted, in an article titled "Saudi Arabia: The Double-Act Wears Thin"—winked at indirect fund-raising for Mr. bin Laden in the kingdom as a way of currying favor with its hard-line Islamist critics.

I don't want to see the Saudi regime destabilized. I'm sure it wants to be part of the solution now. But how about a little candor? *Yes*, America should look deeper into its policies and actions—*but, but, but* we're not the only ones who need to look in the mirror.

October 5, 2001

IT'S FREEDOM, STUPID

I happened to be reading Richard Reeves's compelling new biography of Richard Nixon last week when a paragraph about Israel caught my eye. It was a memo that Nixon wrote to Henry Kissinger in 1969, describing his, and America's, feelings about Israel: "[The Israelis] must recognize that our interests are basically pro-freedom and not just pro-Israel because of the Jewish vote . . . [Golda] Meir . . . must trust [Nixon] completely. He will see to it that Israel always has 'an edge.' This is going to be the policy of this country. Unless [Israelis] understand it, and act as if they understood it right now, they are down the tubes."

I find this quote so revealing because Nixon didn't like Jews, but he understood Americans—you don't get elected President without that. And what he understood was that the animating vision of America in the world is the promotion and protection of freedom—freedom of speech, freedom of religion, freedom of markets, and freedom of politics. And that while America might align itself with all sorts of countries for economic or strategic reasons, in the end it was those who were "basically pro-freedom" whom America would never abandon and with whom America would always share a special bond.

I am not sure all our coalition partners in the war against Osama bin Laden understand that. The truth is, our real coalition partners can be counted on a few fingers: Britain, France, Canada, Germany, Australia, Japan. The Saudis, Egyptians, and Syrians are not, and will not be, members of this coalition in any equal sense—not because they don't have military power to contribute, but because deep down, these Arab regimes do not share the values that we're trying to defend.

These Arab regimes are whispering members of the coalition—they whisper their support in our ear—but they cannot be full-throated members, they cannot openly tell their people they are on our side. Because our side is out for the defense of freedom, and their goal is not the preservation of freedom—for their own societies or for others. Their goal is self-preservation.

"Regimes such as Egypt, Saudi Arabia, or the Palestinian Authority have a legitimate fear of democracy—they fear that free elections would be exploited by Islamist extremists who are basically undemocratic," said the Middle East specialist Stephen P. Cohen. "But these Arab leaders have to understand that if we root out these extremists—who've been produced by their own bad governance—we are not doing it so these regimes can keep their countries free of democracy for everyone else. We want to make the world safe for democracy, and they want to make the Arab world safe from democracy."

The other guy who doesn't get it is Prime Minister Ariel Sharon of Israel. His suggestion that America was in danger of acting like those who appeased Hitler on the eve of World War II—because Mr. Bush reiterated U.S. support for a Palestinian state—was stupid and offensive.

Yes, Mr. Bush should have elaborated by saying, "We favor a Palestinian state, but after the last year we don't know whether we have a serious Palestinian leader ready to live in peace with Israel in such a state." Still, it's outrageous to suggest that after all the military, diplomatic, and economic support America has given Israel over decades, America is now going to sell Israel out.

Attention, Mr. Sharon: America is now fighting for its freedom—the same battle we have aided Israel in all these years—and when we are fighting for our freedom, there is only one thing for Israel to say: How can we help? Period.

There's one more thing Mr. Sharon needs to understand: Americans want to destroy this terrorist menace so that we and all other free nations, including Israel, can really enjoy our freedom. That's what it's all about. But we are not out to destroy this extremist menace so that Israel will be free to build more settlements or to eat up more Palestinian land. Today the Palestinians are literally at war with each other over whether to make peace with Israel. But if and when the Palestinians ever get their peace act together, Mr. Sharon needs to realize that we are out to make the world safe for Israel to be free, not safe for Israel to occupy the West Bank according to his biblical map—and saying that is not appeasement, it's American.

October 9, 2001

BUSH TO BIN LADEN

The White House has asked U.S. networks to limit broadcasts of statements by Osama bin Laden. I wish that instead of censorship, the President would respond to him. Here's what Mr. Bush could say:

Dear bin Laden: I've listened to the statement you released through Al Jazeera TV. Since I know that no Arab or Muslim leader will dare answer you, I thought I would do it. Let me be blunt: Your statement was pathetic. It's obvious from what you said that you don't have a clue why we're so strong or why the Arab regimes you despise are so weak.

You spoke about the suicide attacks on us as being just revenge for the "eighty years of humiliation and disgrace" the Islamic nation has gone through. You referred to the hijackers as a Muslim vanguard sent "to destroy America," the leader of the "international infidels," and you denounced the Arab regimes as "hypocrites" and "hereditary rulers."

What was most revealing, though, was what you didn't say: You offered no vision of the future. This was probably your last will and testament—I sure hope so—and you could have said anything you wanted to future generations. After all, it was your mike. Yet you had nothing to say. Your only message to the Muslim world was whom to hate, not what to build—let alone how.

In part it's because you really don't know much about Islamic history. The Muslim world reached the zenith of its influence in the Middle Ages—when it preserved the best of classical Greek and Roman teachings, and inspired breakthroughs in mathematics, science, medicine, and philosophy. That is also when Islam was at its most open to the world, when it enriched, and was enriched by, the Christian, Greek, and Jewish communities in its midst—whom you now disparage as infidels—and when it was actively trading with all corners of the world. Your closed, inward, hate-filled version of Islam—which treats women as cattle and all non-Muslims as enemies—corresponds with no period of greatness for Islam, and will bring none.

It was also revealing that the only Arab state you mentioned was Iraq. Interesting—Iraq is led by a fascist dictator, Saddam Hussein, who used poison gas against his own people, who squandered Iraq's oil wealth to build himself palaces, and who raped Kuwait. But you are silent about all that. What bothers you is our targeted sanctions to end such a regime—not the regime itself.

In other words, you not only don't understand the Muslim past, you don't understand its present. The reason these past eighty years have been so stagnant for the Arab-Muslim world is not because we in America have been trying to keep you down. Actually, we haven't been thinking about you much at all.

No, the difference between American power, Chinese power, Latin American power, and Arab-Muslim power today is what we've each been doing for these past eighty years. We and others have been trying to answer many questions: How do we best educate our kids? How do we increase our trade? How do we build an industrial base? How do we increase political participation? And we judged our leaders on how well they answered all those questions.

But people like you want Arabs and Muslims to ask only one question of their leaders: How well did you fight the infidels and Israelis? I know that who rules Jerusalem is a deeply important part of your heritage, and every Arab-Muslim leader must address it. But it can't be the only question. Yet because people like you have reduced it to the only question, and tried to intimidate every Arab who wanted to ask other questions, you have allowed your region to be led by scoundrels like Saddam.

Yes, you've wreaked some havoc, bin Laden, but don't flatter yourself into thinking you can destroy us. You have to build something strong to destroy something strong. But you can't. Because all the intellectual and creative energies in the Arab-Muslim world—which are as bountiful as in any other region—can never reach their full potential under repressive regimes like Iraq or leaders like yourself.

Stalin and Mao killed a lot of their own people, but even these thugs had a plan for their societies. You, bin Laden, are nothing but a hijacker—a hijacker of Islam, a hijacker of other people's technology, a hijacker of a vast Arab nation's anger at its own regimes. But you have no vision and no plan for your people. Which is why your epitaph will be easy to write:

Osama bin Laden—he destroyed much, he built nothing. His lasting impact was like a footprint in the desert.

October 12, 2001

SAUDI ROYALS AND REALITY

Three cheers for Mayor Rudy Giuliani for returning the $10 million donation made by a Saudi billionaire, Prince Alwaleed bin Talal, after he toured the World Trade Center ruins, handed the mayor a check, and then declared that it was time to get at the "roots" of this terrorism—which the Saudi royal defined as the U.S. failure to push Israel to make peace with the Palestinians and to stop Israel from "slaughtering" Palestinians.

No doubt there is deep Arab anger over U.S. support for Israel. I've gotten angry myself over the failure of successive U.S. governments to restrain Israel's voracious settlement-building program. But to suggest that Israel is slaughtering Palestinians for sport, as if a war were not going on there that Israel did not court, in which civilians on both sides are being killed—or to suggest that President Clinton didn't spend the whole end of his term forging a real plan for a Palestinian state, which Yasir Arafat ran away from, with the Saudi government only a few steps behind him, because it required some fair compromises on Jerusalem—or to suggest that somehow Arab anger over any of this justified people blowing up buildings in New York—is just a lie.

Normally, such casual lying doesn't bother me. It's a staple of Middle East politics, and in the end only hurts the liars. But this particular version is dangerous, because it masks a deeper lie that can hurt us. I call it "the virgin birth problem."

To listen to Saudi officials or read the Arab press, you would never know that most of the hijackers were young Saudis, or that the main financing for Osama bin Laden—a Saudi—has been coming from other wealthy Saudis, or that Saudi Arabia's government was the main funder of the Taliban. No, to listen to them you would think that all these young men had virgin births: They came from nowhere, no society is responsible for them, and no Arab state need reflect on how perpetrators of such a grotesque act could have come from its womb.

Attention, Prince Alwaleed: These young men came from your country, and while the Palestinian issue no doubt angers them, it does not compare to their hatred of what Mr. bin Laden called the corrupt, "hypocritical," "hereditary" Arab regimes, starting with Saudi Arabia.

So if you want to do something useful with your $10 million, then endow an anticorruption campaign in Saudi Arabia, or endow American Studies departments in all Saudi universities, or endow a center of Islamic learning in Saudi Arabia that would focus on the teachings of reformist Islamic scholars. Or give the money to Seeds of Peace, which brings Arab and Israeli youth together, or invest in development inside Saudi Arabia or Palestine so young Saudis and Palestinians can find fulfilling jobs.

Or persuade King Fahd to say publicly that if Israel withdraws to the 1967 borders, Saudi Arabia would lead the Muslim world into diplomatic relations with Israel.

But whatever you do, stop lying to us and to yourselves. Because we're sick of it, and we're not alone.

So many Arab citizens, seeking a better future for their kids, are also starved for the truth. Consider this letter, written by a Sudanese, Hashem Hassan. It was published last week in the London-based Arabic daily *Al-Quds Al-Arabi*, and translated by the invaluable MEMRI research service.

"We must stop presenting [Mr. bin Laden] as a stepson of American and Western hegemony. He is the lawful son of Arab-Muslim helplessness. He is a completely legal son, to whom we, with our rigidity, gave birth—we, the supporters of pan-Arabism; you, the Marxists; you, the Islamists; and you, the other educated individuals. We undermined our homeland and our peoples to the point where they became easy prey to the interests of America, Israel, and others . . . Renouncing these prodigal sons and attempting to lay them at the door of the West is shirking responsibility. It would be better to admit our paternity, and [admit] that our primary mistake in the education that we gave them was that we closed our societies, our schools, and our media to freedom and knowledge, to the possibility of learning from mistakes."

If you really want to honor the terrorists' victims, Prince Alwaleed, set up a newspaper and TV station in Saudi Arabia—not in London—that can freely publish such thoughts. Then we'll start to feel that the roots of this tragedy are being addressed.

Until then, I'm with Rudy—here's your money back.

October 16, 2001

A TWEEZER DEFENSE SHIELD?

We've all had a Eureka! moment in recent days when we realized the new world we're living in post–September 11. For me it came at National Airport the other day when, while checking in for the Delta Shuttle to New York, my small overnight bag was searched and the security agent found my tweezers.

"I'm sorry," she said. "You have to check this."

For a moment, as I stared at the tiny red tweezers, my mind drifted forward: I imagined myself returning to the check-in counter and telling the Delta agent, "I would like to check these tweezers to La Guardia, please." She would then ask me, "Did you pack these tweezers yourself? Have they been in your possession at all times?" I would nod and then watch as she wrapped a Delta luggage tag around one arm of my tweezers while I wrapped my name tag around the other. Then she would delicately lay my tweezers on the conveyer belt, next to all the big suitcases, and it would head off to the plane like a mouse among elephants. I would then claim it at La Guardia, waiting patiently as it came down the luggage carousel.

But what if it didn't arrive? I thought. What if I had to go to the lost-baggage counter and say, "Excuse me, I checked my tweezers in Washington and they didn't arrive." What would I tell the lost-luggage agent when she asked what model they were, Samsonite or Louis Vuitton? And I would have to answer, "Rite-Aid Pharmacy."

With such thoughts in mind, I just checked my whole overnight bag—tweezers and all. But this is not a column about tweezers. It's about the world we now live in, which can make tweezers so dangerous.

We have moved from a cold war system to a globalization system. And in this new networked, integrated world without walls, a pair of tweezers in the hands of the wrong person can turn an airplane into a missile, which, if it hits the right building, can set off dominoes that destabilize the whole world. Being poor or uneducated no longer means being weak. Because this new system is an incredible force-multiplier that can super-empower evil people so they can destabilize a super-power.

How do we deal with such a world?

First, we need to eliminate the Osama bin Ladens, who are dedicated to using any sharp instrument to super-empower themselves to do us harm. We will not get the backing of our Arab allies by winning an argument with them about the necessity of this war. We will win their backing and respect if we win the war and uproot bin Laden and the Taliban.

Second, we need to toughen up. Shame on Speaker Dennis Hastert for closing the House of Representatives because of the anthrax scare. We have U.S. troops in the field all around Afghanistan.

It can't be easy duty. But the House is running scared. Just what the terrorists wanted. The House members should be meeting on the Capitol steps, popping Cipro if they have to, telling America's troops and America's enemies that nothing—N-O-T-H-I-N-G—will derail our democracy.

Third, we need to start changing hearts and minds abroad. I'm not talking about the people who are angry at us for what we do. People are entitled to oppose us for what we do. I am talking about the growing number of people who are being taught to hate us for who we are—"infidels" who don't share their faith.

This requires a multipronged approach. On one track, we need to understand that so many of these angry people are living in failed states, with rotten, repressive regimes tacitly supported by the United States. America needs to triple its development assistance and begin taking seriously the task of improving governance in these failing states, where too many young people are being raised in Taliban-like schools, being taught an angry version of Islam and no life skills.

But we cannot succeed without Muslim allies. We need political leaders ready to provide an ideological alternative to the politics of resentment that is peddled by bin Laden—leaders ready to look their own regimes in the mirror, not just use the mirror to deflect their people's wrath at them onto America. We also need Muslim spiritual leaders who will vigorously challenge those who insist that Islam is about jihad and martyrdom—not a religion with a long history of enriching, and being enriched by, different faiths, cultures, and ideas.

If we don't do our part, and if our allies don't do theirs, this will become a war of civilizations—and that's a war we cannot win: Too many angry people. Too many tweezers.

October 19, 2001

DEAR ARIEL AND YASIR

From: George W. Bush
To: Ariel Sharon and Yasir Arafat

I'm writing you both urgently because I fear your conflict is deteriorating so far and fast that it's going to undermine my ability to sustain the war against Osama bin Laden.

Ariel, let me start with you. I'm still not sure you understand that America is now under attack. We're fighting for our self-defense. We are fighting to maintain the free and open society that is the basis of all that is good in America and Israel. And when your friend America is at war for its survival, there is only one question Israel should ask: How can we help?

We're not interested in debating with you whether or not Arafat is your Osama bin Laden, as you've been saying. Clearly, you can't make up your own mind. After all, you've been secretly negotiating with Arafat, and have sent your own son, Omri, to meet him several times. I've never sent my daughters to meet bin Laden.

I know exactly who Arafat is. He's like many of the Arab leaders in my coalition. He's a corrupt, authoritarian, impossible figure, easily influenced by his "street," who is awful to deal with—but whose domestic opponents are even worse. He's part of the problem and part of the solution.

What worries me is, Who is Israel? I have no problem with Israel retaliating against Palestinians who murder Israeli civilians. No one can object to that. When your snipers assassinated the Palestinian terrorist who organized the suicide bombing of the Tel Aviv disco, my spokesmen made clear we had no problem with that. But there's a red line for us. And the red line is if you try to use this situation, as some in your cabinet are urging, to destroy the Palestinian Authority and end Arafat's control in the West Bank and Gaza.

If you do that now, and if total chaos erupts in the territories or, worse, Islamist radicals take over, which then forces you to reoccupy these areas, and that inflames the Arab-Muslim world, you will be seriously undermining our coalition against bin Laden. And whoever undermines that coalition undermines us.

I fear, Ariel, that your American friends and your ambassador—do you even have an ambassador here?—have not conveyed to you how serious this war is for America. I know the Palestinian radicals are trying to goad you. I know you were working for a cease-fire before they killed your minister. I truly appreciate that. But don't let the assassination of your minister goad Israel into doing crazy things. That is exactly what the terrorists want.

Ariel, don't you get it? We know bin Laden didn't attack us to liberate Palestine. We know the roots of this story are in the anger of Arab citizens at their own bad regimes. We know the roots are with the fanatics who want to twist Islam into a religion of anger and martyrdom. These truths are too big to hide—unless you get in the way and make Israel the story. Get off the radar screen! Our resolve is now being tested by our enemies—we don't need it tested by our friends. If you do—especially after Americans start dying in Afghanistan—it will seriously damage the special U.S.-Israeli relationship.

As for you, Yasir, you say you want to join the world's nonsmoking section—those who oppose terrorism. Well, then don't come near me smoking cigars. I made clear that I'm ready to support a Palestinian state, but if you're not supportive of us in this war, you can forget about that.

If your people want to throw stones at Israeli soldiers, that's your business. But if you won't crack down on Palestinians who blow up Israeli discos or assassinate Israeli ministers and take some of the pressure off Sharon, as I have asked him to take it off you, then I'll assume you're on the side of bin Laden and the Taliban—just another thug who harbors terrorists. And please don't tell me you can't control your own people. You've sold us that carpet one too many times. If you won't, Congress eventually will force me to cut off all aid to you, put you on the terrorism list, and use all our means to delegitimize you. And why not? The cult of martyrdom and suicide that you have recklessly allowed to grow among Islamist Palestinians is not just a threat to Israel and to you. It's now a threat to us.

For so many years, boys, it's always been about you. Well, now it's about us. I need you both to postpone your war now. If you won't do that for us, we'll assume you're against us.

October 23, 2001

WE ARE ALL ALONE

So let me see if I've got this all straight now: Pakistan will allow us to use its bases Mondays, Wednesdays, and Fridays—provided we bomb only Taliban whose names begin with Omar and who don't have cousins in the Pakistani secret service. India is with us on Tuesdays and Fridays, provided it can shell Pakistani forces around Kashmir all other days. Egypt is with us on Sundays, provided we don't tell anyone and provided we never mention that we give the Egyptians $2 billion a year in aid.

Yasir Arafat is with us only after 10 p.m. on weekdays, when Palestinians who have been dancing in the streets over the World Trade Center attack have gone to bed. The Northern Alliance is with us, provided we buy all its troops new sandals and give U.S. passports to the first one thousand to reach Kabul.

Israel is with us provided we never question the lunacy of seven thousand Israeli colonial settlers living in the middle of a million Palestinians in the Gaza Strip. Kuwait would like to be with us, it really would, since we saved Kuwait from Iraq, but two Islamists in the Kuwaiti Parliament spoke out against the war, so the emir just doesn't want to take any chances. You understand. The Saudis, of course, want to be with us, but Saudis are not into war-fighting. That's for the household help. Don't worry. Prince Alwaleed has promised to rent us some Bangladeshi soldiers through a Saudi temp agency—at only a small markup.

The Saudi ruling family would love to cooperate by handing over its police files on the fifteen Saudis involved in the hijackings, but that would be a violation of its sovereignty, and, well, you know how much the Saudis respect sovereignty—like when the Saudi Embassy in Washington rushed all of Osama bin Laden's relatives out of America after September 11 on a private Saudi jet before they could be properly questioned by the FBI.

And then there's my personal favorite: All our Arab-Muslim allies would love us to get bin Laden quickly, but the Muslim holy month of Ramadan is coming soon, and the Muslim "street" will not tolerate fighting during Ramadan. Say, do you remember the 1973 Middle East war, launched by Egypt and Syria against Israel? Remember what that war was called in the Arab world? "The Ramadan war"—because that's when it was started. Oh, well. I guess the Arab world can launch wars on Ramadan, but not receive them.

My fellow Americans, I hate to say this, but except for the good old Brits, we're all alone. And at the end of the day, it's U.S. and British troops who will have to go in, on the ground, and eliminate bin Laden.

Ah, you ask, but why did we have so many allies in the Gulf War against Iraq? Because the Saudis and Kuwaitis bought that alliance. They bought the Syrian army with billions of dollars for Damascus. They bought us and the Europeans with promises of huge reconstruction contracts and by covering all our costs. Indeed, with the money Japan paid, we actually made a profit on the Gulf War; Coalitions "R" Us.

This time we'll have to pay our own way, and for others. Unfortunately, killing five thousand innocent Americans in New York just doesn't get the rest of the world that exercised. In part, we're to blame.

The unilateralist message the Bush team sent from its first day in office—get rid of the Kyoto climate treaty, forget the biological treaty, forget arms control, and if the world doesn't like it that's tough—has now come back to haunt us.

And who can blame other countries for wanting to shake down U.S. taxpayers when Dick Armey and his greedy band of House Republicans are doing the same thing—pushing a stimulus bill with more tax breaks for the rich, lobbyists, and corporations, and virtually nothing for the working Americans who will fight this war?

My advice: Try not to focus on any of this. Focus instead on the firemen who rushed into the Trade Center towers without asking "How much?" Focus on the thousands of U.S. reservists who have left their jobs and families to go fight in Afghanistan without asking "What's in it for me?" Unlike the free-riders in our coalition, these young Americans know that September 11 is our holy day—the first day in a just war to preserve our free, multireligious democratic society. And I don't really care if that war coincides with Ramadan, Christmas, Hanukkah, or the Buddha's birthday—the most respectful and spiritual thing we can do now is fight it until justice is done.

October 26, 2001

DRILLING FOR TOLERANCE

In April 1988 Saudi Arabia asked the United States to withdraw its newly appointed ambassador, Hume Horan, after only six months. News reports said King Fahd just didn't like the U.S. envoy. What the Saudis didn't like about him, though, was that he was the best Arabic speaker in the State Department, and had used his language skills to engage all kinds of Saudis, including the kingdom's conservative religious leaders who were critical of the ruling family. The Saudis didn't want someone so adroit at penetrating their society, so—of course—we withdrew Mr. Horan.

Ever since then we've been sending non-Arabic-speaking ambassadors to Riyadh—mostly presidential cronies who knew exactly how to penetrate the White House but didn't have a clue how to penetrate Saudi Arabia. Yes, sir, we got the message: As long as the Saudis kept the oil flowing, what they taught in their schools and mosques was not our business. And what we didn't know wouldn't hurt us.

Well, on September 11 we learned just how wrong that view was. What we didn't know hurt us very badly. On September 11 we learned all the things about Saudi Arabia that we didn't know: that Saudi Arabia was the primary funder of the Taliban, that fifteen of the hijackers were disgruntled young Saudis, and that Saudi Arabia was allowing fundraising for Osama bin Laden—as long as he didn't use the money to attack the Saudi regime.

And most of all, we've learned about Saudi schools. As this newspaper recently reported from Riyadh, the tenth-grade textbook for one of the five required religion classes taught in all Saudi public schools states: "It is compulsory for the Muslims to be loyal to each other and to consider the infidels their enemy." This hostile view of non-Muslims, which is particularly pronounced in the strict Saudi Wahhabi brand of Islam, is reinforced through Saudi sermons, TV shows, and the Internet.

There is something wrong with this picture: Since September 11, the President of the United States has given several speeches about how Islam is a tolerant religion, with no core hostility to the West. But the leader of Saudi Arabia, the keeper of the Muslim holy places, hasn't given one.

The truth is, there are at least two sides to Saudi Arabia, but we've pretended that there's only one. There is the wealthy Saudi ruling family and upper middle classes, who send their kids to America to be educated and live Western-style lives abroad and behind the veil at home. And there is an Islamist element incubating religious hostility toward America and the West, particularly among disaffected, unemployed Saudi youth.

It is said that truth is the first victim of war. Not this war. In the war of September 11, we've been the first victims of our own inability to tell the truth—to ourselves and to others. It's time now to tell the truth.

And the truth is that with the weapons of mass destruction that are now easily available, how governments shape the consciousness, mentality, and imagination of their young people is no longer a private matter.

We now have two choices. First, we can decide that the Saudi ruling family really is tolerant, strong, and wants to be part of the solution, and thus we can urge its members to educate their children differently and ensure that fund-raising in their society doesn't go to people who want to destroy ours. If so, I don't expect the Saudis to teach their kids to love America or embrace non-Muslim religions.

But if countries want good relations with us, then they have to know that whatever religious vision they teach in their public schools, we expect them to teach the "peaceful" realization of that vision. All U.S. ambassadors need to make that part of their brief. Because if tolerance is not made universal, then coexistence is impossible. But such simple tolerance of other faiths is precisely what Saudi Arabia has not been teaching.

If the Saudis cannot or will not do that, then we must conclude that the Saudi ruling family is not really on our side, and we should move quickly to lessen our dependence upon it. I was for radical energy conservation, getting rid of gas-guzzlers, and reducing oil imports before September 11—but I feel even more strongly about it now.

"Either we get rid of our minivans or Saudi Arabia gets rid of its textbooks," says Michael Mandelbaum, the Johns Hopkins foreign policy specialist. "But one thing we know for sure—it's dangerous to go on assuming that the two can coexist."

October 30, 2001

ONE WAR, TWO FRONTS

A month into the war in Afghanistan, the hand-wringing has already begun over how long this might last. Let's all take a deep breath and repeat after me: Give war a chance. This is Afghanistan we're talking about. Check the map. It's far away.

I have no doubt, for now, that the Bush team has a military strategy for winning a long war. I do worry, though, whether it has a public relations strategy for sustaining a long war. Over time, Arab and Muslim public opinion will matter. The silent majority in Pakistan, which for now is supporting President Pervez Musharraf's newfound alliance with the United States — something that is strategically critical for us — will be influenced by the broad trends in Arab-Muslim public opinion. So too will the next generation in the region. It is critical that this generation see bin Laden as a rogue, not a role model. So how do we fight this P.R. war?

The most important way we win the public relations war is by first winning the real war — by uprooting the Taliban regime and the bin Laden network, and sending the message that this is the fate of anyone who kills five thousand innocent Americans. Quite simply, if we win the war and are seen to be winning, we will have friends and allies in the Arab-Muslim world. If we are seen as losing the war or wavering, our allies will disappear in a flash.

Indeed, to read some of the commentaries in the Arab press is to understand that bin Laden and Saddam Hussein still have a great deal of popular support. It is no easy trick to lose a P.R. war to two mass murderers — but we've been doing just that lately. It is not enough for the White House just to label them "evildoers." We have to take the P.R. war right to them, just like the real one.

When the President or his spokesmen are asked about civilian casualties from our bombing in Afghanistan, they should answer: "Yes, for the thirtieth straight day Osama bin Laden, a mass murderer, has cloaked himself in a human blanket of Afghan civilians. Unfortunately, this has led to some civilian deaths." Or "Yes, for the fourth straight week Osama bin Laden, the man who sends other Muslims to their death but never risks his own life, is now sending Afghans to die for him."

Ditto with Saddam. Whenever U.S. officials speak about Saddam, they should always say: "Saddam Hussein, the man who has killed more Muslims in the twentieth century than any other human being . . ." (He's killed a million Iranians, Iraqi Kurds, and Kuwaitis.) Or they should point out that Saddam and bin Laden are "the world's two biggest hijackers—they have each hijacked a country and are holding its civilians hostage, and we're trying to liberate them."

Besides playing better defense, we also need to play offense. Yes, it's time for the Bush administration to do more to get the poisonous Palestinian-Israeli conflict off TV. It doesn't have to solve it, but it should send a serious, high-level U.S. envoy to work on a real cease-fire or interim deal. Israelis and Palestinians on their own are not going to find a way out of this dead end. Negotiations won't end all the violence, but they might at least create a competing story line and dynamic.

But we can't play offense by ourselves. It is not enough for our allies Egypt, Saudi Arabia, and Kuwait to issue one formal statement in support of the United States and then duck for cover. Not a single Arab-Muslim leader has yet answered bin Laden's taped message, which was heard all over the world. Our Arab-Muslim allies have to give their people a vision of why they are with us—not just secretly let us use their bases while their newspapers fuel anti-American rage.

Bin Laden told the Arabs that the Arab modernizing strategy had failed and all that was left was Islam—particularly his angry, retrograde version. Egypt, the leading Arab country, needs to take on that bin Laden message and insist that there is an Arab vision that can blend modernism with respect for Arab culture and tradition. And Saudi Arabia, the leading Muslim state, has to take on that bin Laden message and insist that there is a Muslim ideal that can blend faith, tolerance, and modernity.

But to sell that vision, they first have to have that vision.

Bottom line: we can't win the P.R. war with polite arguments, passive diplomacy, or allies that are afraid to claim the future from a man who wants to bury it with the past.

November 2, 2001

FIGHTING BIN LADENISM

———

DOHA, QATAR

If you want to know why the United States is hated in the Arab street, read the recent editorial in the semiofficial Egyptian daily, *Al-Ahram*, written by its editor, Ibrahim Nafie. After saying that the United States was deliberately making humanitarian food drops in areas of Afghanistan full of land mines, Mr. Nafie added: "Similarly, there were several reports that the [U.S.] humanitarian materials have been genetically treated, with the aim of affecting the health of the Afghan people. If this is true, the U.S. is committing a crime against humanity by giving the Afghan people hazardous humanitarian products."

This was an editorial written by Egypt's leading editor, personally appointed by President Hosni Mubarak. It basically accuses the United States of dropping poison food on Afghans according to unspecified "reports." So is it any wonder that people on the Egyptian street hate us?

This is the game that produced bin Ladenism: Arab regimes fail to build a real future for their people. This triggers seething anger. Their young people who can get visas escape overseas. Those who can't turn to the mosque and Islam to protest. The regimes crush the violent Muslim protesters, but to avoid being accused of being anti-Muslim, the regimes give money and free rein to their most hard-line, but nonviolent, Muslim clerics, while also redirecting their publics' anger onto America through their press.

Result: America ends up being hated and Islam gets handed over to the most antimodern forces. Have a nice day.

What these Arab regimes still don't get is that September 11 has exposed their game. They think America is on trial now, but in fact it is stale regimes like Egypt and Saudi Arabia, which produced the hijackers, that are on trial. Will they continue to let Islam be hijacked by antimodernists, who will guarantee that the Arab world falls further behind? Will they continue to blame others? Or will they look in the mirror, take on intolerance, and open their societies to a different future?

Here's the good news: Some Arab-Muslim voices are popping up, rejecting the garbage peddled by the regimes. The London-based newspaper *Al-Hayat* just published a letter from an Egyptian film critic,

Samir Farid. It said: "I felt ashamed while reading most, if not all, of the commentary [on September 11], primarily in the Egyptian press . . . Most, if not all, of what I read proves that the poison of the undemocratic military Arab regimes has also entered the bloodstream of the [intellectual] elite. These [people] no longer see . . . destruction for its own sake as disgraceful. What murky future awaits this region?"

Here in Qatar, on the Persian Gulf, Al Jazeera TV, the freest and most popular in the Arab world, recently ran a debate featuring the liberal Kuwaiti political scientist Shafeeq Ghabra versus an Islamist and a radical Arab nationalist. While the latter two tried to excuse Osama bin Laden, Mr. Ghabra hammered back: "The Lebanese civil war was not an American creation; neither was the Iran-Iraq war; neither was bin Laden. These are our creations. We need to look inside. We cannot be in this blame-others mode forever."

Dr. Abdelhameed al-Ansari, dean of Qatar University's law school, wrote in *Al-Raya*: "How does a terrorist [bin Laden] become a hero? What is happening to the collective Arab outlook? What is happening to our famous Islamic scholars? . . . We should solve this problem from its roots. Education is the key."

While Arab leaders have refused to acknowledge any Palestinian responsibility for the stalemate with Israel, a few weeks ago the Jerusalem-based Palestinian leader Sari Nusseibeh had the guts to criticize Palestinian strategy: "We're telling the Israelis, We want to kick you out: it's not that we want liberation, freedom, and independence in the West Bank and Gaza, we want to kick you out of your home. And in order to make sure that the Israelis get the message, people go out to a disco or restaurant and blow themselves up. The whole thing is just crazy, ugly, totally counterproductive. The secret is to get Israelis to side with you. We lost our allies."

The Bush team should tell our Arab partners: Look, we don't need your bases or armies. We just need you to open your societies so the voices of those who want a different Arab future can really be heard.

We'll take care of bin Laden—but you have to take care of bin Ladenism.

November 6, 2001

BEWARE OF ICEBERGS

As I was boarding my Emirates Air flight from Dubai to Pakistan the other day, I noticed a young Pakistani in front of me wearing a brown corduroy jacket, on the back of which was written, in big white letters, TITANIC.

Hmmm, I thought, that's not a good sign. I started to wonder: Is America the *Titanic* and Pakistan the iceberg we're about to hit while we're searching for Osama bin Laden in the fog of Afghanistan? Or is Pakistan the *Titanic*; its president, Pervez Musharraf, the captain; America the only passengers; and Afghanistan the iceberg we're about to hit?

Who knows? But the more I see of Pakistan, the more I realize the iceberg image is useful—because what you see popping out on the surface often bears little relation to what lurks below. Here's what I mean:

On the surface, President Musharraf has made a courageous 180-degree turn, from supporting the Taliban to joining the U.S. coalition to destroy the Taliban and bin Laden. What lurks beneath the Pakistani president, though, is less clear. There is really only one institution in Pakistan—the army. For now, that Pakistani army seems to have moved all 180 degrees with the president—but the Pakistani silent majority has not. And the Pakistani army, whose leadership is still Western-oriented but whose base is increasingly affected by Islamic trends, will be influenced by that silent majority, particularly the religious parties.

Pakistanis like to say that events here are determined by three things: "Allah, America, and the army." Right now America and the army are one side. If their alliance delivers benefits to Pakistanis, the regime will be OK. If not, more and more Pakistanis will look to Allah for direction.

On the surface, we're in the same war with the Pakistanis. But beneath the surface, we're fighting two different wars: "America is fighting Osama bin Laden in Afghanistan and Pakistan is fighting India through Afghanistan," says the Pakistani analyst Husain Haqqani. "The whole reason Pakistan first supported the Taliban in Afghanistan was to gain strategic depth against India, with which it has fought three wars. And the main reason Pakistan is getting involved with the U.S. now is to guarantee that it has more influence in a post-Taliban Afghanistan than

India and is paid by the U.S. in ways that will strengthen Pakistan against India."

On the surface, Saudi Arabia and Iran seem to be on the U.S. side. But beneath the surface, everyone here knows that it was the "war" between Iran and Saudi Arabia about who would have the most influence over the Muslim world that has fueled the rise of Islamic fundamentalism in Afghanistan and Pakistan. This twenty-year Iranian-Saudi struggle for influence was played out with money for schools, mosques, banks, and social welfare groups. These Islamic institutions filled the vacuum left by failing governments, but they also created a generation across this region with a lot more sympathy for bin Laden than for America. Every young person I spoke with in Peshawar, when I asked about arresting bin Laden, had the same answer: "Show me the proof."

On the surface, we see the war in Afghanistan as a just war to end terrorism. Beneath the surface, both Pakistanis and Afghans see it as a war between the Taliban—who are ethnic Pashtuns and who stretch from Afghanistan right across the Pakistani border here into Peshawar—and the Northern Alliance, who are primarily Tajiks and Uzbeks. For us, this is good versus evil; for them, it is the Hatfields versus the McCoys, Round 50. The Pashtun-led Taliban will not break easily, because they think they're fighting for the survival of their tribe in Afghanistan—not for the survival of bin Laden. But bin Laden can take advantage of that.

"You should focus on getting rid of bin Laden and [the Taliban leader] Mullah Omar, but be ready to accept any Taliban ready to play a new role," said Rifaat Hussain, a strategic studies expert at Islamabad University. "Otherwise you will be creating a huge ethnic imbalance in Afghanistan, and if you really pressure all the Pashtun Taliban out of there, they will retreat to their logical fallback position: Pakistan."

None of this means that America can't win in Afghanistan. It can. But it must be smart. Dorothy, this ain't Kansas; to win will require navigating alliances where nothing is called by its real name, where everyone is wearing a mask, and where what you see on the surface is only a sliver of what you might get.

November 9, 2001

IN PAKISTAN, IT'S JIHAD 101

You need only spend an afternoon walking through the Storytellers' Bazaar here in Peshawar, a few miles from the Afghan border, to understand that America needs to do its business in Afghanistan—eliminate Osama bin Laden and his Taliban protectors—as quickly as possible and get out of here. This is not a neighborhood where we should linger. This is not Mr. Rogers' neighborhood.

What makes me say that? I don't know, maybe it was the street vendor who asked me exactly what color Osama bin Laden T-shirt I wanted—the yellow one with his picture on it or the white one simply extolling him as the hero of the Muslim nation and vowing JIHAD IS OUR MISSION. (He was doing a brisk business among the locals.) Or maybe it was the wall poster announcing CALL THIS PHONE NUMBER IF YOU WANT TO JOIN THE 'JIHAD AGAINST AMERICA.' Or maybe it was all the Urdu wall graffiti reading HONOR IS IN JIHAD and THE ALLIANCE BETWEEN THE HUNOOD [Indians] AND YAHOOD [Jews] IS UNACCEPTABLE. Or maybe it was the cold stares and steely eyes that greeted the obvious foreigner. Those eyes did not say "American Express accepted here." They said "Get lost."

Welcome to Peshawar. Oh, and did I mention? This is Pakistan—these guys are on our side. Fat chance. This whole region of northwest Pakistan is really just an extension of Afghanistan, dominated by the same ethnic Pashtuns that make up the Taliban. This is bin Laden land. This is not a region where America is going to sink any friendly roots. In part it's because the Pashtuns here all, understandably, side with their brothers in Afghanistan; in part it's because they were jilted once before by the Americans—after the United States just dropped Pakistan like a used hanky once the Soviets left Afghanistan. But most important, it's because of the education system here.

On the way into Peshawar I stopped to visit the Darul Uloom Haqqania, the biggest madrasa, or Islamic school, in Pakistan, with 2,800 live-in students—all studying the Koran and the teachings of the Prophet Muhammad with the hope of becoming mullahs, or spiritual leaders. I was allowed to sit in on a class with young boys, who sat on the floor, practicing their rote learning of the Koran from holy texts perched on wooden holders. This was the core of their studies. Most will never be exposed to critical thinking or modern subjects.

It was at once impressive and disquieting. It was impressive because the madrasas provide room, board, education, and clothing for thousands of Pakistani boys who would otherwise be left out on the streets because of the gradual collapse of Pakistan's secular state education system. In 1978 there were 3,000 madrasas in Pakistan; today there are 39,000. It was disquieting because their almost entirely religious curriculum was designed by the Mogul emperor Aurangzeb Alamgir, who died in 1707. There was one shelf of science books in the library—largely from the 1920s.

The air in the Koran class was so thick and stale you could have cut it into blocks and sold it like ice. A sign on the wall said this room was "a gift of the Kingdom of Saudi Arabia." The teacher asked an eight-year-old boy to chant a Koranic verse for us, which he did with the beauty and elegance of an experienced muezzin. What did it mean? It was a famous verse: "The faithful shall enter Paradise and the unbelievers shall be condemned to eternal hellfire."

I asked one of the students, an Afghan refugee, Rahim Kunduz, age twelve, what his reaction was to the September 11 attacks, and he said: "Most likely the attack came from Americans inside America. I am pleased that America has had to face pain, because the rest of the world has tasted its pain." And his view of Americans generally? "They are unbelievers and do not like to befriend Muslims, and they want to dominate the world with their power."

The Darul Uloom Haqqania madrasa is famous because the Taliban leader, Mullah Muhammad Omar, once attended it, as did many other top Taliban figures. Mullah Omar never graduated, our guide explained, "but we gave him an honorary degree anyway, because he left to do jihad and to create a pristine Islamic government."

As we were leaving, my Pakistani friend asked the school's rector a question he had posed to me, which I couldn't answer: How come Americans are so good at selling Coke and McDonald's to people all over the world, but can't sell their policies? "Because their policies are poisonous and their Coke is sweet," said Moulana Samiul Haq.

I am all for reviewing our policies, but only the Pakistanis can rebuild their schools so they meld modernity, Islam, and pluralism. Bin Laden is a sideshow, but one we must deal with. The real war for peace in this region, though, is in the schools. Which is why we must do our military operation against bin Laden quickly and then get out of here. When we return, and we must, we have to be armed with modern books and schools—not tanks. Only then might we develop a new soil—a new generation as hospitable to our policies as to our burgers.

Until then, nothing pro-American will grow here.

November 13, 2001

BREAKING THE CIRCLE

ISLAMABAD, PAKISTAN

Although it was never his intention, Osama bin Laden has triggered the most serious debate in years, among Muslims, about Islam's ability to adapt to modernity. In Arab states this debate is still muted. But in Pakistan and other Muslim countries with a relatively free press, writers are raising it openly and bluntly. Nothing could be more important.

Here's why: Many Arab-Muslim states today share the same rigid political structure. Think of it as two islands. One island is occupied by the secular autocratic regimes and the business class around them. On the other island are the mullahs, imams, and religious authorities who dominate Islamic practice and education, which are still based largely on traditional Koranic interpretations that are not embracing of modernity, pluralism, or the equality of women. The governing bargain is that the regimes get to stay in power forever and the mullahs get a monopoly on religious practice and education forever.

This bargain lasted all these years because oil money, or U.S. or Soviet aid, enabled many Arab-Muslim countries to survive without opening their economies or modernizing their education systems. But as oil revenues have declined and the population of young people seeking jobs has exploded, this bargain can't hold much longer. These countries can't survive without opening up to global investment, the Internet, modern education, and emancipation of their women so that they will not be competing with just half of their populations. But the more they do that, the more threatened the religious authorities feel.

Bin Laden's challenge was an attempt by the extreme Islamists to break out of their island and seize control of the secular state island. The states responded by crushing or expelling the Islamists, but without ever trying to reform the Islamic schools—called madrasas—or the political conditions that keep producing angry Islamist waves. So the deadly circle that produced bin Ladenism—poverty, dictatorship, and religious antimodernism, each reinforcing the others—just gets perpetuated.

Some are now demanding the circle be broken. Consider this remarkable open letter to bin Laden that a Pakistani writer and businessman, Izzat Majeed, wrote in last Friday's popular Pakistani daily *The Nation*:

> We Muslims cannot keep blaming the West for all our ills. . . . The embarrassment of wretchedness among us is beyond repair. It is not just the poverty, the illiteracy and the absence of any commonly accepted social contract that define our sense of wretchedness; it is, rather, the increasing awareness among us that we have failed as a civil society by not confronting the historical, social and political demons within us. . . . Without a reformation in the practice of Islam that makes it move forward and not backward, there is no hope for us Muslims anywhere. We have reduced Islam to the organized hypocrisy of state-sponsored mullahism. For more than a thousand years Islam has stood still because the mullahs, who became de facto clergy instead of genuine scholars, closed the door on *itjihad* [reinterpreting Islam in light of modernity] and no one came forward with an evolving application of the message of the Holy Quran. All that the mullahs tell you today is how to go back a millennium. We have not been able to evolve a dynamic practice to bring Islam to the people in the language of their own specific era. . . . Oxford and Cambridge were the "madrasas" of Christendom in the thirteenth century. Look where they are today—among the leading institutions of education in the world. Where are our institutions of learning?

The Protestant Reformation, melding Christianity with modernity, happened only when wealthy princes came along ready to finance and protect the breakaway reformers. But in the Muslim world today, the wealthiest princes, like Saudi Arabia's, are funding antimodern schools from Pakistan to Bosnia, while the dictators pay off the antimodern mullahs (or use them to whack the liberals) rather than reform them. This keeps the soil for bin Ladenism ever fertile.

Addressing bin Laden, Mr. Majeed concluded, "The last thing [Muslims] need is the growing darkness in your caves. . . . Holy Prophet

Muhammad, on returning from a battle, said: 'We return from little Jihad to greater Jihad.' True Jihad today is not in the hijacking of planes, but in the manufacturing of them."

November 16, 2001

TODAY'S NEWS QUIZ

NEW DELHI

So, class, time for a news quiz: Name the second-largest Muslim community in the world. Iran? Wrong. Pakistan? Wrong. Saudi Arabia? Wrong. Time's up—you lose.

Answer: India. That's right: India, with nearly 150 million Muslims, is believed to have more Muslim citizens than Pakistan or Bangladesh, and is second only to Indonesia. Which brings up another question that I've been asking here in New Delhi: Why is it you don't hear about Indian Muslims—who are a minority in this vast Hindu-dominated land—blaming America for all their problems or wanting to fly suicide planes into the Indian Parliament?

Answer: Multiethnic pluralistic free-market democracy. To be sure, Indian Muslims have their frustrations, and have squared off over the years in violent clashes with Hindus, as has every other minority in India. But they live in a noisy, messy democracy, where opportunities and a political voice are open to them, and that makes a huge difference.

"I'll give you a quiz question: Which is the only large Muslim community to enjoy sustained democracy for the last fifty years? The Muslims of India," remarked M. J. Akbar, the Muslim editor of *Asian Age*, a national Indian English-language daily funded by non-Muslim Indians. "I am not going to exaggerate Muslim good fortune in India. There are tensions, economic discrimination, and provocations, like the destruction of the mosque at Ayodhya. But the fact is, the Indian Constitution is secular and provides a real opportunity for the economic advancement of any community that can offer talent. That's why a growing Muslim middle class here is moving up and generally doesn't manifest the strands of deep anger you find in many non-democratic Muslim states."

In other words, for all the talk about Islam and Islamic rage, the real issue is, Islam in what context? Where Islam is embedded in authoritarian societies, it tends to become the vehicle of angry protest, because religion and the mosque are the only places where people can organize against autocratic leaders. And when those leaders are seen as being propped up by America, America also becomes the target of Muslim rage.

But where Islam is embedded in a pluralistic, democratic society, it thrives like any other religion. Two of India's presidents have been Muslims; a Muslim woman sits on India's supreme court. The architect of India's missile program, A. P. J. Abdul Kalam, is a Muslim. Indian Muslims, including women, have been governors of many Indian states, and the wealthiest man in India, the info-tech whiz Azim Premji, is a Muslim. The other day, the Indian Muslim film star and parliamentarian Shabana Azmi lashed out at the imam of New Delhi's biggest mosque. She criticized him for putting Islam in a bad light and suggested he go join the Taliban in Kandahar. In a democracy, liberal Muslims, particularly women, are not afraid to take on rigid mullahs.

Followed Bangladesh lately? It has almost as many Muslims as Pakistan. Over the last ten years, though, without the world noticing, Bangladesh has had three democratic transfers of power, in two of which—are you ready?—Muslim women were elected prime ministers. Result: All the economic and social indicators in Bangladesh have been pointing upward lately, and Bangladeshis are not preoccupied with hating America. Meanwhile in Pakistan, trapped in the circle of bin Ladenism—military dictatorship, poverty, and antimodernist Islamic schools, all reinforcing one another—the social indicators are all pointing down and hostility to America is rife.

Hello? Hello? There's a message here: *It's democracy, stupid!* Those who argue that we needn't press for democracy in Arab-Muslim states and can rely on repressive regimes have it all wrong. If we cut off every other avenue for nonrevolutionary social change, pressure for change will burst out anyway—as Muslim rage and anti-Americanism.

If America wants to break the bin Laden circles across the Arab-Muslim world, then "it needs to find role models that are succeeding as pluralistic, democratic, modernizing societies, like India—which is constantly being challenged by religious extremists of all hues—and support them," argues Raja Mohan, strategic affairs editor of the newspaper *The Hindu*.

So true. For Muslim societies to achieve their full potential today, democracy may not be sufficient, but it sure is necessary. And we, and they, fool ourselves to think otherwise.

November 20, 2001

TERRORIST SOFTWARE

—————

Over coffee the other day here in the Gulf, an Arab friend—a sweet, thoughtful, liberal person—confided to me something that was deeply troubling him: "My eleven-year-old son thinks bin Laden is a good man."

For Americans, Osama bin Laden is a mass murderer. But for many young Arabs, bin Laden, even in defeat, is still Robin Hood. What attracts them to him is not his vision of the ideal Muslim society, which few would want to live in. No, what attracts them to him is his sheer defiance of everything young Arabs and Muslims detest—their hypocritical rulers, Israel, U.S. dominance, and their own economic backwardness. He is still the finger in the eye of the world that so many frustrated, powerless people out here would love to poke.

The reason it is important to eliminate bin Laden—besides justice—is the same reason it was critical to eliminate the Taliban: As long as we're chasing him around, there will never be an honest debate among Muslims and Arabs about the future of their societies. Think of all the nonsense written in the press—particularly the European and Arab media—about the concern for "civilian casualties" in Afghanistan. It turns out many of those Afghan "civilians" were praying for another dose of B-52s to liberate them from the Taliban, casualties or not. Now that the Taliban are gone, Afghans can freely fight out, among themselves, the war of ideas for what sort of society they want.

My hope is that once bin Laden is eliminated, Arabs and Muslims will want to do the same. That is, instead of expressing rage with their repressive, corrupt rulers, or with U.S. policy, by rooting for bin Laden, they will start to raise their own voices. It's only when the Arab-Muslim world sheds the veil of bin Laden as Afghans shed the Taliban, and faces the fact that 9/11 was primarily about anger and problems with their societies, not ours, that we will eradicate not just the hardware of terrorism, but its software.

"We in the West can't have that debate for them, but we can help create the conditions for it to happen," remarked the Middle East analyst Stephen P. Cohen. "America's role is to show the way to incremental change—something that is not, presto, instant democracy or fantasies that enlightened despotism will serve our interests. We can't just go on looking at the Arab world as a giant gas station, indifferent to what happens inside. Because the gas is now leaking and all around people are throwing matches."

Every day I see signs that this war of ideas is possible: it's the Arab journalist who says to me angrily of the Arab world today, "We can't even make an aspirin for our own headache," or it's Ahmad al-Baghdadi, the Kuwaiti professor who just published a remarkable essay in Kuwait's *Al-Anbaa* and Egypt's *Akhbar Al-Youm* titled "Sharon Is a Terrorist—and You?"

"[Ariel] Sharon was a terrorist from the very first moment of the . . . Zionist entity," wrote Mr. Baghdadi. But what about Arab-Muslim rulers?

Persecuting intellectuals in the courtrooms [of Arab countries], trials [of intellectuals] for heresy, . . . all exist only in the Islamic world. Is this not terrorism? . . . Iraq alone is a never-ending story of terrorism of the state against its own citizens and neighbors. Isn't this terrorism?

. . . The Palestinian Arabs were the first to invent airplane hijacking and the scaring of passengers. Isn't this terrorism? Arab Muslims have no rivals in this; they are the masters of terrorism toward their citizens, and sometimes their terrorism also reaches the innocent people of the world, with the support of some of the clerics . . . [Ours] is a nation whose ignorance makes the nations of the world laugh! The Islamic world and the Arab world are the only [places] in which intellectuals—whose only crime was to write—rot in prison. The Arabs and Muslims claim that their religion is a religion of tolerance, but they show no tolerance for those who oppose their opinions . . . Now the time has come to pay the price . . . and the account is long—longer than all the beards of the Taliban gang together. The West's message to the Arab and Muslim world is clear: Mend your ways or else. [Translation by MEMRI]

We must fight the ground war to get bin Laden and his hardware. But Arabs and Muslims must fight the war of ideas to uproot his software. The sooner we help them get on to that war, the better. Ask the folks in Kabul.

November 23, 2001

THE REAL WAR

If 9/11 was indeed the onset of World War III, we have to understand what this war is about. We're not fighting to eradicate "terrorism." Terrorism is just a tool. We're fighting to defeat an ideology: religious totalitarianism. World War II and the cold war were fought to defeat secular totalitarianism — Nazism and Communism — and World War III is a battle against religious totalitarianism, a view of the world that says, My faith must reign supreme and can be affirmed and held passionately only if all others are negated. That's bin Ladenism. But unlike Nazism, religious totalitarianism can't be fought by armies alone. It has to be fought in schools, mosques, churches, and synagogues, and can be defeated only with the help of imams, rabbis, and priests.

The generals we need to fight this war are people like Rabbi David Hartman, from the Shalom Hartman Institute in Jerusalem. What first attracted me to Rabbi Hartman when I reported from Jerusalem was his contention that unless Jews reinterpreted their faith in a way that embraced modernity, without weakening religious passion, and in a way that affirmed that God speaks multiple languages and is not exhausted by just one faith, they would have no future in the land of Israel. And what also impressed me was that he knew where the battlefield was. He set up his own schools in Israel to compete with fundamentalist Jews, Muslims, and Christians, who used their schools to preach exclusivist religious visions.

After recently visiting the Islamic madrasa in Pakistan where many Taliban leaders were educated and seeing the fundamentalist religious education the young boys there were being given, I telephoned Rabbi Hartman and asked: How do we battle religious totalitarianism?

He answered: "All faiths that come out of the biblical tradition — Judaism, Christianity, and Islam — have the tendency to believe that they have the exclusive truth. When the Taliban wiped out the Buddhist statues, that's what they were saying. But others have said it too. The opposite of religious totalitarianism is an ideology of pluralism — an ideology that embraces religious diversity and the idea that my faith can be nurtured without claiming exclusive truth. America is the Mecca of that ideology, and that is what bin Laden hates, and that is why America has to be destroyed."

The future of the world may well be decided by how we fight this war. Can Islam, Christianity, and Judaism know that God speaks Arabic on Fridays, Hebrew on Saturdays, and Latin on Sundays, and that he welcomes different human beings approaching him through their own history, out of their language and cultural heritage? "Is single-minded fanaticism a necessity for passion and religious survival, or can we have a multilingual view of God—a notion that God is not exhausted by just one religious path?" asked Rabbi Hartman.

Many Jews and Christians have already argued that the answer to that question is yes, and some have gone back to their sacred texts to reinterpret their traditions to embrace modernity and pluralism, and to create space for secularism and alternative faiths. Others—Christian and Jewish fundamentalists—have rejected this notion, and that is what the battle is about within their faiths.

What is different about Islam is that while there have been a few attempts at such a reformation, none have flowered or found the support of a Muslim state. We patronize Islam, and mislead ourselves, by repeating the mantra that Islam is a faith with no serious problems accepting the secular West, modernity, and pluralism, and the only problem is a few bin Ladens. Although there is a deep moral impulse in Islam for justice, charity, and compassion, Islam has not developed a dominant religious philosophy that allows equal recognition of alternative-faith communities. Bin Laden reflects the most extreme version of that exclusivity, and he hit us in the face with it on 9/11.

Christianity and Judaism have struggled with this issue for centuries, but a similar internal struggle within Islam to reexamine its texts and articulate a path for how one can accept pluralism and modernity—and still be a passionate, devout Muslim—has not surfaced in any serious way. One hopes that now that the world spotlight has been put on this issue, mainstream Muslims too will realize that their future in this integrated, globalized world depends on their ability to reinterpret their past.

November 27, 2001

PAY ATTENTION

I really enjoyed those pictures of President Bush and President Vladimir Putin of Russia backslapping and barbecuing down at the Bush ranch in Crawford the other day. It was heartwarming. You don't see that very often. But you know what else you don't see very often? Such a personal, important summit meeting that doesn't reach any agreement. Now that's unusual. But because the Taliban were falling at the time, no one paid attention. We should.

Houston, we have a problem here. And the problem can best be framed as follows: How much of President Bush's pre–September 11 foreign policy agenda is he ready to abandon in order to advance his post–September 11 agenda?

The Bush team came to office obsessed with building a ballistic missile shield. In order to test missiles for such a shield, the Bushies insist they must remove the restrictions set by the 1972 ABM treaty with Russia. Many experts argue that the United States could do all the testing it needs now within the ABM treaty, but the Bush hard-liners don't care. Because what they really want is to get rid of the ABM treaty, and all nuclear arms control, so they can be free to pursue Ronald Reagan's fantasy of a total Star Wars missile shield.

The Russians initially resisted changing ABM. The ABM treaty is critical to Russia as confirmation of its superpower status, and for maintaining nuclear predictability. By keeping ABM, the Russians feel they have a legal barrier that would prevent the United States from developing something more than just the "limited" shield the Bush team claims to want. What the Russians fear is a total Star Wars umbrella that might make the United States invulnerable to missile attack and thus able to strike Russia without fear of retaliation. This would upset the nuclear balance that has kept the peace since World War II.

Now for a brief aside: While the Bush administration was pushing missile defense as its priority before September 11, some of us were arguing otherwise. We began by asking a simple question: What are the real threats to U.S. security? The answers were nuclear proliferation, missile proliferation, terrorism, mafias, rogue states, and financial contagion. Then we asked: Is there any way the United States could effectively deal with any of these threats without a cooperative relationship with Russia? Since the answer was no, we argued that missile defense, not to mention NATO expansion, should be subordinated to forging a strategic relationship with Moscow. Nothing has vindicated that view more than the events since September 11, when Russia's support has been essential for fighting the Taliban, and would be even more critical for fighting Iraq.

The good news is that since September 11 Mr. Bush has developed a greater appreciation of Russia's importance for U.S. foreign policy. So Mr. Bush offered Mr. Putin two choices in Crawford: We can keep the ABM treaty around for a limited period, but you have to allow us an unprecedented degree of missile testing and assured deployment later; or we can rip up ABM now and reach a handshake agreement on how to reduce nuclear weapons and manage testing. Mr. Putin said no to both. He could not sell his generals on the amount of testing the United States envisaged, and the idea of arms control by handshake seemed totally wacky to the Russians.

"The idea that we would get rid of the ABM treaty and replace it with a handshake between Bush and Putin is ludicrous," said Michael Mandelbaum, the Johns Hopkins foreign policy expert. "Would any member of the Bush team buy a house that way—with a handshake and no contract? What happened to Reagan's 'Trust but verify'?"

The Bush team is about to make a big mistake. Mr. Putin has made the decision to "go west." But he's way out ahead of his generals and his public. He needs the continued cover of the ABM treaty to keep them moving west too. But he's willing to concede limited testing under ABM. Give him what he wants. Let's have more Putin and less testing.

Because more testing buys us nothing, but less Putin really hurts us. If we had had a complete Star Wars missile shield on September 11, it would not have saved a single American life. But if we put our priorities right and begin by forging a strategic partnership with Russia, we can still test antimissile systems and have real Russian cooperation to meet the threats of September 12 and beyond—which is so much more important.

November 30, 2001

RIGHTS IN THE REAL WORLD

I was being interviewed the other day by an Arab satellite TV station when the host drifted into a line of questioning that one hears so often in the Arab-Muslim world today: "What proof do you have that bin Laden is guilty? How can you be sure the Arab passengers were the hijackers? Won't you be embarrassed if in a couple of years it turns out that the hijackers were really from Colombia?"

The host was a serious Arab journalist, who was partly playing devil's advocate—but he was certainly reflecting his Arab viewers' opinions. As I absorbed those questions, a famous picture came to my mind. It was the snapshot of American black and white college students reacting at the moment O. J. Simpson was pronounced "not guilty"—the blacks exploding in celebration, the whites grim-faced and angry.

Remember that picture? Well, that picture is us and the Arab-Muslim world today. Just as many African-Americans felt abused for decades by the U.S. judicial system and expressed their anger by rallying to O.J. and refusing to acknowledge his apparent guilt, many Arabs and Muslims now passively back bin Laden to express their rage at U.S. support for Israel and repressive Arab regimes. America is to many Arabs and Muslims today what the LAPD was to many African-Americans—an unfair power structure.

This is why so many intelligent Arabs and Muslims refuse to acknowledge bin Laden's guilt. They don't endorse his murders, but they relish his trying to beat the system. If bin Laden were to have a trial by his peers, he would be acquitted faster than you could say "Marcia Clark."

I raise this issue to make a simple point: Attorney General John Ashcroft is not completely crazy in his impulse to adopt unprecedented draconian measures and military courts to deal with suspected terrorists. Do not get me wrong: I am glad critics are in Mr. Ashcroft's face, challenging his every move. His draconian measures go against our fundamental notion that people have a right to be left alone by government when there is no evidence that they have committed a crime, and if there is evidence, to be charged and tried in public, with judicial oversight, not in some secret proceeding. When our officials deviate from those norms they should be grilled and grilled again.

But having said that, I find myself with some sympathy for Mr. Ashcroft's moves. Listening to the debate, it is almost as if people think we're safe now: the Taliban have fallen, we've won, and we can act as if it were September 10—with no regard to the unique enemy we're up against.

At some level our legal system depends on certain shared values and assumptions between accusers and accused. But those simply do not apply in this case. When we were at war with the Soviet Union, we saw the world differently, but there were still certain basic human norms that the two sides accepted. With bin Laden and Al Qaeda we are up against radical evil—people who not only want to destroy us but are perfectly ready to destroy themselves as well. They are not just enemies of America; they are enemies of civilization.

Before we totally repudiate what Mr. Ashcroft is doing, we need to remember something very basic: Most of these hijackers came from big families. They left behind parents, brothers, sisters, and, in at least one case, a fiancée. What does that say? It says they hate us more than they love their own families.

As the Israeli author Ari Shavit noted, they hate us more than they love life itself. In the cold war, we could always count on the fact that at the end of the day, the Soviets loved life as much as we did—which is why the Soviets finally backed down in the Cuban missile crisis. That is not the kind of enemy we are up against here at all.

So, yes, let us grill Mr. Ashcroft and President Bush every time they propose deviating from our legal norms. And let us certainly demand judicial oversight for their steps. But let's not debate all this in a vacuum. Let's not forget what was surely the smile on those hijackers' faces as they gunned the engines on our passenger planes to kill as many Americans as possible in the World Trade Center. Let's not forget what they would do had they had access to even bigger weapons. And let's not forget how long they lived among us and how little they absorbed—how they went to their deaths believing that American laws were only something to be eluded, American citizens only targets to be killed, and American society only something to be destroyed.

December 2, 2001

THE INTIFADA IS OVER

The Palestinian Intifada II is finished.

It ended with last weekend's spasm of suicide bombings against Israeli kids—a signal that the Palestinian national movement was being taken over by bin Ladenism, which is the nihilistic pursuit of murderous violence against civilians, without any political program and outside of any political context. If there is anything left of the Palestinian national movement for independence, it better act now to rescue itself. Otherwise it's headed for the same dark cave as Osama bin Laden.

How so? Actually, I thought Intifada II was idiotic from the start. Why? Context. It came in the face of the most far-reaching U.S. and Israeli offers ever for a Palestinian state. While those offers of more than 90 percent of the West Bank, Gaza, and part of East Jerusalem may not have been sufficient for Palestinians, they were a serious opening bid. The right response was a Palestinian overture to the Israeli people to persuade them to give up 100 percent—not murderous violence. That's still true. Two weeks ago, a Gallup poll showed nearly 60 percent of Israelis favoring a Palestinian state—a remarkable figure after a year of violence. Also, President Bush just publicly endorsed the idea of a Palestinian state.

In other words, it's not as if Palestinians' aspirations were being ignored and their only alternative was violence. The Israeli silent majority and the world's silent majority were both poised for a serious deal, and had Prime Minister Ariel Sharon spurned a Palestinian peace bid he would have been swept aside. But instead, Palestinians offered a suicide package. It leads to only one conclusion: that the priority of the Palestinians is not achieving an independent state. Their priority, apparently, is to kill Jews and get revenge for Israel's assassination of a Hamas leader whose only claim to fame was organizing previous suicide bombings—a regular Thomas Jefferson.

So Intifada II, which was supposedly an uprising to prompt Israel to give Palestinians 100 percent of the West Bank, Gaza, and East Jerusalem, has morphed into Bin Laden II, a Palestinian attempt to eliminate 100 percent of Israel. There are authentic Arab and Muslim voices who understand how self-destructive this is. Take *The Jordan Times*, which said in its editorial Monday: "There is mounting sympathy world-wide, even solid support for the Palestinians' legitimate fight for independence and freedom. . . . But resorting to suicide attacks that have mainly targeted civilians has been harmful to the cause itself."

Arab leaders know this too, but they won't speak the truth to the Palestinians. Sad. Because if it is impossible anymore for Arab-Muslim leaders to distinguish between Palestinian resistance directed at military targets and tied to a specific peace proposal, and terrorism designed to kill kids without regard to a peace plan or political alternatives, then over time no moral discourse will be possible between America and the Arabs. You can already see the cleavage starting with the White House's unqualified defense of Israel's retaliation.

Mr. Sharon is right to send the Arabs and the world the message that Israel is going to do whatever it takes to defend itself. But he would make a huge error—huge—if he eliminated Yasir Arafat. That is a job for Palestinians. Israel should not take ownership of their misfortune, and Mr. Arafat and his leadership are their misfortune. They need to face up to that. Mr. Sharon's job is to dispel any fantasies they have about eliminating Israel and to make clear that if Palestinians adopt a different leadership, with a different approach, Israel will offer them a fair and dignified peace.

Egypt and Saudi Arabia, which keep telling America that Israel is the problem, need to help now too—by giving Palestinians support and cover for a fair compromise. America just told Israel publicly that it must end settlements, end the occupation, and accept a Palestinian state to end the conflict. When will Egypt and Saudi Arabia tell the Palestinians publicly that their game is up and they have to accept a Jewish state and end the conflict? (When will they tell *themselves*?)

Because if they won't, if they only blame Israel and sit by while the Palestinian national movement is hijacked by Hamas and Islamic Jihad—which want no end of the conflict except when all Jews are gone—then America too will retreat and simply adopt the view that Israel's occupation is a matter of self-defense, and may the stronger nation win.

December 5, 2001

ASK NOT WHAT...

News anchor Tom Brokaw tells the story of meeting a young New York City fireman a week after September 11. The fireman had just participated in a memorial service for some of his fallen colleagues, and the two of them talked about the tragedy. "As I said good-bye," Mr. Brokaw recalled, "he grabbed my arm and his expression took on a tone of utter determination as he said, 'Mr. Brokaw, watch my generation now, just watch us.'" As the author of the acclaimed *The Greatest Generation*, the story of the World War II cohort that saved America from Nazism, Mr. Brokaw told me he knew just what the man was saying: "'This is our turn to be a greatest generation.'"

There is a lot of truth to that. I have nothing but respect for the way President Bush has conducted this war. But this moment cannot just be about moving troops and tracking terrorists. There is a deep hunger in post–September 11 America in many people who feel this is their war in their backyard and they would like to be summoned by the President to do something more than go shopping. If you just look at the amount of money spontaneously donated to victims' families, it's clear that there is a deep reservoir of energy out there that could be channeled to become a real force for American renewal and transformation—and it's not being done. One senses that President Bush is intent on stapling his narrow, hard-right September 10 agenda onto the September 12 world, and that is his and our loss.

Imagine if tomorrow President Bush asked all Americans to turn down their home thermostats to 65 degrees so America would not be so much of a hostage to Middle East oil? Trust me, every American would turn down the thermostat to 65 degrees. Liberating us from the grip of OPEC would be our Victory Garden.

Imagine if the President announced a Manhattan Project to make us energy independent in a decade, on the basis of domestic oil, improved mileage standards, and renewable resources, so we Americans, who are 5 percent of the world's population, don't continue hogging 25 percent of the world's energy?

Imagine if the President called on every young person to consider enlisting in some form of service—Army, Navy, Marines, Air Force,

Coast Guard, Peace Corps, Teach for America, AmeriCorps, the FBI, the CIA? People would enlist in droves. Imagine if the President called on every corporate chieftain to take a 10 percent pay cut, starting with himself, so fewer employees would have to be laid off? Plenty would do it.

I don't toss these ideas out for some patriotic high. There is a critical strategic point here: If we are going to be stomping around the world wiping out terrorist cells from Kabul to Manila, we'd better make sure that we are the best country, and the best global citizens, we can be. Otherwise, we are going to lose the rest of the world.

That means not just putting a fist in the face of the world's bad guys, but also offering a hand up for the good guys. That means doubling our foreign aid, intensifying our democracy promotion programs, increasing our contributions to world development banks (which do microlending to poor women), and lowering our trade barriers for textile and farm imports from the poorest countries. Imagine if the President called on every U.S. school to raise money to buy solar-powered lightbulbs for every village in Africa that didn't have electricity so African kids could read at night? And let every one of those lightbulbs carry an American flag decal on it, so when those kids grew up they would remember who lit up their nights?

The world's perception of us and our values matters even more now, and it is not going to be changed by an ad campaign, or just by winning in Afghanistan, as important as that is. It will be changed only by what we do—at home and abroad. This war can't end with only downtown Kabul on the mend, and not downtown Washington, Chicago, and Los Angeles. Remember: the victims on September 11 were a cross section of America—black, white, Hispanic, rich, poor, and middle-class—and that same cross section has to share in the healing. If we've learned anything from September 11, it is that if you don't visit a bad neighborhood, it will visit you.

The first Greatest Generation won its stripes by defending America and its allies. This Greatest Generation has to win its stripes by making sure that the America that was passed on to us, and that now claims for itself the leadership of a global war against evil terrorists, is worthy of that task.

Mr. President, where do we enlist?

December 9, 2001

DEAR SAUDI ARABIA

From: President Bush
To: Sheik Saleh al-Sheikh, Saudi Arabian Minister of Islamic Affairs

Dear Minister: I'm sure you find it unusual to be receiving a letter from me. In the past, U.S. Presidents have been interested in writing only the Saudi oil minister, because we just looked on Saudi Arabia as a big gas station to be pumped and defended but never to be taken seriously as a society. But we've learned from the terrorist attacks of September 11 that you are the minister we need to talk with because, sadly, fifteen young Saudis were involved in these attacks — or, to put it another way, fifteen recent graduates of your schools and religion classes.

First, let me make something very clear: America has not suddenly decided to become anti-Saudi. There is no "Zionist" plot here to sour our relations. I beg you not to fall prey to such conspiracy nonsense. There's actually broad recognition here that Saudi Arabia has been a good ally and that many Saudis have studied here and are pro-American. More important, we know it will be impossible for us to counter radical Islamism without Saudi help. Saudi Arabia is the keeper of the Muslim holy places and leader of the Islamic world; it finances thousands of Islamic schools and mosques around the globe; we can't be effective without you.

But having said all that, you would also be dead wrong to think there's no problem between us, or that the only thing you need is better P.R. and a few meetings with Washington elites to smooth things over.

You have a problem with the American people, who, since September 11, have come to fear that your schools, and the thousands of Islamic schools your government and charities are financing around the world, are teaching that non-Muslims are inferior to Muslims and must be converted or confronted.

I want to be sensitive here. We can't tell you how to teach your children, but we can tell you that several thousand American children are without parents today because they were hit by radical Islamists educated in your schools, who justified their mass murder in the name of Islam. We can't tell you how to teach your children, but we can tell you that in a wired world—in which tools for mass destruction are increasingly available to individuals—we need you to interpret Islam in ways that sanctify religious tolerance and the peaceful spread of your faith. If you can't do that, then we will have a problem—then Saudi Arabia will become to our war on terrorism what the Soviet Union was to our war on Communism: the source of the money, ideology, and people who are threatening us.

What encourages us is that you seem to understand that and are taking steps to curtail incitement in your mosques and media. I notice that Crown Prince Abdullah recently called on your country's leading clerics "to examine with restraint every word that leaves our mouths, [because] Allah has said in the Koran: 'We have made you a moderate nation.'" I also noticed that you told a group of Saudi religious leaders that "what is important here is for a centrist trend [in Islam] to grow gradually. If this trend grows rationally, other trends will become weak." And I was also heartened that Sheik al-Sabil, the imam of the Holy Mosque in Mecca, denounced the suicide killing of civilians as against Islamic law.

These are important words. We hope that they will enter your textbooks and classrooms. And we invite you to come over and look at our public schools, and if there are texts that you find offensive to Islam, tell us. Look, in the age of globalization, how we each educate our kids is a strategic issue. In the 1990s we learned that another country's faulty financial software could harm our Wall Street portfolios. On September 11 we learned that another country's faulty education software could destroy all of Wall Street.

We understand that the issue of Palestine is also very important for you. But you can't come here and tell us that it must be America's business how Israel behaves, but it is none of our business how you behave, or what you teach, when fifteen of your sons helped to kill four thousand Americans. We do not want you as an enemy, and we don't want a war *with* Islam. We want a war *within* Islam—a war against intolerance and extremism. We want you to be the voice for moderation that we and Muslims will listen to. But we can only listen to what you say about us when you talk honestly about yourselves. Good luck.

Sincerely, George W. Bush—the first U.S. President who wants to be your friend, not just your customer.

December 12, 2001

SPIRITUAL MISSILE SHIELD

————

I and a group of friends in Maryland recently started a new synagogue—
so new that we have nowhere to meet yet and had to rent space for our
Hanukkah party. When our weekly bulletin came out, it contained the
following announcement: "Our Friday night service/Shabbat dinner/
Hanukkah party will be held December 14 at Trinity Presbyterian
Church." What struck me when I read those words was how absolutely
routine both the writer and the readers thought they were: We're having
a Hanukkah party. It will be in the neighborhood church. See you there.

Whenever I encounter the reality of religious tolerance in America,
it strikes me almost as a miracle. I know that religious intolerance is also
alive and well in this country, but it is not the norm. The norm is that
our floating synagogue can hold its Hanukkah party in the local church
and nobody thinks it's unusual. The norm is that my daughter's county
orchestra, which is predominantly Asian-American, ended its holiday
concert with a Hanukkah medley—including a solo by the Hispanic
concertmaster that was so beautifully rendered it would have made the
Fiddler on the Roof weep—and nobody thought it was any more
unusual than the "Jingle Bells" encore.

And that brings me to the Osama bin Laden tape just released. What
was most chilling about that tape was not bin Laden's boasting about his
mass murder. What was most chilling was the unidentified Saudi sheik
sitting next to him who so eagerly nodded his head in agreement with
everything bin Laden said, and who assured him that in the mosques in
Saudi Arabia, the reaction to the terror acts had been "very positive."

Look, bin Laden is finished. But there are thousands of those fawning
sheiks still out there who sympathize with his religious totalitarianism,
and we have not even begun to design a strategy for changing their
minds. (Listening to their conversation was like eavesdropping on the
Middle Ages.) Everyone is asking: Which country does America attack
next? Iraq? Somalia? The more important question is, How do we delegitimize the ideas espoused by the sheik and bin Laden, who kept invok-
ing Allah while discussing a mass murder?

That is a task that must begin with Muslims themselves, which some
are eager to do. They are eager for a language and a leadership that can

reform Islam in a way that will make it more compatible with modern education, pluralism, and religious tolerance. An e-mail arrived the other day from a young Pakistani-American woman about a column I wrote decrying religious totalitarianism. She said: "You basically articulate the views of myself and many American Muslims that I know. I am only saddened that more Muslims do not come forward and articulate the same truth publicly—that an Islamic enlightenment (I prefer 'enlightenment' to your choice of 'reform') is long overdue and this enlightenment should nurture a dynamic, progressive Islamic thought that embraces plurality and modernity. . . . These ideas would be most persuasive to the masses of Muslims if conveyed by other Muslims."

On Al Jazeera TV the other night there was a debate on this subject in which the Arab journalist Ahmad al-Sarraf asked: "Why don't we have tolerance? This rhetoric of hatred is in all sermons, in all schoolbooks. . . . We don't need America to interfere and teach us how to worship, but we need a certain element to force us to change our curriculum that calls for extremism."

The question is, Will any Arab-Muslim leaders rise to address these feelings, or will they all duck and hope that the storm blows over? Will the United States raise these issues of pluralism and tolerance with our Muslim allies, or will we duck as long as the oil keeps flowing?

I thought it was ironic that President Bush announced that he was scrapping the ABM treaty—in order to build a missile shield—just a few minutes before he released the bin Laden tape. The President's emphasis on a missile shield reminded me of a man whose house had just been burned down by his neighbor's son and his response was to call a plumber, because that was the only phone number he could remember.

A missile shield? Thanks a lot. Unless we do our part, and our Muslim friends do theirs, to foster religious tolerance and pluralism, no wall will be high enough and no missile shield accurate enough to protect us from the next wave of human missiles that will be launched at us—not by bin Laden, but by that unidentified sheik or his students.

December 16, 2001

ALL ALONE, AGAIN

MOSCOW

Anyone in Washington planning to take the war on terrorism to Iraq after Osama bin Laden is eliminated should not count on Russia's help—at least for now. The word here when you ask about marching on Baghdad is very simple: "Nyet."

In case you missed it, President Vladimir Putin of Russia told *The Financial Times* Monday that the next priority for the war on terrorism should be to "block the financing of terrorist activities. And so far I have no confirmation, no evidence that Iraq is financing the terrorists that we are fighting against."

Mr. Putin is not alone in this view. If one looks at the core U.S. coalition against bin Laden, what the different countries have in common is both outrage at the terror acts in America and their own national interest in seeing bin Laden and the Taliban defeated. When it comes to Iraq, that sense of outrage is missing for most coalition members, and more important, their national interests work against an anti-Saddam crusade.

Turkey, which does a big business selling smuggled Iraqi oil, is concerned that a war in Iraq could lead to the creation of a Kurdish ministate in northern Iraq that would link up with Turkish Kurds. Saudi Arabia is unnerved by the thought of Iraq being weakened as the Sunni Arab counterweight to Iran and the possible creation of an independent Shiite enclave in southern Iraq that would stir up the Shiites of eastern Saudi Arabia.

Jordan, which is badly infiltrated with Iraqi agents and depends heavily on trade with Iraq, fears being destabilized by any war over Baghdad. Egypt is not eager to see a "nice" leader in Iraq, which would fully reintegrate Baghdad into the Arab state system and enable it to resume its natural rivalry with Egypt for influence over the Arab world. Syria would never support a war on Iraq that, if it succeeded, could lead to Damascus's being targeted next. I could go on.

Russians were never keen on hitting Iraq, but since the Bush team embarrassed Mr. Putin by unilaterally pulling out of the ABM treaty, both he and other Russians generally seem even less inclined to help the United States attack Baghdad—absent a taped confession by Saddam.

And without the Russians, many European and Arab allies would shy away too.

"What America is doing in Afghanistan corresponds to our interests and understanding of the situation," said Aleksandr Bovin, a former Russian ambassador to Israel. "Iraq is a different matter. We had well-developed economic ties. We don't want to lose them, and we don't see any danger now from Iraq. Iraqi missiles won't hit either Russia or the U.S. I personally don't care for the ABM treaty, but Bush put Putin in a difficult position that was not necessary. [He scrapped ABM] right when Putin was saying to people here: 'Look, we're friends with the U.S. now.' It disappointed me and many Russians—as if [Bush] wanted to offend someone on purpose. The next time there is a choice to help America, [Putin] may choose not to help."

Mr. Bush looked into Putin's eyes, but he didn't look at the world through Putin's eyes. Shortsighted "R" U.S.

Don't get me wrong. There is no love lost here for Saddam. The Russians could, at best, be brought around to what the foreign affairs analyst Aleksei Pushkov calls "a negative neutralism" toward any U.S. action against Iraq. But the rubles would have to be sorted out in advance. Iraq ran up an $8 billion debt with the Soviet Union that Russia wants paid. The Russians want assurances that Washington will back their view that this debt was incurred by Iraq, and not just by Saddam, in case he is removed and a new Iraqi government says it's not responsible. The Russians also want assurances that if a pro-Western regime is installed in Baghdad, Russian oil companies will not be frozen out of lucrative oil exploration there. With bin Laden, our allies said: "Show me the proof." With Saddam, they will say: "Show me the proof and show me the money. Then we'll think about it."

Bottom line: the shooting-fish-in-a-barrel part of this antiterrorism war is over. Unlike the Taliban, Saddam has real money to buy off adversaries. Unlike Afghanistan, his country is strategically critical to all its neighbors, most of whom fear any change to the status quo. And unlike bin Laden, Saddam may not make himself an easy, obvious target. That doesn't mean America can't, or shouldn't, look for ways to oust him, but it does mean we should start by planning to do it alone.

December 19, 2001

RUSSIA'S LAST LINE

MOSCOW

Because of Moscow's exploding middle class, you quickly notice two things while driving around this increasingly European city—sushi bars are opening all over (yes, from borscht to Big Macs to California-Kremlin rolls in one decade!) and so many people have cars now that traffic is permanently snarled (imagine Jakarta with snow and ice and you've got today's Moscow). So sitting in gridlock the other day in Pushkin Square, I had plenty of time to ask my Russian friend Viktor a cosmic question: Is your life easier or harder now than it was under Communism?

"Both," he remarked. "It's easier because I don't have to hunt for food every day and wait in lines for everything. Stores are full now. No lines. But it all costs a lot of money. The saying here now is that there is only one line left in Russia—the line for money."

So Karl Marx's theories have finally triumphed in today's Russia: It's all about money. That's the key to understanding President Vladimir Putin too. He's not a tougher Mikhail Gorbachev, or a more sober Boris Yeltsin. He is Russia's first Deng Xiaoping—Mao's pragmatic successor who first told the Chinese that "to get rich is glorious" and put in place the modernizing reforms to do it.

Abba Eban once said that men and nations will always do the right thing in the end—after they exhaust every other possibility. That is Mr. Putin's basic message to Russians: "For a decade, we've tried every bad idea, from default to devaluation to shock therapy. Now there's only one idea left: passing real reform legislation so we can get real investment to build a real modern economy. Because in this world, without a real economic foundation, you're nothing. So we're going to focus now on the only line that matters—the line for money." This is Putinism: from *Das Kapital* to DOScapital.

And it explained to me why Mr. Putin rolled over so meekly on President Bush's decision to walk away from the ABM treaty, limiting missile defenses. In 1972, when that treaty was forged, Russian foreign policy was about one thing—geopolitics, the ideologically driven global competition for influence with the United States, and everything, particularly economics, was subordinated to that. Hence all the food lines. Today, Russian foreign policy is about two things—geopolitics and geo-economics—and there is a real competition between the two. So if Russia can save money and win Western help by walking away from the ABM treaty, then walk it will.

Don't be fooled, though. Russia's military and foreign policy elite considered Mr. Bush's ABM move "a slap in the face," said the Russian pollster Igor Bunin. If the United States doesn't come through now with what Mr. Putin believes he's been promised—a new accord for deep cuts in nuclear weapons and a real Russia-NATO partnership, plus debt relief, WTO membership, and Western investment—Mr. Putin will be seen as another Gorbachev—always giving and never receiving. "Then elites could start to form a front against him," added Mr. Bunin. But for now, Mr. Putin is ignoring the whispers because in his view Russia will never again be a player in geopolitics unless it first masters geoeconomics.

What's new in today's Moscow is that there are young capitalists coming of age, and they believe they can get rich the Chinese way, by making things, not the old Russian way, by taking things from the state or from the ground. And without anyone noticing, in 2001 Russia's Parliament quietly passed a lot of the judicial and tax-reform legislation that America was beating on it to pass for a decade.

I had lunch the other day in a combination art gallery–restaurant, Ulitsa OGI, which is part of a successful new chain started by Dmitry Jekovich and his partner. "The difference between us and the oligarchs is that we're oriented toward creating something new, not just privatizing something that existed before," he explained.

The confidence of Russia's new generation that it can actually do this "capitalist thing" has enormous geopolitical significance. One reason that Russia was so zealous about keeping so many nukes and reflexively opposing the United States was because these were the only currency that defined it as a superpower. If Russians believe they can be powerful on the basis of geoeconomics, they aren't going to surrender all their nukes or quest for influence, but the chances of their being real partners with the West will be much, much greater.

So keep rootin' for Putin—and hope that he makes it to the front of Russia's last line.

December 23, 2001

NAKED AIR

In the wake of the attempted bombing last week of the American Airlines flight from Paris by a terrorist nut with explosives in his shoe, I'm thinking of starting my own airline, which would be called Naked Air. Its motto would be "Everybody flies naked and nobody worries." Or "Naked Air—where the only thing you wear is a seat belt."

Think about it. If everybody flew naked, not only would you never have to worry about the passenger next to you carrying box cutters or exploding shoes, but no religious fundamentalists of any stripe would ever be caught dead flying nude, or in the presence of nude women, and that alone would keep many potential hijackers out of the skies. It's much more civilized than racial profiling. And I'm sure that it wouldn't be long before airlines would be offering free dry cleaning for your clothes while you fly.

Well, you get the point: If the terrorists are just going to keep using technology to become better and better, how do we protect against that while maintaining an open society—without stripping everyone naked? I mean, what good is it to have a free and open America when someone can easily get on an airplane in Paris and bring a bomb over in the heel of his shoe or plot a suicide attack on the World Trade Center from a cave in Kandahar and then pop over and carry it out?

This is America's core problem today: A free society is based on openness and on certain shared ethics and honor codes to maintain order, and we are now intimately connected to too many societies that do not have governments that can maintain order and to people who have no respect for our ethics or our honor codes.

Remember the electronic ticket machines that were used for the Boston–New York–Washington shuttles? Ever use one? Not only were you automatically issued your ticket with a credit card by pressing a screen, but they asked you—electronically—"Did you pack your bags yourself?" and "Did any strangers give you anything?" And you answered those security questions by touching a screen! Think about the naïve trust and honor code underlying those machines.

If I had my way, they would now take all those machines and put them in a special exhibit in the Smithsonian called "Artifacts from America Before September 11, 2001."

We're not alone. I just flew in and out of Moscow, where you now have to fill out a detailed customs form. It asks the usual questions: Are you carrying any fruits, plants, large amounts of foreign currency, special electronics, or weapons? But there was one box that unnerved me a bit. It asked: Are you carrying any radioactive materials? Hmm, I wondered, how many people (i.e., smugglers) are going to check that box? Can you imagine going through Moscow customs and the couple in front of you turning to each other and asking: "Dear, did we pack the nuclear waste in your suitcase or mine?" Or "Honey, is the plutonium in your purse or the black duffel?" I don't think so.

Which is why we are entering a highly problematic era, one that we are just beginning to get our minds around. We are becoming much more keenly aware of how freedom and order go together (see the Ashcroft debates). For America to stay America, a free and open society intimately connected to the world, the world has to become a much more ordered and controlled place. And order emerges in two ways: It is either grown from the bottom up, by societies slowly developing good democratic governance and shared ethics and values, or it is imposed from the top down, by nondemocratic authoritarian regimes rigidly controlling their people.

But in today's post–cold war world, many, many countries to which we are connected are in a transition between the two—between a rigid authoritarian order that was imposed and voluntary self-government that is being homegrown. It makes for a very messy world, especially as some countries—Afghanistan being the most extreme example—are not able to make the transition.

"The problem with top-down control is that more governments around the world are fragmenting today, rather than consolidating," said the Israeli political theorist Yaron Ezrahi. "At the same time, America's technologies are being universalized—planes that go faster and faster and electronics that are smaller and smaller—but the American values and honor system that those technologies assume have not been universalized. In the hands of the wrong people they become weapons of mass destruction."

So there you have our dilemma: Either we become less open as a society, or the world to which we are now so connected has to become more controlled—by us and by others—or we simply learn to live with much higher levels of risk than we've ever been used to before.

Or we all fly naked.

December 26, 2001

LET'S ROLL

All hail to President Bush for how he has conducted the war against Osama bin Laden. Mr. Bush has emerged a far better commander in chief than anyone predicted. In the war on terrorism he has shown steely resolve, imagination, leadership, and creativity. Thank you, Mr. Bush.

And now, I wish Al Gore were President.

Why? Quite simply because instead of showing resolve, imagination, leadership, and creativity on the domestic front, Mr. Bush has done just the opposite. He has tried to use the tremendous upsurge in patriotism, bipartisanship, and volunteerism triggered by the tragedy of September 11 to drive a narrow, right-wing agenda from September 10 into a September 12 world. It's wrong. It won't work. It sells the country short and it will ultimately sell the Bush presidency short.

I have no problem with nation-building in Afghanistan, but what I'm really interested in is nation-building in America—using the power of September 11 to make our country stronger, safer, and a better global citizen in the world of September 12, beginning with how we use energy.

But so far, all that's happening is that we've made the world safer for Saudi Arabia and OPEC to raise oil prices again. In case you missed it, last Friday the Saudi-led cartel cut production by 6.5 percent to boost oil prices, while the world is struggling to get out of a recession induced in part by the terrorism of Osama bin Laden and fifteen Saudi hijackers.

Frankly, the thought that U.S. taxpayers, who have had to bail out the airline industry (which was devastated by September 11 and by higher gas prices) and to finance the $1 billion–a–month war against bin Laden, will now have to pay more for oil because the Middle East regimes we're protecting want to hike the price, is an *outrage*.

You'd think maybe the leader of Saudi Arabia would say: "America, we're as upset as you that Osama bin Laden and fifteen Saudi youth were involved in the terrible attack on your shores. So we want to help America—the engine of the global economy—recover, as well as the developing world. As such, we're going to keep oil prices extremely low for the next six months, then we'll slowly lift them back to the $24–$28 range. It will cost us, but that's our tax cut for the world."

Is that too much to ask? Well, it seems so—which leads me back to President Bush.

The most obvious bold national project that Mr. Bush could launch now—his version of the race to the moon—would be a program for energy independence, based on developing renewable resources, domestic production, and energy efficiency. Not only would every schoolkid in America be excited by such a project, but it also would be Mr. Bush's equivalent of Richard Nixon going to China—the Texas oilman weaning America off of its dependence on Middle East oil. That would be a political coup!

It would also be Mr. Bush's best response to foreigners who are enraged by America's refusal to join the Kyoto treaty to stop global warming. Mr. Bush could say that by weaning America away from oil gluttony he would be doing more for the environment than Kyoto ever would, which would greatly improve America's standing as a global good citizen.

There are lots of ways Mr. Bush could go. "Today one out of every seven barrels of oil produced in the world is consumed on American highways," says the respected oil consultant Philip Verleger. "We could cut that by a third in five years if Washington were to offer tax incentives for manufacturers to produce more efficient vehicles and for consumers to buy them. Such tax cuts could be paid for with a higher gas tax, gradually phased in. Then we could replace all those American flag bumper stickers with ones that read I CUT MY OIL USE BY A THIRD, HOW ABOUT YOU?"

I don't want to be dependent on Mideast oil anymore. Countries in that region haven't had a good century in seven hundred years—and they're not going to soon. Oil is their curse, as well as ours. It's corrupted their rulers, enabled them to keep their women backward and out of the workforce, and prevented them from developing innovative economies that make things instead of just take things from the ground. They have a lot of homework to do before they will be stable allies.

We will all benefit if they succeed, but for now we have to look after ourselves. So, Mr. Bush, "let's roll." Ultimately, presidential greatness is measured by what you do at home. If this war on terrorism ends with nation-building only in Afghanistan and not in America, it will be no victory at all.

January 2, 2002

SOMEONE TELL THE KIDS

President Bush has warned us that the war on terrorism will be a long struggle. But how will we know when we've won even round one? Simple. We will have won round one once we've killed Osama bin Laden and his allies and once the leaders of the Arab-Muslim world have killed his ideas. That's the division of labor: We have to eliminate the killers and they have to delegitimize his ideas. I fear, though, that we'll do our part, but Arab-Muslim leaders won't do theirs. And if that's how round one ends, then on your next flight keep an eye on the tennis shoes of the guy next to you.

Bin Laden and his key cohorts Ayman al-Zawahiri, Muhammad Atef, and Taliban leader Mullah Muhammad Omar must all be eliminated for a very important reason—beyond sheer justice. Because the four of them have made a career of sending young Muslim men to commit suicide while they sit back, relishing the fallout on their homemade videos.

We need to send the message that anyone who orders suicide bombings against Americans, or protects those who do, commits suicide himself. And U.S. marines will search every cave in Afghanistan to make that principle stick. You order, you die—absolutely, positively, you die.

Yet round one cannot end with the leaders of Al Qaeda eliminated but their ideas still intact. One would think that killing these ideas would be easy. The most striking thing about bin Laden's tapes is how little the man has to say. There is no program for Arab-Muslim development, just venom built on the mantras of "jihad," "infidels," and "Allah."

Yet, to this day, the only two leaders to directly take on bin Laden and his warped view of Islam have been George W. Bush and Tony Blair. Why? One reason is that the leaders of the Middle East have no tradition of talking frankly to their people, particularly about religion. In times of trouble, their instinct is to button up the tent and let the sandstorm blow over. Some leaders are also afraid of directly challenging bin Laden for fear of becoming his main target. After all, this man has taken on two superpowers.

But the biggest reason is this: Give bin Laden his due; he is an authentic person who gave up a life of riches in Saudi Arabia to go live in a cave and fight the Soviets and Americans. To counter his authentic message of hate, you need an authentic messenger of progress, tolerance, and modernism.

But there are very few such messages or messengers in the Arab-Muslim world today. To begin with, it's hard to develop an authentic voice in authoritarian societies where thought-leaders—imams, academics, politicians, and columnists—are either owned by the regime or jailed by the regime. Moreover, the natural answer to bin Laden's religious totalitarianism is an ideology that's also grounded in Islamic tradition and values, but is progressive and forward-looking—and no Arab-Muslim leader today has articulated such a vision. To the contrary, bin Laden is just an extreme form of the same austere religious ideology many of these Arab regimes have used to legitimize themselves.

It was Israel that executed Nazi leader Adolf Eichmann. But it was modern Germany that executed Nazism, by writing one of the world's most democratic constitutions and living up to it. In so doing, Germans transformed Germany from a destructive to a constructive force for themselves, Europe, and the world.

Bin Ladenism has to be fought the same way. There are some faint signs of hope. The Arab world has gone through three phases since September 11: shock that Arab Muslims could have done this; then denial, blaming Israel or the CIA; and now, finally, the first stirrings of introspection. Saudi Arabia's Crown Prince Abdullah told a meeting of Gulf leaders last week: "Catastrophes are in fact opportunities that make it incumbent upon us to conduct self-scrutiny, review our attitudes, and repair errors . . . The real and deadly risk is to face crises with hands folded and blame others instead of confronting the crises and taking responsibility for our role."

This is healthy talk and needs to be encouraged. Up to now, the Bush team has let our key Arab-Muslim allies cooperate with us secretly, while never calling on them to answer bin Laden or to tell their own people that this view of America is a sick perversion. In effect, we let these leaders carry on an illicit relationship with us, while always making sure that no one told their kids. We can't afford that anymore. Someone needs to tell the kids.

January 6, 2002

WHO'S HOME, WHO'S NOT

Two world-renowned figures have been on the run, living in "undisclosed locations" since September 11. There are occasional sightings of both, but then they vanish. One figure is named Osama bin Laden. The other is named Dick Cheney.

I understand why there was concern just after September 11 to keep Vice President Cheney largely in hiding so that America's chain of command couldn't be decapitated with one blow. It was the prudent thing to do. And I'm sure it hasn't been easy for the Vice President, who's been a good soldier for putting up with it. But there is a fine line between looking prudent and looking nervous and vulnerable, and Mr. Cheney's continued cave-dwelling—while the President is urging the rest of us to go about our lives—is starting to seem like the latter. It's bin Laden and his gang who are supposed to be on the run, not our Vice President.

I think it's symbolically important that Mr. Cheney return to a normal life and routine in his well-protected residence—before bin Laden is captured in his cave or confirmed dead. I would hate to see us sound the all-clear for Mr. Cheney only after bin Laden is killed. Because sooner or later there will be another bin Laden or some other Al Qaeda roaming around, and the sooner we get used to that, the better.

At a certain point, playing hide-and-seek with our Vice President isn't protecting America. Because protecting America now means preparing every citizen and every child to live in an open society with a much higher level of personal risk.

This new reality comes as a shock. We've had it so easy all these years, with lax borders and cursory airport checks. But the open society we enjoyed was built on freedom and trust. After September 11, it's not so simple. Now we have a choice. One option is to build a closed society, based not on freedom and trust but on fear and mistrust. This would probably wipe out terrorism, but it would be an awful place to live. The other option is to accept slightly less freedom, tolerate a little less trust, and continue living in a basically open society—but accept that there will be terrorism in the cracks.

That's what the Israelis and the British have done, and they're right. The culture of freedom and openness is not for softies. I'd rather steel myself to live in an open society with greater risks than live in a steel cage.

Sure, President Bush can promise normalcy after the war with terrorism is won. But there's no such thing. America can defeat another country. But terrorism is such an individual sport, based on so many different grievances and requiring so little to perpetrate, that you can never conclusively defeat it in an open society.

So Mr. Bush can't really deliver normalcy again. What he can do is redefine normalcy—teach us how to maintain a free and open society while being a little less open, a little less trusting, a little more vigilant, and a little less risk-averse.

That's why I'm still angry that after September 11 my daughter's county orchestra abruptly canceled its planned trip to Italy this summer. Would I have worried every day that she was gone? Sure. But in the new normalcy, I'd rather accept the worry than rob her of the experience.

The Israeli political theorist Yaron Ezrahi said to me recently: "Every time I walk in Jerusalem I know that a car might blow up next to me. But I still go out, because life without affirmation is no life at all. Even my daughter, when I plead with her not to go to restaurants in central Jerusalem, says to me: 'Dad, you can't live constantly trying to protect me and worrying whether I'm protecting myself.'"

It's true. We all, parents and politicians, have to learn how to thrive in a riskier world—not how to simply survive until the utopia of a risk-free world is created. Let's start the dialogue about it with a town hall meeting led by Dick Cheney—in his house.

It's a great home, and there's lots of room. In fact, it was just featured in the December issue of *Architectural Digest*, with an essay by Lynne Cheney that notes that their white nineteenth-century house "has much to commend it: a lovely setting, a wide veranda from which to view the acres of surrounding greenery [and] gracious high-ceilinged rooms that manage to be both stately and inviting."

Sounds perfect, and that's where the Cheneys should be. It is bin Laden who belongs out in the cold, where the only magazine featuring his home will be *Guns & Ammo*.

January 9, 2002

THE TALK OF KABUL

KABUL, AFGHANISTAN

I've got good news and bad news from Afghanistan. The good news is that America doesn't need a lot to satisfy its basic security interest here, which is that this distant land never again be so uncontrolled that a tumor like Osama bin Laden can grow in its midst and then metastasize into the world and threaten us. We really don't need much to get that—just a loose Afghan federal government, some basic police and army units, a functioning economy, and a few institutions.

The bad news: it's not clear that we can get even that.

It is impossible to exaggerate how broken this place is. You know what Ground Zero looks like, where the World Trade Center once stood? Well, probably half of Kabul looks the same way, thanks to twenty-two years of civil war. And the "good" half—with its scant electricity, no phones, no mail, a 10 p.m. curfew, and only a bare minimum of food—looks like a caravan ghost town. We might as well be doing nation-building on the moon.

You see sad and bizarre scenes here: a white donkey galloping down the main street right behind our car; a man with one leg peddling a bicycle; people washing a car with water from a Porta Potti; thousands of refugees crammed into the fetid old Soviet Embassy, living in subzero temperatures with nothing but plastic wrap for windows. The central government is so broke it has less money than most American network crews here, so the government can't even pay salaries. "When some ministers come to see me, they have to take a taxi," said Lakhdar Brahimi, the senior UN envoy here.

This is a travesty. Afghanistan needs a quick infusion of cash. (Maybe the Muslim world, which was so worried about Afghan civilians when America was bombing here, could send some cash now that the bombing is over and people need to eat?) In addition, though, Afghanistan needs a multinational force that can forge a secure environment in its major cities—so refugees will return home, commerce will resume, and people will consider investing. Such a force could buy the frail Afghan government time to build up an army and police force of its own. Already, Afghanistan's carnivorous neighbors smell a power vacuum developing here, and some, like Iran, have begun brazenly sending people across Afghanistan's borders to buy influence. No good will come from that.

And that brings me to the Bush team. Right now there is a fight within the administration over whether to allow a robust multinational force here, and whether to participate in it ourselves. Let me be blunt: If the Bush team thinks our allies are going to send peacekeeping troops here in any numbers for any length of time without U.S. leadership and participation, they're crazy. And if they think that Afghanistan is going to pull itself together without the aid of such a force — just pour in money and stir — they're equally mistaken.

The United States won the war in Afghanistan by remote control, with air power, pilotless drones, local tribal fighters, and a few U.S. Special Forces. The Bush team now seems to hope that it can win the peace in Afghanistan by remote control as well. It's not going to happen. The Pentagon's reluctance to put troops on the ground here to go cave by cave has already resulted in the vanishing of bin Laden and most of his key aides. A reluctance to create some kind of multinational security force here could end up costing us the peace.

Interior Minister Yunus Qanooni told visiting U.S. Senator Joe Biden, "We expect from the U.S. that it won't leave Afghanistan alone." Interim President Hamid Karzai told me in an interview: "I received delegations from every province after I was elected. I must have received twenty-five hundred people. People from every province asked me to help get a multinational force here. People are desperate for security. One mullah opposed the idea."

I appreciate Mr. Bush's wariness about becoming involved here. We barely know who's who here, and the history of this place doesn't offer much hope. I wandered into an English bookstore in Kabul and was struck by how many books had "Afghan wars" in the title. I picked up one called A History of the War in Afghanistan and discovered it was part of a thick two-volume set that covered only the years 1800 to 1842.

Naturally, the Bush team doesn't want to "own" this problem. But unless we at least "rent" it for a while and make at least a limited commitment to a security force here, for a limited period of time, this country will go right back to what it was: Mr. bin Laden's neighborhood.

January 13, 2002

CRACKS IN THE RUBBLE

———

KABUL, AFGHANISTAN

I've got more good news and bad news from Kabul. The good news is that sporting events have returned to the city, even before electricity or law and order have been fully restored.

The bad news is that the sport is cockfighting.

A match took place last week at Babur's Gardens, a once beautiful, now decayed botanical park. About a hundred Afghan men—captured in stunning photographs by the *Times*'s Chang W. Lee—gathered to watch two huge fighting roosters go four rounds against each other before the match was finally called a draw.

Unfortunately, these aren't the only fighting roosters strutting around the Afghan ruins. There's also the human variety—the Afghan warlords, and the neighboring powers that support them, who've been fighting over Afghanistan for two decades. The reason the Afghan war went so smoothly for the United States was because the geopolitical roosters—Iran, Pakistan, Uzbekistan, and Russia—either overtly or tacitly cooperated with us to destroy the Taliban and Osama bin Laden, which was in each of their interests. And the local roosters—the key Tajik, Pashtun, Hazara, and Uzbek warlords—did the same.

But now that the war is largely finished, the struggle over Afghanistan is resuming, and America has a big decision in front of it: Will it show the same resolve in winning the peace here as it did in winning the war here? Will it support and join a multinational force to stay here and stabilize Afghanistan, and create some law and order, until the fledgling new government can get on its feet? This is the question of the day. If America hesitates, well, you can already see the roosters sharpening their claws.

I just met the new interior minister, Yunus Qanooni, in his office. Above his desk, where an American cabinet secretary would have a picture of President Bush, he had a photograph of Ahmed Shah Massoud, the charismatic leader of the Tajik-dominated Northern Alliance who was killed by the Taliban just before September 11. The foreign minister and defense minister, also Tajiks, also hang Ahmed Shah Massoud's picture. The finance minister, an ethnic Pashtun, does not. I have a rule:

When a minister has his favorite warlord's picture over his desk, and not that of the new president (who is a Pashtun), that's not a good sign.

Meanwhile, Afghan Ministry of Education officials have had their eyebrows raised by urgent approaches from Iran about acquiring land for Iranian-funded schools here. The Iranians have also been pumping money to their favorite Persian-speaking warlords so their Afghan allies will be able to resist any orders of the central government that hard-liners in Iran don't like—such as Afghanistan becoming a close U.S. ally.

But here's what's also interesting: Every Afghan you stop tells you this country is so war-weary and starved for security that he would much rather have a multinational force police the whole place, over any ethnic militia or local rooster. One Special Forces officer told me he was ordered to poll local leaders about whom they would like as peacekeepers: Germans, Canadians, Turks? And they all answered, "We want you."

Sure, some will take potshots at us, but even those warlords who might think of challenging a U.S.-led peacekeeping force admit that they were wowed by the incredible power America displayed here. For all the talk about the vaunted Afghan fighters, this was a war between the Jetsons and the Flintstones—and the Jetsons won, and the Flintstones know it. (There are Al Qaeda prisoners held near Bagram, guarded by U.S. Army MPs, some of whom are women. Imagine going overnight from a society where you never see a woman's face to being guarded by one with an M16. "At first some of them [make faces]," one woman MP told me, "but then they realize there's nothing they can do.")

The Taliban and Osama bin Laden lost the war because they mistakenly thought the Americans were the Russians, and could be defeated as easily. The Americans could lose the peace by also mistakenly thinking that they're the Russians—just another superpower that will automatically be resisted if it stays behind, so it better not even try.

It is by no means certain that, even if we stay for a limited period to provide security while the Afghans rebuild, they will make it. They may just be too divided after twenty-two years of civil war. But if we don't try, it is absolutely certain that this whole country will become just one big cockfight again.

January 16, 2002

PAKISTAN'S CONSTITUTION AVENUE

JACOBABAD, PAKISTAN

Pakistani President Pervez Musharraf's January 12 speech to his nation has the potential—the potential—to be the kind of mindset-shattering breakthrough for the Muslim world that has not been seen since Anwar el-Sadat's 1977 visit to Israel.

Why? Because for the first time since September 11, a Muslim leader has dared to acknowledge publicly the real problem: that Muslim extremism has been rooted in the educational systems and ruling arrangements of many of their societies, and it has left much of the Muslim world in a backward state. But he also laid out a road map for doing something about it—not just throwing extremists in jail, but confronting their extremist ideas with modern schools and a progressive Islam.

Ever since September 11 it has been clear that we need a war *within* Islam, not *with* Islam, and at least one leader has finally declared it. It would be nice if some Arab-Muslim leaders now did the same.

"The day of reckoning has come," Mr. Musharraf told his people. "Do we want Pakistan to become a theocratic state? Do we believe that religious education alone is enough for governance, or do we want Pakistan to emerge as a dynamic Islamic state? The verdict of the masses is in favor of a progressive Islamic state." The Pakistani president vowed to reform those madrasas, or Islamic schools, that teach only the Koran, and not science, math, and literature. From bazaars to barbershops, Pakistan's silent majority responded: "It's about time."

Scholars have long argued that as a country's domestic policies change, so too will its foreign policy. What happened in Pakistan is just the reverse. Because of September 11 and the subsequent attack on the Indian Parliament by pro-Pakistan Kashmiri terrorists, the United States and India made clear that Pakistan's foreign policy had to change—or America would destroy it economically and India militarily. There is nothing like the prospect of being hanged in the morning to concentrate the mind. So President Musharraf abruptly ended both Pakistan's support of the Taliban and of militants seeking to liberate Kashmir.

Having created a new Pakistani foreign policy, Mr. Musharraf's challenge now is to build broad domestic support. The old Pakistani foreign policy was forged in the 1980s under dictator General Zia ul-Haq. General Zia knew he was an illegitimate ruler so, as the Pakistani political analyst Husain Haqqani put it, "he based his rule on a military-mosque alliance." He used Muslim clerics and militant Islam to bless his dictatorship.

But Mr. Musharraf realized that using the militants in Kashmir and Afghanistan would destroy Pakistan from without and that relying upon them to legitimize his military regime would destroy Pakistan from within. So he has laid out a vision that caters to the aspirations of Pakistan's broad secularized or moderately religious mainstream. But to win the backing of these people, he will have to empower them, and that requires a gradual return to democracy.

"When you are relying on the military and the militants to stay in power, then all you have to do is give orders," Mr. Haqqani said. "But when you want to rely on the broader moderate public, you have to lead, you have to persuade, and you have to empower people to think and speak for themselves."

To put it another way, now that Pakistan has changed its foreign policy, Mr. Musharraf can either remake all of Pakistan's jails—arrest as many militant Islamists as possible—or he can remake Pakistan's politics and move from a military-mosque alliance to a military–Main Street one. To do that, though, he will have to share power, attract better people into politics, and dare to hold elections, which would also expose how little support radical Islamists actually have. When not propped up by the army, they have never drawn more than 5 percent.

Driving into Pakistan's capital, Islamabad, I am always struck by how the Parliament, presidency, and Supreme Court are all on one wide boulevard: Constitution Avenue. The only thing not on Constitution Avenue is Pakistan's Constitution, which is suspended. That is the road Mr. Musharraf has to reopen, because it is the only one that will lead him from an alliance with the mosques to an alliance with Main Street. And if he succeeds, well, who knows what other leaders may follow?

January 20, 2002

RUN, OSAMA, RUN

On the way back from Kabul, I passed through Pakistan, the Persian Gulf, London, and Belgium, where I had a variety of talks with Arab and Muslim journalists and businesspeople and Muslim community leaders in Europe. All of them were educated, intelligent, and thoughtful—and virtually none of them believed that Osama bin Laden was guilty.

Let's see, there was the serious Arab journalist in Bahrain who said that Arabs could never have pulled off something as complex as September 11; there was the Euro-Muslim woman in Brussels who looked at me as if I was a fool when I said that the bin Laden tape in which he boasted of the World Trade Center attack was surely authentic and had not been doctored by the Pentagon; there was the American-educated Arab student who insisted that somehow the CIA or Mossad must have known about September 11 in advance, so why didn't they stop it? There was the Saudi businessman who declared that there was a plot in the U.S. media to smear Saudi Arabia, for absolutely no reason. And there was the Pakistani who confided that his kids' entire elementary school class believed the canard that four thousand Jews who worked in the World Trade Center were warned not to go to the office on September 11.

Frankly, these views have been present across the Arab-Muslim world ever since September 11, but I somehow hoped that after the fall of the Taliban, or bin Laden's confessional tapes, they would have melted away. But they have not. Indeed, they have congealed into an iron curtain of misunderstanding separating America and the Arab-Muslim world, and are now as deeply held as they were on September 11—even if people are slightly more reticent about airing them.

And they add up to a simple point: that while America has won the war in Afghanistan, it has not won the hearts and minds of the Arab-Muslim world. The cultural-political-psychological chasm between us is wider than ever. And if you don't believe that, ask any U.S. ambassador from Morocco to Islamabad—any one of them. They will share with you cocktail party chatter about the "American conspiracy" against the Muslim world that will curl your ears.

Yes, there are exceptions in every country. When I sat with Bahraini friends in Manama last week, I found many of them deeply introspective and ready to look reality in the eye. But these are not the rule. Why? What produced this iron curtain of mistrust and misunderstanding?

There are many rivets in it. One is our own failure over the past two decades to really explain ourselves in Arabic and to puncture canards about U.S. policy with hard facts. The Bush team has yet to provide a dossier, in Arabic, detailing all the evidence against bin Laden. It is not too late for that, although facts alone will not be enough.

There is enormous cultural resistance to believing anything good about America. Some of this is deliberately fanned by the state-run press in certain Arab countries to deflect criticism from the regime. Some is revenge for America's support for Israel, particularly at this time when the Israeli-Palestinian conflict has turned into such a human meat grinder, aired every night on Arab TV. Not acknowledging America's version of reality, or undercutting its sense of victory in Afghanistan, is a way for Arabs and Muslims to get revenge for America's support for Israel, which they feel so powerless to affect.

At the same time, there does seem to be a certain strain of self-loathing at work in parts of the Arab-Muslim world today. What else can one think when someone tells you that Arabs or Muslims could never have been clever enough to pull off September 11 — only the Mossad or CIA? It is a sad fact that Arab self-esteem is very low these days because of the lagging state of Arab political systems and economies, and that feeds the free-floating anger that bin Laden has been surfing on.

Finally, we have to admit that bin Laden touches something deep in the Arab-Muslim soul, even among those who condemn his murders. They still root for him as the one man who was not intimidated by America's overweening power, as the one man who dared to tell certain Arab rulers that they had no clothes, and as the one man who did something about it.

Quietly today, many in the Arab-Muslim world are rooting for bin Laden to get away. They are whispering in their hearts, "Run, Osama, run!" That's what's really going on out there. I just wish we knew how to change it.

January 23, 2002

THE TWO DOMES OF BELGIUM

BRUSSELS

For all that has been written about September 11, there is still one big hole in our knowledge. We know who Osama bin Laden is. He is a unique cult figure—a Muslim Charles Manson with the organizational skills of Jack Welch. We also know who bin Laden's passive supporters are—all those Muslims who sympathize with him out of anger with their own leaders, America, or Israel. But who were the guys in the middle—the killer pilots who went beyond passive support to become suicidal mass murderers?

In search of that answer, I came to Europe. Why? Look at the biographies of many of the key hijackers or Al Qaeda agents: Mohamed Atta, Ziad al-Jarrah, Marwan al-Shehhi, etc. It's the same story: He grew up in a middle-class family in the Arab world, was educated, went to Europe for more studies, lived on the fringes of a European society (many in Belgium), gravitated to a local prayer group or mosque, became radicalized there by Islamist elements, went off for training in Afghanistan, and presto—a terrorist was born. The personal encounter between these young men and Europe is the key to this story.

A female Arab friend who also studied abroad with young Muslim men described them this way: "They are mostly men who grew up in an environment where the rules were very clear. They grew up never encountering anything that shakes their core. Suddenly they are thrown into Europe, and there is a whole different set of social rules that shakes their core. They don't know how to adapt because they've never had to, so they become more insular and hold on to their [Islamic] core even more."

This trend is reinforced by the fact that Muslim immigrants are often perennial outsiders in Europe. In America, Muslims can enjoy a fairly rapid transition to citizenship, but in Europe there is no melting pot. "Our problem in Belgium is that there is Islamophobia," said Nordin Maloujahmoum, president of the Muslim Executive Council of Belgium. "Some 54 percent of the population here say they don't believe non-Belgian ethnic groups could ever be real Belgians. A woman wearing a veil here finds it impossible to get a job."

Fauzaya Talhaoui, the only Muslim woman in the Belgian Parliament, told me that her parents' generation came from North Africa and just wanted to assimilate but that many in her generation, after being frozen out, have turned to Islam. "They took the view—if you want to treat us differently, we will act differently," she said.

Here's the truth: What radicalized the September 11 terrorists was not that they suffered from a poverty of food, it was that they suffered from a poverty of dignity. Frustrated by the low standing of Muslim countries in the world, compared with that of Europe or the United States, and the low standing in which they were personally held where they were living, they were easy pickings for militant preachers who knew how to direct their rage.

"Many of the terrorists we are now confronting are a Western phenomenon, existing inside the Islamic diaspora in the U.S. and Europe," wrote Adrian Karatnycky, the president of Freedom House, in a highly original essay in *National Review*. These men are not "sleepers" planted within Europe years in advance by bin Laden, he argues; instead, they are minted right there, when they encounter the West.

"Like the leaders of America's Weather Underground, Germany's Baader-Meinhof Gang, Italy's Red Brigades, and Japan's Red Army Faction, the Islamic terrorists were university-educated converts to an all-encompassing neo-totalitarian ideology," Mr. Karatnycky argues. "For them, Islamism is the new universal revolutionary creed, and bin Laden is Sheikh Guevara."

Mr. Karatnycky is right: The real challenge of the West is to understand what is happening not just in Iraq or Saudi Arabia, but also in its own backyard, in the chemical reaction between Western societies and their own mosques and Muslim diasporas. That's where the killer pilots were conceived, and that's where they must be tracked—but in a way that respects the fact that 99.9 percent of the Muslims in Europe or America are good citizens, not militants.

Belgium is a microcosm of the whole story. There are three hundred mosques in Belgium today, with three hundred domes. But there is another famous dome here: the huge radar dome at NATO headquarters in Mons. Somewhere in the cultural encounter between these two domes of Belgium—the dome of NATO and the dome of the mosques—lies the key to this September 11, and maybe the next.

January 27, 2002

DEAD MAN WALKING

Yasir Arafat is a dead man walking. Few American, Israeli, or Arab leaders, not to mention Palestinians, really believe anymore that he will ever lead his people into a peace deal with Israel. The only thing keeping Mr. Arafat afloat today is that no one wants to own his demise—neither Israel nor America nor the Arabs nor his own aides want responsibility for finishing him off. That's why this conflict has left the realm of diplomacy and entered the realm of biology—everyone is just waiting for Mr. Arafat to pass away. Too bad he eats yogurt and takes regular naps.

Mr. Arafat is a dead man walking because he shot himself—three times. First, he spurned Bill Clinton's peace offer, which would have given the Palestinians a state in the West Bank, Gaza, and East Jerusalem. And he spurned it primarily because he not only wanted a Palestinian state in Gaza and the West Bank, he also wanted the right of return of hundreds of thousands of Palestinian refugees to pre-1967 Israel.

"It turns out Arafat wanted two Palestinian states," notes the Middle East expert Stephen P. Cohen. "He wanted a Palestinian state for the West Bank and Gaza to be negotiated with Israel today. And he wanted a Palestinian state inside Israel that would be brought about by a return of Palestinian refugees and their soaring birthrate tomorrow. Israel was ready to give him one Palestinian state, but not two. And Arafat didn't have the courage to tell his people that."

Second, when Mr. Arafat couldn't get his two states at Camp David, he decided to give up the monopoly of force within the Palestinian areas. A monopoly of force is the definition of a state, or a "Palestinian Authority." Mr. Arafat gave up that monopoly so Hamas and Islamic Jihad could carry out suicide attacks against Israel to pressure Israel into accepting his terms—but in a way that he wouldn't have to take responsibility for. In doing so, Mr. Arafat undercut any notion that he could be a responsible sovereign for a Palestinian state. Who would trust a leader who gives up his authority whenever it suits him?

And finally, by importing the Ship of Fools—a boatload of advanced weapons from Iran—while he was insisting that he was abiding by a cease-fire, Mr. Arafat destroyed a central argument of Israeli doves: that

Israel could accept a Palestinian state on the West Bank and Gaza because it would be "demilitarized" and unable to threaten either Israel or Jordan. Says the Middle East writer David Makovsky, "Everyone hoped Arafat would be Nelson Mandela, but he turns out to be Robert Mugabe."

This leaves us with five options. Option one: The Arab leaders will get together and try to replace Mr. Arafat as the relevant negotiating partner with Israel and offer Israelis a pan-Arab comprehensive peace in return for total withdrawal. Option two: Palestine is Jordan—Israel will invite Jordan to replace Mr. Arafat and reassume its sovereignty in the West Bank as the only Arab party Israel could trust there. Option three: Jordan is Palestine—Ariel Sharon will reoccupy the West Bank and drive Palestinians into Jordan. Option four: The Palestinians will oust Mr. Arafat and replace him with a new leadership that will restore Palestinian credibility with Israel as a responsible peace partner and authority. Option five: NATO takes over the West Bank and Gaza.

In the meantime, Israeli and American Jews would be well advised not to get too smug. Yes, Mr. Arafat is now discredited and isolated. But let that not obscure the fact that he isn't the only one who wanted more than one state. Because what Mr. Sharon and the Jewish right have been doing by building so many settlements in the territories is saying to the Arabs: We also want two states—a Jewish state in Israel and a Jewish state in the West Bank and Gaza.

Right now there is no Palestinian partner to call this bluff. But be advised: These settlements are a cancer for the Jewish people; they threaten the entire Zionist enterprise. If Israel tries to retain them, it will end up either as a non-Jewish state, because it will be absorbing so many Palestinians, or a nondemocratic apartheid state, because the only way to rule so many Palestinians will be à la the old South African model. So let us root for the rapid emergence of a real Palestinian peace partner. It is not only the Palestinians' future that rides on that, but also the Israelis'.

January 30, 2002

THE END OF NATO?

Flying in and out of Afghanistan is a harrowing business. When I tried to get out of Kabul a few weeks ago, bad weather closed Bagram Air Base and the UN canceled its flight, so my only way out was to hitchhike on a U.S. military transport. The trip turned out to be a real insight.

For security reasons, the U.S. military flies all its transports in and out of Afghanistan at night. In this case, the runway lights were kept off until just before the C-130, guided by infrared sensors and radar, dipped below the low clouds and hit the tarmac.

As soon as it cut its engines, U.S. soldiers, wearing special night-vision goggles that made them look like bug-eyed Martians, unloaded and then reloaded the plane entirely in the dark. It then took off completely in the dark, save for a few seconds of runway lights to guide it out. There is only one air force in the world that can operate so effectively in the pitch dark this way, using night-vision equipment: the U.S. Air Force.

It's a great thing—and it's destroying the NATO alliance.

Yes, you read that right. Visiting Brussels after Kabul, I found only one issue dominating the buzz at NATO headquarters, and it was this: The United States has become so much more technologically advanced than any of its NATO allies that America increasingly doesn't need them to fight a distant war, as it demonstrated in Afghanistan, where it basically won alone, except for small but important contributions from Britain, Canada, and Australia. And when you add to that the unilateralist impulses of the Bush team—which instinctively doesn't want to fight with aid from allies who might get in the way or limit America's room for maneuvers—you have many, many people in Brussels asking whether NATO nations can ever fight together again.

"In the 1960s, it was France under Charles de Gaulle that threatened NATO's cohesion—in 2001, it is Don Rumsfeld's America that is doing so," argued Dominique Moisi, the French expert on international relations. "Basically, the question before us is this: What happens to a creature when its creator no longer trusts it? What is the meaning of an alliance if the immediate reaction of its leader is, 'Don't call us, we'll call you, because we basically don't trust you.' Look, I am all for NATO, but if the Americans are not, what am I to do?"

As Afghanistan and Kosovo showed, to fight a modern war today you need four key assets: many large transport aircraft to deploy troops to far-flung battlefields; precision-guided bombs and missiles that can hit enemy targets with a high degree of certitude, thereby shortening the war and reducing civilian casualties; large numbers of Special Operations teams that can operate at night using night-vision equipment; and secure, encrypted communications so ground and air units can be knit together in a high-tech war without the enemy listening in.

No other NATO country has all four of these. Britain comes closest. Germany, France, and Italy are barely in the ball game, and the others are a joke. In part this is because European defense industries are not as sophisticated as America's today. But in part it's because the Europeans, deep down, don't feel threatened by America's enemies, particularly by the "axis of evil" (Iran, Iraq, and North Korea) that Mr. Bush identified. Therefore, they don't want to spend much on defense. If President Bush gets the defense budget increase he asked for in his State of the Union address, U.S. defense spending will equal the defense budgets of the next fifteen highest countries—combined.

As a result, we are increasingly headed for a military apartheid within NATO: America will be the chef who decides the menu and cooks all the great meals, and the NATO allies will be the busboys who stay around and clean up the mess and keep the peace—indefinitely. As one French diplomat put it to me bluntly, "That is not going to be sustainable."

He's right. Brussels, we have a problem.

But if the Europeans truly want to be in on the takeoff of military operations, they had better invest in the planes and equipment that can take off with us—including in total dark. Otherwise they will have no credibility when they complain about U.S. unilateralism. At the same time, though, the Bush team would do well to restrain some of its unilateralist instincts, from NATO to Kyoto, to make clear that we don't intend to fly solo everywhere and we want others in on the landing.

Because, frankly, I'm glad America can fight everywhere in the dark, but I wouldn't want it to have to fight everywhere alone.

February 3, 2002

DEAR ARAB LEAGUE

To: President Hosni Mubarak, Crown Prince Abdullah,
   King Abdullah, President Bashar al-Assad,
   and the rest of the Arab League
From: President Bush

Dear Friends: You've all warned me privately about the foul wind of anti-Americanism that is now blowing through your region, fed by the perception that I've bowed out of Mideast diplomacy and given a blank check to Prime Minister Ariel Sharon of Israel. So let me explain to you exactly my position: I believe your problems with us grow from a misreading of Arab-Israeli history. You think somehow that if we just squeezed the Israelis they would roll over and do whatever the Palestinians demanded. You're wrong.

The relevant balance of power is not between us and Israel, but between you and Israel. All the peace breakthroughs happened not when we threatened Israelis, but when you enticed them. That is, when Arab leaders—Anwar el-Sadat, King Hussein, and even Yasir Arafat in Oslo—made clear to the Israeli silent majority that they were interested in real peace in return for real Israeli withdrawal, they got exactly what they wanted from Israel.

Remember, some Israeli rightists resisted giving back all of the Sinai to Sadat, some even resisted the land swaps with Jordan, and many, as you know, resisted Oslo I and II. But when you, the Arab leaders, persuaded mainstream Israelis that you were offering real peace for real withdrawal, you shifted them to your side of the bargaining table and the Israeli rejectionists were defeated. That's the only balance of power that matters.

We're just bystanders. You're the ones with the power to really reshape the diplomacy, not me. And here is my advice for how to do it. You have an Arab League summit set for March in Lebanon. I suggest your summit issue one simple resolution: "The twenty-two members of the Arab League say to Israel that in return for a complete Israeli withdrawal to the June 4, 1967, lines—in the West Bank, Gaza, Jerusalem, and on the Golan Heights—we offer full recognition of Israel, diplomatic relations, normalized trade, and security guarantees. Full peace with all twenty-two Arab states for full withdrawal."

Since you've all told me privately that this is your position, why not make it public and get the benefit? This is how to bury Osama bin Laden and define for the world who the Arabs really are. If you can't take that risk, why should I?

You need to face up to something: Ehud Barak gave us an Israeli peace plan, however rough. Bill Clinton then followed up with an American peace plan. Now is the time for an Arab peace plan. It's time you guys stopped sitting back and complaining about everyone else's peace plans. It's time for you to put on the table not only what you want from Israel—an end to occupation—but what you collectively are ready to give in return. Arafat can't do it alone.

You know what bugs me, guys? You want to pretend that Sharon just reappeared from outer space and that's when all the trouble started, and I'm just supporting him for no reason. That's not what happened. Sharon was unelectable in Israeli politics. What allowed him to reemerge was Arafat's rejection of the Barak plan and the Clinton plan, and then his launching of an intifada with suicide bombings of Israeli pizza parlors. Did Sharon provoke the Palestinians by going to the Temple Mount? You bet. But he wasn't prime minister at the time. Barak was. How could you let Sharon provoke you and lose the best opportunity ever for a Palestinian state?

Some of you have asked me privately: If we do this, can you guarantee Israel will respond positively? No, I can't guarantee it, but every ounce of history tells me Israel's silent majority will insist that its leader respond positively to you, and if he doesn't, Israelis will vote him out, and I will back them.

There is one thing I can guarantee, though. If you don't make this offer, nothing will change, the Israeli silent majority will continue following Sharon into a dead end, and the Arab League will fall further and further behind the rest of the world. Guys, you know that the peace process was about so much more than just Israelis and Palestinians. It was also a cover and an engine for all the progressive forces in the Arab world that want to integrate, trade, and modernize. Without the peace process, all those forces are now on the run. That's why you all need this as much as Israelis and Palestinians do. The future is in your hands—not mine. Good luck. W.

February 6, 2002

BLUNT QUESTION,
BLUNT ANSWER

LONDON

We were just finishing a lunch hosted by a U.S. diplomat for Arab editors in London when one of the editors turned to me and said: "I hope you will not be insulted, but I have to ask you this question because it's around: Are Jews in the media behind the campaign to smear Saudi Arabia and Islam?"

Wow. It is not a question I often get over coffee, but it was asked sincerely, by a serious Arab journalist who wanted a serious answer. I said that I was not insulted and that I knew this question was everywhere—everywhere—in the Arab-Muslim world today, so let me take a stab at it.

My first instinct was to ask a question back: When Jewish reporters in Beirut and Israel were at the forefront in covering such stories as the Sabra and Shatila massacre of Palestinians, why did no one in the Arab world ask whether they were part of a Jewish conspiracy? When Jewish congressmen and commentators led the campaign for U.S. intervention to save the Muslims of Bosnia and Kosovo and to roll back the Iraqi invasion of Kuwait and protect Saudi Arabia in the Persian Gulf war, why did no one in the Muslim world complain about a Jewish conspiracy?

The truth is that Jewish commentators and lawmakers have probably been more outspoken in support of using American force to rescue Muslims in the last fifteen years than any other group—including American Muslims.

So, to begin with, maybe—just maybe—there is no Jewish conspiracy against Muslims or Saudi Arabia at work here. Maybe, just maybe, many Americans are upset because fifteen Saudis took part in the September 11 attacks, private Saudi charities financed Osama bin Laden, and hundreds of Saudis fought with Al Qaeda against America in Afghanistan. And these hard facts have hardened U.S. opinion against them.

It will be a tragedy if Arabs and Muslims adopt the position that there is no conceivable reason why Americans might be upset with them today and that any criticism they face in the U.S. media is entirely the result of some Jewish campaign of vilification.

Why a tragedy? First, because it will reinforce all the reasons why the Arab-Muslim world has fallen behind in economic development, education, science, and democratization. Because whenever a people reduces all its problems to a conspiracy by someone else, it absolves itself and its leaders of any responsibility for its predicament—and any need for self-examination. No civilization has ever prospered with that approach. (And several courageous Arab journalists have started to point that out.)

Blaming someone else is not a substitute for analyzing or coping. (That also applies to Israelis who say Yasir Arafat alone is the source of all their problems.) Only in a society that embraces self-criticism can the political process produce real facts to cope with real problems. Look at the excruciating process of analysis, self-criticism, and accountability that America went through after Vietnam. Few Arab-Muslim countries have ever done anything like that after a war, let alone after 9/11. Until they do, their conclusion that America or the Jews are behind all their problems is escapism, not analysis.

Second, persisting in this will only widen the gulf between America and the Muslim world, because such conspiracy theories are based on a total misunderstanding of America. The standard view of America in the Arab-Muslim world is that America is rich and powerful because it is crass and materialistic. And since America is just about material interests—not values—why can't it understand that its real material interests are with the Arabs, not with Israel? The Jews must be manipulating things.

The truth is exactly the opposite. America is successful and wealthy because of its values, not despite them. It is prosperous because of the way it respects freedom, individualism, and women's rights and the way it nurtures creativity and experimentation. Those values are our inexhaustible oil wells. Americans naturally gravitate toward societies that share those same values, and they recoil from those that don't.

There are two kinds of blame: one that is a result of self-analysis and self-criticism, and one that is an attempt to avoid self-analysis and self-criticism. We have all known people who endlessly blame their mothers or fathers for all their shortcomings, never themselves. Some eventually grow out of it and thrive. Some never do—and they go through life angry, miserable, and never achieving their full potential.

February 10, 2002

CRAZIER THAN THOU

LONDON

Reading Europe's press, it is really reassuring to see how warmly Europeans have embraced President Bush's formulation that an "axis of evil" threatens world peace. There's only one small problem. President Bush thinks the axis of evil is Iran, Iraq, and North Korea, and the Europeans think it's Donald Rumsfeld, Dick Cheney, and Condi Rice.

I'm not kidding. Chris Patten, the European Union's foreign policy czar, told *The Guardian* that the Bush "axis of evil" idea was dangerously "absolutist and simplistic," not "thought through," and "unhelpful," and that the Europeans needed to stop Washington before it went into "unilateralist overdrive."

So what do I think? I think these critics are right that the countries Mr. Bush identified as an axis of evil are not really an "axis," and we shouldn't drive them together. And the critics are right that each of these countries poses a different kind of threat and requires a different nuanced response. And the critics are right that America can't fight everywhere alone. And the critics are right that America needs to launch a serious effort to end Israeli-Palestinian violence, because it's undermining any hope of U.S.-Arab cooperation.

The critics are right on all these counts—but I'm still glad President Bush said what he said.

Because the critics are missing the larger point, which is this: September 11 happened because America had lost its deterrent capability. We lost it because for twenty years we never retaliated against, or brought to justice, those who murdered Americans. From the first suicide bombing of the U.S. Embassy in Beirut in April 1983, to the bombing of the Marine barracks at the Beirut airport a few months later, to the TWA hijacking, to the attack on U.S. troops at Khobar Towers in Saudi Arabia, to the suicide bombings of two U.S. embassies in East Africa, to the attack on the U.S.S. *Cole* in Yemen, innocent Americans were killed and we did nothing.

So our enemies took us less and less seriously and became more and more emboldened. Indeed, they became so emboldened that a group of individuals—think about that for a second: not a state but a group of individuals—attacked America in its own backyard. Why not? The terrorists and the states that harbor them thought we were soft, and they were right. They thought that they could always "out-crazy" us, and they were right. They thought we would always listen to the Europeans and opt for "constructive engagement" with rogues, not a fist in the face, and they were right.

America's enemies smelled weakness all over us, and we paid a huge price for that. There is an old Bedouin legend that goes like this: An elderly Bedouin leader thought that by eating turkey he could restore his virility. So he bought a turkey, kept it by his tent, and stuffed it with food every day. One day someone stole his turkey. The Bedouin elder called his sons together and told them: "Boys, we are in great danger. Someone has stolen my turkey." "Father," the sons answered, "what do you need a turkey for?"

"Never mind," he answered, "just get me back my turkey." But the sons ignored him, and a month later someone stole the old's camel. "What should we do?" the sons asked. "Find my turkey," said the father. But the sons did nothing, and a few weeks later the man's daughter was raped. The father said to his sons: "It is all because of the turkey. When they saw that they could take my turkey, we lost everything."

America is that Bedouin elder, and for twenty years people have been taking our turkey. The Europeans don't favor any military action against Iraq, Iran, or North Korea. Neither do I. But what is their alternative? To wait until Saddam Hussein's son Uday, who's an even bigger psychopath than his father, has bio-weapons and missiles that can hit Paris?

No, the "axis of evil" idea isn't thought through—but that's what I like about it. It says to these countries and their terrorist pals: "We know what you're cooking in your bathtubs. We don't know exactly what we're going to do about it, but if you think we are going to just sit back and take another dose from you, you're wrong. Meet Don Rumsfeld—he's even crazier than you are."

There is a lot about the Bush team's foreign policy I don't like, but their willingness to restore our deterrence, and to be as crazy as some of our enemies, is one thing they have right. It is the only way we're going to get our turkey back.

February 13, 2002

AN INTRIGUING SIGNAL
FROM THE SAUDI CROWN PRINCE

RIYADH, SAUDI ARABIA

Earlier this month, I wrote a column suggesting that the twenty-two members of the Arab League, at their summit in Beirut on March 27 and 28, make a simple, clear-cut proposal to Israel to break the Israeli-Palestinian impasse: In return for a total withdrawal by Israel to the June 4, 1967, lines and the establishment of a Palestinian state, the twenty-two members of the Arab League would offer Israel full diplomatic relations, normalized trade, and security guarantees. Full withdrawal, in accord with UN Resolution 242, for full peace between Israel and the entire Arab world. Why not?

I am currently in Saudi Arabia on a visit—part of the Saudi opening to try to explain themselves better to the world in light of the fact that fifteen Saudis were involved in the September 11 attacks. So I took the opportunity of a dinner with Saudi Arabia's crown prince and de facto ruler, Abdullah bin Abdulaziz al-Saud, to try out the idea of this Arab League proposal. I knew that Jordan, Morocco, and some key Arab League officials had been talking about this idea in private but had not dared to broach it publicly until one of the "big boys"—Saudi Arabia or Egypt—took the lead.

After I laid out this idea, the crown prince looked at me with mock astonishment and said, "Have you broken into my desk?"

"No," I said, wondering what he was talking about.

"The reason I ask is that this is exactly the idea I had in mind—full withdrawal from all the occupied territories, in accord with UN resolutions, including in Jerusalem, for full normalization of relations," he said. "I have drafted a speech along those lines. My thinking was to deliver it before the Arab summit and try to mobilize the entire Arab world behind it. The speech is written, and it is in my desk. But I changed my mind about delivering it when Sharon took the violence, and the oppression, to an unprecedented level.

"But I tell you," the crown prince added, "if I were to pick up the phone now and ask someone to read you the speech, you will find it virtually identical to what you are talking about. I wanted to find a way to make clear to the Israeli people that the Arabs don't reject or despise them. But the Arab people do reject what their leadership is now doing to the Palestinians, which is inhumane and oppressive. And I thought of this as a possible signal to the Israeli people."

Well, I said, I'm glad to know that Saudi Arabia was thinking along these lines, but so many times in the past we've heard from Arab leaders that they had just been about to do this or that but that Ariel Sharon or some other Israeli leader had gotten in the way. After a while, it's hard to take seriously. So I asked, What if Mr. Sharon and the Palestinians agreed to a cease-fire before the Arab summit?

"Let me say to you that the speech is written, and it is still in my drawer," the crown prince said.

I pass all of this on as straightforwardly as I can, without hype or unrealistic hopes. What was intriguing to me about the crown prince's remarks was not just his ideas—which, if delivered, would be quite an advance on anything the Arab League has proposed before—but the fact that they came up in the middle of a long off-the-record conversation. I suggested to the crown prince that if he felt so strongly about this idea, even in draft form, why not put it on the record—only then would anyone take it seriously. He said he would think about it. The next day his office called, reviewed the crown prince's quotations, and said, Go ahead, put them on the record. So here they are.

Crown Prince Abdullah is known as the staunchest Arab nationalist among Saudi leaders, and the one most untainted by corruption. He has a strong Arab following inside and outside the kingdom, and if he ever gave such a speech, it would have a real impact on Arab public opinion, as well as Israeli. Prince Abdullah seemed to be signaling that if President Bush took a new initiative for Middle East peace, he and other Arab leaders would be prepared to do so as well.

I also used the interview with the Saudi leader to ask why his country had never really apologized to America for the fact that fifteen Saudis were involved in 9/11.

"We have been close friends for so long, and we never expected Americans to doubt us," he said. "We saw this attack by bin Laden and his men as an attack on us too, and an attempt to damage the U.S.-Saudi relationship," the crown prince said. "We were deeply saddened by it, and we never expected it to lead to tensions between us. But we've now learned that we respond to events differently . . . It is never too late to express our regrets."

As for the "axis of evil" and reports of a possible U.S. military strike against Iraq, the Saudi leader said: "Any attack on Iraq or Iran should not be contemplated at all, because it would not serve the interests of America, the region, or the world, as there is no clear evidence of a present danger. Iraq is contemplating the return of the inspectors, and the United States should pursue this because inspectors can determine if Iraq is complying with the UN resolutions."

February 17, 2002

THE SAUDI CHALLENGE

JIDDA, SAUDI ARABIA

I could tell that Saudi Arabia had undergone a big change since I last visited when I checked into the Sheraton Hotel here and the desk clerk was a Saudi. Five years ago, the hotel owner would have been a Saudi, but the clerks and key hotel personnel all would have been imported labor from the Philippines, Pakistan, or Lebanon. Not anymore.

Today, with the oil boom over, the Saudi economy can no longer afford the welfare net that once guaranteed every Saudi a government job. Since 1980 Saudi Arabia's population has exploded from 7 million to 19 million, thanks to one of the highest birthrates in the world and zero family planning.

Meanwhile, per capita oil income has fallen from $19,000, at the height of the oil boom in 1981, to about $7,300 today. With less money trickling down to sustain extended families or bloated government offices, several million Saudis are now unemployed, underemployed, or taking jobs they never would have before.

To soak up all the unemployed here, Saudi Arabia will have to learn how to drill human oil wells. That is, its crude oil wells built an impressive infrastructure, but they can't sustain the future. Saudi Arabia will be able to thrive only if it can reform its schools to build young people who can innovate and create wealth from their minds—not just from their wells.

That means revamping the overcrowded Saudi universities, which right now churn out endless graduates in Islamic studies or liberal arts, but too few with the technical skills a modern economy demands. It also means revamping the Saudi legal system to attract foreign investors to create jobs. That means real transparency, rule of law, independent courts, and anticorruption measures.

Without those changes, this country is going to get poorer and poorer, because 40 percent of the population is under fourteen—meaning the biggest population bulge hasn't even hit the labor market yet. This could be dynamite. In December an end-of-Ramadan youth brawl erupted on the Jidda coastal road, during which the crowd turned against the police and shouted antigovernment and anti-U.S. slogans, leading to some three hundred arrests.

The good news is that a move was already afoot before September 11 to begin English education—and more teaching about the world beyond the domain of Islam—in the fourth grade instead of the seventh, which will start next year. But with extensive class time devoted here to teaching Islam, often by rote, shifting students to more independent thinking in other areas won't be simple, and already has conservatives grumbling. "We are now in the middle of a major change of our education system," said Khalid al-Awwad, the deputy education minister for curriculum. "It will be based on the idea: Think global, act local."

The bad news is that the only top leader of the al-Saud ruling family who has reformist instincts, and is untainted by corruption, is the aging Crown Prince Abdullah. But he is often stymied by his brothers or traditionalists. When the crown prince proposed letting women drive—so Saudi Arabia would not have to employ 500,000 expatriate chauffeurs to shuttle women—he was blocked by conservatives.

This is also a problem for middle-class Saudis who can't afford chauffeurs. "I have a man who works for me who has three daughters," said a Saudi businessman. "He's constantly having to leave work to drive his daughters home from school or somewhere else. It affects productivity." Imagine being a Saudi man with six daughters and no chauffeur—that's a soccer dad on steroids.

Leaders like to make changes here the gradual "Saudi way" to keep the peace, but that may no longer be possible. "You can make people change with time, but do we have the time?" asks oil minister Ali al-Naimi. "With globalization, I don't think we have time. We are living in a crystal ball now. People see what's happening worldwide on every screen."

We have a stake in Saudi success. Almost all of the fifteen Saudi hijackers on September 11 came from one of the country's poorer regions, Asir, which has recently undergone a rapid but socially disruptive modernization. As one middle-class Saudi put it to me: "The problem here is not Islam. The problem is too many young men with no job and no university and nowhere to go except to the mosque, where some [radical preachers] fill their heads with anger for America. Every home now has two or three not working. This is the real problem."

February 20, 2002

A TRAVELER TO SAUDI ARABIA

RIYADH, SAUDI ARABIA

I was riding the elevator the other day in my hotel when a Saudi gentleman got in on the floor below me. He was wearing a traditional Saudi robe and red headdress, and I was in a suit and tie. He looked me up and down for a second before asking, "American?" Yes, I nodded. Then, reaching out his huge hand to me and smiling warmly, he said, "Saudi." It was a kind gesture, meant to say, "We still like you—we hope you still like us."

Over eight days of discussions here I've had many memorable encounters, not all so friendly. One thing I learned was that this is a deceptively insular place. For centuries the desert kept outsiders at bay, and then, with the coming of oil wealth, the Saudis had the luxury of only letting the world in on their own terms, and those who were let in often told the Saudis only what they wanted to hear.

After September 11, though, and the disclosure that fifteen of the hijackers were Saudis, the world kicked down Saudi Arabia's door and arrived without a visa. Suddenly, Saudis got a raw taste of what many outsiders, who did not need to be polite to them, thought of their country—that it had become the source of the money, Islamist ideology, and people who were now threatening us.

This shocked many Saudis and, though they received me hospitably, they hammered me with their pain. I heard it from a female doctor who spoke of the shame she now felt when the foreign border police looked twice at her once-respected Saudi passport and of how much she wanted me to understand that Saudis were "a moderate people." I heard it from a senior official who asked me at the end of an interview: "What is to become of us?"—the thousands of U.S.-educated Saudis who enjoy America, send their kids there, vacation there, and now feel severed from an essential part of their identity.

And I heard it most passionately from a female Saudi professor. (Don't be fooled by the veils; it was the women here who got most in my face.) She almost brought me to tears at the *Okaz* newspaper office when she spoke from the heart of how important Islam was for her identity and the deep hurt she felt from seeing her faith denigrated and misunderstood by outsiders.

But they also heard my pain—my pain at the fact that fifteen Saudis came over to my country and helped kill three thousand Americans, and that to this day Saudi Arabia has never really explained who the hijackers were and what motivated them. At best, I was told they were "deviants." But there are two kinds of deviants—deviants who believe what everyone else around them believes and the only difference is that they act on it, and deviants who believe in things no one around them does. If they were deviants, I asked, why did a U.S. hospital worker here tell me he was appalled to see Saudi doctors and nurses around him celebrating on 9/11?

I was told this was not the true feeling here. I was told the hijackers were actually educated in America. I was told they were sent by the Mossad or the CIA. I was told in one session that the Jews control the U.S. government and that was the real problem, a statement that prompted me to walk out. I was told the hijackers were responding to Arab anger over blind U.S. support for Israel's brutality to Palestinians. If that was the case, I asked, why did Osama bin Laden say that what motivated him was a desire to drive the United States out of Arabia and topple the corrupt Saudi ruling family? I got no good answers.

I would have concluded that the cultural gap between us was unbridgeable, had I not also met a few U.S.-educated Saudis who, when alone with me, confided what I think is the truth. One put it like this: "The tribal mentality here is very strong, and in the desert, when the tribe is attacked, you'd better stick together or you're dead. People know there are problems with our [Islamic] education system, and part of them is glad you're raising it. But they feel under attack, so they won't talk frankly to you [or want to be seen as making] changes because you demand them. The problem is not the books, but the preachers who use their Friday sermons to tell [young] people that America wants to destroy Islam.

"Before 9/11 the government thought they were just talking, so let them talk. Now they're dealing with it. These people need to be controlled. But always it has to be in secret—never tell the outsiders you have a problem. No, I say—let's fix the problem and tell people we've fixed it, and they should fix theirs. Until we get over this tribal outlook, we will never develop."

February 24, 2002

ONE COUNTRY, TWO FUTURES

RIYADH, SAUDI ARABIA

An acquaintance here in Saudi Arabia told me this story: He was touring the countryside by car and got slightly lost. He saw a car down the road and approached it to ask directions, but each time he drew near, the car sped away. Eventually he caught up to it, the car pulled over, and a terrified driver jumped out to flee: It was a Saudi woman dressed like a man. In a country where it is illegal for women to drive, that's the only way for a lady to get behind the wheel.

This story is a good reminder that not everything here operates in real life as it appears on paper—which is what makes predicting Saudi Arabia's future a very inexact science. As such, I've concluded that there are two possible models for Saudi Arabia's future. I call them "the Soviet school" and "the China school."

The Soviet school argues that Saudi Arabia is an Islamic version of the Soviet Union: an absolute monarchy that is, like the Soviet Union, ultimately unreformable. The core of this regime is an alliance between a modernizing, but corrupt, theocracy, led by the al-Saud family, and the ultraconservative Wahhabi religious establishment, which provides the al-Sauds with legitimacy. The minute you try to reform it, the whole system will come unglued.

This is how the Soviet school sees it: The ruling al-Saud brothers are like the old Soviet Politburo; the fifty thousand al-Saud princes and relatives are the equivalent of the Communist Party. Wahhabism, the puritanical Saudi Arabian brand of Islam, is used by the al-Sauds to unite the forty fractious tribes of the Arabian Peninsula, just as Communism was used by Lenin to unite the one hundred fractious nationalities of Russia and its neighboring republics. Osama bin Laden is just the evil version of Andrei Sakharov—the insider who steps outside the system to declare that the king has no clothes. Sakharov was exiled to Gorky for that, and bin Laden to Kabul. And ultimately, both systems went into decline after unhappy encounters where? In Afghanistan.

The intense Saudi competition with Iran for dominance over the Muslim world—which involves financing competing conservative Muslim schools and mosques from Pakistan to Indonesia—is identical to the Soviet competition with China for influence over the Communist world.

The Soviet school concludes that Saudi Arabia has about five more years before its population boom, declining per capita income, need for education reform to create skilled workers and attract foreign investors, excessive defense spending, and influx of satellite TV and the Internet combine to explode the Saudi system, just as they did the Soviet one.

The China school, by contrast, begins with the assumption that Saudi Arabia is a country that makes no sense on paper but in real life has a lot more cushions and ballast, which enable it, like China, to pursue two seemingly contradictory policies at once. In China it's Communism and capitalism, and in Saudi Arabia it's Wahhabism and rapid modernization. Oil is to Saudi Arabia what huge direct foreign investment is to China—a natural resource that allows the system to buy off a lot of discontent and enables people to cheat on the system, and thereby let off steam, behind closed doors.

In the China school, Saudi Arabia's Crown Prince Abdullah is the equivalent of China's reformist prime minister, Zhu Rongji. In particular, like Zhu, Abdullah is trying to push Saudi Arabia into the World Trade Organization to create external pressure for more rule of law and transparency—but this move is resisted by more corrupt elements of the elite, who benefit from the status quo.

Finally, like China's rulers, the Saudi ruling elite knows how to stay in power and will do whatever it takes to do so. In China's case that meant bringing capitalists into the Communist Party and crushing students at Tiananmen, and in Saudi Arabia's case it will mean confronting the radical Islamists—just as the al-Sauds did before when they wanted to introduce radio, television, and women's education.

Like China's leaders, the Saudi monarchy can garner support from members of the middle class—not only by buying them off, but also by arguing that the alternative to its rule would be chaos or extremists.

The China school dismisses the idea that Saudi Arabia will collapse in five years. It notes, instead, that for fifty years, someone has come out with a study every five years that says Saudi Arabia has only five more years.

Which school would I bet on? Ask me in five years.

February 27, 2002

WALL OF IDEAS

I've spent the last six weeks traveling around the Arab-Muslim world, talking with people about September 11 and U.S.-Muslim relations. So I didn't know whether to laugh or cry when I got home and read that the Pentagon was considering putting out false stories that might advance America's antiterrorism campaign. I didn't know whether to laugh or cry because if you spend five minutes in the Arab-Muslim world these days, you'll instantly discover that people there don't believe us when we tell the truth! The idea that they might believe our lies is ludicrous. (Fortunately, the Pentagon has dropped this idea.)

Ladies and gentlemen, in 1989 the Berlin Wall came down, and on the other side we found millions of people receptive to U.S. ideals and perceptions. Well, there is another wall in the world today. It's not on the ground, it's in people's heads—and it divides America from the Arab-Muslim world. Unlike the Berlin Wall, though, this wall was built by both sides and it can be taken down only by both.

Just go anywhere—Egypt, Saudi Arabia, Pakistan—and you'll hit your head against this wall. You say the problem is Islamist terrorism; they will say it is Israeli brutality to Palestinians. You say America liberated Afghans from the Taliban; they will say we bombed innocent Afghan civilians. You say Saddam Hussein is evil; they will say Ariel Sharon is worse. You say America is a democracy; they will say it's a country whose media and politics are controlled by Jews. You say President Bill Clinton devoted the end of his presidency to creating a Palestinian state; they will tell you that America never showed them the plans. You say the problem is their lack of democracy; they will say that must be what America prefers—given the sorts of Arab-Muslim regimes it backs.

From my own experience, the only thing surprising about last week's Gallup poll from nine Muslim countries—which showed that 61 percent of Muslims believe that Arabs were not involved in the 9/11 attack and 53 percent view the United States unfavorably—is that the numbers aren't worse.

How was this iron wall of ideas built? By many hands. Let's start with ours. We've been pathetic at telling Arabs and Muslims who we are. Have U.S. diplomats pointed out in any sustained way how, for the last decade, America has fought to save Muslims in Bosnia, Kosovo, Somalia, and Kuwait?

Has America ever told the world exactly how the Clinton peace plan, which Yasir Arafat rejected, would have produced a Palestinian state on close to 100 percent of the land sought by Palestinians?

U.S. officials rightly say that Israel is our friend because it is a democracy. But for thirty years, these same officials have failed to speak out against Israeli settlements in the occupied territories, even though they know those settlements, if unrestrained, are going to destroy Israel as a Jewish democratic state and deprive Palestinians of any potential homeland. Do we ever press our values—democracy, freedom, women's rights—in the Arab-Muslim world? No. We talk about them only for China or North Korea, never for countries whose oil or bases we may need. Is there any wonder some people there see us as hypocrites?

But our Arab-Muslim allies also helped erect this wall. Their leaders have encouraged their press to print the worst lies about America, as well as blatant anti-Jewish and Holocaust-denial articles, as a way of deflecting their people's anger away from them. That's why these regimes can now cooperate with us only in secret. And they have let their conspiracy theories about America and Israel become easy excuses for why they never have to look at themselves—why they never have to ask, How is it that we had this incredible windfall of oil wealth and have done so poorly at building societies that can tap the vast potential of our people?

Next week a key Arab-Muslim leader, President Hosni Mubarak of Egypt, will meet here with President Bush. No doubt he will whisper all the great things Egypt is doing in secret to help us in the war on terrorism. And we will whisper back. But that's not what we need.

We need Mr. Mubarak to articulate publicly a progressive, modern-looking Arab-Muslim vision to counter bin Ladenism. We need him to get Egypt's act together, to stop riding on its past and start leading the Arab world into the future. And we need Mr. Bush to talk to the Egyptian people, and to Arab societies—not just to their rulers—about how that future can also be theirs.

Hosni Mubarak, George Bush, tear down this wall.

March 3, 2002

THE CORE OF MUSLIM RAGE

The latest death toll in the Indian violence between Hindus and Muslims is 544 people, many of them Muslims. Why is it that when Hindus kill hundreds of Muslims it elicits an emotionally muted headline in the Arab media, but when Israel kills a dozen Muslims, in a war in which Muslims are also killing Jews, it inflames the entire Muslim world?

I raise this point not to make some idiot press critique or engage in cheap Arab-bashing. This is a serious issue. In recent weeks, whenever Arab Muslims told me of their pain at seeing Palestinians brutalized by Israelis on their TV screens every night, I asked back: Why are you so pained about Israelis brutalizing Palestinians, but don't say a word about the brutality with which Saddam Hussein has snuffed out two generations of Iraqis using murder, fear, and poison gas? I got no good answers.

Because the real answer is rooted in something very deep. It has to do with the contrast between Islam's self-perception as the most ideal and complete expression of the three great monotheistic religions—Judaism, Christianity, and Islam—and the conditions of poverty, repression, and underdevelopment in which most Muslims live today.

As a U.S. diplomat in the Middle East said to me, Israel—not Iraq, not India—is "a constant reminder to Muslims of their own powerlessness." How could a tiny Jewish state amass so much military and economic power if the Islamic way of life—not Christianity or Judaism—is God's most ideal religious path?

When Hindus kill Muslims it's not a story, because there are a billion Hindus and they aren't part of the Muslim narrative. When Saddam murders his own people it's not a story, because it's in the Arab-Muslim family. But when a small band of Israeli Jews kills Muslims it sparks rage—a rage that must come from Muslims having to confront the gap between their self-perception as Muslims and the reality of the Muslim world.

I have long believed it is this poverty of dignity, not a poverty of money, that is behind a lot of Muslim rage today, and the reason this rage is sharpest among educated, but frustrated, Muslim youth. It is they who perpetrated 9/11 and who slit the throat of the *Wall Street Journal* reporter Danny Pearl—after reportedly forcing him to declare on film, "I am a Jew and my mother is a Jew."

This is not to say that U.S. policy is blameless. We do bad things sometimes. But why is it that only Muslims react to our bad policies with suicidal terrorism, not Mexicans or Chinese? Is it because Arab-Muslim conspiracy theories state that Jews could not be so strong on their own—therefore the only reason Israel could be strong, and Muslims weak, is because the United States created and supports Israel?

The Muslim world needs to take an honest look at this rage. Look what it has done to Palestinian society, where the flower of Palestinian youth now celebrate suicide against Jews as a source of dignity. That is so bad. Yes, there is an Israeli occupation, and that occupation has been hugely distorting of Palestinian life. But the fact is this: If Palestinians had said, "We are going to oppose the Israeli occupation with nonviolent resistance, as if we had no other options, and we are going to build a Palestinian society, schools, and economy, as if we had no occupation," they would have had a quality state a long time ago. Instead they have let the occupation define their whole movement and become Yasir Arafat's excuse for not building jobs and democracy.

Only Muslims can heal their own rage. But the West, and particularly the Jewish world, should help. Because this rage poses an existential threat to Israel. Three broad trends are now converging: (1) the worst killing ever between Israelis and Palestinians; (2) a baby boom in the Arab-Muslim world, where about half the population is under twenty; (3) an explosion of Arab satellite TV and Internet, which are taking the horrific images from the Intifada and beaming them directly to the new Arab-Muslim generation. If 100 million Arab-Muslims are brought up with these images, Israel won't survive.

Some of this hatred will remain no matter what Israel does. But to think that Israel's exiting the occupied territories—and abandoning its insane settlement land grab there—wouldn't reduce this problem is absurd.

Israel cannot do it alone. But it has to do all it can to get this show off the air. It would take away an important card from the worst Muslim anti-Semites and it would help strengthen those Muslims, and there are many of them, who know that the suicidal rage of their fanatics is dragging down their whole civilization.

March 6, 2002

A FOUL WIND

There is something about this new, intensely violent stage of the Palestinian-Israeli conflict that is starting to feel like the fuse for a much larger war of civilizations. You can smell it in the incredibly foul wind blowing through the Arab-Muslim world these days. It is a wind that is fed by many sources: the (one-sided) Arab TV images of Israelis brutalizing Palestinians, the Arab resentment of America's support for Israel and its threat against Iraq, the frustrations of young Arabs with their own lack of freedom and jobs. But once these forces are all bundled together, they express themselves in the most heated anti-Israeli and anti-American sentiments that I've ever felt.

This is dangerous. The notion is taking hold—it started with Osama bin Laden, was refined by Palestinian suicide bombers, and is cheered on by Hezbollah, Iran, and other radicals—that with a combination of demographics (a baby boom) and terrorism, the Arabs can actually destroy Israel. Some radicals even fantasize that they can undermine America.

A visiting Egyptian official told me that he was recently speaking to Arab students about Middle East peace and one of them interrupted to say that with just "eight small, suitcase-size nuclear bombs," the whole problem of Israel could be eliminated.

"The question is whether Palestinian extremists will do what bin Laden could not: trigger a civilizational war," said the Middle East analyst Stephen P. Cohen. "If you are willing to give up your own life and that of thousands of your own people, the overwhelming power of America and Israel does not deter you anymore. We are now on the cusp of the extremists' realizing this destructive power, before the majority is mobilized for an alternative. That's why this Israeli-Palestinian war is not just a local ethnic conflict that we can ignore. It resonates with too many millions of people, connected by too many satellite TVs, with too many dangerous weapons."

I still believe that a majority of Israelis and Palestinians, Americans and Muslims, do not want this war. But until the passive majorities are ready to act against the energetic minorities, the minorities will have their way. That's why our choices are becoming clear: Either we have civil wars within the communities—with Israel uprooting most of the Jewish settlements, the Palestinians uprooting Hamas, and the Arab regimes dealing with their fundamentalists—or we could end up in a war of civilizations, between communities, with America also being pulled in.

It doesn't have to end this way. In the mid-1990s, Yitzhak Rabin was ready to take on the Jewish settlers, and he paid for it with his life. But that was the same period when Yasir Arafat took on Hamas, and eight Arab countries opened trade or diplomatic ties with the Jewish state. For a brief moment, we saw Israeli and Arab moderates working against Israeli and Arab extremists.

The recent peace overture by Crown Prince Abdullah was intended to improve Saudi Arabia's badly sullied post–September 11 image. But it wasn't only that. My sense was that Abdullah understood that if the Arab moderates didn't step up with a peace idea of their own, they were going to be dragged into a collision with America. Abdullah's statement was the opening shot in what could be a post–September 11 inter-Arab struggle.

We have a huge interest in that struggle's being fought and won by moderates. That will depend in part on how much courage the Saudis and others display, and in part on what the United States and Israel do. With all the passive support shown for bin Laden in the Arab-Muslim world, it's not so easy anymore to understand who is a moderate or who is an extremist out there. But if we don't force ourselves, and Arab moderates, to make that distinction and live by it, we're heading for a war of civilizations.

Some in Israel and in the American Jewish right argue that it is already a war of civilizations and that the only thing to do is kill Palestinians until they say uncle. That is called "realism." Well, let me tell you something else that is real: If this uncompromising view becomes dominant in Israel and among American Jews, then cash in your Israel Bonds right now—the country is doomed. Because there are so many more Muslims than Jews to be killed, and weapons of mass destruction are becoming so much smaller and so much cheaper, it won't be long before the student in my Egyptian friend's story gets one of his eight bombs and wipes Israel off the map.

Is that real enough for you?

March 10, 2002

SAY THAT AGAIN?

When Egypt's president, Hosni Mubarak, visited Washington last week, he used his White House press conference to stress what was new about the peace overture by Saudi Arabia's Crown Prince Abdullah. "This is the first time in the history of the Saudis that they say we are ready to normalize relations with Israel, in case a peace prevails," said Mr. Mubarak. "We should underline this."

Mr. Mubarak emphasized that when the leader of Saudi Arabia, the birthplace of Islam, says in English, and in Arabic to his own press, that he is ready, in exchange for a total Israeli withdrawal, to have a "full normalization of relations" with the Jewish state — meaning trade, tourism, and embassies — that is noteworthy, and is what caused all the buzz.

But will the Arab League adopt Abdullah's formula? Last weekend Arab foreign ministers met in Cairo to prepare for the March 27–28 Arab summit, where the Abdullah initiative is to be endorsed. In Cairo the Saudi foreign minister, Saud al-Faisal, was asked about the Abdullah proposal. He said that in return for Israel's withdrawing to pre-1967 lines and creating a Palestinian state with Jerusalem as its capital, the Arab League would offer Israel "full peace."

That jarred my ear. Say that again? "Full peace"? Words are important here. "Full peace" is not what Abdullah offered. He said "full normalization of relations," and there is a difference. Ask Hosni Mubarak. Syria could live in "full peace" with Israel and not have any relations. Are the Saudis backpedaling? Not clear.

What's clear is that a fight has started in the Arab League, where Syria is trying to water down Abdullah's initiative, and in Saudi Arabia, where Abdullah made his "normalization" proposal in an interview — without consulting anyone else. This was because, whether Abdullah was out for just better P.R. or a real breakthrough, he knew he had to use a psychological breakthrough word—"normalization"—to get any traction. Having done so, though, he is now seeing conservatives at home and abroad trying to dial down his initiative before it gets to a summit vote. Will Abdullah let them?

The fight now is between three different views. The first is Osama bin Laden's. His view is that there is no place for a Jewish state or other "infidels," particularly Americans, in the Muslim world.

Second is the view of the Syrians, who want to prove that they can get as much out of Israel as Anwar el-Sadat did, while giving less—like no normalization of relations, trade, or tourism.

The third view, the one adopted by Egypt and Jordan and alluded to by Abdullah, is the notion that the only way you can have peace is if there is a real Israeli withdrawal and a real acceptance of Israel as a Jewish state in the region. That means using the term "normalization of relations."

This is an important fight, because it's about more than just P.R. or a peace proposal. It's about whose vision is going to dominate Arab politics. If Abdullah lets his message get watered down, it will signal not only that the Palestinians can't make real peace with Israel, but that the Arabs can't either. Therefore, no real acceptance of a Jewish state in the Middle East is possible—even if Israel fulfills all Arab requirements. For the Arab world, that would mean that bin Laden and Syria are in the driver's seat and that the Arab past will continue to bury the Arab future.

That's why the real question before this Arab summit is: Can the Arabs answer bin Laden by positing a different vision? Can the Arab-Muslim world show a willingness to live with pluralism—with a Jewish state in fair boundaries? Or must the area be free of all "infidels"? An Arab League that can't live with a pluralism of people can't live with a pluralism of ideas. If it can't live with a pluralism of ideas, it will never develop and will remain, at some level, alienated from the West and Israel.

Israel will have to do its part and withdraw on the basis of the 1967 lines. But it's time for the Arab League to get real: Anwar el-Sadat also demanded full withdrawal. The reason he got it, though, was not because of what he demanded, but because of the psychological breakthrough to Israelis that he offered first. The reason Abdullah's remarks tantalized some Israelis was because they offered "full normalization." This needs to be elaborated. If, instead, it's washed out by the Arab League, the whole exercise will be remembered as wasted breath. Stay tuned.

March 13, 2002

BETTER LATE THAN...

The last time America dominated the world as overwhelmingly as it does today was in the wake of World War II. So why did that America not inspire the sort of global anger that today's America does? Partly it's because the rest of the world was flat on its back then. But more important, it's because America after World War II took responsibility for making the world both a more secure place to live and a better place to live. And it expended a lot of resources, as in the Marshall Plan, to do both.

Since September 11, the Bush team has focused on making the world safer, but has shown little interest in making it more healthy, less poor, and more environmentally sound. As a result, there has been little chance that it was going to end up safer for Americans.

Therefore, President Bush's speech on Thursday announcing a $5 billion increase in foreign aid for poor countries is important—not only as a substantive breakthrough for this administration, but also, one hopes, as a psychological one. Since September 11, President Bush has often noted that the world has fundamentally changed. Yet, time after time, he has exploited the shock of September 11 to argue why his same old pre–September 11 policies were still the only way to proceed—only more so. Because of September 11, he has argued, we need even deeper tax cuts for the wealthy, even more money for a pie-in-the-sky missile defense that would have been of no use on September 11, an even bigger defense budget, and even more drilling for oil in wilderness areas.

The most obvious conclusion from September 11—that fighting terrorism around the globe will require a new, multidimensional strategy, not just a defense strategy—was the one Mr. Bush seemed least inclined to draw, and that's why his speech should be welcomed.

It will be relevant, though, only if it really signals an understanding by the Bush team that there are no walls for us to hide behind anymore, that everything is connected to everything else and that we cannot win a global war against terrorism without global allies, but we will have those allies only if we practice what the architects of the Marshall Plan practiced: enlightened self-interest, not just self-interest. Those postwar wise men persuaded others to follow us because they not only respected our power but also our wisdom and moral example.

The 9/11 terrorists did not hit us because they were poor. But millions of poor people gave passive support to those terrorists because they resented our greed or our support for their bad regimes. That's why it was important that the President said our increased foreign aid must be conditioned on countries' improving their governance, rule of law, social safety nets, investment climates, and anticorruption practices.

We can't force elections, but we can use our aid to pressure developing countries to give their people more voice, more rule of law, and a fairer slice of the pie, which are their people's real priorities. Here's a tip: The reason Islam seems like such an angry religion today is because so many Muslims are angry. The reason so many Muslims are angry is because most of them live under antidemocratic regimes backed by America, with lagging economies and shrinking opportunities for young people.

Beyond just aid, though, we should also be forging free trade accords with as many Muslim nations as possible (instead of throwing up insane protectionist walls around our steel industry). At the World Economic Forum, one expert noted that Muslim countries made up 20 percent of the world's population, yet only 4 percent of the world's trade. Trade in goods brings trade in ideas. The most open, tolerant places in the Muslim world today are all trading centers: Dubai, Istanbul, Bahrain, Amman, Beirut, Jakarta, coastal India.

But enlightened self-interest is not just about generosity; it's also about self-restraint. We need to find a way to ratify the Kyoto climate change treaty. It's not only the right thing to do, it would also send a hugely positive signal to the world—that America understands that if it's going to have lasting allies in a global war on terrorism, it has to be the best global citizen it can be. The attitude that we are entitled to consume 25 percent of the world's energy, while we're only 4 percent of the world's population, is obnoxious. Selfishness and hubris are a terrible combination.

Mr. Bush has repeatedly told the world: If you're not with us, you're against us. He needs to remember this: The rest of the world is saying the same thing to us.

March 17, 2002

PULL UP A CHAIR

We need to talk.

Are you sitting down? OK, I'm not going to beat around the bush. I'm just going to say it straight: There is no way that America will be able to sustain a successful Middle East policy, whether it wants to invade Iraq or do anything else in the region, unless the United States is prepared to station American troops on the ground, indefinitely, around both Afghanistan and Israel.

No, I haven't lost my mind.

The logic here is very simple. There is no way that the United States will be able to garner any sustained support for taking out Saddam Hussein in Iraq unless it can stabilize both Israel-Palestine and Afghanistan. We don't need to make Afghanistan into Switzerland. We just need to make the new Afghanistan into something slightly more stable, slightly more decent, and slightly more prosperous than it was under the Taliban. If we cannot do that minimum, we will have no legitimacy, no credibility, and no support for taking apart Iraq.

If we shrink from this task, Afghanistan will revert right back to what it was before September 11, only worse. And this open sore of Afghanistan will dog us, and the U.S. antiterror campaign, forever. The only way to make the new Afghanistan a slightly better place than the old one is with a U.S. troop presence that will bolster the government and serve as the anchor for a wider peacekeeping force manned by our allies. Enough said.

The same is true for the Israeli-Palestinian theater. This is our dilemma there: Israel cannot stay in the occupied territories and remain a Jewish democracy. But the Palestinians cannot yet be trusted to control these areas on their own if Israel withdraws. Would you trust Yasir Arafat to police your neighborhood?

So the only solution is that Israel gradually withdraw from the West Bank and Gaza Strip, to be replaced by a joint American-Palestinian security force. Palestinians would be responsible for internal security, and the joint U.S.-Palestinian security force would control all borders and entryways to ensure that no heavy weapons can be imported and that any Palestinian state could never become a base of operations against Israel. The most sensitive area of Jerusalem, the Temple Mount, would be protected by U.S. troops, with Palestinians having sovereignty and operational control over the mosques and the Jews over their holy sites.

Israelis and Palestinians do not have the resources, or mutual trust, ever to find their way out of this problem alone—not after the collapse of Oslo. And the United States can no longer afford to just let them go on killing each other. It will undermine America's whole position in the Middle East, as more and more Muslims will blame us for what Israel does to protect itself. It will spin off more and more suicide craziness that will land at our door. And it will make it impossible for the United States to take on Saddam.

Those who think Israel needs to just wear the Palestinians down with more military action and everything will be fine should pay attention to something that has happened in the past month. Palestinians have destroyed two Israeli-made Merkava tanks during the fighting, using homemade but sophisticated land mines detonated in the most vulnerable spot on the tank's underbelly. Israeli generals were shocked.

What the hawks don't understand is that the escalating friction between the Israeli and Palestinian forces is enabling Palestinians to steadily improve their military skills. This is a natural phenomenon seen in many prolonged wars between a more sophisticated and a less sophisticated army. It was the long friction between Hezbollah, a ragtag Lebanese militia, and Israel that eventually improved Hezbollah's skills to the point where it was able to force Israel to withdraw unilaterally from Lebanon, without any agreement, by lowering the casualty ratio between Hezbollah and Israel from 10 to 1 down to 1 to 1.

Israel can kill Palestinians till the cows come home and that will not alter its central dilemma—it can't stay in the territories and remain a Jewish democracy, and it can't just leave and stay alive as a Jewish democracy. The only way it can safely leave is if U.S. troops are protecting its borders and those of the Palestinian state. It's also the only way the Palestinians are going to get a state. If American Jews really care about Israel, if Arab leaders really care about the Palestinians, if Iraq hawks really want to get rid of Saddam, this is what they will lobby President Bush to offer.

I told you you needed to be sitting down.

March 20, 2002

NO MERE TERRORIST

There was something symbolic about the fact that the U.S. Immigration and Naturalization Service sent out letters approving visas for the terrorist leaders Mohamed Atta and Marwan al-Shehhi and that those letters arrived at their Florida flight school on the six-month anniversary of the September 11 massacre, which the two of them directed. Some things you just can't make up.

It was symbolic precisely because we are forgetting some of the most important truths about September 11 — so why shouldn't the INS? September 11 was about a very new kind of threat. And it wasn't mere terrorism.

Real terrorists don't want to kill a lot of people. Rather, they use limited, but indiscriminate, violence or hijacking to create noise or fear that draws attention to their cause and ultimately builds political or diplomatic pressure for a specific objective.

That's why Osama bin Laden is not a mere terrorist. He has much larger aspirations. He is a super-empowered angry man who has all the geopolitical objectives and instincts of a nation-state. He has employed violence not to grab headlines but to kill as many Americans as possible to drive them out of the Islamic world and weaken their society. That's why the September 11 hijackers never left a list of demands, as terrorists usually do. Their act was their demand. Their demand is total victory.

What enabled bin Laden, as a super-empowered angry man, to challenge a superpower was his ability to invent his own missile delivery system to rival ours. We have computer-guided missiles. He had human guided missiles: nineteen young, educated Arab men ready to hijack an airliner and commit suicide with it against a major target. But always remember that September 11 could have been worse. One of bin Laden's human missiles could have carried a nuclear device. The only reason it didn't happen was because the hijackers couldn't get one.

Since that is the case, the proper, long-term U.S. strategic response to September 11 should be twofold: First, we must understand exactly who these nineteen suicide bombers were and how they were recruited. We need to know how these human guided missiles are assembled. Second, we need to launch an all-out global effort to make sure that all nuclear and biological warfare materials are under as tight a control as possible.

"Historically, there has always been a gap between people's individual anger and what they could do with their anger," said the Harvard University strategist Graham Allison. "But thanks to modern technology and the willingness of people to commit suicide, really angry individuals can now kill millions of people if they can get the right materials. We can't change their intentions overnight, but we can make sure that the materials that can transform their rage into something that threatens us all are locked away in places as secure as Fort Knox."

That means investing even more U.S. energy and money in working with Russia to secure its stockpiles, because Russia and America have 99 percent of the world's nuclear and biowarfare materials. And, after Russia, focusing on China, India, Pakistan, Iran, and Iraq. Unfortunately, the Bush team seems to focus only on Iraq. It's not that Iraq is not a problem, but it's not at the top of my list.

What worries me most for my daughters' future is not Saddam Hussein. He's a homicidal dictator who can be deterred, or eliminated, by conventional means. No, what worries me most is the fact that we still don't understand who those nineteen hijackers were. What worries me is that nearly every day for the past six months, Palestinian men and women—many of them secular, not religious—have strapped dynamite around their waists and blown themselves up against Israeli targets. How do you deter young people who hate us, or Israel, more than they love their own families or their own future?

It will take us a long time, and much diplomatic therapy, to cure such intentions. But what we can do now is limit the capabilities of such people. We are not the only ones with an interest in this. If suicidal warfare becomes "normal," the Arab regimes won't be spared. Because once people feel empowered by this sort of thing, they won't stop with just the infidels—they will turn it on their own autocrats. And if it becomes "normal," it will be awful for Palestinians, because how their state is born matters, and a state brought about by suicide bombers will forever be deformed.

And if it becomes "normal" in this integrated world, it will touch your kids and mine in a way that will make Iraq look like a day at the beach.

March 24, 2002

THE FREE-SPEECH BIND

So here's an interesting moral dilemma: I got e-mails last week from Saudi and Egyptian friends encouraging me to write a column about the Saudi poet who had been thrown in jail for writing a fiery poem attacking Saudi judges as corrupt.

The Saudi poet, Abdul Mohsen Musalam, in his poem "The Corrupt on Earth," published March 10 in the newspaper *Al-Medina*, wrote: "It is sad that in the Muslim world, justice is suffering from a few judges who care for nothing but their bank accounts and their status with the rulers." He then added, with amazing bluntness about the judges: "Your beards are smeared with blood. You indulge a thousand tyrants and only the tyrant do you obey."

Not only did the Saudi interior minister throw Mr. Musalam in jail for this poem, but his editor, Mokhtar al-Fal, was fired. So what's my dilemma? I should be all for free speech—right?—especially in Saudi Arabia.

Not so fast. By accident, I met this poet on a recent trip to Saudi Arabia and I tasted some other free speech he has in him. Readers may recall that I noted in an earlier column that at one newspaper I visited in Saudi Arabia, I walked out after being told that the source of all the problems today was that "the Jews control America." The newspaper was *Al-Medina*, and the person who said that to me, during a discussion, was Mr. Musalam. (His editor, who apologized for him, was a good person, and I hope he gets his job back.)

So what to do?

The only thing to do is to call on the Saudis to release Mr. Musalam—not for his sake, but because a government that is afraid of a poem only shows itself to be insecure, and as tyrannical as the poet charged. His charges should be answered—but don't throw him in jail.

This incident, though, actually highlights a larger dilemma: At the Arab summit meeting now being held in Beirut, not one of the twenty-two Arab leaders represented has been elected in a free and fair balloting. But some experts ask: Why would we want to foster democracy and a free press in that part of the world when we know that many of those who would be elected or free to write would be incredibly hostile to us?

After all, we may not like everything that Egypt's Hosni Mubarak or the al-Saud ruling family in Saudi Arabia do—but they are more liberal and pro-American than many of their people.

That's true, but September 11 demonstrates how dangerous it is for us to rely on that. Because the pro-Americanism of these Arab leaders is being bought at a price of keeping their own people so angry, so without voice, and so frustrated by corruption that they are enraged at both their regimes and us. Stability in these countries is achieved by these regimes' letting their people have free speech only to attack America and Israel.

After all, the newspaper *Al-Riyadh* recently published an article by a Saudi "professor" who alleged that Jews make a holiday pastry that requires them to "drain the blood" from a young Christian or Muslim, but the editor of *Al-Riyadh* was not fired. Right now, the only way you get a free voice in most of the Arab press is by denouncing Israel and America or praising your regime. That distorts the whole political discourse.

"There is no way out of the dilemmas of the Arab world without some political opening," says the Stanford University democracy expert Larry Diamond. "But it doesn't start by holding elections now.

"What is needed is a managed political opening, coincident with economic reform, that can generate a middle class with respect for the rule of law and institutions. It requires a gradual process, with a vision from the top, that introduces pluralism into the political life. The objective is to create a body of people who can one day contest for power in a responsible way, with the regimes keeping some reserve of power for themselves as insurance."

Yes, when you open up such closed societies, crazy things do fly out, like bats from a dungeon. Look at Poland and Russia, where two of the first bats out were rabid ultranationalist presidential candidates Stanislaw Tyminski and Vladimir Zhirinovsky. But after a few seasons of democracy, both are now long gone. When given a real choice, people usually don't want to be ruled by jerks.

Sure, these transitions are tricky. They can go wrong. See Serbia. But it's a worthwhile risk. Because context matters. Change the context of how people live and you change everything. And the current Arab context sure isn't working in our favor.

March 27, 2002

SUICIDAL LIES

The outcome of the war now under way between the Israelis and Palestinians is vital to the security of every American, and indeed, I believe, to all of civilization. Why? Quite simply because Palestinians are testing out a whole new form of warfare, using suicide bombers—strapped with dynamite and dressed as Israelis—to achieve their political aims. And it is working.

Israelis are terrified. And Palestinians, although this strategy has wrecked their society, feel a rising sense of empowerment. They feel they finally have a weapon that creates a balance of power with Israel, and maybe, in their fantasies, can defeat Israel. As Ismail Haniya, a Hamas leader, said in *The Washington Post*, Palestinians have Israelis on the run now because they have found their weak spot. Jews, he said, "love life more than any other people, and they prefer not to die." So Palestinian suicide bombers are ideal for dealing with them. That is really sick.

The world must understand that the Palestinians have not chosen suicide bombing out of "desperation" stemming from the Israeli occupation. That is a huge lie. Why? To begin with, a lot of other people in the world are desperate, yet they have not gone around strapping dynamite to themselves. More important, President Clinton offered the Palestinians a peace plan that could have ended their "desperate" occupation, and Yasir Arafat walked away. Still more important, the Palestinians have long had a tactical alternative to suicide: nonviolent resistance, à la Gandhi. A nonviolent Palestinian movement appealing to the conscience of the Israeli silent majority would have delivered a Palestinian state thirty years ago, but they have rejected that strategy too.

The reason the Palestinians have not adopted these alternatives is because they actually want to win their independence in blood and fire. All they can agree on as a community is what they want to destroy, not what they want to build. Have you ever heard Mr. Arafat talk about what sort of education system or economy he would prefer, what sort of constitution he wants? No, because Mr. Arafat is not interested in the content of a Palestinian state, only the contours.

Let's be very clear: Palestinians have adopted suicide bombing as a strategic choice, not out of desperation. This threatens all civilization because if suicide bombing is allowed to work in Israel, then, like hijacking and airplane bombing, it will be copied and will eventually lead to a bomber strapped with a nuclear device threatening entire nations. That is why the whole world must see this Palestinian suicide strategy defeated.

But how? This kind of terrorism can be curbed only by self-restraint and repudiation by the community itself. No foreign army can stop small groups ready to kill themselves. How do we produce that deterrence among Palestinians? First, Israel needs to deliver a military blow that clearly shows terror will not pay. Second, America needs to make clear that suicide bombing is not Israel's problem alone.

To that end, the United States should declare that while it respects the legitimacy of Palestinian nationalism, it will have no dealings with the Palestinian leadership as long as it tolerates suicide bombings. Further, we should make clear that Arab leaders whose media call suicide bombers "martyrs" aren't welcome in the United States.

Third, Israel must tell the Palestinian people that it is ready to resume talks where they left off with Mr. Clinton, before this intifada. Those talks were 90 percent of the way toward ending the occupation and creating a Palestinian state. Fourth, U.S. or NATO troops must guarantee any Israeli-Palestinian border.

"The Spanish Civil War was the place where the major powers all tested out their new weapons before World War II," said the Israeli political theorist Yaron Ezrahi. "Well, the Israeli-Palestinian conflict today is the Spanish Civil War for the twenty-first century. A big test is taking place of whether suicide terrorism can succeed as a strategy for liberation. It must be defeated, but that requires more than a military strategy."

The Palestinians are so blinded by their narcissistic rage that they have lost sight of the basic truth civilization is built on: the sacredness of every human life, starting with your own. If America, the only reality check left, doesn't use every ounce of energy to halt this madness and call it by its real name, then it will spread. The Devil is dancing in the Middle East, and he's dancing our way.

March 31, 2002

THE HARD TRUTH

———

A terrible disaster is in the making in the Middle East. What Osama bin Laden failed to achieve on September 11 is now being unleashed by the Israeli-Palestinian war in the West Bank: a clash of civilizations.

In the wake of repeated suicide bombings, it is no surprise that the Israeli army has gone on the offensive in the West Bank. Any other nation would have done the same. But Ariel Sharon's operation will succeed only if it is designed to make the Israeli-occupied territories safe for Israel to leave as soon as possible. Israel's goal must be a withdrawal from these areas captured in the 1967 war; otherwise it will never know a day's peace, and it will undermine every legitimate U.S. effort to fight terrorism around the globe. What I fear, though, is that Mr. Sharon wants to get rid of Mr. Arafat in order to keep Israeli West Bank settlements, not to create the conditions for them to be withdrawn.

President Bush needs to be careful that America doesn't get sucked into something very dangerous here. Mr. Bush has rightly condemned Palestinian suicide bombing as beyond the pale, but he is not making it clear that Israel's war against this terrorism has to be accompanied by a real plan for getting out of the territories.

Why? Because President Bush, like all the other key players, doesn't want to face the central dilemma in this conflict—which is that while Israel must get out of the West Bank and Gaza, the Palestinians cannot, at this moment, be trusted to run those territories on their own without making them a base of future operations against Israel. That means some outside power has to come in to secure the borders, and the only trusted powers would be the United States or NATO.

Palestinians who use suicide bombers to blow up Israelis at a Passover meal and then declare "Just end the occupation and everything will be fine" are not believable. No Israeli in his right mind would trust Yasir Arafat, who has used suicide bombers when it suited his purposes, not to do the same thing if he got the West Bank back and some of his people started demanding Tel Aviv.

"The only solution is a new UN mandate for U.S. and NATO troops to supervise the gradual emergence of a Palestinian state—after a phased

Israeli withdrawal—and then to control its borders," says the Middle East expert Stephen P. Cohen.

People say that U.S. troops there would be shot at like U.S. troops in Beirut. I disagree. U.S. troops that are the midwife of a Palestinian state and supervise a return of Muslim sovereignty over the holy mosques in Jerusalem would be the key to solving all the contradictions of U.S. policy in the Middle East, not new targets.

The Arab leaders don't want to face this hard fact either, because most are illegitimate unelected autocrats who are afraid of ever speaking the truth in public to the Palestinians. The Arab leaders are as disingenuous as Mr. Sharon; he says ending "terrorism" alone will bring peace to the occupied territories, and the Arab leaders say ending "the occupation" alone will end all terrorism.

Like Mr. Sharon, the Arab leaders need to face facts—that while the occupation needs to end, they independently need to address issues like suicide terrorism in the name of Islam. As Malaysia's prime minister, Mahathir Mohamad, courageously just declared about suicide bombing: "Bitter and angry though we may be, we must demonstrate to the world that Muslims are rational people when fighting for our rights, and do not resort to acts of terror."

If Arab leaders have only the moral courage to draw lines around Israel's behavior, but no moral courage to decry the utterly corrupt and inept Palestinian leadership or the depravity of suicide bombers in the name of Islam, then we're going nowhere.

The other people who have not wanted to face facts are the feckless American Jewish leaders, fundamentalist Christians, and neoconservatives who together have helped make it impossible for anyone in the U.S. government to talk seriously about halting Israeli settlement-building without being accused of being anti-Israel. Their collaboration has helped prolong a colonial Israeli occupation that now threatens the entire Zionist enterprise.

So there you have it. Either leaders of goodwill get together and acknowledge that Israel can't stay in the territories, but can't just pick up and leave without a U.S.-NATO force helping Palestinians oversee their state, or Osama wins—and the war of civilizations will be coming to a theater near you.

April 3, 2002

LIFELINES TO THE FUTURE

Shortly after Yitzhak Rabin was assassinated, I got an e-mail note from an Israeli who was writing to her friends about her grief. She explained that when she had sat down at the computer to write her thoughts, she had labeled the file "Rabin," and when she was done and went to save it, the computer software automatically asked her: "Save Rabin?" She wrote us about how much she wished she could "Save Rabin" by just pressing a key.

I was thinking about her as I read all my angry e-mail from friends in the Middle East. This is the most polarizing moment I've ever experienced. The volcanic rage on both sides—intensified by the live TV coverage from the West Bank and the ability of the Internet to transmit people's immediate reactions—is terrifying, and it is spilling, like lava, out of the Middle East into Europe and beyond. It leaves me wishing there were a "Return" key I could hit to take us back to some point before all this craziness.

Remember, it hasn't always been like this. Since the late 1970s, Israel has enjoyed long stretches of peace, or at least quiet, with Egypt, Jordan, and even the Palestinians. These moments all had one thing in common: They were based on a mutual willingness to draw clear lines and defend them—border lines, moral lines, and lines to the future.

Oslo gradually collapsed because everyone started blurring the lines. Israel built peace with one hand and continued to build Jewish settlements in the West Bank and Gaza with the other, to a degree that made Palestinians feel their living space was shrinking while Israel's was constantly expanding, all under the umbrella of "peace."

Ariel Sharon played a major role in building those settlements and blurring those lines. The Jewish right always justified this with its inane mantra "Why shouldn't Jews be able to live anywhere?" The point was not whether Jews should have the right to live everywhere. The point was whether it was smart for them to live everywhere in biblical Israel—when it meant shrinking the Palestinians' opportunity for their own state.

But Oslo also failed because the Palestinians, while talking peace in English, continued to build hate against Israelis in Arabic, in their mosques and textbooks. And they continued to draw maps of a future Palestinian state that erased Israel. Yasir Arafat played a leading role in all this. Recently, the Palestinians' mounting anger with Israel lulled them into their own self-delusional argument: that the Israeli occupation justified any Palestinian tactic for liberation, including suicide bombing of civilians. You can't build a normal state on the backs of suicide bombers.

President Bush's speech last week was particularly important because he put America in exactly the role it should be playing: restoring clear lines. He drew a clear line for Israelis—that no matter how many settlements they've built, any peace deal has to be based on the 1967 lines. He drew a clear line for Palestinians—that suicide bombers are "not martyrs. They're murderers."

But Mr. Bush did not draw the line down the middle. He was more critical of Mr. Arafat than of Mr. Sharon because he knows something the Arabs have consistently tried to ignore: Ariel Sharon did not come from outer space. He was elected only after Mr. Arafat walked away from the best opportunity ever for creating a Palestinian state: the Clinton plan. Mr. Arafat deliberately chose to use military pressure, instead of diplomacy or nonviolence, to extract more out of Israel, and Israelis turned to Mr. Sharon as their revenge. This context is critical, and Mr. Bush has refused to ignore it.

A firm U.S. hand in redrawing all the fudged lines is our only hope. Otherwise the distinction between the sane center and the extremists, in both communities, will become totally blurred, with the hard-liners calling all the shots.

As I said, it wasn't always that way. I attended the 1995 Arab-Israeli Economic Summit in Amman. I was seated in the press gallery, just above the Israeli delegation. A Kuwaiti delegate accidentally sat down in the Israeli section, and Israelis filled in around him. So as I looked down, all I could see was an Israeli yarmulke sitting next to a Kuwaiti Arab headdress. It was an image I'll never forget.

That's the only blurring of lines we want: the one that brings the Israeli center and the Arab center together in the middle. But it can be done only if we restore all the other lines—the border lines and the moral lines. If only there were an "Insert Lines" key on my computer, I'd press it now.

April 7, 2002

GEORGE W. SADAT

So Colin Powell goes out to the Middle East and tries to stop the killing and what happens? Let's see, first he gets embarrassed by the boy king of Morocco. Then he arrives in Israel to be greeted by editorials in the hysterical *Jerusalem Post* about how his mission is "doomed to failure" because he doesn't see things exactly as Ariel Sharon and some of the right-wing maniacs in his cabinet do. Even before Mr. Powell arrives in Jerusalem, he is treated to the news that Yasir Arafat's wife, Suha, has declared (from her luxury bunker in Paris) that had she had a son, she would have been happy to see him "martyred" for Palestine, and the news that the Palestinian who recently blew herself up in a Jerusalem supermarket was a mere teenager. I have a teenage daughter. There is no teenager capable of making the political decision to commit suicide. You can bet it was older men who encouraged her to do this and who wrapped her in dynamite. That is not martyrdom, that is ritual sacrifice.

Do they know how twisted all this looks to the rest of the world?

There is only one positive thing about this moment, when all boundaries of civilized behavior have been breached: It may have created an opportunity, which I hope President Bush will seize.

Here's what I mean: Mr. Arafat and his boys, by cynically employing suicide bombers, have proved that they can unsettle the Israeli public more than any Arab army has in fifty years—by sacrificing Palestinian kids. In doing so, though, they have punctured the last myths of the Israeli right that somehow Palestinians would reconcile themselves to Israeli settlements, or that with enough force Palestinians could be cowed into accepting any Israeli terms.

At the same time, Israel, under Mr. Sharon, has counter-punctured the fantasy that was taking wing among Palestinians, that through suicide bombing they might finally have found the weapon to drive the Jews out of the Middle East. By mercilessly going after the perpetrators of suicide bombing in the West Bank, even when they were hiding among Palestinian civilians, Mr. Sharon should have ended any illusions that Palestinians can terrorize the Jews into fleeing without being terrorized themselves.

The Arab leaders have been taught a lesson too. For decades they have used the Palestinian cause to buttress their own legitimacy or to deflect attention from their own failures. But in the old days, they could regulate how their own people saw the conflict through their state-controlled media. No more. This is the cyber-intifada in the age of globalization. Thanks to independent Arab satellite TV beaming images from Palestine to Arab youths twenty-four hours a day, and thanks to the Internet, which allows those youths to tell each other exactly how they feel about those images, the Arab regimes are losing their grip on public opinion. No, these regimes will not be toppled tomorrow, but they are being shaken, and their economies devastated by fleeing investors.

Finally, this unrestrained explosion of Palestinian-Israeli violence has taught the Bush team something as well: As much as they prefer to ignore this conflict, they can't, and if they try, it will undermine their global war on terrorism.

All this adds up to an opportunity, not unlike the one that arose after Egypt crossed the Suez Canal in 1973 and punctured Israel's sense of invulnerability, and then Israel, led by Ariel Sharon's tanks, crossed the canal into Egypt, grabbed Egypt's army by the throat, and made it clear that Egypt was just as vulnerable.

This is not a time for some two-bit international conference. The United States and the Soviets tried that after the 1973 war, and Anwar el-Sadat, realizing it was a waste of time, decided instead to go to Jerusalem and put everything on the table. Mr. Bush has to do the same right now. He has to be the Anwar el-Sadat of this moment, because no one else will be. That means laying down a clear American peace plan calling for a new UN mandate for the West Bank and Gaza to develop a new Palestinian Authority capable of ruling those areas; a phased withdrawal of Israeli troops, à la the Clinton plan; and U.S. or NATO forces to cement the deal.

I believe one of Don Rumsfeld's Washington rules is: If you have a problem and you can't solve it, enlarge it. Either we now go all the way toward peace and demand that every party step up to it—Palestinians, Israelis, and Arabs—or they will keep going all the way the other way, blowing out one civilizational barrier after another until their war touches us.

April 17, 2002

CHANGING THE CHANNEL

As the fighting between Israelis and Palestinians has intensified, I've found it increasingly impossible to watch TV news. Lately, whenever Middle East stories come on CNN or MSNBC, I reach for the remote and switch to the Golf Channel. Everyone needs a break from the all-too-real suffering that surrounds this story.

I happened to mention this in a chat with Jim Bouton, the former Yankees pitcher and author of *Ball Four*. Mr. Bouton says he's had the same reaction, and as we talked we came up with ten reasons for why the Golf Channel is actually the perfect antidote to Middle East news:

1. All the commentators, particularly the instructors, on the Golf Channel actually know what they're talking about, and no one on the Golf Channel is identified by the phony and meaningless title of "Terrorism Expert." Indeed, the only spin you see on the Golf Channel comes from Titleist and Nike golf balls. You have to perform your way onto the Golf Channel—you don't get on through a P.R. firm or by running for President and losing or by having been part of the O.J. trial.

2. There's no religion on the Golf Channel. The only time God or Jesus Christ is mentioned is in anger after somebody hits a bad shot.

3. There is no history on the Golf Channel and no arguments about history. As with golf itself, it doesn't really matter what you did yesterday on the Golf Channel; every day starts with a fresh slate. Indeed, success in golf requires that you erase the history of what you did yesterday and focus only on today's round. In golf, unlike Arab-Israeli politics, the future always buries the past—the past doesn't bury the future.

4. There are long, glorious silences on the Golf Channel. And the commentators who cover their events—rather than shouting at each other across a split screen—actually spend a lot of their airtime whispering, so as not to disturb the players. Nobody interrupts anybody on the Golf Channel.

5. There are no uniforms on the Golf Channel—only golf

shirts with swooshes, alligators, and umbrellas—because, refreshingly, the players there represent only themselves and their achievements, not cities, countries, or religions. Also, the only flags waved on the Golf Channel are green, with the numbers 1 through 18 on them (except during the European-American Ryder Cup matches).

6. On the Golf Channel, no one blames America for everything bad that happens to them. In golf, you alone are responsible for what happens to you. No whining is allowed on the Golf Channel. Your ball ended up in a divot or took a crazy bounce? Too bad, that's golf—that's life. Unlike on CNN, Fox, or MSNBC, where guests can wail that whatever went wrong was caused by an American conspiracy, on the Golf Channel they tell you to get over it and move on.

7. On the Golf Channel, the only "settlements" are "fairway condos," and "the right of return" is what you ask for after you've played Augusta for the first time. The only bunkers on the Golf Channel are the kind you need a sand wedge to blast out of, not a bazooka. And the only time the Middle East makes the Golf Channel is in March, when the Dubai Desert Classic and Qatar Masters are played in the Persian Golf, er, I mean, Persian Gulf.

8. The Golf Channel is devoted to a game that respects rules and clearly defines what is inbounds and what is out of bounds. Unlike in the Middle East, where America is supposed to be the referee and all the parties cheat as much as they can get away with, in golf you are expected to call penalties on yourself. On the Golf Channel, there are real consequences for cheating, lying, or breaking the rules: no one will play with you or have you on the air. In the Middle East, the more outrageously you behave, the more likely you are to be elected to high office or invited to appear on *Crossfire*.

9. On the Golf Channel, people want to beat up the course, not one another. It's man (and woman) against nature and man against himself, but not man against man.

10. No one on the Golf Channel is afraid of compromise or change. On the contrary, golf is a game where the very best players engage in never-ending self-criticism, self-reflection, and self-correction, constantly adapting to changes in courses, conditions, or age. That's all they talk about on the Golf Channel. The best golfers spend a lot of time looking at themselves in the mirror to

check their swings—unlike in the Middle East, where self-reflection and self-criticism are as common as a three-hump camel.

April 21, 2002

WHAT DAY IS IT?

JERUSALEM

President Bush recently lamented that in the Middle East "the future is
dying." Being out here now, I can confirm that. There is only one way to
reclaim that future: It is for America to get Saudi Crown Prince Abdullah, Ariel Sharon, and Yasir Arafat to face up to what each wants to
ignore. Abdullah wants to ignore yesterday, Sharon wants to ignore
tomorrow, and Arafat wants to ignore today.

The Saudi leader will be meeting Mr. Bush tomorrow and will no
doubt want to focus on one thing—the Arab-Israeli conflict and the
Saudi peace initiative. I'm glad the crown prince has put forward a peace
plan. It can only help create possibilities, and those who say it is only
P.R. don't know what they're talking about.

But as Americans we still have some "yesterday" business to clear up
with him: namely, who were those fifteen Saudi hijackers on September
11, and what were the forces inside Saudi Arabia that produced them?
The FBI still doesn't know. Saudi Arabia refuses to take any responsibility for its citizens who participated in September 11. A society that won't
acknowledge responsibility isn't likely to engage in self-correction—in
terms of how it educates its youth and what opportunities it offers them
for the future.

Think about two recent stories. The *Times*'s Education Life supple-
ment just reported that the best-selling book in China for the past sixteen
months has been a book, in Chinese, about how to get your teenager into
Harvard, titled *Harvard Girl Yiting Liu*. In this book a Chinese mother
shares her "scientifically proven methods" for getting her daughter into
Harvard. It has sold more than 1.1 million copies and triggered fifteen
copycats about how to get into Columbia, Oxford, or Cambridge. In the
same week it was reported that the normally intelligent Saudi ambassador
in London, Ghazi Algosaibi, had published a poem in *Al-Hayat* in praise

of the eighteen-year-old Palestinian girl who blew herself up outside an Israeli supermarket, saying to her, "You died to honor God's word."

A society that makes a best-seller about how to get its teenagers into Harvard will eventually build Harvards of its own. But leaders who glorify a teenager who committed suicide in front of a supermarket full of civilians will never build a country that can live on anything other than oil; their priorities will be too messed up. Israel did not "honor" God in Jenin, and neither do suicide bombers.

As for Mr. Sharon, he only wants to talk about how to crush Palestinian suicide terrorism today, but he has no apparent plans for tomorrow. I find a split mood here: After months of Israelis' swallowing suicide bombs and wondering whether Jews would be able to go on living here, Israel's recent military operation has buoyed them with the feeling that they can still defend themselves. But there is also a deep depression here, because there is also a sense, as many Israelis have commented to me, that their leader has no plan, no road map, beyond his iron fist.

Many Israelis feel Mr. Sharon is so paralyzed by his obsession with eliminating Mr. Arafat, by his commitment to colonial settlements, and by his fear that any Israeli concession now would be interpreted as victory for the other side, that he can't produce what most Israelis want: a practical, nonideological solution, one that says, "Let's pull back to this line, abandon these settlements, and engage the Palestinians with this proposal, because that is what will preserve our Jewish democracy, and forget about the other stuff."

As for Mr. Arafat, he only wants to talk about yesterday, and what the Palestinians have suffered—or about tomorrow, how one day the Palestinian flag will fly over Jerusalem. But Mr. Arafat has no plans for today, no plans for preparing his people for a historic compromise, no plans for building institutions, and no diplomatic strategy for how to cash in this intifada for a peace deal with Israel. Someone should tell the European fools who now rush to protect Mr. Arafat that when this intifada started it was directed partly at his corrupt leadership, but he redirected it all onto Israel—with Mr. Sharon's help—decimating both the Palestinian economy and the very Israeli peace camp that is the only force that can deliver Palestinians a state.

Bill Clinton said at Camp David, "We may not succeed, but we're sure going to get caught trying." Mr. Bush cannot remake Abdullah, Sharon, or Arafat, but he can get caught trying by speaking the truth to them and their societies—where there are still many, many people desperate to save the future from leaders who can't figure out what day it is.

April 24, 2002

REELING, BUT READY

BETHLEHEM, WEST BANK

Israel's former absorption minister, Yuli Tamir, told me this story: After a recent suicide bombing in Jerusalem in which three Israelis were killed, a friend called to ask her whether her teenage daughter was safe because the suicide bomb had gone off next to a youth group office her daughter frequented. "I told my friend: 'Thank God, she's safe. She's in Auschwitz,'" Yuli said.

Yuli's daughter was in Poland at the time, visiting the Nazi death camp with her youth group, but the irony of her words of relief was not lost on her. It's that kind of moment for Israelis. The last two months of almost nonstop suicide bombings have turned this country upside down, puncturing Israel's sense of security more than anything any Arab army has done in fifty years, and leaving Israelis more willing than ever to give up territory but less willing than ever to trust Yasir Arafat & Company.

If you look at the polls in Israel today, you find there is now a two-thirds majority for every option: Two-thirds want to eliminate Mr. Arafat, and two-thirds want to withdraw from the West Bank in return for real security; two-thirds support the current crackdown, and two-thirds fear that it won't provide a long-term solution. There is such a hunger here for a leader with the pragmatic wisdom to find a way out of this, and such a worry that Mr. Sharon, who last week reaffirmed his eternal commitment to the insane Israeli settlements in Gaza, is not the man.

An Israeli major in Bethlehem expressed the mood well when he said to me in one breath: "I am so upset. [The suicide bombers] broke my dream. We don't have a home now," and then added, "but I am a settler in Efrat, and I told my son if the government tells us to leave for real peace, we have to obey."

At the same time, though, Mr. Sharon's smashing of the camps and offices used by the suicide bombers and Palestinian militants has left Palestinians reeling. Ever since the unilateral Israeli withdrawal from Lebanon, Palestinians have watched too much Hezbollah TV from Lebanon, which had peddled the notion that Israel had become just a big, soft Silicon Valley, and that therefore, with enough suicide bombs, the Jews could be forced from Palestine, just as they had been from

South Lebanon. The recent Israeli military operations were an exercise in showing the Palestinians not only the real power of the Israeli Army, but also the fact that Israeli commandos and reservists were ready to fight house-to-house in Palestinian refugee camps to protect their state.

This has also left Palestinians confused. "People cannot agree even on where we are, let alone where we should go," said Sari Nusseibeh, the head of the Palestinian Authority office in Jerusalem. "Some people look at where we are now and say we're winning, and others say we're losing."

I believe it is precisely such a moment that is ripe with diplomatic opportunity—very much like the opportunity that Henry Kissinger exploited when Egypt and Israel had each other by the throat, and were both bleeding badly, at the end of the 1973 war.

"Both sides feel they've made a point—Palestinians made the point that they can make life in Israel unlivable, and Israelis believe they have made the same point back," said the political theorist Yaron Ezrahi. "Neither side feels it lost this last round, but both are deeply worried over what happens if the war resumes. It would be criminal negligence for world diplomacy to miss taking advantage of such a moment."

Attention President Bush: Do not listen to what people out here are saying; they're all confused. The important thing is to understand how they are feeling—which is more open to a realistic diplomatic solution than ever before. Their leaders don't know how to move, so America has to chart the way with a big idea.

President Bush laid out a vision in his speech two weeks ago. Saudi Arabia's crown prince has done the same. But they are way too vague. As Israel's foreign minister, Shimon Peres, observed, the Bush vision and the Saudi vision are "like lights at the end of a tunnel—but with no tunnel." What's needed now is a U.S. plan that offers a clear-cut, phased program for a two-state solution.

Without it, I can tell you what will happen next. The current leaders here have only Plan A—and you saw it played out over the past three months. They have no Plan B. Plan B is more Plan A, and that will be really dangerous. If there is no creative diplomacy to take advantage of this moment, creative depravity will fill the void.

April 28, 2002

THE HIDDEN VICTIMS

———◆———

In recent months, the explosion of Arab satellite TV stations and Web sites has had a profound impact on Arab public opinion by showing live, nonstop images of the Israeli crackdown on Palestinians in the West Bank. These TV and e-mail images have fueled massive demonstrations across the Arab world, and in both Egypt and Bahrain protesters have been shot. Could this roiling Arab street actually topple a regime? No— none of the Arab regimes are in any danger right now. But Arab regimes' surviving or not surviving is not the right question. The right question is how they will survive.

What many are having to do to survive is to slow down whatever modernization, globalization, or democratization initiatives they were either pursuing or contemplating and to focus, at least rhetorically, on the old agenda of the Arab-Israeli conflict. The biggest victims of the West Bank war will not be Arab leaders, but Arab liberals—as fledgling democratic experiments are postponed, foreign investment reduced, security services given more leeway to crack down, and all public discussion dominated by the Palestine issue.

Jordan's King Abdullah, one of the most progressive leaders in the Arab world today, told me: "I have no intention of putting Jordan's modernization program on hold. We are moving ahead, but I cannot do this by myself. I need the public with me."

But keeping the public and politicians focused on modernization today is not as easy as it was a year ago. Jordan, like all other Arab countries, has been bombarded by independent Arab satellite TV stations, which compete for audiences by showing the most gruesome, one-sided images of Israel brutalizing Palestinians.

When I covered the Israeli invasion of Lebanon in 1982, it took hours or days for film footage to get out, and Arab regimes could tightly control what was shown. A few weeks ago, by contrast, Arab News Network carried live, from a Palestinian village next to Jenin, a report from a Palestinian family that had been locked into a room by Israeli forces who were sweeping the area. The mother, who had a cell phone, called ANN, pleading for help for her kids. The whole Arab world listened in—live.

"You hear the screams," said a Jordanian editor. "It comes right into your bedroom. You go to bed seeing Palestinians killed and you wake up seeing them killed . . . If you put anything else on the front page other than this, people will laugh at you."

This was not the case a year ago, when Jordanian news was dominated by the king's innovative modernization program, which is supposed to kick off this year with a radical reform of the Jordanian education system, connecting every Jordanian school to the Internet, and new investments in rural development. Once the initiative was running, the king was planning to hold elections in the fall for a new parliament that would endorse this progressive agenda.

As part of this whole push, Microsoft signaled its intent to invest $2 million in a creative Jordanian software firm. Microsoft conditioned its investment, though, on Jordan's first amending its copyright, labor, and company laws to bring them up to world standards. The cabinet amended the laws by fiat, but was hoping a new parliament would ratify them.

But with the Jordanian population so inflamed about events in the West Bank—"The most popular TV program here now is Hezbollah television, can you believe that?" said a Jordanian businessman—ministers cannot talk publicly, the way they need to, about the domestic reform agenda, the press isn't interested, and the palace is rethinking whether to hold elections. It's worried that in the current mood, Islamists could sweep the day instead of progressives.

This is the real Arab street story. Progressive Arab states, like Jordan, Morocco, and Bahrain, which want to build their legitimacy not on how they confront Israel but on how well they prepare their people for the future, are being impeded. And retrograde Arab regimes, like Syria, Saudi Arabia, and Iraq, can now feed their people more excuses why not to reform.

The Palestinians have been experts at seducing the Arab world into postponing its future until all the emotive issues of Palestine are resolved. Three generations of Arabs have already paid dearly for only being allowed to ask one question—"Who rules Palestine?"—not "How are we educating our young?" or "What kind of democracy or economy should we have?" It would be a tragedy if a fourth generation suffered the same fate.

May 1, 2002

LISTENING TO THE FUTURE?

JAKARTA, INDONESIA

Last Thursday, I sat in the garden of the Pesantren Darunnajah, one of Jakarta's finest Islamic boarding schools, with twenty thoughtful young Indonesians to ask them for their views of America. I wanted to understand how the world's largest Muslim nation was reacting to September 11 and the Middle East crisis. I could tell you in my own words, but let me instead run the tape of my chat with the most articulate student: eighteen-year-old Wisam Rochalina.

"Most Muslims are afraid of America because they think America is against Islam," she began. "You can see that America is backing the Israelians, and the enmity between Islam and Israel, the Jews [and] Judaism, is obvious. It is not that Americans are afraid of Muslims, but that Muslims are afraid of Americans. As for the [September 11] tragedy, we can't prove that Muslims did it. Because up to now they have not found evidence to prove that [bin Laden] is the one who did it. Also, I read in some newspaper that the real people who did that tragedy are Americans. . . . I don't know [what] percent of the Congress are Jewish, [but] America is backing Israel, and I think therein lies the feeling of enmity toward America."

Where do you get your news?

"I get most information from the TV, from the Internet too. . . . I really like to read the [on-line] Arabic magazines because they give a different point of view. If I read Indonesian magazines, they don't have a lot of information about Muslims and Islam."

Why are so many Muslims so angry with America and Israel now?

"I think it is because Israel has gone beyond limits and [Muslims] just got fed up and decided they have to do something about it. I think it has something to do [with] Muslims feeling like they are being called murderers and they are being treated in the U.S. like they are terrorists — they are being blamed for something they haven't done . . . and I think that's why they hate America — it's not hate, it's this feeling that the American media is spreading everywhere, so I think it has something to do with spreading the image of Islam and distorting that image."

What do you think of President Bush?

"At the beginning, when George Bush became President, some people thought he is only going to be like his father and he's not going to make anything new—and also people did not want Al Gore to win because he was Jewish. So people said, 'OK, George Bush is better. . . .' He promised a lot of really good things but [has] not realized them up to now."

Would you like to study in America?

"Of course I would! Because if I go there, I can understand how that world really thinks. Because until now I only read about it in newspapers and only see it on TV."

Wisam's views are widely shared by millions of Muslim youth. They are a product of many things: a reaction to America's war on terrorism and Ariel Sharon's war on Yasir Arafat, the failure of Muslim states to master modernity, Muslim resentment at being blamed for 9/11, unquestioning Congressional support for Israel, and outright incitement against Israel and Jews in Arab and European media and Web sites. Stir it all together, and what comes out is a single big idea melding in the minds of many young Muslims: America, Israel, and the Jews are working together to undermine Islam and dominate the world.

This is not good. But how does one reverse it? Spreading democracy in the Muslim world would help enormously, but that's not going to happen soon. In the near term, Israel has got to get out of the West Bank and Gaza any way it can—just get out—and get this war with Palestinians off TV. It will not end Muslim hostility to the Jewish state, but it will eliminate a good chunk of raw material.

At the same time, America needs to make a much bigger investment in public diplomacy in the Muslim world, and vigorously challenge what is published there. In an era when blind rage can become a weapon of mass destruction, this is as important as any missile shield. We can make a difference with young people. Their views are easily acquired and easily shed. The one time Wisam's eyes lit up was when she talked about studying in America.

A U.S. diplomat in Jakarta told me she had just visited the town of Malang, in East Java, and had seen an Indonesian boy there wearing an Osama bin Laden T-shirt and a New York Yankees cap. So all isn't lost. But we must make sure that he grows into the cap, not the T-shirt.

May 5, 2002

THE WAR ON WHAT?

———

JAKARTA, INDONESIA

Spend a few days in Indonesia and you'll find many people asking you a question you weren't prepared for: Is America's war on terrorism going to become a war against democracy?

As Indonesians see it, for decades after World War II America sided with dictators, like their own President Suharto, because of its war on Communism. With the fall of the Berlin Wall, America began to press more vigorously for democracy and human rights in countries like Indonesia as the United States shifted from containing Communism to enlarging the sphere of democratic states. Indonesians were listening, and in 1998 they toppled Mr. Suharto and erected their first electoral democracy.

Today Indonesians are still listening, and they're worried they're hearing America shift again—from a war for democracy to a war on terrorism in which the United States will judge which nations are with it or against it not by the integrity of their elections or the justice of their courts, but by the vigor with which their army and police combat Al Qaeda. For Indonesia, where democracy is still a fragile flower, anything that encourages a comeback by the long-feared, but now slightly defanged, army and police—the tools of Mr. Suharto's long repression—is not good news.

"Indonesian democrats have always depended on America as a point of reference that we could count on to support us," said the prominent Indonesian commentator Wimar Witoelar. "If we see you waffling, whom do we turn to? It is like the sun disappearing from the sky and everything starts to freeze here again."

There is a broad feeling among Indonesian elites that while some of their more authoritarian neighbors, like Malaysia or Pakistan, have suddenly become the new darlings of Washington as a result of the war on terrorism, Indonesia is being orphaned because it is a messy, but real, democracy.

"We sometimes fear that America's democratization agenda also got blown up with the World Trade Center," says the Indonesian writer Andreas Harsono. "Since September 11 there have been so many free riders on this American antiterrorism campaign, countries that want to use it to suppress their media and press freedom and turn back the clock. Indonesia, instead of being seen as a weak democracy that needs support, gets looked at as a weak country that protects terrorists, and Malaysia is seen as superior because it arrests more terrorists than we do."

Indeed, many people here believe that retrograde elements in the army and police have helped stir up recent sectarian clashes in Aceh and the Maluku Islands to spur Parliament to give the security services some of their old powers back.

Says Jusuf Wanandi, who heads a key strategic studies center here: "I just spoke with some senior military people who said to me: 'Why doesn't the government give up all this human rights stuff and leave [the problem] to us?' They said the Americans should normalize relations again [with the Indonesian army] 'and we'll do the job for them.' That is not the right approach, because we do not trust yet that the reforms of the military here have been adequate."

In fairness, the Bush team has kept aid for Indonesia at $130 million and made it the official policy in all diplomatic contacts that Indonesia should continue fighting its war for democracy, while contributing what it can to the war on terrorism. (It's not clear if there are any Al Qaeda cells here.)

Nevertheless, some top Pentagon officials are definitely pushing to let the Indonesian military make a comeback and to restore ties with the Indonesian military that were suspended after the army ran amok in East Timor in 1999. Indonesia is just beginning to try military officers involved in those killings. If there is any hope of senior army officers being held accountable for East Timor, it will certainly be lost if America signals that all it cares about now is that the new antiterrorism laws being debated by the Indonesian Parliament give the army anything it wants.

America needs to be aware of how its war on terrorism is read in other countries, especially those in transition. Indonesia is the world's biggest Muslim country. Its greatest contribution to us would be to show the Arab-Muslim states that it is possible to develop a successful Muslim democracy, with a modern economy and a moderate religious outlook. Setting that example is a lot more in America's long-term interest than arresting a few stray Al Qaeda fighters in the jungles of Borneo.

May 8, 2002

GLOBAL VILLAGE IDIOCY

JAKARTA, INDONESIA

During a dinner with Indonesian journalists in Jakarta, I was taken aback when Dini Djalal, a reporter for the *Far Eastern Economic Review*, suddenly launched into a blistering criticism of the Fox News Channel and Bill O'Reilly. "They say [on Fox], 'We report, you decide,' but it's biased—they decide before us," she said. "They say there is no spin, but I get dizzy looking at it. I also get upset when they invite on Muslims and just insult them."

Why didn't she just not watch Fox when she came to America? I wondered. No, no, no, explained Ms. Djalal: The Fox Channel is now part of her Jakarta cable package. The conservative Bill O'Reilly is in her face every night.

On my way to Jakarta I stopped in Dubai, where I watched the Arab News Network at 2 a.m. ANN broadcasts from Europe, outside the control of any Arab government, but is seen all over the Middle East. It was running what I'd call the "greatest hits" from the Israeli-Palestinian conflict: nonstop film of Israelis hitting, beating, dragging, clubbing, and shooting Palestinians. I would like to say the footage was out of context, but there was no context. There were no words. It was just pictures and martial music designed to inflame passions.

An Indonesian working for the U.S. Embassy in Jakarta who had just visited the Islamic fundamentalist stronghold of Jogjakarta told me this story: "For the first time I saw signs on the streets there saying things like 'The only solution to the Arab-Israel conflict is jihad—if you are true Muslim, register yourself to be a volunteer.' I heard people saying, 'We have to do something, otherwise the Christians or Jewish will kill us.' When we talked to people to find out where [they got these ideas], they said from the Internet. They took for granted that anything they learned from the Internet is true. They believed in a Jewish conspiracy and that four thousand Jews were warned not to come to work at the World Trade Center [on September 11]. It was on the Internet."

What's frightening him, he added, is that there is an insidious digital divide in Jogjakarta: "Internet users are only 5 percent of the population—but these 5 percent spread rumors to everyone else. They say, 'He got it from the Internet.' They think it's the Bible."

If there's one thing I learned from this trip to Israel, Jordan, Dubai, and Indonesia, it's this: Thanks to the Internet and satellite TV, the world is being wired together technologically, but not socially, politically, or culturally. We are now seeing and hearing one another faster and better, but with no corresponding improvement in our ability to learn from, or understand, one another. So integration, at this stage, is producing more anger than anything else. As the writer George Packer recently noted in *The New York Times Magazine*, "In some ways, global satellite TV and Internet access have actually made the world a less understanding, less tolerant place."

At its best, the Internet can educate more people faster than any media tool we've ever had. At its worst, it can make people dumber faster than any media tool we've ever had. The lie that four thousand Jews were warned not to go into the World Trade Center on September 11 was spread entirely over the Internet and is now thoroughly believed in the Muslim world. Because the Internet has an aura of "technology" surrounding it, the uneducated believe information from it even more. They don't realize that the Internet, at its ugliest, is just an open sewer: an electronic conduit for untreated, unfiltered information.

Worse, just when you might have thought you were all alone with your extreme views, the Internet puts you together with a community of people from around the world who hate all the things and people you do. And you can scrap the BBC and just get your news from those Web sites that reinforce your own stereotypes.

A couple of years ago, two Filipino college graduates spread the "I Love You" virus over the Internet, causing billions of dollars in damage to computers and software. But at least that virus was curable with the right software. There is another virus going around today, though, that's much more serious. I call it the "I Hate You" virus. It's spread on the Internet and by satellite TV. It infects people's minds with the most vile ideas, and it can't be combated by just downloading a software program. It can be reversed only with education, exchanges, diplomacy, and human interaction—stuff you have to upload the old-fashioned way, one-on-one. Let's hope it's not too late.

May 12, 2002

NINE WARS TOO MANY

If I were making a movie of the Arab-Israeli conflict today, I would call it *Ten Wars and a Funeral*. Because the biggest problem in resolving this conflict is that there are at least ten different wars being fought over Israel-Palestine, and we need to reduce them to just one to have any chance of making peace.

Let's run down the list: A majority of Israelis are fighting a war for the right of a Jewish state to exist in the Middle East, roughly along the pre-1967 borders. But a minority in Israel today want a Jewish state within the pre-1967 lines and a Jewish state in the West Bank and Gaza. This was amply demonstrated by Bibi Netanyahu's stunt at the recent Likud Party convention, where he tried to advance his political career and embarrass Ariel Sharon by getting the lunatic core of the Likud to reject any Palestinian state ever in the West Bank. These Israeli rightists and settlers deliberately label any Palestinian resistance to the Israeli occupation of the West Bank as "terrorism" in order to rope the United States into supporting Israel's continued hold on the occupied territories as part of America's global war on terrorism. Beware.

The same is true inside the Bush administration. The State Department sees the Mideast war as a war over Israel's 1967 boundaries, and its focus is on "conflict resolution"—diplomacy aimed at getting Israel to trade occupied land for peace. But over at the Pentagon, the view is that Yasir Arafat is no different from Osama bin Laden, and the other Arab leaders are worthy only of contempt. The Pentagon sees the Israeli war to crush Mr. Arafat as an extension of the U.S. war on terrorism and believes that the most you can do with Arabs and Israelis today is "conflict management," not conflict resolution.

This view is reinforced by the fact that the Palestinians *are* fighting two wars. Yes, many Palestinians are simply fighting to get Israel out of the West Bank, Gaza, and East Jerusalem so they can establish a state there—not because they acknowledge the legitimacy of a Jewish homeland in pre-1967 Israel, but because they know they lack the power to eliminate it. But some Palestinians, and Mr. Arafat is among them, have not abandoned hope of establishing a Palestinian state in the West Bank and Gaza today—through diplomacy and armed struggle—and a Palestinian state in pre-1967 Israel tomorrow—through a baby boom and securing the right of return of millions of Palestinian refugees. Israel still does not appear on many of Mr. Arafat's maps. So let's cut the nonsense that the only thing that *all* Palestinians want is an "end to the Israeli occupation." I wish that were true.

Ditto the Arabs. Egypt, Saudi Arabia, and Syria all claim they just want Israel to withdraw to the pre-1967 borders, but anyone reading their official media, which regularly spew articles comparing Israel to Nazi Germany and extolling the virtues of Palestinian girls who commit suicide amid Israeli civilians in Tel Aviv, would hardly be assured that for them the only problem is the Israeli occupation—and not the Jewish people's right to a homeland in the Middle East.

And ditto-ditto the Europeans. Yes, yes, many Europeans really do just want an end to the Israeli occupation, but the anti-Semitism coming out of Europe today suggests that deep down some Europeans want a lot more: They want Mr.Sharon to commit a massacre against Palestinians, or they want to describe what he did in Jenin as a massacre, so that the Europeans can finally get the guilt of the Holocaust off their backs and be able to shout: "Look at these Jews, they're worse than we were!"

I just attended an Arab media conference and was on a panel with Eric Rouleau, the former Middle East correspondent of *Le Monde*, who said he had recently spoken to some French generals who told him that what Israel did in Jenin was worse than anything France did during the Algerian war. One million Algerians were killed in that war and two million were made homeless. So far, sixty bodies have been recovered in Jenin, many of them fighters. You do the math.

Frankly, I'm happy President Bush is getting more involved in Mideast peacemaking. But he'll get nowhere unless he can get the parties (including his own aides) to abandon all the other wars they're fighting and to tell their own people, and each other, that there's only one war left—a war to determine the border between a Jewish state and a Palestinian state. Anyone who's fighting any other war is an enemy of peace and an enemy of America's national interest.

May 15, 2002

A FAILURE TO IMAGINE

If you ask me, the press has this whole story about whether President Bush had a warning of a possible attack before 9/11, and didn't share it, upside down.

The failure to prevent September 11 was not a failure of intelligence or coordination. It was a failure of imagination. Even if all the raw intelligence signals had been shared among the FBI, the CIA, and the White House, I'm convinced that there was no one there who would have put them all together, who would have imagined evil on the scale Osama bin Laden did.

Osama bin Laden was (or is) a unique character. He's a combination of Charles Manson and Jack Welch—a truly evil, twisted personality, but with the organizational skills of a top corporate manager, who translated his evil into a global campaign that rocked a superpower. In some ways, I'm glad that America (outside Hollywood) is not full of people with bin Laden–like imaginations. One Timothy McVeigh is enough.

Imagining evil of this magnitude simply does not come naturally to the American character, which is why, even after we are repeatedly confronted with it, we keep reverting to our natural, naïvely optimistic selves. Because our open society is so much based on trust, and that trust is so hardwired into the American character and citizenry, we can't get rid of it—even when we so obviously should.

So someone drives a truck bomb into the U.S. Embassy in Beirut and we still don't really protect the Marine barracks there from a similar, but much bigger, attack a few months later. Someone blows up two U.S. embassies in East Africa with truck bombs and we still don't imagine that someone would sail an exploding dinghy into a destroyer, the U.S.S. *Cole*, a few years later. Someone tries to blow up the World Trade Center in 1993 with a truck bomb, and the guy who did it tells us he had also wanted to slam a plane into the CIA, but we still couldn't imagine someone doing just that to the Twin Towers on 9/11.

So I don't fault the President for not having imagined evil of this magnitude. But given the increasingly lethal nature of terrorism, we are going to have to adapt. We need an "Office of Evil," whose job would be to constantly sift all intelligence data and imagine what the most twisted mind might be up to.

No, I don't blame President Bush at all for his failure to imagine evil. I blame him for something much worse: his failure to imagine good.

I blame him for squandering all the positive feeling in America after 9/11, particularly among young Americans who wanted to be drafted for a great project that would strengthen America in some lasting way—a Manhattan Project for energy independence. Such a project could have enlisted young people in a national movement for greater conservation and enlisted science and industry in a crash effort to produce enough renewable energy, efficiencies, and domestic production to wean us gradually off oil imports.

Such a project would not only have made us safer by making us independent of countries who share none of our values. It would also have made us safer by giving the world a much stronger reason to support our war on terrorism. There is no way we can be successful in this war without partners, and there is no way America will have lasting partners, especially in Europe, unless it is perceived as being the best global citizen it can be. And the best way to start conveying that would be by reducing our energy gluttony and ratifying the Kyoto treaty to reduce global warming.

President Bush is not alone in this failure. He has had the full cooperation of the Democratic Party leadership, which has been just as lacking in imagination. This has made it easy for Mr. Bush, and his oil-industry paymasters, to get away with it.

We and our kids are going to regret this. Because a war on terrorism that is fought only by sending soldiers to Afghanistan or by tightening our borders will ultimately be unsatisfying. Such a war is important, but it can never be definitively won. Someone will always slip through. But a war on terrorism that, with some imagination, is broadly defined as making America safer by also making it better is a war that could be won. It's a war that could ensure that something lasting comes out of 9/11, other than longer lines at the airport—and that something would be enhanced respect for America and a country and a planet that would be greener, cleaner, and safer in the broadest sense.

Too bad we don't have a President who could imagine that.

May 19, 2002

COOL IT!

Ah, excuse me, but could we all just calm down here?

What started as a story about how the Bush team handled unspecific warnings about possible terrorist attacks in the United States before 9/11 has now prompted the Bushies not only to defend themselves from charges of irresponsibility—which they are entitled to do—but to go on a Chicken Little warnings binge that another attack is imminent, inevitable, and around the corner, but we can't tell you when, where, or how.

Look, in the wake of 9/11, I would never rule out any kind of attack. That would be foolhardy. But I'm no more interested in indicting the Bush team for failing to respond to an unspecific warning about a possible terrorist attack before 9/11 than I'm interested in having the Vice President and FBI director warn us about the certainty of an unspecified attack sometime in the future.

What are we supposed to do with this information? Never go into another apartment building, because reports suggest an Al Qaeda cell may rent an apartment just to blow up the whole structure? Don't go outside? Don't go near national monuments? Pat the belly of every pregnant woman to check if she's a suicide bomber?

Who wants to live that way? Let's make a deal: We won't criticize the administration for not anticipating 9/11 if it won't terrorize the country by now predicting every possible nightmare scenario, but no specific ones, post-9/11. Not only are these "warnings" just unnerving the public when people were finally starting to calm down, but they are also obscuring something very important: We are winning this war.

No, it's not over. And yes, I too will say for the record that sometime, somewhere, there will be another attack. But in the meantime we've actually accomplished a lot. If Osama bin Laden is alive—a big *if*—his ability to direct acts of terrorism against U.S. targets has been disrupted. It is doubtful that he would dare even use a telephone.

That is important, because bin Laden and his top deputies were a unique and very smart, creative, and daring group of terrorists, who do not come along every day. And whether they are all dead or deep in hiding, there is no indication they are in business right now. Yes, probably less-professional cells still exist and still can wreak havoc. But when you decapitate an organization like Al Qaeda and disrupt its money flow, you've done a lot. And when you oust the Taliban in Afghanistan and take away the one true safe harbor for bin Laden—for training and operations—you've also done a lot.

We have put in place reasonable precautions at airports; we have instituted better coordination between the FBI, CIA, and INS; we are tracking foreign students more closely; and we and our allies have detained thousands of suspects. The fact that there has been no other major incident since 9/11 is surely not because the terrorists have abandoned their intentions. It is because we have hampered their capabilities. That is a good thing.

But the very nature of this war against small groups and individuals bent on terrorism is that you can never win it definitively. It will be with us forever. But we can limit the number of attacks—and keep terrorist cells on the run and disrupted enough to reduce their capabilities—if our public officials responsible for this war are not spending all day looking in their rearview mirrors or mindlessly terrorizing the public with unspecified cover-your-behind warnings about future terrorism.

This is absolutely not an argument for a free pass for the Bush team. Given the stories about intelligence failures that have come out already, we clearly need a special commission, led by professionals, not politicians, that will look into the decade-long history of our handling of Al Qaeda and explore why we did not have better intelligence, why the dots were not connected, and how to improve in the future.

But the other thing we need to do is grow up. If we're going to maintain an open society, all we can do is take all reasonable precautions and then suck it up and learn to live with a higher level of risk. That is our fate, so let's not drive ourselves crazy.

I don't know about you, but my Memorial Day weekend plans are set: golf Saturday, bike trip Sunday, barbecue Monday. If the FBI director wants to interrupt my weekend with a specific warning, I'll be all ears; otherwise, pipe down and chill out. Remember it's supposed to be Al Qaeda that's running scared, not us.

May 22, 2002

WEBBED, WIRED, AND WORRIED

Ever since I learned that Mohamed Atta made his reservation for September 11 using his laptop and the American Airlines Web site, and that several of his colleagues used Travelocity.com, I've been wondering how the entrepreneurs of Silicon Valley were looking at the 9/11 tragedy—whether it was giving them any pause about the wired world they've been building and the assumptions they are building it upon.

In a recent visit to Stanford University and Silicon Valley, I had a chance to pose these questions to techies. I found that at least some of their libertarian technology-will-solve-everything cockiness was gone. I found a much keener awareness that the unique web of technologies Silicon Valley was building before 9/11—from the Internet to powerful encryption software—can be incredible force multipliers for individuals and small groups to do both good and evil. And I found an acknowledgment that all those technologies had been built with a high degree of trust as to how they would be used, and that that trust had been shaken. In its place is a greater appreciation that high-tech companies aren't just threatened by their competitors—but also by some of their users.

"The question 'How can this technology be used against me?' is now a real R-and-D issue for companies, where in the past it wasn't really even being asked," said Jim Hornthal, a former vice chairman of Travelocity.com. "People here always thought the enemy was Microsoft, not Mohamed Atta."

It was part of Silicon Valley lore that successful innovations would follow a well-trodden path beginning with early adopters, then early mass-appeal users, and finally the mass market. But it's clear now that there is also a parallel criminal path—starting with the early perverters of a new technology up to the really twisted perverters. For instance, the 9/11 hijackers may have communicated globally through steganography software, which lets users e-mail, say, a baby picture that secretly contains a 300-page compressed document or even a voice message.

"We have engineered large parts of our system on an assumption of trust that may no longer be accurate," said Stanford law professor Joseph A. Grundfest. "Trust is hardwired into everything from computers to the Internet to building codes. What kind of building codes you need depends on what kind of risks you thought were out there. The odds of someone flying a passenger jet into a tall building were zero before. They're not anymore. The whole objective of the terrorists is to reduce our trust in all the normal instruments and technologies we use in daily life. You wake up in the morning and trust that you can get to work across the Brooklyn Bridge—don't. This is particularly dangerous because societies which have a low degree of trust are backward societies."

Silicon Valley staunchly opposed the Clipper Chip, which would have given the government a back-door key to all U.S. encrypted data. Now some wonder whether they shouldn't have opposed it. John Doerr, the venture capitalist, said, "Culturally, the Valley was already maturing before 9/11, but since then it's definitely developed a deeper respect for leaders and government institutions."

At Travelocity, Mr. Hornthal noted, whether the customer was Mohamed Atta or Bill Gates, "our only responsibility was to authenticate your financial ability to pay. Did your name and credit card match your billing address? It was not our responsibility, nor did we have the ability, to authenticate your intent with that ticket, which requires a much deeper sense of identification. It may be, though, that this is where technology will have to go—to allow a deeper sense of identification."

Speaking of identity, Bethany Hornthal, a marketing consultant, noted that Silicon Valley had always been a multicultural place where young people felt they could go anywhere in the world and fit in. They were global kids. "Suddenly after 9/11, that changed," she said. "Suddenly they were Americans, and there was a certain danger in that identity. [As a result] the world has become more defined and restricted for them. Now you ask, Where is it safe to go as an American?" So there is this sense, she concluded, that thanks to technology and globalization, "the world may have gotten smaller—but I can't go there anymore."

Or as my friend Jack Murphy, a venture capitalist, mused to me as we discussed the low state of many high-tech investments, "Maybe I should have gone into the fence business instead."

May 26, 2002

THE SUICIDE WAR

It's clear now that the Israeli-Palestinian clashes that erupted in the spring of 2002 qualify as the sixth Arab-Israeli war—going down in history with the 1948, 1956, 1967, 1973, and 1982 wars. The 2002 war doesn't have a proper name yet (the Suicide War?). But like all previous Arab-Israeli wars, it is having a proper aftermath—shaking up Arab, Israeli, and Palestinian politics as much as the five previous wars did.

Let's start with the Palestinians. Well before this war, there was already bubbling Palestinian criticism that their "Al-Aksa intifada" had no clearly defined goals and that Yasir Arafat, instead of developing them, was just surfing on his people's anger and trying to direct it away from his own misrule. Yes, Mr. Arafat is still the most nimble survivor of his own mistakes. But this time he has really hurt the Palestinian cause, and Palestinians know it.

First, by provoking Israel with repeated suicide bombings, Mr. Arafat triggered an Israeli retaliation that didn't just destroy Arab cities—as he did in Amman in 1970 and Beirut in 1982. This time he provoked the destruction of Palestinian cities: Ramallah, Nablus, Jenin, and Bethlehem. Second, by encouraging this Suicide War—after rejecting a clearcut U.S. plan for a Palestinian state—Mr. Arafat has badly damaged Palestinian ties with America. President Bill Clinton met with Mr. Arafat more times than with any other foreign leader. Today Mr. Arafat couldn't get to see President Bush if he signed up for a White House tour.

Third, this Suicide War has badly alienated the only party that can deliver the Palestinians a state—the Israeli silent majority. The whole history of the peace process can be reduced to one simple point: If the Palestinians persuade the Israeli center that they are ready to live side by side in peace, they will get a state; if they don't, they won't. Everything else is just commentary.

The aftermath of the Suicide War on Israeli politics has been equally profound. "It has ended the deep political debate between the left and the right that has dominated Israeli politics since 1967," said Moshe Halbertal, a Hebrew University philosophy professor and fellow of the Hartman Institute. "The two big ideas that have dominated Israeli politics have both collapsed."

Indeed, the idea of the Jewish right that Israel could maintain a colonial occupation of the West Bank and continue to seize Palestinian land for more settlements, and that the Palestinians would just roll over and take it, has been exploded. But the idea of the Israeli left that Mr. Arafat, if returned to the West Bank, would build a decent government and civil society that would end the conflict with Israel on the basis of a two-state solution has also been undermined.

As a result, Israel today, instead of being divided around two ideas, is united around two ideas: a clear majority of Israelis are ready to smash the Palestinians as long as they persist in suicide bombings, and an equally clear majority of Israelis are ready to consider the Saudi peace initiative—full withdrawal in return for normal relations—as the basis for a settlement if the Palestinians ever persuade them that they are ready to end the violence.

The big impact on Arab leaders is their realization that the explosion of Arab satellite TV stations and the Internet means they can no longer control public opinion. The tabloid Arab media have inflamed the Arab street with images of the West Bank fighting. No, this inflamed street won't topple any leaders soon. But popular discontent over the Arabs' weakness in the face of Israel is melding with popular discontent about the weakness of Arab economies and dictatorial regimes in ways that are worrying moderate Arab leaders and making them eager to get this Palestinian show off the air.

Bottom line: The region is more ripe than ever for a big U.S. initiative. Unfortunately, none of the leaders—American, Israeli, or Palestinian—seem willing to step up to what's needed. That is, to create a transition structure in the West Bank and Gaza—a new mandate under U.S. or NATO supervision—that would oversee the gradual building of a responsible Palestinian Authority and the gradual unbuilding of settlements. If we shirk that task, we'll just be setting the stage for the seventh Arab-Israeli war.

May 29, 2002

WAR OF IDEAS

I'm glad that frustrated FBI agents are banging away at all the missed signals that might have tipped us off to 9/11, but we need to remember something: Not all the signals for 9/11 were hidden. Many were out there in public, in the form of hate speech and conspiracy theories directed at America and preached in mosques and schools throughout the Muslim world. If we are intent on preventing the next 9/11, we need to do more than just spy on our enemies better in secret. We need to take on their ideas in public.

Frankly, I hope Saddam Hussein disappears tomorrow. But even if he does, that's not going to solve our problem. Saddam is a conventional threat who can be eliminated by conventional means. He inspires no one. The idea people who inspired the hijackers are religious leaders, pseudo-intellectuals, pundits, and educators, primarily in Egypt and in Saudi Arabia, which continues to use its vast oil wealth to spread its austere and intolerant brand of Islam, Wahhabism.

But here's the good news: These societies are not monoliths, and there are a lot of ordinary people, and officials, inside both who would like to see us pressing their leaders and religious authorities to teach tolerance, modernize Islam, and stop financing those who won't.

Too bad President Bush has shied away from this challenge. After recently visiting Saudi Arabia, I got an e-mail note from a young Saudi woman (who signed her name) that began: "Thank you as a moderate Saudi for your efforts to expose what's going on in Saudi Arabia . . . Mr. Friedman, our schools teach religious intolerance, most of our mosques preach hate against any non-Muslims, our media is exclusively controlled by the government and religious people. Our moderate ideas have no place to be presented. Our government is not doing anything really to stop the religious control from paralyzing our lives. Mr. Friedman, we need help."

On May 8, the Saudi-owned Arabic daily *Al-Sharq Al-Awsat* ran an essay by an anonymous Arab diplomat who asked: "What would happen if every Arab country had, since 1948, turned its attention to building itself up from within, without making Palestine its main issue? What would happen if every Arab country focused on educating its citizens, and on improving their physical and emotional health and cultural level? I am amazed at the clerics who raise a hue and cry about Jihad against Israel and compete with each other in issuing religious rulings [in support of] suicide, but do not encourage their citizens to wage spiritual Jihad to build up their own countries." [Translation by MEMRI]

In short, America and the West have potential partners in these countries who are eager for us to help move the struggle to where it belongs: to a war within Islam over its spiritual message and identity, not a war with Islam.

And that war within Islam is not really a religious war. It is a war between the future and the past, between development and underdevelopment, between authors of crazy conspiracy theories versus those espousing rationality, between advocates of suicide bombing and those who know you can't build a society out of gravestones. Only Arabs and Muslims can win this war within, but we can openly encourage the progressives. Instead, we're looking for some quick fix. Just get rid of Saddam and all the fanatics will fall. I doubt it.

The only Western leader who vigorously took up this challenge was actually the Dutch politician Pim Fortuyn, who was assassinated on May 6—for other reasons. Mr. Fortuyn questioned Muslim immigration to the Netherlands (which by 2010 will have more mosques than churches), not because he was against Muslims but because he felt that Islam had not gone through the Enlightenment or the Reformation, which separated church from state in the West and prepared it to embrace modernity, democracy, and tolerance.

As a gay man, Mr. Fortuyn was very much in need of tolerance, and his challenge to Muslim immigrants was this: I want to be tolerant, but do you? Or do you have an authoritarian culture that will not be assimilated, and that threatens my country's liberal, multicultural ethos?

Zacarias Moussaoui, accused of being the twentieth hijacker, told a U.S. court that he "prayed to Allah for the destruction of the United States." That is an ugly idea—one many Muslims would not endorse. But until we and they team up to fight a war of ideas against those who do, there will be plenty more Moussaouis where he came from—and there will never be enough FBI agents to find them.

June 2, 2002

THE LAND OF DENIAL

I read in yesterday's *Times* that Egypt's president, Hosni Mubarak, says he warned the U.S. of a plot by Al Qaeda before 9/11 and that he has a new plan for a Palestinian state. I suppose that's all to the good, but frankly, none of it leaves me feeling reassured, for one simple reason: We don't need Egypt to be our policeman, we need it to be our progressive.

What I mean is that we need Egypt to play the role that it played in Arab politics in the nineteenth and early twentieth centuries, the role that history assigned it and for which it has no replacement: to lead the Arab-Muslim world into modernity with an ideological message that is rooted in Arab and Muslim tradition but is progressive, pluralistic, and democratic. That is the most important thing Egypt can do for us, and that is precisely what it has not been doing for decades now.

Let me be blunt. Egypt is the center of gravity of the Arab world. It has the biggest middle class, the best-educated population, and the people with the most potential. Egypt should be the Taiwan of the Mediterranean. But it is a country that has been stagnating, to the degree that smaller Arab countries are now passing it by.

Jordan was the first Arab country to secure a free-trade agreement with America; Bahrain is the Arab country doing the most innovative experiments with democracy; Qatar was the pioneer of free satellite television, with Al Jazeera; and Tunisia, despite its authoritarian regime, has led the way in economic liberalization and in forging closer ties with the EU.

All these innovations should have come from Egypt, and had they, they would have had a modernizing effect on the entire Arab world, particularly its other big stagnating countries—Iraq, Syria, and Saudi Arabia. But they are not happening. Egypt, which in the last century produced such towering Arab intellectuals as Naguib Mahfouz, Taha Hussein, and Tawfik al-Hakim, has produced no successors to them. The intellectual air has gone stale in Egypt from too many years of controlled press and authoritarian politics.

President Mubarak says, "We have all kinds of democracy." Really? All kinds but genuine democracy, because a genuine democracy wouldn't be putting on trial an Egyptian democracy expert, Saad Eddin

Ibrahim, for wanting the right to speak freely, press for social change, and question official policy.

In the mid-1990s Mr. Mubarak seemed to realize that Egypt needed to reform and privatize its economy, to keep pace with a population that will double in twenty years. But after a little reform produced a little boomlet, he backed off doing the really hard stuff. Since 2000, Egypt's economic growth has been anemic; it has seemed unable to attract much foreign or domestic investment. Costa Rica, with 4 million people, exports more than Egypt, with 68 million; and Thailand, with the same population as Egypt, exports ten times as much.

Yes, Egypt has been threatened by Al Qaeda too. But Egypt's way of cracking down has been to either arrest or expel radical Islamic leaders and then leave an ideological vacuum in their wake. The reason a psychopath like Osama bin Laden—with his Arab-Islamic but backward-looking message—could gain such currency is because no one in the Arab world, particularly Egypt, has articulated a progressive, democratic Arab-Islamic alternative to counter him.

The Bush team wants to spend money on TV or advertisements to broadcast our message in Arabic to the Arab world. Frankly, there is no modern, progressive message we could broadcast in Arabic that would begin to compare in influence to one that would come from Egypt. But it's not coming.

Look, Hosni Mubarak is not our enemy. He is authentically pro-American and a bulwark against another Arab-Israeli war. But if he really wants to help us, and we really want his help, we don't need to talk to him about Al Qaeda or Israel. We need to talk to him about Egypt.

If we've learned one thing since 9/11, it's that terrorism is not produced by the poverty of money. It's produced by the poverty of dignity. It is about young middle-class Arabs and Muslims feeling trapped in countries with too few good jobs and too few opportunities to realize their potential or shape their own future—and blaming America for it. We have to break that cycle, and no one could help us do it more effectively than the Egyptians. Does President Bush dare say that, or are we going to keep lying to ourselves and to them?

June 5, 2002

THE BEST OF ENEMIES?

TEHRAN, IRAN

Quick quiz: Which Muslim Middle East country held spontaneous candlelight vigils in sympathy with Americans after September 11? Kuwait? No. Saudi Arabia? No. Iran? Yes. You got it! You win a free trip to Iran. And if you come, you'll discover not only a Muslim country where many people were sincerely sympathetic to America after September 11, but a country where so many people on the street are now talking about—and hoping for—a reopening of relations with America that the ruling hard-liners had to take the unprecedented step two weeks ago of making it illegal for anyone to speak about it in public.

No matter. Despite the official ban, Iran-U.S. relations are still the number one political subject here, and are still being openly discussed in Parliament and in the reformist press. And no conversation between an Iranian and a visiting American seems to be complete without some variation of the question "When do you think we will have relations again?"

What's fueling this discussion? To begin with, there's an overall sense, probably unrealistic, that everything that ails Iran today and frustrates average Iranians—from the widespread unemployment to a sense of isolation from the world, a lack of foreign investment, and a general political malaise—would somehow be reversed if Iranian-U.S. relations were restored and the U.S. embargo on Iran were lifted.

But what is striking is how much President Bush's branding of Iran as part of an "axis of evil" (along with Iraq and North Korea) intensified this discussion. At first, reformers in Parliament and the media were embarrassed by Mr. Bush's statement, which hard-liners used against them as "proof" that America would never have ties with the Islamic Republic. But since then, reformers have retaliated by pointing to the "axis of evil" accusation and saying to the hard-liners: "Look where your policies have led us."

Add to this the reduction in U.S. visas for Iranians since September 11, which has dispirited many Iranian college students, and the shock the Iranians had two weeks ago when Russia, their longtime backer, effectively joined NATO, and you can understand why a lot of people here are rethinking ties with Washington.

What's striking is how much the debate within Iran mirrors that in Washington. There are three schools in Washington: the Engagers, who argue that since America helped to ignite this debate in Iran, we should now pour fuel on it by actively seeking diplomatic ties; the Embargoers, who see Iran's clerical regime as an overripe fruit that will fall from the tree if the United States just keeps isolating it; and the Rollbackers, who would like to force a regime change in Iran, just as they would in Iraq.

In Iran there are also Engagers, who see American ties as the key to Iran's modernization; Isolators, who distrust America and believe Iran is better off going it alone; and Provokers—conservatives who believe they would be strengthened by a confrontation with the United States.

Diplomats here insist that even Ayatollah Ali Khamenei, Iran's hard-line spiritual leader, is no longer against relations with the United States—he can smell the mood here too, and he knows how badly Iran's economy needs U.S. investment and trade—but he wants to find a way to do it whereby he, not the reformers, gets the credit and is in control, so that any U.S. opening doesn't end up as a boost to his political opponents.

For now, though, the different factions in both countries each have just enough power to block the others from any fundamental move that would really make relations better or worse.

It's too bad, because the silent majority in both countries is for engagement. Last year the Iranian hard-liners decided to completely renovate the U.S. Embassy in Tehran, which had not been touched since Iranian students took it over in 1979. The idea was to turn it into a museum for the revolution. The museum opened last November 4, but nobody came, so now it's closed again. Most Iranians don't want a U.S. Embassy museum. They want a U.S. Embassy.

In short, I don't know what the final outcome will be, but I do know this: If Secretary of State Colin Powell were to announce tomorrow that he was ready to fly to Tehran and put everything on the table—an end to sanctions, Iran's nuclear program, its support for Palestinian terrorists, diplomatic relations—he would light this place on fire.

June 12, 2002

IRAN'S THIRD WAVE

TEHRAN, IRAN

Iran has the bomb. I know. I found it.

No, no—not that bomb. This bomb is hiding in plain sight—in high schools, universities, and coffeehouses. It is a bomb that is ticking away under Iranian society, and over the next decade it will explode in ways that will change the face of this Islamic Republic. It's called here, for short, "The Third Generation."

The first generation of Iranian revolutionaries overthrew the shah in 1979 and founded the Islamic Republic. They are now old, gray, and increasingly tired, a clerical regime clinging to power more by coercion than by any popular acceptance of their plan to Islamize all aspects of Iranian life. The second generation came of age during the 1980s Iran-Iraq war, which left 286,000 Iranians dead and 500,000 injured. This is a lost generation, deflated and quiescent.

The Third Generation are those Iranians from sixteen to thirty years old who have come of age entirely under Islamic rule. They never knew the shah's despotism. They have known only the ayatollahs'. There are now 18 million of them—roughly a third of Iran's population—and they include 2 million university students and 4 million recent university grads.

"As with most revolutions, this Third Generation has no special sympathy for the founders of the revolution—in fact, they blame our generation for bringing them a government they feel doesn't know how to run the country properly," observed Mohsen Sazgara, a former aide to Ayatollah Khomeini and now a top reformer. "They are the most significant population group in Iran [until the fourth generation, the 24 million Iranians under sixteen, comes of age] and wherever this generation decides to go is where Iran will go in the next decade."

Where this Third Generation wants to go is already apparent. While some of them are religious conservatives, most are not. They are young, restless, modern-looking, and often unemployed, because there are not enough good jobs. They are connected to the world via the Internet or satellite dishes—and they like what they see. They want the good life, a good job, more individual freedom and more connections with the outside world—and they are increasingly angry that they don't have those things. They embrace Islam, but they don't want it to occupy every corner of their lives.

"They are not antireligious, but they are anti-fundamentalism—they refuse to be blind followers of anything," says Hamidreza Jalaeipour, a sociology professor. His nineteen-year-old son, Mohammadreza, nods vigorously in agreement.

The government has already had to ease up in response to them. When I was last here, six years ago, a friend took me to see an Iranian guitarist who had an electric guitar but could only play songs in his bedroom, because pop music had been banned. Today he is giving public concerts of Iranian pop songs and cutting CDs. When I was last here, women had to be covered in black robes and their hair could not show. Now the robes are multicolored and many push back their head scarves to show their hair. When the mullahs shout at them, many young women shout right back. The most popular Iranian films today are those that mock the hypocrisy of the theocracy, including one now playing in Tehran about a fifteen-year-old Iranian girl who has a child out of wedlock and decides to keep the baby, and another about a mother who runs off with her daughter's fiancé.

This Third Generation of Iranians is quite different from its counterpart in Saudi Arabia. Saudi Arabia is a country getting younger, poorer, more Islamic, and more anti-American—as young Saudis react against what they consider a corrupt, irreligious, pro-American regime. Iran is a country getting younger, poorer, less Islamic, and less anti-American— as young Iranians react against an anti-American theocracy that isolates them from the world.

When Iran got the telegraph in the early 1900s, that helped trigger the first constitutional revolution, against the despotic Qajar regime. When telephones and tape cassettes spread around Iran in the 1970s, they became tools through which Ayatollah Khomeini spread his revolution against the shah. Today the Internet and satellite TV have come to Iran, bringing with them new appetites and aspirations for Iran's Third Generation.

This Third Generation hoped President Khatami's reformist candidacy would satisfy those aspirations, but he proved to be a bust, unwilling to confront the conservatives. No matter. The Third Generation will eventually find a new political horse to ride, and when it does, Iran will change—with or without the ayatollahs' blessings.

June 16, 2002

IRAN AND THE WAR OF IDEAS

TEHRAN, IRAN

What if a theocracy and a democracy had a baby? What would it look like? It would look like Iran.

What makes Iran so interesting is that it's not a real democracy, but it's not a real Islamic theocracy either. It is, though, just enough of a democracy for many Iranians to know that they want more of it, and just enough of an Islamic theocracy for many Iranians to know they want less of it.

And if you listen to what's going on behind all the noise here, what you find are a lot of thinkers, both democrats and religious conservatives, looking for a way to synthesize these two aspirations.

You find democratic reformers who have learned from the shah's failed attempt at imposed secularism, and from the past twenty-three years of Islamic rule, that no democracy will take root in Iran that doesn't find a respected place for Islam.

And you find religious thinkers who have also learned from the last twenty-three years that Iranians have lived through enough incompetent clerics trying to run a government—and trying to tell people what they should wear, think, and speak—to know that Islam can't regulate every aspect of a nation's life in the modern age without producing a backlash. Many young Iranians are now running away from the mosques and dislike clerics so much that some mullahs take off their turbans and robes when they walk around certain neighborhoods, to avoid being insulted or harassed.

But precisely because Iran is this crazy semi-democracy (unlike Iraq or Saudi Arabia)—precisely because people here get arrested every day for speaking out, then go to prison and write books, then get released, then run for Parliament, speak out, start a reformist newspaper, and get arrested again—there is a lively debate about how to find a better balance between state and religion.

One day I went to see Amir Mohebian, the political editor of *Ressalat*, a religious conservative newspaper, who told me: "At the time of the revolution we offered certain [religious] values to the society in a maximalist way . . . Now we are witnessing a backlash. So I am proposing a new definition for an Islamic society. In this definition we won't try converting people into religious people. We just don't want to have a deviant society. If we go on pressing for maximalist religious values, we will increase the gap between the generations. If we articulate a minimalist definition, we can have a lot in common with the new generation."

The same day I visited Mohsen Sazgara, a former aide to Ayatollah Khomeini, now a reformer, who is opening a paper staffed by and directed at Iranian students. He said: "We believed that we would overthrow the shah and establish a new government, an Islamic government, that would show the world a new way. But what we did after the victory of the revolution was not a new way. We did not succeed in marrying democracy and Islam. That led to the reform movement . . . but it has failed, because it had no constitutional power. In the Constitution there was a religious authority above everything that could always block changes. So now we have to push for real constitutional democracy—not religious democracy but real democracy, with a respected place for religion under it."

Such a synthesis will take a long time to play out here. For now, the Islamic regime is still deeply entrenched, thanks to oil money that can buy friends, and an iron fist that can crush all domestic foes. The hard-line clerics will not give way easily, and they are not afraid to make enemies abroad, because tensions help them militarize Iranian society and shut down criticism. Yet even the hard-line clerics seem to realize that they cannot survive indefinitely on coercion alone, which is why they let the debate go on.

It's ironic that the war of ideas that the West hoped would be fought in the Arab-Muslim world after September 11—a war against the Islamic fascism of Osama bin Laden that would be waged by Arabs offering a democratic, progressive Islamic alternative—has not happened, because there is not enough democracy in most places there for that war to even begin. But it is being fought in Iran—not in response to September 11 but in response to Iran's own bad experiences with secular despotism and religious despotism.

Wish them well. If Iranian thinkers and politicians were ever to blend constitutional democracy with a redefined Islam that limited itself to inspiring social norms, not running a state, it could have a positive impact on the whole Muslim world, from Morocco to Indonesia, that Iran's Islamic revolution never had.

June 19, 2002

IRAN BY THE NUMBERS

TEHRAN, IRAN

The most striking thing about Iran today is the honesty you can find in the newspapers. Some mornings, they take your breath away. Consider the mainstream paper *Entekhab*, which ran a long piece the other day, headlined "Skyrocketing Figures," that ticked off the following statistics: There are now 84,000 prostitutes operating on the streets of Tehran and 250 brothels, including some linked to high officials. There are 60 new runaway girls hitting Tehran's streets every day—a 12 percent increase over last year. Forty percent of all drug-addicted women in Iranian prisons have AIDS. Two sisters, ages sixteen and seventeen, recently gave AIDS to 1,100 people in a two-month period. Four million youths under the age of twenty suffer from depression. Unemployment (which is already around 30 percent) is steadily rising.

All of these problems are symptoms of a floundering economy, or, as the newspaper *Iran News* baldly put it two weeks ago: "The nation's entire economic structure is fundamentally bankrupt and in desperate need of urgent and sweeping reforms. Some of the graver and more prominent problems include lack of sufficient foreign investment, mismanagement in all tiers of our economic system, political isolation leading to [a] deteriorating economic situation, atrocious unemployment, [and] high inflation."

This deterioration is not primarily the result of U.S. sanctions. Iran has plenty of oil wealth and can buy anything from Europe or the black market. It is primarily the result of mismanagement by Iran's theocratic rulers—their corruption, incompetence, arbitrary decisions, religious legal codes, and anti-globalization instincts. Which is why the biggest internal drama playing out in Iran today is this: Will the ayatollahs peacefully reform their system, or will it explode beneath their feet from social unrest?

In a poll published by the *Noruz* newspaper last month, 6.2 percent of those surveyed in Tehran said they were satisfied with the current state of affairs, 48.9 percent favored "reform," and 44.9 percent favored "fundamental change."

The problem for Iran's ruling clerics is that they cannot provide enough new jobs without privatizing their state-dominated economy and attracting foreign investment. And they cannot reform the economy and attract foreign investors, who will bring new technology and new markets, without reforming every pillar of their ruling system. This system includes vast monopolies awarded to their allies—the bazaar merchants, clerics, and children of the clergy—as well as Islamic charities that serve as front organizations for huge business conglomerates that pay no taxes and import everything from cigarettes to cars duty-free. Iran also can't attract investors, particularly for industry, without some transparent rule of law, which means curbing the arbitrary rule of the Guardian Council of clerics and the judges they appoint, who sit atop the system here, dominating the courts and Parliament.

The Islamic revolution urbanized millions of rural Iranians and made them real citizens, in a way the shah never did. "Now they have education, roads, transport, and health facilities," said the manager of an auto-parts company. "Sixty percent of university students today are girls. But now these new citizens are looking for a citizens' regime, not a rural regime. A citizens' regime is a secular government, which respects the religion of the people but also the rights of the people."

For the moment, the ruling clerics have enough oil money—and enough support in the rural areas, in their seminaries, and in the bazaar—to stay on top. But given Iran's soaring population—there were 30 million Iranians when the shah left twenty-three years ago, and there are 66 million today, with 70 percent under age thirty—something will have to give if Iran hopes to create enough jobs.

"The establishment has two choices," said the opposition economist Rahim Oskui, "but they have the same result: Either the establishment will resist international and national changes—in that case it will crash—or it will become flexible and adapt. But in that case it cannot remain what it is now . . . [My feeling is] the clergy will reach the conclusion that they will have to secularize the system in order to survive, but this will take time. . . . All our modern revolutions came from inside the country, and given the level of demands inside the society today, a backward establishment like we have now cannot resist these forces forever—provided there is no outside interference."

June 23, 2002

THE VIEW FROM TEHRAN

TEHRAN, IRAN

So a senior Iranian official is explaining to me how the world looks from Tehran: Let's see, he says, Iran helps the United States organize the Northern Alliance, a longtime Iranian ally, to oust the Taliban in Afghanistan—a regime Iran staunchly opposed. ("We are civilized fundamentalists," unlike the Taliban, sniffed an Iranian official.) Once the Taliban were out, Iran quietly aided the United States in forming the interim government in Kabul. Not a single Iranian was involved in September 11, not a single Iranian has been found in Al Qaeda, and Iran's nuclear reactor is under international inspection. Iran has the most democracy and freest press of any Muslim country in the Middle East. And as a thank-you, President Bush labeled Iran part of the "axis of evil."

Pakistan, meanwhile, created the Taliban, gave sanctuary to members of Al Qaeda, supported Islamist terrorists in Kashmir, built an Islamic nuclear bomb, and its leader, a military dictator, got $1 billion in aid from America. Saudi Arabia financed the Taliban, has hundreds of its citizens in Al Qaeda, has private charities that support Hamas and Islamic Jihad, funds Islamic fundamentalist schools all over the world, was home to fifteen of the nineteen hijackers of 9/11, has no democracy, and its leader, Crown Prince Abdullah, was invited to President Bush's ranch.

I confess, I did laugh when it was all put that way. But I am not here to defend Iran, which has supported terrorism both against its own citizens and abroad. I would, though, defend the notion that Iran is the one Muslim Middle East country that is politically alive, full of ferment, with certain overlapping interests with the United States, and worth a fresh look as to how it might be nudged in the right direction—not just branded evil and ignored.

Iran has three power centers. There is Iran-E—the evil conservative clerics, intelligence services, and shock troops of the regime, who still have a monopoly on all the tools of coercion and are responsible for Iran's support for Hamas and Islamic Jihad and the killing of Iranian intellectuals a few years ago.

Then there is Iran-C—the rational conservatives among the clerics and bazaar merchants who backed the Islamic revolution out of a real revulsion for the shah's secular despotism, but who favor democracy and the rule of law. For now, Iran-C is aligned with Iran-E.

Finally, there is Iran-R, all the reformers—the economically strapped middle class, the rising student generation, and the former revolutionaries who are fed up with clerical rule. They want more democracy and less imposed religion, and are leading the opposition in Parliament, but have the least power.

That's why the key to peaceful change in Iran is a break within the conservative ruling elite. The key is to get Iran-C, the rational conservatives, to break with Iran-E, the dark conservatives, and forge a new alliance with the reformers. It's not impossible. There are many members of Iran-C who realize that clerical rule—particularly of the incompetent, isolating, and arbitrary variety found in Iran today—is increasingly resented by the population and could eventually threaten the whole Islamic revolution.

What can the United States do? Most reformers said they would be helped if the United States resumed diplomatic ties and eased economic sanctions. Others told me the United States should go to the UN and publicly identify, with evidence, any Iranian officials involved in terrorism. "We ourselves don't know who's doing what, and if the United States put out the names, it would freeze these people inside," said one reformer. (When an Iranian cleric recently proposed a small new tax to support the Palestinian uprising, it was rejected by the Iranian Parliament.) Others said the United States should speak up in defense of every Iranian who wants to run for office, or start a newspaper, and is being blocked by the clerics. The clerics claim Iran is a Muslim democracy, and America should constantly challenge them to prove it.

I don't know if all this advice is correct, but I do know that Iran is in flux and worth a new look from Washington—not because the dark forces here are innocent of supporting terrorism, but because they are guilty of it; not because it would strengthen those dark forces, but because many here think it would weaken them; not because Iranians themselves have been unwilling to courageously confront those dark forces, but because they have; not because it would delay the demise of those dark forces, but because it might just hasten it.

June 26, 2002

THE END OF SOMETHING

Recent events in the Middle East leave me wondering whether we're witnessing not just the end of the Oslo peace process, but the end of the whole idea of a two-state solution to the Israeli-Palestinian conflict.

When the Palestinians' Intifada II began over a year ago, in the wake of a serious proposal for a Palestinian state by President Clinton, I argued that Palestinians were making a huge mistake. When the party to a conflict initiates an uprising and then suicide bombing at a time when the outlines of a final peace are on the table—as the Palestinians did—it shatters everything, present and future. In this case, it shattered the Israeli peace camp, it blew apart all the fragile confidence-building measures that took years to build, and it generally left the Israeli public feeling it had opened the gates to a Trojan horse.

This is particularly true in the case of the Palestinians because they never articulated why their uprising was necessary, given the diplomatic alternatives still available, or what its precise objectives were. They seem to have been heavily influenced by Hezbollah's success at driving Israel out of Lebanon and seem to have bought into the fantasy that they could give birth to their own state in similar blood and fire. And Yasir Arafat went along for the ride.

"This Intifada II was Yasir Arafat's 1967 war," says the Middle East expert Stephen P. Cohen. "Like Egypt's President Nasser, Arafat got completely swept up in the fantasies of the moment and failed to distinguish between what was real and what was not. And like Nasser, it will be the beginning of his end."

But here's the rub: Even if Mr. Arafat went away, and even if a majority of Israelis were ready to give his successor all of the West Bank, Gaza, and East Jerusalem, the security requirements and limitations on Palestinian sovereignty that Israelis would insist upon—in the wake of the total breakdown in trust over the last year—would probably be so high that no Palestinian leader would be able to accept them.

If that is the case, it means that a negotiated two-state solution is impossible and Israel is doomed to permanent occupation of the West Bank and Gaza. And if that is the case, it means Israel will have to rule the West Bank and Gaza permanently, the way South African whites ruled blacks under apartheid. Because by 2010, if current demographic patterns hold, there will be more Palestinians in Israel, the West Bank, Gaza, and East Jerusalem than Jews. And if that is the case, it means an endless grinding conflict that poses a mortal danger to Israel.

Because there are three trends converging in the Middle East today. The first is this vicious Israeli-Palestinian war. The second is a population explosion in the Arab world, where virtually every Arab country has a population bubble of under-fifteen-year-olds who are marching toward a future where they will find a shortage of good jobs and a surplus of frustration. The third is an explosion of Arab satellite TV stations, the Internet, and other private media.

Basically, what's happening is that this Arab media explosion is taking images of the Israeli-Palestinian conflict and beaming them to this population explosion, nurturing a rage against Israel, America, and Jews in a whole new Arab generation. Of that new generation there are going to be ten who will go to Dad one day and say, "Dad, there is a Pakistani gentleman at the door selling a suitcase nuclear bomb. He wants a check for $100,000, and I would like to personally deliver the suitcase to Tel Aviv." And Dad is going to write the check.

The only hope for Israel is to get out of the territories—any orderly way it can—and minimize its friction with the Arab world as the Arabs go through a wrenching internal adjustment to modernization. I applaud President Bush's call for Mr. Arafat to be replaced, in what amounts to Mr. Bush's last-ditch attempt to "reaccredit" the Palestinians as a partner for a two-state solution with Israel. But it is a travesty that Mr. Bush did not act to "reaccredit" Israel too, as a peace partner for a two-state solution with the Palestinians, by insisting that Israel begin pulling back from some of its far-flung settlements in Gaza and the West Bank. It would help the Palestinians undertake their reforms, and it would put Israel in a better position to withdraw unilaterally, if it has to.

Mr. Bush blinked because he didn't want to alienate Jewish voters. Sad. Because George Bush may be on Israel's side, but history, technology, and demographics are all against it.

June 30, 2002

ARABS AT THE CROSSROADS

President Bush was right to declare in his recent speech that the Palestinians need to produce decent governance before they can get a state. Too bad, though, that the President didn't have the courage to say that it's not only the Palestinians who need a radical reform of their governance—it's most of the Arab world.

By coincidence, though, some other important folks have had the courage to say that just this week: the UN Development Programme (UNDP), which Tuesday copublished, along with the Arab Fund for Economic and Social Development, a brutally honest Arab Human Development Report analyzing the three main reasons why the Arab world is falling off the globe. (The GDP of Spain is greater than that of all twenty-two Arab states combined.) In brief, it's due to a shortage of freedom, a shortage of women's rights, and a shortage of quality education. If you want to understand the socioeconomic milieu that produced bin Ladenism—and will reproduce it if nothing changes—read this report.

While the twenty-two Arab states currently have 280 million people, soaring birthrates indicate that by 2020 they will have 410 to 459 million. If this rising new generation is not to grow up angry and impoverished in already overcrowded cities, the Arab world will have to overcome its poverty—which is not a poverty of resources but a "poverty of capabilities and poverty of opportunities," the report argues.

Though the report pays homage to the argument that the ongoing Arab-Israeli conflict and Israeli occupation have been both a cause and an excuse for lagging Arab development, it refuses to stop with that explanation.

To begin with, it notes that "the wave of democracy that transformed governance in most of Latin America and East Asia in the 1980s and early 1990s has barely reached the Arab states. This freedom deficit undermines human development." Using a standard freedom index, the report notes that out of seven key regions of the world, the Arab region has the lowest freedom score—which includes civil liberties, political rights, a voice for the people, independence of the media, and accountability of government. In too many Arab countries, women still can't vote, hold office, attain senior management positions, or get access to capital for starting businesses. "Sadly, the Arab world is largely depriving itself of the creativity and productivity of half its citzens," the report notes, in reference to Arab women.

On education, the report reveals that the whole Arab world translates about three hundred books annually—one-fifth the number that Greece alone translates; investment in research and development is less than one-seventh the world average; and Internet connectivity is worse than in sub-Saharan Africa. In spite of substantial progress in school enrollment, 65 million Arab adults are still illiterate, almost two-thirds of them women. This is why average per capita output in the Arab world was higher than that of the "Asian Tigers" in 1960, and today is half that of Korea.

The report concludes: "What the region needs to ensure a bright future for coming generations is the political will to invest in Arab capabilities and knowledge, particularly those of Arab women, in good governance, and in strong cooperation between Arab nations. . . . The Arab world is at a crossroads. The fundamental choice is whether its trajectory will remain marked by inertia . . . and by ineffective policies that have produced the substantial development challenges facing the region; or whether prospects for an Arab renaissance, anchored in human development, will be actively pursued."

Well said, and here's the best part: This report, according to its introduction, was researched and written by a "group of distinguished Arab intellectuals" who believed that only an "unbiased, objective analysis" could help the "Arab peoples and policymakers in search of a brighter future."

There is a message in this bottle for America: For too many years we've treated the Arab world as just a big dumb gas station, and as long as the top leader kept the oil flowing, or was nice to Israel, we didn't really care what was happening to the women and children out back— where bad governance, rising unemployment, and a soaring birthrate were killing the Arab future.

It's time to stop kidding ourselves. Getting rid of the Osamas, Saddams, and Arafats is necessary to change this situation, but it's hardly sufficient. We also need to roll up our sleeves and help the Arabs address all the problems out back. The bad news is that they've dug themselves a mighty deep hole there. The good news, as this report shows, is that we have Arab partners for change. It's time we teamed up with them, and not just with the bums who got them into this mess.

July 3, 2002

BUSH'S SHAME

———

Watching the pathetic, mealy-mouthed response of President Bush and his State Department to Egypt's decision to sentence the leading Egyptian democracy advocate to seven years in prison leaves one wondering whether the whole Bush foreign policy team isn't just a big bunch of phonies. Shame on all of them.

Since September 11 all we've heard out of this Bush team is how illegitimate violence is as a tool of diplomacy or politics, and how critical it is to oust Saddam Hussein in order to bring democracy to the Arab world. Yet last week, when a kangaroo court in Egypt, apparently acting on orders from President Hosni Mubarak, sentenced an ill, sixty-three-year-old Saad Eddin Ibrahim to seven years at "hard labor" for promoting democracy—*for promoting the peaceful alternative to fundamentalist violence*—the Bush-Cheney team sat on its hands.

The State Department, in a real profile in courage, said it was "deeply disappointed" by the conviction of Mr. Ibrahim, who holds a U.S. passport. "Disappointed"? I'm disappointed when the Baltimore Orioles lose. When an Egyptian president we give $2 billion a year to jails a pro-American democracy advocate, I'm "outraged" and expect America to do something about it.

I'm also frightened, because if there is no space in Egypt for democratic voices for change, then Egyptians will only be left with the mosque. If there is no room in Egypt for Saad Ibrahims, then we will only get more Mohamed Attas—coming again to a theater near you.

Mr. Ibrahim's "crime" was that his institute at the American University in Cairo was helping to teach Egyptians how to register to vote, how to fill out a ballot, and how to monitor elections. The Egyptian court accused him of embezzling funds from the European Union, which supported his efforts. The outraged EU said no such thing ever happened.

This monkey trial was really about an insecure, isolated Mr. Mubarak quashing any dissenters, and it is much more important than it looks—because so many more people are watching than we think. The other day, I interviewed a leading Sri Lankan human rights activist, Radhika

Coomaraswamy, director of the International Center for Ethnic Studies. We started out talking about Sri Lanka but ended up talking about Mr. Ibrahim, whom she knew, and America.

"What is the nonviolent alternative for expressing discontent [and promoting change]?" she asked me. "It's democracy. When you remove any democratic alternative, the only route left in many countries for expressing discontent is religious fundamentalism. Saad is the alternative democratic voice, and if we don't protect it we're just inviting more violence."

This ties in with a larger concern that human rights activists share toward America today—a concern that post-9/11 America is not interested anymore in law and order, just order, and it's not interested in peace and quiet, but just quiet. I am struck by how many Sri Lankans, who are as pro-American as they come, have made some version of this observation to me: America as an idea, as a source of optimism, and as a beacon of liberty, is critical to the world—but you Americans seem to have forgotten that since 9/11. You've stopped talking about who you are, and are only talking now about whom you're going to invade, oust, or sanction.

"These days," said Mrs. Coomaraswamy, "none of us in the human rights community would think of appealing to the U.S. for support for upholding a human rights case—maybe to Canada, to Norway, or to Sweden—but not to the U.S. Before there were always three faces of America out in the world—the face of the Peace Corps, the America that helps others, the face of multinationals, and the face of American military power.

"My sense is that the balance has gone wrong lately and that the only face of America we see now is the one of military power, and it really frightens the world. . . . I understand that there is always a tension between security concerns and holding governments accountable for human rights. But if you focus on security alone and allow basic human rights violations in the name of security, then, well, as someone who grew up in America and went to law school there, I find that heartbreaking."

So do I. How about before we go trying to liberate a whole country—Iraq—we first liberate just one man, one good man, who is now sitting in an Egyptian jail for pursuing the very democratic ideals that we profess to stand for.

August 4, 2002

LESSONS FROM SRI LANKA

COLOMBO, SRI LANKA

It's often forgotten that while suicide bombing started in the Middle East, the people who perfected suicide as a weapon of war were the Tamil Tigers militia here in Sri Lanka, the island-state off the southern tip of India. In the last decade, Tamil suicide bombers, many of them women, killed some 1,500 people, including an Indian prime minister and a Sri Lankan president. And in a bizarre twist, the Tigers filmed many of their suicide bombings to show and motivate their troops.

But since last December a cease-fire between the Tigers—who have been militating for a separate state for Sri Lanka's Tamil Hindu minority in the northeast—and the government, which is dominated by the Buddhist Sinhalese majority, has halted all suicide bombings. No one can be sure it will last, after eighteen years of civil war. But it's still worth examining how suicide was defused here, and whether any of this might apply to Palestinians and Israelis.

To begin with, one of the key factors in halting Tamil suicide bombings was the Tamil diaspora, living in North America, Europe, and India. This Tamil diaspora had been the main source of funding for the Tamil Tigers. But the Tamil diaspora is made up largely of middle-class merchants and professionals, and when in the late 1990s the U.S., Britain, and India all declared the Tigers a "terrorist" group, not freedom fighters, the Tamil diaspora became embarrassed by them and started choking off their funds.

"The Tamil diaspora started out as a force encouraging Tamil radicalism, but eventually it evolved into a source for moderation," said Suresh Premachandran, head of a Tamil rights party in Sri Lanka. "September 11 changed that even more. People here knew after that there would never be any sympathy for any suicide bombers."

Unfortunately, in the Middle East Arabs and Muslims continue to indulge, justify, praise, or provide religious legitimation for Palestinian suicide bombers, even after 9/11. The Palestinians have convinced themselves, with the help of many Arabs and Europeans, that their grievance is so special, so enormous, that it isn't bound by any limits of civilized behavior, and therefore they are entitled to do whatever they want to Israelis. And Israelis have convinced themselves that they are entitled to do virtually anything to stop it.

Second, Sri Lankans had to pay retail for their extremism. They had no oil or foreign powers to finance their war. And because so much domestic savings was diverted to the war, Sri Lanka's roads and infrastructure today are decrepit. It is not surprising, therefore, that the peace movement, which blossomed in the last two years, was led by the business community—particularly after the Tamil Tigers blew up Colombo's airport in July 2001 and sent the country into an economic tailspin.

"The business community finally said, 'Enough is enough,'" said Mahesh Amalean, chairman of MAS Holdings, Sri Lanka's leading apparel maker. "That turned the tide. Our motto became 'Sri Lanka first.'"

Israelis and Palestinians, by contrast, got to buy their extremism wholesale. Palestinians could engage in suicide bombings without becoming destitute because the Arab states are always ready to pass the hat for them. Israelis have been able to build insane settlements in the heart of the West Bank, because the U.S. was ready to provide aid with no limits attached.

Third, in Sri Lanka the government realized it had no military solution for suicide bombers—that the only way they could be stopped was if the Tigers themselves could be induced to turn them off. The Tigers, meanwhile, realized they while they could terrify the government with suicides, they couldn't even hold their own ethnic capital, Jaffna. So they both finally opted for negotiations. Unfortunately, the Palestinians abandoned a peace offer and opted instead for the delusion that suicide bombing will get them more, and Ariel Sharon has opted for a purely military response.

Finally, while Jews and Arabs have carried out their war with all the world watching—and often meddling in ways that prolonged the conflict—Sri Lankans have conducted their war, in which 64,000 people have died, with almost no coverage.

"Ours has been a forgotten war, and we've had to live with our mistakes and to find our own way out," said Milinda Moragoda, one of the government's peace negotiators. "It had its disadvantages, but also its advantages."

August 7, 2002

INDIA, PAKISTAN, AND G.E.

BANGALORE, INDIA

Two months ago India and Pakistan appeared headed for a nuclear war. Colin Powell, the U.S. secretary of state and a former general, played a key role in talking the two parties back from the brink. But here in India, I've discovered that there was another new, and fascinating, set of pressures that restrained the Indian government and made nuclear war, from its side, unthinkable. Quite simply, India's huge software and information technology industry, which has emerged over the last decade and made India the back room and research hub of many of the world's largest corporations, essentially told the nationalist Indian government to cool it. And the government here got the message and has sought to de-escalate ever since. That's right—in the crunch, it was the influence of General Electric, not General Powell, that did the trick.

This story starts with the fact that, thanks to the Internet and satellites, India has been able to connect its millions of educated, English-speaking, low-wage, tech-savvy young people to the world's largest corporations. They live in India, but they design and run the software and systems that now support the world's biggest companies, earning India an unprecedented $60 billion in foreign reserves—which doubled in just the last three years. But this has made the world more dependent on India, and India on the world, than ever before.

If you lose your luggage on British Airways, the techies who track it down are here in India. If your Dell computer has a problem, the techie who walks you through it is in Bangalore, India's Silicon Valley. Ernst & Young may be doing your company's tax returns here with Indian accountants. Indian software giants in Bangalore, like Wipro, Infosys, and MindTree, now manage back-room operations—accounting, inventory management, billing, accounts receivable, payrolls, credit card approvals—for global firms like Nortel Networks, Reebok, Sony, American Express, HSBC and G.E. Capital.

You go to the Bangalore campuses of these Indian companies and they point out: "That's G.E.'s back room over here. That's American Express's back office over there." G.E.'s biggest research center outside the U.S. is in Bangalore, with 1,700 Indian engineers and scientists. The brain chip for every Nokia cell phone is designed in Bangalore. Renting a car from Avis on-line? It's managed here.

So it was no wonder that when the State Department issued a travel advisory on May 31 warning Americans to leave India because the war prospects had risen to "serious levels," all these global firms who had moved their back rooms to Bangalore went nuts.

"That day," said Vivek Paul, vice chairman of Wipro, "I had a CIO [chief information officer] from one of our big American clients send me an e-mail saying: 'I am now spending a lot of time looking for alternative sources to India. I don't think you want me doing that, and I don't want to be doing it.' I immediately forwarded his letter to the Indian ambassador in Washington and told him to get it to the right person."

No wonder. For many global companies, "the main heart of their business is now supported here," said N. Krishnakumar, president of MindTree. "It can cause chaos if there is a disruption." While not trying to meddle in foreign affairs, he added, "what we explained to our government, through the Confederation of Indian Industry, is that providing a stable, predictable operating environment is now the key to India's development."

This was a real education for India's elderly leaders in New Delhi, but, officials conceded, they got the message: Loose talk about war or nukes could be disastrous for India. This was reinforced by another new lobby: the information technology ministers who now exist in every Indian state to drum up business.

"We don't get involved in politics," said Vivek Kulkarni, the information technology secretary for Bangalore, "but we did bring to the government's attention the problems the Indian IT industry might face if there were a war. . . . Ten years ago [a lobby of IT ministers] never existed."

To be sure, none of this guarantees there will be no war. Tomorrow, Pakistani militants could easily do something so outrageous and provocative that India would have to retaliate. But it does guarantee that India's leaders will now think ten times about how they respond, and if war is inevitable, that India will pay ten times the price it would have paid a decade ago.

In the meantime, this cease-fire is brought to you by G.E. — and all its friends here in Bangalore.

August 11, 2002

WHERE FREEDOM REIGNS

BANGALORE, INDIA

The more time you spend in India the more you realize that this teeming, multiethnic, multireligious, multilingual country is one of the world's great wonders—a miracle with a message. And the message is that democracy matters.

This truth hits you from every corner. Consider Bangalore, where the traffic is now congested by all the young Indian techies, many from the lower-middle classes, who have gotten jobs, apartments—and motor scooters—by providing the brainpower for the world's biggest corporations. While the software designs of these Indian techies may be rocket science, what made Bangalore what it is today is something very simple: fifty years of Indian democracy and secular education, and fifteen years of economic liberalization, produced all this positive energy.

Just across the border in Pakistan—where the people have the same basic blood, brains, and civilizational heritage as here—fifty years of failed democracy, military coups, and imposed religiosity have produced thirty thousand madrasas—Islamic schools, which have replaced a collapsed public school system and churn out Pakistani youth who know only the Koran and hostility toward non-Muslims.

No, India is not paradise. Just last February the Hindu nationalist BJP government in the state of Gujarat stirred up a pogrom by Hindus against Muslims that left six hundred Muslims, and dozens of Hindus, dead. It was a shameful incident, and in a country with 150 million Muslims—India has the largest Muslim minority in the world—it was explosive. And do you know what happened?

Nothing happened.

The rioting didn't spread anywhere. One reason is the long history of Indian Muslims and Hindus living together in villages and towns, sharing communal institutions and mixing their cultures and faiths. But the larger reason is democracy. The free Indian press quickly exposed how the local Hindu government had encouraged the riots for electoral purposes, and the national BJP had to distance itself from Gujarat because it rules with a coalition, many of whose members rely on Muslim votes to get reelected. Democracy in India forces anyone who wants to succeed nationally to appeal across ethnic lines.

"Even when Gujarat was burning, practically the whole of India was at peace—that is the normal pattern here," said Syed Shahabuddin, editor of *Muslim India*, a monthly magazine, and a former Indian diplomat. "India is a democracy, and more than that, India is a secular democracy, at least in principle, and it does maintain a certain level of aspiration and hope for Muslims. . . . If there were no democracy in India, there would be chaos and anarchy, because so many different people are aspiring for their share of the cake." It is precisely because of the "constitutional framework here," added Mr. Shahabuddin, that Indian Muslims don't have to resort to terrorism as a minority: "You can always ask for economic and political justice here."

It is for all these reasons that the U.S. is so wrong not to press for democratization in the Arab and Muslim worlds. Is it an accident that India has the largest Muslim minority in the world, with plenty of economic grievances, yet not a single Indian Muslim was found in Al Qaeda? Is it an accident that the two times India and Pakistan fought full-scale wars, 1965 and 1971, were when Pakistan had military rulers? Is it an accident that when Pakistan has had free elections, the Islamists have never won more than 6 percent of the vote?

Is it an accident that the richest man in India is an Indian Muslim software entrepreneur, while the richest man in Pakistan, I will guess, is from one of the fifty feudal families who have dominated that country since its independence? Is it an accident that the only place in the Muslim world where women felt empowered enough to demand equal prayer rights in a mosque was in the Indian city of Hyderabad? No, all of these were products of democracy. If Islam is ever to undergo a reformation, as Christianity and Judaism did, it's only going to happen in a Muslim democracy.

People say Islam is an angry religion. I disagree. It's just that a lot of Muslims are angry, because they live under repressive regimes, with no rule of law, where women are not empowered, and youth have no voice in their future. What is a religion but a mirror on your life?

Message from India to the world: Context matters—change the political context within which Muslims live their lives and you will change a lot.

August 14, 2002

FOG OF WAR

A remarkable news article from Gaza appeared in *The Washington Post* last week, and it deserved more attention than it got. The article reported that for the past month, the twelve main Palestinian factions had been holding secret talks to determine the "ground rules for their uprising against Israel, trying to agree on such fundamental issues as why they are fighting, what they need to end the conflict and whether suicide bombings are a legitimate weapon."

Let me repeat that in case you missed it: Two years into the Palestinian uprising, Palestinian factions were meeting to determine *why they are fighting* and whether their means are legitimate.

I can't say I'm surprised. From the moment this uprising began, I, and others, argued that it was a reckless, pointless, foolish adventure. Why? Because at the time the Palestinians had before them on the table, from the U.S. and Israel, a credible diplomatic alternative to war—a peace offer that would have satisfied the vast majority of their aspirations for statehood.

From the moment this intifada got rolling, Palestinians have never been able to explain why they were adopting armed struggle, killing Israeli civilians with suicide bombs, and exposing their own people and institutions to utter devastation—when they had a credible opening diplomatic offer to end the occupation.

Oh, yes, Palestinian spokesmen, and their chorus in the Western diplomatic corps and media, would tell you things like this: The U.S. offer wasn't for 96 percent of the West Bank, it was for only 90 percent (not true), or the U.S. and Israeli proposals did not offer the Palestinians a contiguous state in the West Bank, but just a collection of "Bantustans" (not true). But even if the opening U.S. and Israeli offers were as insufficient as the Palestinians claim, they never justified this ruinous war. A Palestinian peace overture to improve those offers would have gotten them so much more and spared them so much pain.

But the Arab and European "friends" of the Palestinians, instead of confronting them on this issue, became their apologists and enablers, telling us why the Palestinians' "desperation" had led them to suicide bombing. It was their enabling that helped produce this situation where the Palestinians, two years into a disastrous war, are meeting to decide what it is about.

And where was Yasir Arafat's leadership? Resting as usual on his motto: "It doesn't matter where my people want to go, even if it's into a ditch. All that matters is that I get to drive."

But there is a message in this bottle for America, too. It's the first rule of warfare: Never launch a war that you can't explain to your people and the world on a bumper sticker. If it requires an explanation from a Middle East expert on CNN, you're on the wrong track. The Palestinians could never explain why they were killing Jews to end an occupation that the U.S. and Israel were offering to end through diplomacy. There is only one bumper-sticker phrase that can explain such behavior: "Death to Israel." And if that is their real strategy, then a war to the death it will be. If it's not, then what have they been up to?

Attention President Bush: What is your bumper sticker for justifying war with Iraq? I've heard a lot of different ones lately: We need to preemptively attack before Saddam deploys weapons of mass destruction. We need to change the Iraqi regime to give birth to democracy in Iraq and the wider Arab world. We need to eliminate Saddam because he is evil and may have been behind 9/11. We need to punish Saddam for not living up to the UN inspection resolutions.

All of these are legitimate rationales, but each would require a different U.S. military and diplomatic strategy. If the Bush team is serious about Iraq, it needs to zero in on one clear objective, produce a tightly focused war plan around it and then sell it—with a simple bumper sticker—to America and the world. If the Bush administration's different factions—which are as divided as the Palestinians—can't do that in advance, they shouldn't move.

When you don't know where you're going, any road will get you there—just ask the Palestinians. But when you're talking about an unprovoked war to dismantle a government half a world away, any road just won't do. You need a clearly focused end, means, and rationale.

Because we certainly don't want to pick up a newspaper two years from now and read that there was just a heated meeting of Bush advisers about what the war in Iraq was supposed to be about.

August 18, 2002

BUSH'S MIDEAST SAND TRAP

Two weeks ago I was in New Delhi watching CNN, when on came President Bush talking about the need to deal with the threat from Iraq. I had no problem with what the president was saying. What bothered me, though, was that he was saying it in a golf shirt, standing on the tee with his golf clubs. Up to now Mr. Bush has conducted the war against terrorism with serious resolve. But he shows real contempt for the world, and a real lack of seriousness, when he says from the golf tee, as he did on another occasion: "I call upon all nations to do everything they can to stop these terrorist killers. Thank you. Now watch this drive."

But it is not just the physical backdrop for our Iraq policy that we need to be more serious about if we want to win greater world backing. It's also the political one—in particular, how we talk about democracy.

When the Bush team insists that Saddam Hussein must be ousted to bring democracy to Iraq and the Arab world—but says nothing about democratizing Saudi Arabia or Egypt—people there notice. And it undercuts our support and credibility. To his credit, Mr. Bush has finally decided to withhold an aid increase to Egypt, in response to its jailing of Egypt's leading democracy advocate.

"This will be a good move if it is the start of a more consistent application of shared values," the Jordanian columnist Rami Khouri wrote the other day. In the meantime, many Arabs are wondering: Why is America pushing democracy only in Iraq? Maybe it's because America really doesn't care about democracy in the Arab world, but is just pursuing some naked interests in Iraq and using democracy as its cover.

Ditto in the West Bank. The Bush team is pushing democracy on Yasir Arafat and the Palestinian Authority, but it will not utter a word against an Israeli settlement policy in the West Bank that helps poison the atmosphere there, empowering Palestinian radicals and weakening the liberals.

"Up to now, the Bush administration has been using democracy-promotion in the Mideast only as a tool to punish its enemies, not to create opportunities for its friends," notes the Middle East expert Stephen P. Cohen.

It's true. The Bush team is advocating democracy only in authoritarian regimes that oppose America, not in authoritarian regimes that are ostensibly pro-American—even though it is America's support for the autocratic regimes in Egypt and Saudi Arabia that has made many of their citizens so anti-American and contributed to the fact that fifteen Saudis and one Egyptian played key roles in 9/11.

Some argue that if you have elections in these countries you will end up with "one man, one vote, one time"—in other words, the Islamists would win and never cede power back. I disagree. I think you would have one man, one vote, one time—*for one term*. Because sooner or later even the Islamists would have to deliver or be ousted.

People cite Iran for what happens when democracy goes wrong. Sorry, Iran is not a democracy. Iran is a dictatorship of conservative Iranian clergy, financed by oil wealth, that uses voting for pre-selected candidates to give it a patina of democracy.

Iran, though, is living proof of why, in a country with a long legacy of authoritarianism, you need a process of democratization before democracy. Which is why I would not favor America's demanding elections tomorrow in Saudi Arabia or Egypt.

What we should be advocating (and what democrats in these countries seek) is a soft landing, notes Larry Diamond, a democracy expert at the Hoover Institution. "That means," he said, "encouraging these regimes to gradually introduce authentic political parties, competitive and fair elections, even if they are initially only at the municipal level, more freedom of the press and greater judicial independence—as a way of laying the groundwork for democracy."

For a period of years the current ruling families could retain key powers—over the army and security services—as a check to make sure elected governments act responsibly. (The army in Turkey and the king in Thailand have played that kind of guardian role, as their societies gradually built the habits of democracy.) Constrained by powerful oversight institutions, competing parties could learn the limits and obligations of power. Then, gradually, more power could be transferred to them.

But that is not the Bush policy. The Bush policy today is to punish its enemies with the threat of democracy and reward its friends with silence on democratization. That's a surefire formula for giving democracy a bad name.

August 21, 2002

DROWNING FREEDOM IN OIL

On a recent tour of India, I was visiting with an Indian Muslim community leader, Syed Shahabuddin, and the conversation drifted to the question of why the Muslim world seems so angry with the West. "Whenever I am in America," he said, "people ask me, 'Why do they hate us?' They don't hate you. If they hated you, would they send their kids to be educated by you? Would they look up to you as a model? They hate that you are monopolizing all the nonrenewable resources [oil]. And because you want to do that, you need to keep in power all your collaborators. As a consequence, you support feudal elements who are trying to stave off the march of democracy."

The more I've traveled in the Muslim world since 9/11, the more it has struck me how true this statement is: Nothing has subverted Middle East democracy more than the Arab world's and Iran's dependence on oil, and nothing will restrict America's ability to tell the truth in the Middle East and promote democracy there more than our continued dependence on oil.

Yet, since September 11, the Bush-Cheney team has not lifted a finger to make us, or the Arab-Islamic world, less dependent on oil. Too bad. Because politics in countries dependent on oil becomes totally focused on who controls the oil revenues—rather than on how to improve the skills and education of both their men and women, how to build a rule of law and a legitimate state in which people feel some ownership, and how to build an honest economy that is open and attractive to investors.

In short, countries with oil can flourish under repression—as long as they just drill a hole in the right place. Think of Saudi Arabia, Libya, or Iraq. Countries without oil can flourish only if they drill their own people's minds and unlock their energies with the keys of freedom. Think of Japan, Taiwan, or India.

Do you think the unpopular mullahs in Iran would be able to hold power today if they didn't have huge oil revenues to finance their merchant cronies and security services? Do you think Saudi Arabia would be able to keep most of its women unemployed and behind veils if it didn't have petrodollars to replace their energies? Do you think it is an accident that the most open and democratizing Arab countries—Lebanon, Jordan, Bahrain, Morocco, Dubai, and Qatar—are those with either no oil or dwindling oil reserves? They've had to learn how to tap the talents of their people rather than their sand dunes.

The Pentagon is now debating whether Saudi Arabia is our enemy. Yes and no. There is a secularized, U.S.-educated, pro-American elite and middle class in Saudi Arabia, who are not America's enemies. They are good people, and you can't visit Saudi Arabia without meeting them. We should never forget that.

But the Saudi ruling family stays in power not by a democratic vote from these progressives. It stays in power through a bargain with the conservative Wahhabi Muslim religious establishment. The Wahhabi clerics bless the regime and give it legitimacy—in the absence of any democratic elections. In return, the regime gives the Wahhabis oil money, which they use to propagate a puritanical version of Islam that is hostile to the West, to women, to modernity, and to all non-Muslim faiths.

This bargain suits the Saudi rulers well. If they empowered the secularized, pro-American Saudis, it would not be long before they demanded things like transparency in budgeting, accountability, and representation. The Wahhabi religious establishment, by contrast, doesn't care how corrupt the ruling family is in private—as long it keeps paying off the clerics and gives them a free hand to impose Wahhabi dogma on Saudi society, media, and education, and to export it abroad.

So while there are many moderate Saudis who do not threaten us, there is no moderate Saudi ruling bargain. The one that exists does threaten us by giving huge oil resources to the Wahhabi conservatives, which they use to build mosques and schools that preach against tolerance, pluralism, and modernity across the Muslim world—and in America. And it is our oil addiction that keeps us from ever confronting the Saudis on this. Addicts never tell the truth to their pushers.

Until we face up to that—and curb our consumption and encourage alternative energies that will slowly bring the price of oil down and force these countries to open up and adapt to modernity—we can invade Iraq once a week and it's not going to unleash democracy in the Arab world.

August 25, 2002

CUCKOO IN CAROLINA

The ruckus being raised by conservative Christians over the University of North Carolina's decision to ask incoming students to read a book about the Koran—to stimulate a campus debate—surely has to be one of the most embarrassing moments for America since September 11.

Why? Because it exhibits such profound lack of understanding of what America is about, and it exhibits such a chilling mimicry of what the most repressive Arab Muslim states are about. Ask yourself this question: What would Osama bin Laden do if he found out that the University of Riyadh had asked incoming freshmen to read the New and Old Testaments?

He would do exactly what the book-burning opponents of this UNC directive are doing right now—try to shut it down, only bin Laden wouldn't bother with the courts. It's against the law to build a church or synagogue or Buddhist temple or Hindu shrine in public in Saudi Arabia. Is that what we're trying to mimic?

As a recent letter to the *Times* observed, the problem with the world today is not that American students are being asked to read the Koran, it is that students in Saudi Arabia and many other Muslim lands are still *not* being asked to read the sacred texts of other civilizations—let alone the foundational texts of American democracy, like the Bill of Rights, the Constitution, or the Federalist Papers.

The fact that they ignore such diverse texts is the source of their weakness, and the fact that we embrace them is the source of our strength. What we should be doing is driving that point home, not copying their obscurantism.

The notion that UNC violated constitutional prohibitions against state-sponsored religion—by asking freshmen to simply read a book, *Approaching the Qur'an: The Early Revelations*—has been rightly dismissed by the courts as nonsense.

I discovered the other day that my seventeen-year-old daughter, who is a twelfth grader at a Washington-area public high school, was reading Genesis, Luke, Psalms, and Job as part of a summer assignment for her AP English class. I'm glad. I wish she had also been assigned the Koran.

I understand that some people feel it's not right that terrorists kill three thousand Americans—in the name of Islam—and then we go out and make the Koran a bestseller to try to figure out who *they* are. But that doesn't bother me as an American. It would bother me, though, if I were Muslim. It would bother me that people have been awakened to my faith by an outrageously destructive act perpetrated in its name—rather than by some compelling attractiveness of countries that claim to reflect Islam's vision of a just society.

The freedom of thought and the multiple cultural and political perspectives we offer in our public schools are what nurture a critical mind. And it is a critical mind that is the root of innovation, scientific inquiry, and entrepreneurship.

Right after 9/11, the majority of books on Amazon.com's top 100 bestseller list were about the Middle East and Islam. But there has been no parallel upsurge in interest in American studies, no new intellectual ferment in the blinkered, monochromatic universities and madrasas of the Arab and Muslim worlds since 9/11. One is reminded of Harry Lime's famous quip in the movie *The Third Man*—that thirty years of noisy, violent churning under the Borgias in Italy produced Michelangelo, Leonardo da Vinci, and the Renaissance, while five hundred years of peace, quiet, and harmony in Switzerland produced the cuckoo clock.

"A monolithic framework does not create a critical mind," remarked the religious philosopher David Hartman. "Where there is only one self-evident truth, nothing ever gets challenged and no sparks of creativity ever get generated. The strength of America has always been its ability to challenge its own truths by presenting alternative possibilities. That forces you to justify your own ideas, and that competition of ideas is what creates excellence."

I would bet that Islam is taught in virtually every state university in America—and was before 9/11. I first studied Islam and Arabic at the University of Minnesota in 1971.

America will always be a strong model for how a nation thrives in the modern age, as long as our culture of curiosity, free inquiry, and openness endures. And the Arab Muslim world will continue to struggle with modernity as long as twelfth graders in public schools there are never challenged to read Genesis, Luke, Job, and Psalms over their summer vacations.

August 28, 2002

IRAQ WITHOUT SADDAM

As I think about President Bush's plans to take out Saddam Hussein and rebuild Iraq into a democracy, one question gnaws at me: Is Iraq the way it is today because Saddam Hussein is the way he is? Or is Saddam Hussein the way he is because Iraq is the way it is?

I mean, is Iraq a totalitarian dictatorship under a cruel, iron-fisted man because the country is actually an Arab Yugoslavia—a highly tribalized, artificial state, drawn up by the British, consisting of Shiites in the south, Kurds in the north, and Sunnis in the center—whose historical ethnic rivalries can be managed only by a Saddam-like figure?

Or has Iraq, by now, congealed into a real nation? And once the cruel fist of Saddam is replaced by a more enlightened leadership, Iraq's talented, educated people will slowly produce a federal democracy.

The answer is critical, because any U.S. invasion of Iraq will leave the U.S. responsible for nation-building there. Invade Iraq and we own Iraq. And once we own it, we will have to rebuild it, and since that is a huge task, we need to understand what kind of raw material we'll be working with.

It is instructive in this regard to quickly review Iraq's history before Saddam. Romper Room it was not. It was a saga of intrigue, murder, and endless coups involving the different ethnic and political factions that were thrown together inside Iraq's borders by the British. In July 1958, Iraq's King Faisal was gunned down in his courtyard by military plotters led by Brig. Abdel Karim Kassem and Col. Abdul Salam Arif. A few months later, Kassem ousted Arif for being too pro-Nasserite. Around the same time a young Saddam tried, but failed, to kill Kassem, who himself executed a slew of Iraqi Nasserites in Mosul in 1959.

In 1963, Arif came back from exile and killed Kassem. A short time later Arif, and the Baath Party thugs around him, savagely slaughtered and tortured thousands of left-wingers and Communists all across Iraq. Arif ruled until 1966, when he was killed in a helicopter crash and was succeeded by his brother, who was toppled in 1968 by Saddam and his clan from the village of Tikrit. That's when Saddam first began sending away his opponents to a prison called Qasr al-Nahiya—"the Palace of the End." Since 1958, every one of these Sunni-dominated military regimes in Baghdad began with a honeymoon with the Kurds in north-ern Iraq and ended up fighting them.

The point here is that we are talking about nation-building from scratch. Iraq has a lot of natural resources and a decently educated pop-ulation, but it has none of the civil society or rule-of-law roots that enabled us to quickly build democracies out of the ruins of Germany and Japan after World War II. Iraq's last leader committed to the rule of law may have been Hammurabi—the King of Babylon in the eighteenth century B.C. So once Saddam is gone, there will be a power vacuum, revenge killings, and ethnic pulling and tugging between Kurds, Sunnis, and Shiites.

This is not a reason for not taking Saddam out. It *is* a reason for prepar-ing the U.S. public for a potentially long, costly nation-building opera-tion and for enlisting as many allies as possible to share the burden. There is no avoiding nation-building in Iraq. Because to get at Iraq's weapons of mass destruction we'll need to break the regime open, like a walnut, and then rebuild it.

What's worrying about the Bushies is that they seem much more adept at breaking things than building things. To do nation-building you need to be something of a naïve optimist. I worry that the Bushies are way too cynical for nation-building.

My most knowledgeable Iraqi friend tells me he is confident that the morning after any U.S. invasion, American troops would be welcomed by Iraqis, and the regime would fold quickly. It's the morning after the morning after that we have to be prepared for.

In the best case, a "nice" strongman will emerge from the Iraqi Army to preside over a gradual transition to democracy, with America receding into a supporting role. In the worst case, we crack Iraq open and it falls apart in our hands, with all its historical internal tensions—particu-larly between its long-ruling Sunni minority and its long-frustrated Shi-ite majority. In that case, George Bush will have to become Iraq's strongman—the iron fist that holds the country together, gradually redis-tributes the oil wealth, and supervises a much longer transition to democracy.

My Iraqi friend tells me that anyone who tells you he knows which scenario will unfold doesn't know Iraq.

September 1, 2002

9/11 LESSON PLAN

The *Times* just ran an article about the trouble teachers were having in deciding what to tell students on September 11. That's a serious question. This is a moment for moral clarity, and here are the three lessons I would teach:

Lesson #1: Who are they? This lesson would emphasize that while most people in the world are good and decent, there are evil people out there who are not poor, not abused—but envious. These extremists have been raised in societies that have failed to prepare them for modernity, and the most evil among them chose on September 11 to lash out at the symbol of modernity—America. As the Egyptian playwright Ali Salem put it in *Time* magazine, "Beneath their claims . . . these extremists are pathologically jealous. They feel like dwarfs, which is why they search for towers and all those who tower mightily." Their grievance is rooted in psychology, not politics; their goal is to destroy America, not reform it; they can only be defeated, not negotiated with.

Assigned reading: Larry Miller's January 14, 2002, essay in *The Weekly Standard*: "Listen carefully: We're good, they're evil, nothing is relative. Say it with me now and free yourselves. You see, folks, saying 'We're good' doesn't mean 'We're perfect.' Okay? The only perfect being is the bearded guy on the ceiling of the Sistine Chapel. The plain fact is that our country has, with all our mistakes and blunders, always been and always will be the greatest beacon of freedom, charity, opportunity, and affection in history. If you need proof, open all the borders on Earth and see what happens. In about half a day, the entire world would be a ghost town, and the United States would look like one giant line to see *The Producers*. . . . So here's what I resolve: to never forget our murdered brothers and sisters. To never let the relativists get away with their immoral thinking. After all, no matter what your daughter's political science professor says, we didn't start this."

Lesson #2: Who are we? We Americans are not better than any other people, but the Western democratic system we live by is the best system on earth. Unfortunately, in the Arab-Muslim world, there is no democracy, too few women's rights, and too little religious tolerance. It is the values and traditions of freedom embraced by Western civilization, and the absence of those values and traditions in the Arab-Muslim world, that explain the main differences between us.

Assigned reading: *An Autumn of War*, by the military historian Victor Davis Hanson: "Our visionaries must be far clearer about the nature of our struggle. In their understandable efforts to say what we are not doing—fighting Islam or provoking Arab peoples—they have failed utterly to voice what we are doing: preserving Western civilization and its uniquely tolerant and human traditions of freedom, consensual government, disinterested inquiry and religious and political tolerance. . . . We must cease the apologetic tone we have developed with the Arab world, and make it clear that their ministers who hector us are not legitimate without elections, their spokesmen are not journalists without a free press, and their intellectuals are not credible without liberty. The right to admonish Americans on questions of morality is not an entitlement, but something earned only through a shared commitment to constitutional government."

Lesson #3: Why do so many foreigners reject the evil perpetrators of 9/11 but still dislike America? It's because, while we have the best system of governance, we are not always at our best in how we act toward the world. Because we want to drive big cars, we support repressive Arab dictators so they will sell us cheap oil. Because our presidents want to get votes, they readily tell the Palestinians how foolishly they are behaving, but they hesitate to tell Israelis how destructive their West Bank settlements are for the future of the Jewish state. Because we want to consume as much energy as we please, we tell the world's people they have to be with us in the war on terrorism but we don't have to be with them in the struggle against global warming and for a greener planet.

The point, class, is that while evil people hate us for who we are, many good people dislike us for what we do. And if we want to win their respect we need to be the best, most consistent, and most principled global citizens we can be.

Assigned readings: The U.S. Constitution, Woodrow Wilson's Fourteen Points speech, and the Declaration of Independence.

September 4, 2002

NOAH AND 9/11

Over the past year several friends have remarked to me how much they still feel a pit in their stomachs from 9/11. One even said she felt as if this was the beginning of the end of the world. And no wonder. Those suicide hijackings were such an evil act that they shattered your faith in human beings and in the wall of civilization that was supposed to constrain the worst in human behavior. There is now a big jagged hole in that wall.

What to do? For guidance, I turned to one of my mentors, Rabbi Tzvi Marx, who teaches in the Netherlands. He offered me a biblical analogy. "To some extent," said Tzvi, "we feel after 9/11 like we have experienced the flood of Noah—as if a flood has inundated our civilization and we are the survivors. What do we do the morning after?"

The story of Noah has a lot to offer. "What was the first thing Noah did when the flood waters receded and he got off the ark?" asked Tzvi. "He planted a vine, made wine, and got drunk." Noah's first response to the flood's devastation of humanity, and the challenge he now faced, was to numb himself to the world.

"But what was God's reaction to the flood?" asked Tzvi. "Just the opposite. God's reaction was to offer Noah a more detailed set of rules for mankind to live by—rules which we now call the Noahite laws. His first rule was that life is precious, so man should not murder man." (These Noahite laws were later expanded to include prohibitions against idolatry, adultery, blasphemy, and theft.)

It's interesting—you would have thought that after wiping out humanity with a devastating flood, God's first postflood act wouldn't have been to teach that all life is precious. But it was. Said Tzvi: "It is as though God said, 'Now I understand what I'm up against with these humans. I need to set for them some very clear boundaries of behavior, with some very clear values and norms, that they can internalize.'"

And that is where the analogy with today begins. After the deluge of 9/11 we have two choices: We can numb ourselves to the world and plug our ears, or we can try to repair that jagged hole in the wall of civilization by insisting, more firmly and loudly than ever, on rules and norms—both for ourselves and for others.

"God, after the flood, refused to let Noah and his offspring indulge themselves in escapism," said Tzvi, "but he also refused to give them license to live without moral boundaries, just because humankind up to that point had failed."

The same applies to us. Yes, we must kill the murderers of 9/11, but without becoming murderers and without simply indulging ourselves. We must defend ourselves—without throwing out civil liberties at home, without barring every Muslim student from this country, without forgetting what a huge shadow a powerful America casts over the world and how it can leave people feeling powerless, and without telling the world we're going to do whatever we want because there has been a flood and now all bets are off.

Because imposing norms and rules on ourselves gives us the credibility to demand them from others. It gives us the credibility to demand the rule of law, religious tolerance, consensual government, self-criticism, pluralism, women's rights, and respect for the notion that my grievance, however deep, does not entitle me to do anything to anyone anywhere.

It gives us the credibility to say to the Muslim world: Where have you been since 9/11? Where are your voices of reason? You humbly open all your prayers in the name of a God of mercy and compassion. But when members of your faith, acting in the name of Islam, murdered Americans or committed suicide against "infidels," your press extolled them as martyrs and your spiritual leaders were largely silent. Other than a few ritual condemnations, they offered no outcry in their mosques; they drew no new moral red lines in their schools. That's a problem, because if there isn't a struggle within Islam—over norms and values—there is going to be a struggle between Islam and us.

In short, numbing ourselves to the post-9/11 realities will not work. Military operations, while necessary, are not sufficient. Building higher walls may feel comforting, but in today's interconnected world they're an illusion. Our only hope is that people will be restrained by internal walls—norms and values. Visibly imposing them on ourselves, and loudly demanding them from others, is the only viable survival strategy for our shrinking planet.

Otherwise, start building an ark.

September 11, 2002

IRAQ, UPSIDE DOWN

Recently, I've had the chance to travel around the country and do some call-in radio shows, during which the question of Iraq has come up often. And here's what I can report from a totally unscientific sample: Don't believe the polls that a majority of Americans favor a military strike against Iraq. It's just not true.

It's also not true that the public is solidly against taking on Saddam Hussein. What is true is that most Americans are perplexed. The most oft-asked question I heard was some variation of: "How come all of a sudden we have to launch a war against Saddam? I realize that he's thumbed his nose at the UN, and he has dangerous weapons, but he's never threatened us, and, if he does, couldn't we just vaporize him? What worries me are Osama and the terrorists still out there."

That's where I think most Americans are at. Deep down they believe that Saddam is "deterrable." That is, he does not threaten the U.S. and he never has, because he has been deterred the way Russia, China, and North Korea have been. He knows that if he even hints at threatening us, we will destroy him. Saddam has always been homicidal, not suicidal. Indeed, he has spent a lifetime perfecting the art of survival—*because he loves life more than he hates us.*

No, what worries Americans are not the deterrables like Saddam. What worries them are the "undeterrables"—the kind of young Arab-Muslim men who hit us on 9/11, and are still lurking. Americans would pay virtually any price to eliminate the threat from the undeterrables— the terrorists *who hate us more than they love their own lives,* and therefore cannot be deterred.

I share this view, which is why I think the Iraq debate is upside down. Most strategists insist that the reason we must go into Iraq—and the only reason—is to get rid of its weapons of mass destruction, not regime change and democracy building. I disagree.

I think the chances of Saddam being willing, or able, to use a weapon of mass destruction against us are being exaggerated. What terrifies me is the prospect of another 9/11—in my mall, in my airport, or in my downtown—triggered by angry young Muslims, motivated by some pseudo-religious radicalism cooked up in a mosque in Saudi Arabia,

Egypt, or Pakistan. And I believe that the only way to begin defusing that threat is by changing the context in which these young men grow up—namely all the Arab-Muslim states that are failing at modernity and have become an engine for producing undeterrables.

So I am for invading Iraq *only* if we think that doing so can bring about regime change and democratization. Because what the Arab world desperately needs is a model that works—a progressive Arab regime that by its sheer existence would create pressure and inspiration for gradual democratization and modernization around the region.

I have no illusions about how difficult it would be to democratize a fractious Iraq. It would be a huge, long, costly task—if it is doable at all, and I am not embarrassed to say that I don't know if it is. All I know is that it's the most important task worth doing and worth debating. Because only by helping the Arabs gradually change their context—a context now dominated by antidemocratic regimes and antimodernist religious leaders and educators—are we going to break the engine that is producing one generation after another of undeterrables.

These undeterrables are young men who are full of rage, because they are raised with a view of Islam as the most perfect form of monotheism, but they look around their home countries and see widespread poverty, ignorance, and repression. And they are humiliated by it, humiliated by the contrast with the West and how it makes them feel, and it is this humiliation—this poverty of dignity—that drives them to suicidal revenge. The quest for dignity is a powerful force in human relations.

Closing that dignity gap is a decades-long project. We can help, but it can succeed only if people there have the will. But maybe that's what we're starting to see. Look at how Palestinian legislators just voted no confidence in Arafat; look at how some courageous Arab thinkers produced an Arab Human Development Report, which declared that the Arab-Muslim world was backward because of its deficits of freedom, modern education, and women's empowerment.

If we don't find some way to help these countries reverse these deficits now—while access to smaller and smaller nuclear weapons is still limited—their young, angry undeterrables will blow us up long before Saddam ever does.

September 18, 2002

GLOBALIZATION, ALIVE AND WELL

If one were having a contest for the most wrongheaded prediction about the world after 9/11, the winner would be the declaration by the noted London School of Economics professor John Gray that 9/11 heralded the end of the era of globalization. Not only will September 11 not be remembered for ending the process of global financial, trade, and technological integration, but it may well be remembered for bringing some sobriety to the anti-globalization movement.

If one thing stands out from 9/11, it's the fact that the terrorists originated from the least globalized, least open, least integrated corners of the world: namely, Saudi Arabia, Yemen, Afghanistan, and northwest Pakistan. Countries that don't trade in goods and services also tend not to trade in ideas, pluralism, or tolerance.

But maybe the most important reason why globalization is alive and well post-9/11 is that while pampered college students and academics in the West continue to debate about *whether* countries should globalize, the two biggest countries in the world, India and China—who represent one-third of humanity—have long moved beyond that question. They have decided that opening their economies to trade in goods and services is the best way to lift their people out of abject poverty and are now focused simply on *how* to globalize in the most stable manner. Some prefer to go faster, and some prefer to phase out currency controls and subsidies gradually, but the debate about the direction they need to go is over.

"Globalization fatigue is still very much in evidence in Europe and America, while in places like China and India, you find a great desire for participation in the economic expansion processes," said Jairam Ramesh, the Indian Congress Party's top economic adviser. "Even those who are suspicious now want to find a way to participate, but in a way that manages the risks and the pace. So we're finding ways to 'glocalize,' to do it our own way. It may mean a little slower growth to manage the social stability, but so be it. . . . I just spent a week in Germany and had to listen to all these people there telling me how globalization is destroying India and adding to poverty, and I just said to them, 'Look, if you want to argue about ideology, we can do that, but on the level of facts, you're just wrong.'"

That truth is most striking in Bangalore, India's Silicon Valley, where hundreds of thousands of young Indians, most from lower-middle-class families, suddenly have social mobility, motor scooters, and apartments after going to technical colleges and joining the Indian software and engineering firms providing back-room support and research for the world's biggest firms—thanks to globalization. Bangalore officials say each tech job produces 6.5 support jobs, in construction and services.

"Information technology has made millionaires out of ordinary people [in India] because of their brainpower alone—not caste, not land, not heredity," said Sanjay Baru, editor of India's *Financial Express*. "India is just beginning to realize that this process of globalization is one where we have an inherent advantage."

Taking advantage of globalization to develop the Indian IT industry has been "a huge win in terms of foreign exchange [and in] self-confidence," added Nandan Nilekani, chief executive of Infosys, the Indian software giant. "So many Indians come and say to me that 'when I walk through immigration at JFK or Heathrow, the immigration guys look at me with respect now.' The image of India changed from a third-world country of snake charmers and rope tricks to the software brainy guys."

Do a majority of Indians still live in poor villages? Of course. Do we still need to make globalization more fair by compelling the rich Western countries to open their markets more to those things that the poor countries are best able to sell: food and textiles? You bet.

But the point is this: The debate about globalization before 9/11 got really stupid. Two simple truths got lost: One, globalization has its upsides and downsides, but countries that come at it with the right institutions and governance can get the best out of it and cushion the worst. Two, countries that are globalizing sensibly but steadily are also the ones that are becoming politically more open, with more opportunities for their people, and with a young generation more interested in joining the world system than blowing it up.

September 22, 2002

DEAD END

I happened to be in Israel on September 11, 2001, and on September 12 went to the Israeli Defense Ministry to talk to security experts there about what Israel had learned from dealing with Palestinian suicide bombers that might help America. The main lesson, they said, was this: In the end, the only people who can effectively stop suicide bombers are those in the community they come from. Only if their political and spiritual leaders delegitimize suicide bombing, only if their security forces and intelligence agencies are mobilized to prevent it, can it really be stopped. Israel, they told me, could never penetrate Palestinian society the way Palestinians could. Therefore, the ultimate task for Israel was to find the right pressures and incentives to get the Palestinians themselves to stop the bombings.

Unfortunately, that message does not seem to have reached Prime Minister Ariel Sharon, who, I believe, has never had a plan for how to reach a stable accommodation with the Palestinians, is only interested in making the West Bank safe for Israeli settlers to stay, not to leave, and is going to lead Israel into a dead end—if he sticks to his present course—and will take America along for the ride.

I have enormous sympathy for Israel's plight today. There is no society in the world that has ever been exposed to what Israel has over the past two years—repeated suicide bombings of its civilians in their buses, restaurants, and city centers, compounded by anti-Semitic attacks by Europeans, who call for a severing of ties with Israeli universities when Israel retaliates. That is enough to make any civilized society crazy.

But the Sharon response is not working. Months ago Mr. Sharon dismissed Yasir Arafat as "irrelevant," smashed his security services, and announced Israel's intention to assume responsibility for its own security in the West Bank. But when Palestinian suicide bombers from Hamas and Islamic Jihad then perpetrate more suicide bombings, Mr. Sharon attacks Mr. Arafat's headquarters as if he sent the bombers himself.

If Mr. Sharon believes that Mr. Arafat sent these bombers, then he should evict him. If he thinks Mr. Arafat is irrelevant, then he should ignore him. But what makes no sense is to treat Mr. Arafat as if he's totally irrelevant and totally responsible. Because all that does is get

Palestinians to rally around the feckless Mr. Arafat and abort any possibility of Palestinians producing a new leadership that would be relevant to negotiations and to Israeli security.

That's not a pipe dream. Thanks to President Bush's blunt call for Palestinians to dump Mr. Arafat—and thanks to Mr. Sharon's crackdown on Palestinians to prove that the foolish intifada they launched two years ago (in the wake of President Clinton's peace overture) will not pay—Israel and the U.S. had begun to sow the first seeds of internal Palestinian reform that were needed for them to rein in the suicide bombers.

For the past months a few Palestinian leaders and commentators have been speaking about what a mistake it was for Mr. Arafat to have turned down the Clinton plan for a Palestinian state; Palestinian legislators have voted no confidence in Mr. Arafat's cabinet and pushed forward more responsible alternatives; and secular Palestinians have begun openly questioning suicide bombing. All of these trends are bad news for Hamas, Islamic Jihad, Iraq, and Iran. So they have been pushing out even more suicide bombers to trigger a Sharon reaction that would rally Palestinians around Mr. Arafat's failed leadership and abort the emergence of any new consensus. Mr. Arafat is celebrating.

Mr. Sharon has a tough job. He has to pursue a peace settlement with the Palestinians, as if there were no terrorism, and to hunt the terrorists, as if no peace settlement were possible. That requires subtle distinctions. But Mr. Sharon's policy seems to be to ignore all distinctions—between Hamas and Arafat and between Hamas and the secular Palestinian mainstream, which would like to see change.

One has to wonder whether Mr. Sharon isn't really out to undermine the whole Palestinian national movement in hopes that one day some quisling Palestinian Authority simply surrenders to the Israeli occupation. He sure doesn't seem interested in nurturing a more responsible Palestinian Authority to cede land to.

If that is where Mr. Sharon is going, it will come to tears, and the Bush team, if it goes along for the ride, will be very sorry. Always remember, the leading Hebrew biography of Mr. Sharon is entitled *He Doesn't Stop at Red Lights*.

September 25, 2002

YOU GOTTA HAVE FRIENDS

While in Nebraska this week, I asked a Republican official there about the mood in his state on going to war with Iraq. He had a quick answer: "Ambivalence." People know that Saddam Hussein is a bad guy with bad weapons, he said, but they feel no threat from him. The lingering threats from 9/11 and the weakening economy and stock market are what have Nebraskans on edge. They will, he added, follow the president's lead— if he makes the case—but they are ambivalent, and they really don't want to fight this war alone.

Having just visited a dozen states, I have found this same ambivalence everywhere, and President Bush would do well to heed it. Mind you, I think some of Mr. Bush's wild and crazy unilateralist rhetoric— STOP ME BEFORE I INVADE AGAIN!—can be useful now. Suggesting to allies that you will go it alone is often the only way to get them to come along with you. I just hope the Bush team doesn't really intend to implement its new preemption strategy *alone*, because in the case of Iraq, most Americans would be very uneasy. Our national interest is best served now by taking on Saddam with as many allies, and as much UN cover, as possible—for four reasons.

First, Americans understand that the war against Al Qaeda in Afghanistan was a war of "no choice"—and millions of Americans would have volunteered to fight there. Iraq, however, is widely perceived as a war of "choice." Yes, Saddam is dangerous, but he poses no immediate threat to us and has proved to be deterrable. Removing him is a legitimate choice, but it is still perceived as precisely that: a choice. Getting the backing of the UN and key allies for that choice would be the best way to reassure Americans that it's the right choice at the right time, and rally more of the nation behind any war.

Second, easing that ambivalence by adding allies is critical because of what could be the prolonged nature of this war. The success of any war in Iraq all depends on what happens on Day 3. That is, on Day 1, the U.S. military will topple the Iraqi regime. On Day 2, the Iraqi people will throw rice on U.S. troops for liberating them. Everything depends on what happens on Day 3—when, having broken Iraq, we own Iraq.

As I've argued before, America and the world have a real interest in helping Iraqis build a more stable, democratic, decent government on Day 3. Setting up the first progressive Arab state, at the heart of the Arab world, could have a very positive effect on the whole region. It would be a huge undertaking, though, and maybe impossible, given Iraq's fractious history. But to my mind it's the only thing worth debating or doing there—and to keep the American people on board for such a long-haul project, and to defray the costs, we need allies.

To put it differently, nation-building in Iraq could go one of two ways: like Beirut or like Bosnia. In Beirut in 1982, America was a reluctant nation-builder and had little help, and it all ended badly. In Bosnia, working under a UN mandate—with NATO allies to share the risks and the costs—America and its friends have been able to sustain a long-term nation-building effort. Bosnia still has a long way to go, but it's no longer an open sore destabilizing Eastern Europe.

Third, it is impossible to predict how Iraqis would react to a prolonged U.S. nation-building occupation, but it is safe to assume that the sooner such an operation would be put under a UN umbrella, or some other non-U.S. international framework, the less it would look like American neocolonialism, the less opposition it would engender in the region, and therefore the longer it would be sustainable.

And fourth, it's OK for the Bush team to talk about its new philosophy of preemptive war. But I wouldn't want to live in a world where that became the strategy of every country. At times, preemption is necessary, but the more it can be done with allies and UN approval, the less likely it is that the doctrine will be abused and the more stable the world will be.

Bottom line: Iraq is a war of choice, not a war of no choice, and it is a war of choice that will require a lot of nation-building if it is to produce a more peaceful Iraq. If the Bush team can enlist the backing of the UN and key allies, there is a real chance that such an operation can be successful. If the U.S. can't do that, it should keep Saddam in his box through deterrence and wait for a better strategic environment. Because launching a war of choice in Iraq, with an ambivalent U.S. public and no allies, could make for a frustrating, dangerous, and endless Day 3.

September 29, 2002

ANYONE SEEN ANY
DEMOCRATS LATELY?

Ever since President Bush took office I've had this feeling that the only serious opposition party in America, at least in foreign policy, was made up of three people, and none of them were Democrats. The only three people Mr. Bush really worries about—the only three people who could take big constituencies with them if they openly parted company with the president on an issue like Iraq—are Colin Powell, Tony Blair, and John McCain.

What happened to the Democrats? Well, I don't buy their whining that their voices have been cynically drowned out by Mr. Bush's focus on Iraq. The problem with the Democrats is not that they are being drowned out by Iraq. The problem is that the Democrats have nothing compelling to say on all the issues *besides* Iraq. Iraq is winning control of the agenda by Democratic default, not by Republican design.

I spent the last month traveling the country on a book tour, during which I said that what worried me most after 9/11 was what kind of world my girls were going to grow up in. I ran into so many Americans who share that concern. After a talk in Atlanta, one guy came up to me, just opened his wallet and showed me the picture of his daughter. He didn't say a word.

The point is that I can assure the Democrats that while Mr. Bush may be obsessed with Iraq, most Americans are worrying about their jobs, the stock market, the environment, and the fact that their kids may not grow up in as open and peaceful a world as they did.

The biggest security concern of Americans today is not Iraq or Osama. It's the fear that America itself could be weakened by short-term, greedy decisions, taken by politicians squandering our hard-won surplus or corporate executives squandering our pensions and undermining our markets. And Americans are right to be concerned. Because without a strong America holding the world together, and doing the right thing more often than not, the world really would be a Hobbesian jungle.

Because I believe that is what is really gnawing at Americans, and because I believe that Mr. Bush is not really addressing this broader concern—but is still running on the momentum of his strong military performance right after 9/11—there is a leadership opportunity for bold Democrats. But where are they?

Where are the Democrats who are ready to argue forcefully that the future tax cuts that Mr. Bush pushed through are utterly reckless and need to be repealed—because they will erode the resources the government needs to remain a Great Power in this age of uncertainty? And they send a terrible signal to our kids, corporate leaders, and the world: that all that matters is short-term, me-first gratification.

Where are the Democrats who would declare that the best way to enhance our security, make us better global citizens, reduce our dependence on Middle East oil, and leave a better planet for our kids is a Manhattan Project to develop a renewable energy source, along with greater conservation? Mr. Bush has totally ignored the longing by young Americans to be drafted for such a grand project to strengthen America. And so, too, have the Democrats.

Where are the Democrats who would declare that confronting Saddam is legitimate, but it must not be done without real preparation of the U.S. public? Decapitating Saddam's regime will take weeks. Building Iraq into a more decent state, with a real civil society, will take years. But it is this latter project that is the most important—the one that really gets at the underlying threat from the Middle East, which is its failed states. But do we know how to do such nation rebuilding, and if we do, do Americans want to pay for it? We need to go in prepared for this task (which is unavoidable if we really intend to disarm Iraq) or stay out and rely instead on more aggressive containment, because halfhearted nation-building always ends badly and would surely weaken us. Why aren't the Democrats clarifying this?

At the moment, the Bush team is leading the nation much more by fear than by hope. The Democrats can only win, or only deserve to win, if they can offer a bold alternative. That would be a program for strengthening America based on hope not fear, substance not spin, a program that addresses the primary concern of Americans now: the future for the kids whose pictures they carry around in their wallets.

October 6, 2002

CHICKEN À L'IRAQ

To be successful in dealing with Iraq, President Bush has to tread the most unusual line one could imagine for a statesman: He has to be wild, but not crazy.

How so? Well, it all goes back to a well-known concept in strategic theory: how to win a game of chicken between two drivers barreling head-on at one another. If you are one of the drivers, the best way to win is, before the race even starts, to take out a screwdriver and very visibly unscrew your steering wheel and throw it out the window. The message to the other driver is: "Hey, I'd love to chicken out and get out of your way, but I just threw out my steering wheel—so unless you want to crash head-on, you better get out of the way."

We are witnessing a similar situation between President Bush and Saddam Hussein. To push the UN, the Arabs, and the Europeans to finally get serious about forcing Saddam to comply with the UN inspection resolutions, Mr. Bush had to appear wild—as if he had thrown out America's steering wheel and was ready to invade Iraq tomorrow, alone. It was a very smart tactic, and if it produces a serious, united international front it may yet pressure Saddam into chickening out and allowing unconditional inspections. It may even turn up the pressure inside Iraq so much that someone there is emboldened to take Saddam down. You never know.

But in order to cultivate allies ready to keep the pressure on Saddam and, more important, to join a U.S.-led coalition to overthrow him if he continues to snub the UN, and, even more important, to join with America in rebuilding Iraq after his government is ousted—President Bush has to be ready to take yes for an answer from Saddam, and give him a chance to comply. The Bush team has to be willing, if Saddam swerves aside by accepting unconditional inspections, not to also swerve off the road, chase his car, and crash into it anyway. That is, Mr. Bush has to appear wild, but not crazy.

This is a very delicate strategy to pull off, and what is worrying is that while the Bush team is agreed about the need to be wild, it still seems divided on how crazy to get. Secretary of State Colin Powell appears ready to accept a yes from Saddam if he agrees to unconditional inspections. Even if we don't believe Saddam, even if we think he will cheat in the end, Mr. Powell seems to understand that we need to appear to be making a reasonable offer and taking yes for an answer—if we want to retain allied and U.S. public support.

But to listen to Mr. Bush, Don Rumsfeld, and Dick Cheney, a "yes" from Saddam on inspections is not sufficient. In his speech Monday, Mr. Bush detailed a list of conditions—that Saddam allow witnesses to illegal activities in Iraq to be interviewed outside the country, end the "persecution" of Iraq's civilians, and stop "illicit trade."

These add-ons are a mistake. First of all, most of America's Arab allies persecute their people, and many Arabs, Turks, and Europeans thrive from illicit trade with Iraq. We should be focusing on Saddam's non-compliance with UN inspection demands—period. It's very unlikely that Saddam will comply, and that is what we want the world to see clearly. We don't want to give the Europeans or the Arabs a chance to muddy the waters by saying, "Well, of course Saddam wouldn't agree to inspections—you asked him to commit suicide as well."

We don't want the allies to be able to say that the Bush team is wild and crazy, so let them go alone. Many allies would love that: America eliminates Saddam, the world gets to criticize the U.S. for being a bully, and the U.S. has to pick up the bill for rebuilding Iraq. That's a European trifecta!

It's also a trap for America: If we invade Iraq alone, we own Iraq alone—we own the responsibility of rebuilding it into a more progressive Arab state alone. As worthwhile a project as I believe that is, I don't think Americans are up for doing it alone, without UN cover or NATO allies to help pay. Mr. Bush knows that, which is why he stressed: "We will act with allies at our side and we will prevail." I would say, "*If* we act with allies, we will prevail." If we can't, we should opt instead for aggressive containment (which means: Don't ask, don't tell, just bomb any suspicious Iraqi weapons sites).

It's OK to throw out your steering wheel as long as you remember you're driving without one. It's OK to be wild to spur our allies to join us. But if they won't, we must not go from wild to crazy and invade Iraq alone. Because the folks in the Middle East do crazy so much better than we do.

October 9, 2002

WARS OF NERVES

Living in Montgomery County, Maryland, these days with a sniper on the loose is an unnerving experience. We've all gotten to know our police chief, Charles Moose, through his news conferences during the past two weeks of random shootings. We've also gotten to know our pizza deliveryman better. Last Monday night my wife ordered pizza from the California Pizza Kitchen. When the deliveryman arrived, I was in the living room watching President Bush address the nation about Iraq. As my wife paid the pizza guy, she remarked to him that the pizza smelled great, "but I don't think my husband will get up because he's watching the news conference."

"Oh," the deliveryman said, "has there been another shooting?"

No, no, no, my wife explained, my husband is watching *the president* speak about Iraq.

But who can blame the deliveryman for assuming that I must be watching a news conference about the shooter. If you had to drive around here at night, standing on people's doorsteps with your back to the street, all you'd be worried about would be the shooter, too. But he's hardly alone. There is something about these shootings that is touching deeper nerves in us all.

The fact that the president speaks only about Iraq, while his neighbors down the street speak only about the shooter, reinforces the sense that this administration is so obsessed with Saddam it has lost touch with the real anxieties of many Americans. Mr. Bush wants to rally the nation to impose gun control on Baghdad, but he won't lift a finger to impose gun control on Bethesda, six miles from the White House.

Personally, I'm glad Mr. Bush is focused on disarming Iraq's madman and tracing Iraq's Scud missiles and weapons of mass destruction. It's a worthy project. I just wish he were equally focused on disarming America's madmen, and supporting laws that would make it easier to trace their .223-caliber bullets and their weapons of individual destruction. A lot of us would like to see more weapons inspectors on the streets *here*, and in the gun shops *here*, not just in Baghdad.

What's also frightening about this shooter, with his high-powered rifle, is that he could be the first real domestic copycat of 9/11, in terms of technique. That is, this shooter doesn't seem to be a serial killer with a political agenda or the perverse lust to look into the eyes of his victims before he snuffs out their lives.

No, like Osama bin Laden, this shooter seems to get his thrills from seeing the fear in the eyes of *the survivors*—after he randomly kills his victims as if they were deer. And like bin Laden, this shooter is a loser who combines evil, cunning, technical prowess, a world stage, and a willingness to kill everyday people doing everyday things to magnify that fear. By gunning down people pumping gas, mowing lawns, and walking to school, the shooter is making America's capital area squirm. That's power. No wonder the note he apparently left said, "I am God."

And no wonder the Bethesda *Gazette*, which normally covers school board meetings, carried a big headline that I never thought I'd see in my local paper. It said, "In the Grip of Terror," and the article included little bios of all the people killed. It could have been *The New York Times* on 9/12: "A County Challenged."

Finally, whether or not this shooter is a twisted copycat, he is part of a larger post-9/11 trend. That trend is the steady erosion of our sense of security, our sense that while the world may be crazy, we can always crawl into our American cocoon, our sense that "over here" we are safe, even if "over there" dragons live.

Well, "over here" is starting to feel like "over there" way too much. Over there, they just shot up U.S. marines guarding Kuwaiti oil fields, but over here, when I filled my car with gas the other day, I ducked behind a pillar so no drive-by sniper could see me; others hide in their backseats. Over there, Saddam terrorizes his people, but over here, my kids are now experts in the fine distinctions between Code Blue and Code Red. Code Blue means they're locked in their public school building because a potential shooter is in the area, and Code Red means they are locked in their classroom because there may be a gunman in the building.

Frankly, I don't want to hear another word about Iraq right now. I want to hear that my president and my Congress are taking the real steps needed in this country—starting with sane gun control and sane economic policy—to stop this slide into over here becoming like over there.

October 13, 2002

CAMPUS HYPOCRISY

The Washington Post recently reported that students and faculty at a growing number of universities are pressuring their schools "into selling their holdings in companies that do business with Israel, prompting a counter-campaign among Jewish groups that consider the effort part of a creeping tide of anti-Semitism on campus." Here's what I would say to both sides on this issue:

Memo to professors and students leading the divestiture campaign: Your campaign for divestiture from Israel is deeply dishonest and hypocritical, and any university that goes along with it does not deserve the title of institution of higher learning.

You are dishonest because to single out Israel as the only party to blame for the current impasse is to perpetrate a lie. Historians can debate whether the Camp David and Clinton peace proposals for a Palestinian state were for 85, 90, or 97 percent of the West Bank and Gaza. But what is not debatable is what the proper Palestinian response should have been. It should have been to tell Israel and America that their peace proposals were the first fair offer they had ever put forth, and although they still fell short of what Palestinians feel is a just two-state solution, Palestinians were now prepared to work with Israel and America to achieve that end. The proper response was not a Palestinian intifada and one hundred suicide bombers, which are what brought Ariel Sharon to power.

It is shameful that at a time when some Palestinians are writing that they made a historic mistake in not nurturing the Clinton peace offer, pro-Palestinian professors and students in America and Europe pretend that the only reason the occupation persists is because of Israeli obstinacy. This approach will never gain the Palestinians a state, and those who dabble in it are simply prolonging Palestinian misery.

You are also hypocrites. How is it that Egypt imprisons the leading democracy advocate in the Arab world, after a phony trial, and not a single student group in America calls for divestiture from Egypt? (I'm not calling for it, but the silence is telling.) How is it that Syria occupies Lebanon for twenty-five years, chokes the life out of its democracy, and not a single student group calls for divestiture from Syria? How is it that

Saudi Arabia denies its women the most basic human rights and bans any other religion from being practiced publicly on its soil, and not a single student group calls for divestiture from Saudi Arabia?

Criticizing Israel is not anti-Semitic, and saying so is vile. But singling out Israel for opprobrium and international sanction—out of all proportion to any other party in the Middle East—*is* anti-Semitic, and not saying so is dishonest.

Memo to Israel's supporters: Just because there are anti-Semites who blame Israel for everything that is wrong does not mean that whatever Israel does is right, or in its self-interest, or just. The settlement policy Israel has been pursuing is going to lead to the demise of the Jewish state. No, settlements are not the reason for the Israeli-Palestinian conflict, but to think they do not exacerbate it, and are not locking Israel into a permanent occupation, is also dishonest.

If the settlers get their way, Israel will de facto or de jure annex the West Bank and Gaza. And if current Palestinian birth rates continue, by around the year 2010 there will be more Palestinians than Jews living in Israel, the West Bank, and Gaza combined. When that happens, the demand of the college anti-Israel movements will change.

They won't bother anymore with divestiture. They will simply demand: "One Man, One Vote. Since Israel has de facto annexed the territories, and there is now just one political entity between Jordan and the Mediterranean, we want majority rule." If you think it is hard to defend Israel on campus today, imagine doing it in 2010, when the colonial settlers have so locked Israel into the territories it can rule them only by apartheid-like policies.

This is not a call for unilateral Israeli withdrawal. This is a call for everyone who wants Israel to remain a Jewish state—and not become a binational state—to urge President Bush to renew the U.S. push for a two-state solution. If you think the Bush team is doing Israel a favor with its diplomacy of benign neglect, if you think the only campaign Jews need to be involved in today is with hypocrites on U.S. college campuses—and not with extremists in their own camp—you too are telling yourselves a very big and dangerous lie.

October 16, 2002

DRILLING FOR FREEDOM

A funny thing happened in Iran the other day. The official Iranian news agency, IRNA, published a poll on Iranian attitudes toward America, conducted by Iran's National Institute for Research Studies and Opinion Polls. The poll asked 1,500 Iranians whether they favored opening talks with America, and 75 percent said "yes." More interesting, 46 percent said U.S. policies on Iran—which include an economic boycott and labeling Iran part of an "axis of evil"—were "to some extent correct."

Oops!

You can imagine what happened next. Iran's hard-liners shut down the polling institute and threatened the IRNA official who published the results. Never mind. The fact that the hard-liners had to do such a thing shows how out of touch they are with Iran's courageous mainstream.

I relate this incident because it is very useful in thinking about the task of democratic transition in the Middle East. The Arab and Muslim worlds today are largely dominated by autocratic regimes. If you want to know what it would look like for them to move from autocracy to democracy, check out Iran. In many countries it will involve an Iranian-like mixture of theocracy and democracy, in which the Islamists initially win power by the ballot box, but then can't deliver the jobs and rising living standards that their young people desire, so they come under popular pressure and can only hold on to power by force.

But eventually they will lose, because the young generation in Iran today knows two things: (1) They've had enough democracy to know they want more of it. (2) They've had enough theocracy crammed down their throats to know they want less of it. Eventually, they will force a new balance in Iran, involving real democracy and an honored place for Islam, but not an imposed one.

But why is it taking so long? Why isn't Iran like Poland or Hungary after the fall of the Berlin Wall? And why might Iraq not be like them after the fall of Saddam? The answer is spelled O-I-L.

The transition from autocracy to real democracy in Iran is dragged out much longer than in Europe for many reasons, but the most important is because the hard-line mullahs control Iran's oil wealth. What that means is that they have a pool of money that they can use to monopolize all the instruments of coercion—the army, police, and intelligence services. And their pool of money is not dependent on their opening Iran's economy or political system or being truly responsive to their people's aspirations.

Think of it like this: There are two ways for a government to get rich in the Middle East. One is by drilling a sand dune and the other is by drilling the talents, intelligence, creativity, and energy of its men and women. As long as the autocratic leaders of Iran, Iraq, or Saudi Arabia can get rich by drilling their natural resources, they can stay in power a long, long time. All they have to do is capture control of the oil tap. Only when a government has to drill its human resources will it organize itself in a way that enables it to extract those talents—with modern education, open trade, and freedom of thought, of scientific enquiry, and of the press.

For all these reasons, if we really want to hasten the transition from autocracy to something more democratic in places like Iraq or Iran, the most important thing we can do is gradually, but steadily, bring down the price of oil—through conservation and alternative energies.

I know that Dick Cheney thinks conservation is for sissies. Real men send B-52's. But he's dead wrong. In the Middle East, conservation and alternative energies are strategic tools. Ronald Reagan helped bring down the Soviet Union by using two tactics: He delegitimized the Soviets and he defueled them. He delegitimized them by branding the Soviet Union an "Evil Empire" and by exposing its youth to what was going on elsewhere in the world, and he defueled them by so outspending them on Star Wars that the Soviet Union went bankrupt. In the Middle East today, the Bush team is delegitimizing the worst regimes as an "axis of evil," but it is doing nothing to defuel them. Just the opposite. We *refuel* them with our big cars.

Which was the first and only real Arab democracy? Lebanon. Which Arab country had no oil? Lebanon. Which is the first Arab oil state to turn itself into a constitutional monarchy? Bahrain. Which is the first Arab oil state to run out of oil? Bahrain.

Ousting Saddam is necessary for promoting the spread of democracy in the Middle East, but it won't be sufficient, it won't stick, without the Mideast states kicking their oil dependency and without us kicking ours.

October 20, 2002

UNDER THE ARAB STREET

———

DOHA, QATAR

At a seminar here this week on relations between America and Islam, one of the questions discussed by American and Muslim scholars was that elusive issue: Where is the Arab street and how might it respond to a U.S. invasion of Iraq? For my money, the most helpful answer was provided by the Jordanian columnist Rami Khouri, who said that "what's really important today is not the Arab street, but the Arab basement."

This is an important distinction. The "Arab street" is the broad mass of public opinion, which is largely passive and nonviolent. The "Arab basement" is where small groups of hard-core ideologues, such as Osama bin Laden and his gang, have retreated and where they are mixing fertilizer, C-4 plastic explosives, and gasoline to make the bombs that have killed Westerners all over the world.

Over the years, Arab leaders have become adept at coping with the Arab street, which is why not a single one of them has ever been toppled by it. They know how to buy off, or seal off, its anger and how to deflect its attention onto Israel. They also know that the street's wrath can be defused by progress on the Arab-Israeli front or elections at home.

The Arab basement, though, is a new and much more dangerous phenomenon. These are small groups of super-empowered angry men who have slipped away from the street into underground cells, but with global reach and ambitions. While issues like Israeli and U.S. policy clearly motivate them, what most fuels their anger are domestic indignities—the sense that their repressive societies are deeply failing, or being left behind by the world, and that with a big bang, they can wake them up and win the respect of the world.

"These guys started in their living rooms," said Mr. Khouri, "then they went out into the streets, got pushed back, and now they have retreated to the basements." Unlike the Arab street, no diplomacy can defuse the Arab basement. It doesn't want a smaller Israel, it wants no Israel; it doesn't want a reformed Saudi monarchy, it wants no Saudi monarchy.

So what to do? The only sensible response is to defeat those in the Arab basement, who are beyond politics and diplomacy, while at the same time working to alleviate the grievances, unemployment, and sense of humiliation that is felt on the Arab street, so that fewer young people will leave the street for the basement, or sympathize with those down there—as millions of Arabs do today.

There is no question that America can help by making a more energetic effort to defuse the Israeli-Palestinian conflict and by speaking out for the values that America has advocated everywhere in the world—except in the Arab world—namely democracy. I met yesterday with fifty students from an elite Qatari high school and the new Cornell Medical College in Doha. They were so hungry to talk, to have their voices heard; and what you heard when you listened was how much they still looked up to America, but how much they thought America looked down on them.

But the Arab states have a huge role to play, too. You cannot seal the door between the Arab street and the Arab basement without addressing the reasons for Arabs' backwardness and humiliation cited in the UN's Arab Human Development Report, which are their deficit of freedom, their deficit of women's empowerment, and their deficit of modern education.

"It takes many years of political, social, economic, and human degradation to create a terrorist," notes Mr. Khouri. "So fighting terror can only succeed by rehumanizing degraded societies, by undoing, one by one, the many individual acts of repression, obstruction, denial, marginalization, and autocracy that cumulatively turned wholesome developing societies into freak nations, and decent, God-fearing people into animals that kill with terror."

My guess is that the only way to stop the drift of young Arabs from the street to the basement is by administering some shock therapy to this whole region. Could replacing Saddam Hussein with a progressive Iraqi regime be such a positive shock? I don't know. I don't know if the Bush team really wants to do that, or if the American people want to pay for it. But I do know this: If America made clear that it was going into Iraq, not just to disarm Iraq but to empower Iraq's people to implement the Arab Human Development Report, well, the Arab basement still wouldn't be with us, but the Arab street just might.

October 23, 2002

THERE IS HOPE

MANAMA, BAHRAIN

There is nothing more beautiful than watching people get to vote in a free election for the first time—particularly in the Arab world, where elections have been so rare. That's what happened in Bahrain Thursday, as this tiny island nation off the east coast of Saudi Arabia voted for a parliament that will, for the first time, get to share some decision-making with Bahrain's progressive king, Sheik Hamad bin Isa al-Khalifa.

As I visited polling stations, what struck me most was the number of elderly women who voted, many covered from head to toe in black burka-like robes. Many of them illiterate, they would check the picture of the candidate they wanted to vote for and then stuff the ballot in the box—voting less for a politician than for their own empowerment. One appeared to have her grandchildren with her. As she voted, her grandson, who looked about age ten and wore a soccer outfit, tried to explain to his little sisters what a voting booth was. Thus are seeds of democracy planted.

This is the first election ever in the Arab gulf region where women were allowed to run and vote, and their husbands have quickly discovered what that means. The king's wife, Sheika Sabika—in an unprecedented move in this conservative region—campaigned publicly for women to go out and vote. She visited a Shiite Muslim community center and an elderly woman stood up to say: "Thank you. [Because we can now vote,] for the first time our husbands are asking us what we think and are interested in what we have to say."

It's true that Bahrain's young king has been planning this transition to a constitutional monarchy for several years, as part of a move to spur economic growth and overcome Bahrain's legacy of Sunni-Shiite tension. He prepared the way by releasing all political prisoners, inviting exiles home, loosening reins on the press, and repealing laws permitting arbitrary arrests. Nevertheless, this election is about something larger than Bahrain. It is about how the Arab world confronts the forces that produced 9/11—and all of Bahrain's neighbors, like Saudi Arabia, are watching.

What the more enlightened Arab leaders understand today is that with the mounting pressure of globalization, population explosions, and dwindling oil revenues, their long acceptance of political and economic stagnation—which they managed with repression and by refocusing anger onto Israel and America—is becoming unsustainable. While the first big explosion happened in New York City, these regimes know that unless they get their houses in order, and on a more democratic track, the next explosion will be on their doorsteps.

Not a single person I spoke to at polling centers mentioned foreign policy. Most said they hoped the parliament would improve the economy, end corruption by senior ministers, and give people a voice. "Things have changed in the whole world and we can't just sit around and watch and have no forum to express our views—the pace of change dictates this upon us," said Dr. A. W. M. Abdul Wahab as he waited to vote.

The Bush team needs to pay attention to the Bahrain experiment, because it is a mini-version of what nation-building in Iraq would require. Like Iraq, Bahrain is a country with a Shiite majority, which has been economically deprived, and a Sunni Muslim minority, which has always controlled the levers of power. Historically in this part of the world, democracy never worked because of the feeling that if your tribe or religious community was not in power, it would lose everything—so no rotation in power could be tolerated.

By electing one house of parliament and appointing another, the Bahraini king is taking the first tentative steps to both share decision-making and nurture a political culture in which the country will not be able to move forward without the new lawmakers' building coalitions across ethnic lines. The same would be needed in Iraq, only on a much larger scale.

I heard Harvard's president, Lawrence Summers, say once that "in the history of the world, no one has ever washed a rented car." Ditto for countries. So many Arabs today feel that they are just renting their governments. They have no real ownership, and so don't feel responsible for solving their own problems. Bahrain took a small step last week toward giving its people ownership over their own country, and one can only hope they will take responsibility for washing it and improving it. Nothing could help this region more. There is hope.

October 27, 2002

THE DEMOCRACY THING

MANAMA, BAHRAIN

Think about the contrasting headlines made last week by the biggest Arab state and the smallest Arab state. From the biggest state, Egypt, came the news that its state TV planned to run a forty-one-part series during the month of Ramadan—when TV viewing is at its highest—about a Zionist conspiracy to control Arab lands. From the smallest state, Bahrain, came the news that it had successfully conducted the first democratic parliamentary election in the Arab gulf, to begin empowering Bahrainis to control their own land.

Therein lies the two Arab responses to 9/11. One, the Egyptian model, is to feed their people bread, circuses, and conspiracy theories to explain why they are falling behind in the world. The other, the Bahraini model, is to feed their people more responsibility, a freer press, and greater ability to shape their own future to help them catch up in the world.

Americans have a real stake in Bahrain's democratic experiment working and influencing others. Why? Look, no one should doubt that the rage boiling among Arab youth today—which exploded on 9/11—is due in part to anger at U.S. support for anything Israel does. That anger is real. But the rage is also the result of the way too many Arab regimes, backed by America, have kept their young people without a voice or the tools to succeed in the modern world. Too many young Arabs feel humiliated when they compare themselves with others, and it is their poverty of dignity that also prompts them to lash out.

I just took part in a debate about democracy in the Arab world on Qatar's Al Jazeera TV, which is widely watched in the gulf. As a result, I was stopped all week by people who wanted to tell me what they thought about this subject. Here's a sample: (1) Arab man in my hotel lobby: "I am from Kuwait. I just want to tell you, without democracy, we're lost." (2) Saudi contractor at Bahrain Airport: "Do you think this Bahrain thing could spread to Saudi Arabia?" (3) A young Bahraini banker: "Instead of promoting creative thinking, our public schools here still teach the three R's—read, remember, and regurgitate." (4) Finally, two Bahraini men stopped me on the beach to say how proud they were that tiny Bahrain's election made CNN's world news roundup! "Our democracy made CNN!" I had to smile. The last time Bahrain made CNN was in April, when a Bahraini youth was killed trying to storm the U.S. embassy in an anti-U.S. riot.

And that's the point. How are young Arabs going to find dignity? By holding elections or by holding hostages, by storming embassies or by storming voting booths, by giving them a voice and skills to succeed or by paying them off with oil money but keeping them powerless? These questions are key, and if you give people the freedom to talk about them, they will. I discovered that at *Al Wasat*—the first independent newspaper allowed in Bahrain—when I asked its gutsy young editor, Mansoor al-Jamri, about the roots of 9/11.

"There are domestic roots for what happened [on September 11]," says Mr. Jamri, "and the root is that if you squash freedom, if you stop freedom of expression, insult this person and just give him money, he transfers all this money into revenge, because of having lost his dignity. We have six people from Bahrain in Guantánamo Bay. One is a member of the ruling family. The other five are . . . from the upper class. And for a young man from the ruling family, who receives a monthly salary, who is twenty-three years old, to go to Afghanistan to fight, there must be some sort of an explanation."

"There is a vacuum," he said. "You empty a person, you fill him with money, you fill him with material things, but that does not fulfill his aspirations as a human being. He has some objectives. He has feelings. He is not fulfilled. And all of a sudden someone comes and tells him that the cause of all that is this global power [America], which has insulted us, which continues to look at us as a bunch of nothings, who are basically eating and sleeping and going after women. And all of a sudden he directs his anger at what he thinks is the reason why he doesn't have what he wants—his sense of being a true human able to express himself and having influence on his society and being respected locally and internationally. This lack of respect as a dignified person has resulted in a bin Laden phenomenon."

Little Bahrain is trying to heal that poverty of dignity by introducing a little democracy. If only it would happen to big brothers Egypt, Saudi Arabia, Syria, and Iraq.

October 30, 2002

LET THEM COME TO BERLIN

——◆——

BERLIN

I haven't been to Berlin since the opening of the Berlin Wall, so when I arrived at my hotel near the Brandenburg Gate, my first question was: Where's the wall? My German friend explained that the only trace left is a cobblestone path that snakes across Berlin, drawing a line in the pavement where the wall once ran. It's easy to cross that line without even knowing it.

And therein lies the core of the crisis between America and Germany today—triggered by Chancellor Gerhard Schröder's use of anti-Bush and anti-Iraq-war rhetoric to win reelection, then fueled by a German minister comparing President Bush to Hitler, and now capped by Mr. Bush's refusal to answer two letters from the German leader.

Would somebody please bring back the Berlin Wall? Since World War II, America and Germany have had many disputes, but always within limits, because both sides saw a dangerous foe on the other side of that wall—the Communist totalitarians—and realized we needed to fight together. There is still a dangerous foe out there—now it is religious totalitarians—and we still need to fight together. But without the wall clearly defining our side and the enemy's, all sorts of lines are being crossed.

What is most shocking about the German election is not how the Chancellor ran against America, it's how popular that theme was here. Two things are feeding this. One is the new anti-Americanism, a blend of jealousy and resentment of America's overwhelming economic and military power—the "Axis of Envy," as Josef Joffe, editor of *Die Zeit*, calls it. The other is the new anti-Bushism—resentment of the often contemptuous, unilateralist, anti-green instincts of the Bush team—which was crystallized by Dick Cheney's August speech suggesting that any UN inspections of Iraq were useless and America may have to act alone. "The Cheney speech had a decisive impact on the German election," said Friedburt Pflueger, a top official of the pro-U.S. CDU party, which got creamed.

Bottom line: Many Europeans today fear, or detest, America more than they fear Saddam. That's crazy, but it explains why Mr. Schröder easily moved from raising legitimate questions about how to handle Iraq to taking Germany out of any war against Saddam under any conditions. This put Germany to the left of Saudi Arabia, which at least says it will support an Iraq war if it is approved by the UN. It was the kind of rhetoric that leaves Americans thinking Europeans won't use force under any conditions, and therefore are a danger to themselves and to us.

It is time for both sides to knock it off. We need each other. As Germany's thoughtful foreign minister, Joschka Fischer, said to me, "We are facing a new totalitarianism—the totalitarianism of Al Qaeda and bin Laden," which has emerged from the crisis in Islam. And the goal of these religious totalitarians "is to destroy the open society everywhere and the economy that it's based on."

The war against the religious totalitarians can't be fought with just armies or walls. It must be fought with police, intelligence sharing, development aid, peace diplomacy, and military operations. To win this war the open societies must each play to their strength—America's hard power and Europe's soft power.

When Germany says it's willing to provide the peacekeeping force in Kabul, that is a huge help for us. When Germany funds the expansion of the European Union to lift from poverty ten new democracies of Eastern Europe, that is a huge help to us. But at the same time, some things are true even if a Texas cowboy believes them. I'm still not sure what the right way is to handle Iraq, but I am sure that ruling out war there, under any conditions, against a murderous UN outlaw like Saddam is wrong.

With a nod to JFK, my motto today is simple: "Ich bin ein New Yorker." We are all New Yorkers now. Wherever you live, if you believe in the open society, if you cherish a world of freedom, you are now in World War III—a war against the new totalitarians, who strike at our businesses, discos, airports, and theaters in an attempt to get us to shut ourselves in and our societies down. Either we fight this war together, or we lose it together. To those who forgot what it takes to defend the open society, let them come to Berlin—let them walk the winding path where the Wall once stood and recall the collective effort that brought it down.

November 3, 2002

THE AMERICAN IDOL

—◆—

BERLIN

If you think Germany is turning anti-American, pay attention to what happened here last month when the president visited Berlin. No, not President Bush—President Clinton. Mr. Clinton, who helped unveil the refurbished Brandenburg Gate, was swarmed as Germans clamored to see, hear, or shake hands with him. Elvis was in the house.

If Mr. Bush visited Germany today there would also be street riots—the sort they use tear gas to control.

Why the difference? In fairness to Mr. Bush, it's partly because he had to order the bombing of Afghanistan, and may do the same in Iraq, and these are deeply controversial decisions on this increasingly pacifist Continent. It's much easier to love our presidents when they're not exercising our power. But there is also something deeper.

Bill Clinton is viewed by the world as the epitome of American optimism—naïve optimism maybe, but optimism. And the Bush team—the president, Dick Cheney, Don Rumsfeld, Condi Rice (Colin Powell is an exception)—strike the world as cynical pessimists who believe only in power politics, much like nineteenth-century European statesmen. For the world, Bill Clinton is another JFK and George Bush is another Thomas Hobbes, a man who, after witnessing Europe's religious wars, became deeply pessimistic about human nature and concluded that only one law prevailed in the world: Homo Homini Lupus—every man is a wolf to every other man.

If I've learned anything from living abroad, it's that while other nations often make fun of or scoff at America's naïve optimism, deep down they envy that optimism and rue the day we would give it up and adopt the tragic European view of history. Because our optimism about human nature and its commitment to the rule of law, not just power, is the engine of the modern West. It is also a huge source of U.S. strength and appeal—the soft power that comes from technologies, universities, Disney Worlds, movies, and a Declaration of Independence built on the assumption that the future can bury the past.

This doesn't mean that a true American president would realize that Saddam Hussein or Kim Jong Il are basically good. They are evil. But other American presidents, like JFK, FDR, and Ronald Reagan, faced enemies more evil than Saddam or Osama without losing touch with American optimism and communicating that to the world. The Bush team has lost it—and it's a loss for them and for America.

"Never forget," a top German official said to me, "that it was the *combination* of American hard power and soft power that defeated the Soviet Union. [Europe's] so-called realism is really a deep pessimism that came out of all our religious wars. If you become like us, America will lose its very power and attraction for others—the reason that even people who hate you are attracted to you."

When the Bush folks sneer at things like the World Court or Kyoto, and virtually every other treaty—without offering any alternatives but their own righteous power—"they project an arrogance and obsession with power alone," said the political theorist Yaron Ezrahi. "This undermines the American idealism that made Europe aspire to emancipate itself from the history that brought us World Wars I and II, it delegitimizes American power as an instrument of justice and international order, and it makes it impossible for the rest of the world to stand up and say: 'I am a New Yorker.'"

Al Qaeda's whole strategy is to encourage this, and turn America into a nation of pessimists, by attacking the symbols and sources of American optimism—from the World Trade Center to a Bali disco to the U.S. diplomat in Jordan who was just shot by terrorists. Who was that diplomat? The CIA station chief? No. He was the head of the U.S. aid mission in Jordan—the American helping Jordan make its future better than its past.

The terrorists want us to shutter our windows, reject visa requests from Muslim youth, and turn off our beacon of idealism so we will be less attractive as an alternative to their medieval fanaticism. Because the bin Ladenites know something Mr. Bush doesn't: that it is American optimism and soft power—not American hard power—that really threatens them.

No doubt after 9/11 we can't be naïve optimists anymore. But optimists we must remain. We have to find a way of defending ourselves from others' weapons of mass destruction without losing our own weapon of mass attraction. Our ability to rally the world depends on it.

November 6, 2002

COLIN POWELL'S EYEBROWS

This column is about the foreign policy fallout from the elections. But first, a story. I was recently interviewing a senior European diplomat when he began complaining about the Bush team's imbalanced Mideast policy, which involves telling the truth to Palestinians—that they need a new leader—but not telling the truth to Israel—that it needs to find a secure way to get out of the settlements. He became so passionate that I couldn't resist asking: "What does Colin Powell say when you tell him this?" The diplomat then did an imitation of Mr. Powell raising his eyebrows as if to say, "'You know what I believe, and you know I can't do anything about it with the crazies in this administration.'"

I've been thinking a lot about Colin Powell's eyebrows this week. Let's be blunt: The Democratic Party as a force for shaping U.S. foreign policy is out of business, until that party undergoes regime change. That's not healthy. You can't have a sound foreign policy without an intelligent domestic opposition keeping people honest.

With the Dems out of business, the real opposition party on foreign policy will now be the "De Facto Democrats": Colin Powell, John McCain, and the British prime minister, Tony Blair. They are the only voices that, if raised in opposition to any Bush foreign policy initiative, could restrain the president and sway the public. That is not true of any Democrat today.

What the last election showed us is what a deep trauma of vulnerability 9/11 etched on the American psyche. "While the Democrats failed to articulate a broad range of policy differences with President Bush," said David Makovsky of the Washington Institute, "their key failure was their inability to persuade Americans—in their guts—that they were prepared to deal with the world as it really is now." That is a world full of terrorists and rogue regimes dedicated to our destruction and not responsive to therapy or social work.

Where the Bush hard-liners are out of step is that many people here and abroad don't believe these guys really want to invest in making the world a different place, or that they have any imagination or inspiration to do so. The reason the De Facto Democrats are so important, and have a future, is that people trust that they see the world as it is—but also aspire to make it a better place. That is where the soul of America is.

Mr. Powell and Mr. Blair pushed Mr. Bush to go through the UN before invading Iraq. The hard-liners were angry about that because they fear the inspectors won't find anything and then Iraq will be off the hook. Cool it. Saddam is as likely to *fully* comply with the UN as Mike Tyson is to embrace anger management, and by framing the issue in the UN, Mr. Bush ensured much greater public support for any war. It was good advice by the De Facto Democrats, and more will be needed.

Consider the Predator drone that last week fired a rocket and wiped out a key Al Qaeda cell in Yemen. I'm glad we did that. Sometimes it's the only way justice gets done. Because what you have today is the Arab street and the Arab basement. Predators are very necessary for wiping out the hard-core terrorists who have left the street and gone into the basement, where they are beyond diplomacy and committed to violence. But if you don't try to seal the door between the street and the basement—with diplomacy—what happens is that as soon as you kill four guys in the basement, four more come down from the street and take their place.

Mr. Powell has always understood, better than the Bush hard-liners (who say, Forget about streets, treaties, and institutions—foreign policy is about asserting U.S. power) that Predators are necessary, but not sufficient. You don't have to cater to the Arab street, or the European street, or the Chechen street, but if you don't listen to their legitimate aspirations, you end up refilling the basements with more dangerous characters. If the only outstretched American hand the world sees is the Predator drone, we're in trouble.

This is where the real fight in America is going to be: between those who just want to deal with the world as it is, and those who want to deal with the world as it is—but also really invest in changing it. Until Democrats convince the public that they know how the world really is, we will have to rely on De Facto Democrats to fight this fight. But that means Mr. Powell must step it up. If he and his allies are going to prevail, they are going to have to raise more than just their eyebrows.

November 10, 2002

LIGHT IN THE TUNNEL

For a brief, shining moment last Friday, the world didn't seem like such a crazy place. When all fifteen members of the UN Security Council, including Syria, raised their hands in favor of a UN demand that Iraq submit to unrestricted inspections of its weapons arsenal or else face "serious consequences," it was the first hopeful moment I've felt since 9/11.

It was the first time since then that the world community seemed to be ready to overcome all of its cultural, religious, and strategic differences to impose a global norm—that a country that raped its neighbor and defied UN demands that it give up its weapons of mass destruction not be allowed to get away with it. In a year in which the "I-hate-you" virus has been loosed around the globe, and everyone is either mad at everyone else or telling everyone else to go to his corner—"Muslims, go to your corner"; "Jews, go to your corner"; "Christians, go to your corner"—one could savor a momentary countertrend.

How did it happen? Well, the short answer is that we learned something surprising this past week—that in the world of a single, dominant superpower, the UN Security Council becomes even more important, not less. France, Russia, and China discovered that the most effective way to balance America's overwhelming might was not by defying that power outright, but by channeling it through the UN. And the Bush team discovered that the best way to legitimize its overwhelming might—in a war of choice—was not by simply imposing it, but by channeling it through the UN.

In other words, "to the extent that the world wants to balance American power, without being against America, countries need to make it worth America's while to go through the UN, by producing a credible resolution," said the Mideast expert Stephen P. Cohen. "And to the extent that America wants to take on what it alone defines as the axis of evil, but not have to act alone, it needs to go through the UN as well."

Without the Security Council, we would have to exercise power nakedly—something Americans are ready to do in a war of self-defense (Afghanistan), but not in a war of choice (Iraq). And without the Security Council, others would have to balance our power nakedly, some-thing they are ready to do in self-defense, but reluctant to do in a war of choice.

The superhawks complain that President Bush made a mistake going through the UN, because now he'll never be able to use force if Saddam remains defiant or has hidden his weapons. Not only is this wrong, but Mr. Bush *had no choice*—not because he had to please the Eurowimps, but because he had to please the American and British people.

The American public told Karl Rove, and the British public told Tony Blair, that Iraq was a war of choice, and while it may be a legiti-mate choice, they did not want to fight it without the cover of the UN and the support of its key member states. Because there is no war in Iraq that does not end up with a long-term occupation and nation-building, and that can't be effectively pursued alone or under an exclusively U.S. umbrella. Mr. Rove, Mr. Blair, and Colin Powell communicated that to Mr. Bush—who then balanced a threat to go it alone with a diplomatic effort to avoid having to do so.

As I said, all this made for a pretty good weekend (unless you're Sad-dam). But will it last? That depends entirely on the UN's ability to see this resolution through. Countries could vote in favor of the Iraq resolu-tion for all kinds of reasons: Some powers were seeking balance; Syria was buying life insurance. But to stand together to actually implement a credible inspections resolution—and to endorse the use of force if Sad-dam resists—the parties actually have to believe in it. The Americans have to be prepared to actually stand down if Saddam really complies, and the Europeans and the Arabs actually have to be prepared to stand up—or more likely, stand out of America's way—if he doesn't.

What an improbable moment. There must be some larger forces driving it: The American administration most skeptical of the UN ends up breathing a whole new life into the organization. And the countries most worried about American unilateralism—France, Russia, China, and a nation that just barely missed making the short list for the axis of evil, Syria—end up legitimizing an American threat, if not the Ameri-can use of force.

I wonder what will happen next weekend.

November 13, 2002

THE NEW CLUB NATO

If you want to get a feel for how far ahead the U.S. military is from any of its allies, let alone its enemies, read the fascinating article in the November issue of *The Atlantic Monthly* by Mark Bowden about the U.S. air war over Afghanistan. There is one scene that really sums it up. It involves a U.S. F-15 jet fighter that is ordered to take out a Taliban truck caravan. The F-15's copilot bombardier is a woman. Mr. Bowden, who had access to the communications between pilots, describes how the bombardier locates the truck caravan, and with her laser guidance system directs a five-hundred-pound bomb into the lead truck. As the caravan is vaporized, the F-15 pilot shouts down at the Taliban—as if they could hear him from twenty thousand feet—"You have just been killed by a girl."

I was thinking about that scene as I watched the preparations for this week's NATO summit in Prague, which will expand the alliance from nineteen to twenty-six countries, adding Latvia, Lithuania, Estonia, Bulgaria, Slovakia, Slovenia, and Romania. I wonder how many lady F-15 pilots the Latvians have. Actually, I wonder how many Denmark or Spain have. I suspect the number is zero. And that is the main reason why I don't object anymore to NATO being expanded. Because, as we already saw in the Afghan war, most NATO countries have fallen so far behind the U.S. in their defense spending and modernizations, they really can't fight alongside us anymore anyway. So what the heck, let's invite everybody in.

"It's now Club NATO," said Michael Mandelbaum, author of the new book *The Ideas That Conquered the World*. "And Club NATO's main purpose seems to be to act as a kind of support group and kaffeeklatsch for the newly admitted democracies of Eastern and Central Europe, which suffered under authoritarian rule throughout the cold war."

Indeed, I think of NATO now as "Autocrats Anonymous," a club where all these formerly autocratic nations of Eastern and Central Europe can share their problems as fledgling democracies and buck one another up. Sure it's more Dale Carnegie than Clausewitz, and it means that Club NATO will no longer be a serious fighting force, but don't worry, our Pentagon has known that for a while, which is why it never thought of going through NATO to fight in Afghanistan, and won't in Iraq either.

But there is another reason not to fret: The old NATO has been replaced as a military alliance—not by the expanded NATO but by a totally different NATO. The "new NATO" is made up of three like-minded English-speaking allies—America, Britain, and Australia—with France as a partner for peace, depending on the war. What these four core countries all have in common is that they are sea powers, with a tradition of fighting abroad, with the ability to transport troops around the world, and with mobile special forces that have an "attitude." That is what you need to deal with today's threats.

Also, as one European official noted, all four of these countries play either rugby or American-style football—violent games where success depends on hurting the other team. This should be a prerequisite for joining the new NATO, which should henceforth be called "Nations Allied to Stop Tyrants," or NASTY.

If you talk to U.S. Fifth Fleet sailors in the Persian Gulf, they will tell you that the oil smugglers and pirates down there all know when the Australian Navy takes its monthly turn on patrol, because the Aussie Navy has a real attitude, and the bandits know it. Same with the French. The French can drive you crazy, especially over things that are not important. But when things are important, they usually show up. Said one U.S. official: "The French are bad-weather friends and their troops certainly have an attitude."

While Club NATO countries will never really be able to fight alongside NASTY, they can help, depending on the war. Each of them has certain boutique skills, whether it is an anti–chemical warfare unit from Germany or a peacekeeping unit from Poland or a minesweeper from Spain. They are now Dial-an-Ally, undertaking specific tasks that NASTY does not have the time or energy to do.

In fact, I imagine after this round of expansion that when you call NATO headquarters in Brussels, a recording will answer that will go something like this: "Hello. You have reached NATO. Dial 1 if you want help consolidating your democracy. Dial 2 if you need minesweeping. Dial 3 if you need anti–chemical warfare trucks. If you need to fight a real war, please stay on the line and an English-speaking operator will assist you."

November 17, 2002

CRAZY IN THE 'HOOD

SEOUL, SOUTH KOREA

The best way to understand the North Korea problem is to imagine a small neighborhood in which one of the neighbors, an unemployed loser, has placed dynamite around his house and told all the others that unless they bring him Chinese take-out food every day—and pay his heating bills—he will blow up his house and the neighborhood with it. The local policeman, affectionately called Uncle Sam—whose own house is safely across town but who walks the beat in this neighborhood—is advising the neighbors not to give in. "Very easy for you to say," the neighbors tell Uncle Sam, "but we have to live with this guy."

What strikes you most coming from Washington to South Korea is the contrast between the near-hysteria with which North Korea is viewed in Washington—now that it has disclosed another clandestine nuclear bomb program in violation of its 1994 promise to end it—and the rather ho-hum manner in which South Koreans greet this news.

After decades of living through North Korean threats, and after five recent years of "sunshine" engagement with the North, which has given the South a much clearer idea of how poor the North really is, many South Koreans seem to view North Korea more like a crazy aunt than a strategic threat. They either don't really believe its threats or assume the U.S. will deal with them in the end. This attitude may be delusional, but it is very widespread. A South Korean TV reporter told me that many people she interviews go so far as to ask her why the U.S. is "bullying" the North.

"The young generation, even people in their thirties and forties, they don't remember the [Korean] war; they are a real postwar generation," says former Prime Minister Lee Hong Koo. "North Korea is less dangerous to them. It makes no sense to them to have another war. The older generation still feels a war is a possibility—they feel the Communists can do things that make no sense."

So far, though, more Koreans have mentioned to me the North Korean cheerleaders—with white pom-poms—that the North sent with its soccer team to last month's Asian Games in South Korea than they have the new nuclear threats. Indeed, South Korea is in the midst of a presidential election campaign, yet the "nuclear crisis" is barely mentioned—partly because no candidate wants to be blamed for frightening away foreign investors. "The North is like a Pandora's box," said Chung-in Moon, a Yosei University Korea expert. "You don't know what will happen when you open it. Best to be very careful."

Given these South Korean views, given that China, Russia, and Japan do not want a confrontation with the North either, U.S. policy options are limited. Make no mistake, serious South Korean strategists value President Bush's rhetorical hard line. "South Korea on its own does not have strong enough leverage to change the North's behavior—only the U.S. does," says Taewoo Kim, an expert at the Korea Institute for Defense Analysis. South Korean strategists want the North to hear that tough Bush rhetoric—they just don't want the president to act on it. They want America to brandish a big stick and let its allies talk softly.

And that seems to be the collective strategy that is taking shape. It could best be described as "suspend and talk." President Bush suspended the heavy oil shipments that North Korea needs to heat itself through the winter as punishment for its latest clandestine nuclear program. At the same time, though, the U.S., Tokyo, and Seoul have all—surprisingly—signaled a willingness to address North Korean concerns about its survival if it dismantles its latest nuke program.

How many times are we going to buy this carpet? More than you might think. Sure, some Bush hawks would like to just bash the North, but the neighbors will never go along. Their view is that when dealing with a heavily armed crazy state like North Korea—which will probably never give up some kind of nuclear deterrent—all you can do is steadily reduce its ability to wreak havoc. All you can do is shrink its nuclear programs in exchange for food, and expand trade and investment to alleviate some of its abject poverty—so when it does collapse it does the least damage possible.

A crazy state like the North can have only a crash landing, but the fewer nukes it has lying around when it does, and the fewer starving people, can make the difference between a total mess and a total disaster. And those *are* our choices.

November 20, 2002

WALLING IN, WALLING OUT

OBSERVATION POST DORA, SOUTH KOREA

In the last three weeks I've visited two of modern history's great walls—the Berlin Wall in Germany and the "Green Wall" in Korea, also known as the demilitarized zone separating North and South Korea. It's called the Green Wall here because so little human activity has happened in the 155-mile-long DMZ for the past fifty years that its forests and rivers have become one of the world's richest nature preserves, full of deer, bald eagles, and butterflies. Indeed, my Korean translator, a former cook in the Korean Army, waxed eloquent to me about how his unit, once stationed near here, captured a wild boar that had lost a leg to a DMZ land mine. The men skinned it, smoked it over a fire in an empty oil drum for three days, and then ate it—boar à la DMZ. "The most tasty meal I've ever had," he sighed.

But this is not a cooking column. Visiting these sites in such close proximity prompts one to reflect on the differences among what are actually the three great walls in the world today—the Berlin Wall, which has come down; the Korean Wall, which is still up; and the Wall of Fear in the Middle East, which Israel is erecting to separate itself from the Arabs.

The beauty of the Berlin Wall is that you can barely see any trace of it anymore, just a gray brick path snaking through a united Berlin. That wall was peacefully erased because Mikhail Gorbachev decided not to use military force to resist the will of Berliners to join the world of liberty and reunify their country. But the Berlin Wall was so effectively erased because the people of Berlin took it down—from both sides. Walls brought down by the people tend to stay down. Today, Berlin, rather than being defined by the wall, is defined by the free spirit of those who destroyed it—manifested in its new architecture, museums, and parks.

No such luck for the Green Wall: the DMZ. It remains fifty years after the Korean War because the North Koreans cannot survive without it. Kim Jong Il, North Korea's leader, knows that without that Green Wall to protect his crazy regime from the will of his people—and without the prison camps, land mines, and huge army—North Korea would melt away into the South like a burst dam.

What is so impressive about South Korea is that after several decades of being obsessed with the Korean Wall, it has refused to let itself be defined by it any longer. The South Koreans decided to focus on the sea that linked them to the world instead of the wall that divided them from the North. Putting all their energy into trade and exports has enabled South Korea to recover so effectively from the 1997 Asian economic crisis that it now has the world's fourth-largest foreign reserves—an astounding feat.

And this is the real secret of South Korea's power. When it was obsessed with the wall and North Korea, it had little advantage over the North: South Korea had military rulers, and so did the North; South Korea had a huge standing army, and so did the North. There was a crude symmetry. But once the South became confident enough that it could win any war, and prosperous enough to allow democracy to flourish, there was no more balance. The whole Korean peninsula tilted its way, and much of the South's politics now revolves around preparing for reunification on its terms. It is symbolized by the new four-lane highway that runs from Seoul right up to the DMZ—a dead end just waiting to be brought to life by the North's inevitable demise.

While the South Koreans have not let war or the DMZ define them, that is exactly what the Arabs and Palestinians have done for so long. They had a Gorbachev, Anwar el-Sadat, who tried to take down the wall of hostility with Israel when he declared: "No more war"—let's go on to something else. But too many Arabs refused to embrace Sadat's message. They don't see that the wall of hostility they erected against Israel, and lately against America, has turned into a wall holding the Arabs back from modernity. And the longer the Arab wall of hostility has stood, the more it has debilitated the moderate Israeli majority and emboldened an extremist minority. Today, Israeli-Palestinian relations have turned into a killing field—with no DMZ. Israelis are now trying to protect themselves by building a real wall of concrete—but a wall without a border, accepted by both sides, will never protect.

At the Museum of the DMZ here, they refer to the DMZ as "the world's last wall." If only that were true.

November 24, 2002

"SODOM" HUSSEIN'S IRAQ

The UN inspectors in Iraq have begun their investigation of various Iraqi factories and military sites. Pay no attention. They will find nothing. The key to this whole inspection gambit—indeed, the key to whether we end up in a war with Iraq—will come down not to where the inspectors look *inside* Iraq, but whom they decide to interview *outside* Iraq, and whether that person has the courage to talk. The fate of Iraq will all come down to the least-noticed paragraph in UN Security Council Resolution 1441: Point 5.

The framers of this resolution had learned their lessons from previous Iraqi inspections. They knew that Saddam Hussein was an expert at hiding his war toys and, having had four years without inspections, had probably buried everything good under mosques or cemeteries. That means the only way we can possibly uncover anything important in Iraq is if an Iraqi official or scientist—a Saddam insider—tells the UN where it's hidden.

And that is why the Security Council insisted on Point 5—something I did not appreciate at first, but do now. Point 5 says: "Iraq shall provide [the UN inspectors] and the [International Atomic Energy Agency] . . . immediate, unimpeded, unrestricted, and private access to all officials and other persons whom [the UN] or the IAEA wish to interview in the mode or location of [the UN's] or the IAEA's choice, pursuant to any aspect of their mandates." The UN and IAEA may "conduct interviews inside or outside of Iraq, may facilitate the travel of those interviewed and family members outside of Iraq, and . . . such interviews may occur without the presence of observers from the Iraqi government."

In other words, the chief UN inspector, Hans Blix, can invite any Iraqi general or scientist to come outside Iraq and reveal what he knows. And should that Iraqi worry about personal safety, U.S. officials would be prepared to give his whole family green cards and money to live on. And why not? "I am happy to pay for that," a senior Pentagon official said. "It will be a lot cheaper than going to war to find these weapons."

But there are two weak points to worry about here. The first is Mr. Blix, an IAEA veteran. Although the UN has given him this authority, he is not entirely comfortable with it, UN officials say. The whole IAEA inspection process and culture was never set up to be prosecutorial, and it isn't in most countries. In most countries, the host government provides full cooperation. Mr. Blix, and the UN generally, are not used to such an "aggressive, adversarial approach"—effectively subpoenaing Iraqi officials—one U.S. official said. And that's why it's not clear when—or if—he will opt for interviews.

But this is where the U.S. will have to hold the UN's feet to the fire. "The key is finding a defector" through interviews, a senior U.S. official said. "That's the only way we're going to find anything."

But this leads to the second issue, which is a deeper moral question. Is there an Iraqi Andrei Sakharov? Is there just one Iraqi scientist or official who wants to see the freedom of his country so badly that he is ready to cooperate with the UN by submitting to an interview and exposing the regime's hidden weapons?

It takes just one person in Iraq who wants these inspections to be real, who wants Saddam to be exposed, and the whole house of cards comes down. And that person does not really have to risk his life or his family to do it. He can get everybody out. If there is not one such person in Iraq, well, that tells us something about the Iraqi people's own quest for freedom and a different future.

"In the past year we've seen Arab extremists risking their lives to attack others—is there one Arab democrat willing to risk his life to save his own country?" asked the Middle East expert Stephen P. Cohen. "Think about the refuseniks in Russia who went to prison. Think about the reformers in Iran who speak out every day, knowing that it will land them in jail or with a death sentence. It's really an Abraham-like situation, when God told Abraham he would not destroy Sodom if he could find just ten good men there. Are there ten Iraqi refuseniks who dare to say, 'Enough is enough,' and will whisper to Blix the truth? Is there one?"

Because if there isn't one such Iraqi, we will have to ask, and many Arabs will ask, "Exactly who are we fighting this war for?" And if there is one, or ten, no one will ask that question if we go to war. So watch this issue. This is the real drama.

December 1, 2002

AN ISLAMIC REFORMATION

What's going on in Iran today is, without question, the most promising trend in the Muslim world. It is a combination of Martin Luther and Tiananmen Square—a drive for an Islamic reformation combined with a spontaneous student-led democracy movement. This movement faces a formidable opponent in Iran's conservative clerical leadership. It can't provide a quick fix to what ails relations between Islam and the West today. There is none. But it is still hugely important, because it reflects a deepening understanding by many Iranian Muslims that to thrive in the modern era they, and other Muslims, need an Islam different from the lifeless, antimodern, anti-Western fundamentalism being imposed in Iran and propagated by the Saudi Wahhabi clerics. This understanding is the necessary condition for preventing the brewing crisis between Islam and the West—which was triggered by 9/11—from turning into a war of civilizations.

To put it another way, what's going on in Iran today is precisely the war of ideas *within* Islam that is the most important war of all. We can kill Osama bin Laden and all his acolytes, but others will spring up in their place. The only ones who can delegitimize and root out these forces in any sustained way are Muslim societies themselves. And that will happen only when more Muslim societies undergo, from within, their own struggle for democracy and religious reform. Only the disenchanted citizens of the Soviet bloc could kill Marx; only Muslims fed up that their faith is being dominated by antimodernists can kill bin Ladenism and its offshoots.

This struggle in Iran is symbolized by one man, whose name you should know: Hashem Aghajari, a former Islamic revolutionary and now a college professor, who was arrested November 6 and sentenced to death by the Iranian hard-liners—triggering a student uprising—after giving a speech on the need to rejuvenate Islam with an "Islamic Protestantism."

Mr. Aghajari's speech was delivered on the twenty-fifth anniversary of the death of Ali Shariati, one of the Iranian revolution's most progressive thinkers. In the speech—translated by the invaluable MEMRI service—he often cited Mr. Shariati as his inspiration. He began by noting that just as "the Protestant movement wanted to rescue Christianity from the clergy and the church hierarchy," so Muslims must do something similar today. The Muslim clergymen who have come to dominate their faith, he said, were never meant to have a monopoly on religious thinking or be allowed to ban any new interpretations in light of modernity.

"Just as people at the dawn of Islam conversed with the Prophet, we have the right to do this today," he said. "Just as they interpreted what was conveyed [to them] at historical junctures, we must do the same. We cannot say: 'Because this is the past we must accept it without question.' . . . This is not logical. For years, young people were afraid to open a Koran. They said, 'We must go ask the mullahs what the Koran says.' Then came Shariati, and he told the young people that those ideas were bankrupt. [He said] you could understand the Koran using your own methods. . . . The religious leaders taught that if you understand the Koran on your own, you have committed a crime. They feared that their racket would cease to exist if young people learned [the Koran] on their own."

He continued: "We need a religion that respects the rights of all—a progressive religion, rather than a traditional religion that tramples the people. . . . One must be a good person, a pure person. We must not say that if you are not with us we can do whatever we want to you. By behaving as we do, we are trampling our own religious principles."

Mr. Aghajari concluded: "Today, more than ever, we need the 'Islamic humanism' and 'Islamic Protestantism' that Shariati advocated. While [Iran's clerical leaders] apparently do not recognize human rights, this principle has been recognized by our Constitution. . . . The [Iranian regime] divides people into insiders and outsiders. They can do whatever they want to the outsiders. They can go to their homes, steal their property, slander them, terrorize them, and kill them because they were outsiders. Is this Islamic logic? When there is no respect for human beings?"

Mr. Aghajari refused to appeal his death sentence, saying his whole conviction was a farce. But on Monday his lawyer appealed on his own. Mr. Aghajari's fate now hangs in the balance. Watch this story. It's the most important trial in the world today.

December 4, 2002

BUSH, IRAQ, AND
SISTER SOULJAH

———————

I am worried. And you should be, too.

I am not against war in Iraq, if need be, but I am against going to war without preparing the ground in America, in the region, and in the world at large to deal with the blow back any U.S. invasion will produce.

But I see few signs that President Bush is making those preparations. The Bush team's whole approach was best summed up by a friend of mine: "We're at war—let's party." We're at war—let's not ask the American people to do anything hard.

This can't go on. We *are* at war. We are at war with a cruel, militant Islam, led by Al Qaeda, we are at war with a rising tide of global anti-Americanism, and we will probably soon be at war to disarm Iraq. There is no way we are going to win such a multidimensional conflict without sacrifices and radically new thinking.

For me, the question is whether President Bush, having amassed all this political capital by effectively responding to 9/11, is going to spend any of it—is going to ask Americans to do things that are really hard to win these wars over the long haul. Does Mr. Bush have a Sister Souljah speech in him? If not, if he is just going to rely on the Pentagon to fight this war—and on Karl Rove to exploit it—then we will reap nothing but tears.

What would the president tell the American people if he were preparing them for this multidimensional war?

He would tell the American people that this war could cost over a trillion dollars, and no one should think that we're going to be able to use Iraqi oil to pay for it. It will be paid for by our Treasury—and that means not just changing the faces of the Bush economic team but also reexamining the surplus-squandering tax cuts at the center of the Bush fiscal policy.

He would tell the American people that he is embarking on a Manhattan Project to increase fuel efficiency and slash the cost of alternative energy sources to reduce our dependence on foreign oil. Yes, it will take time, but gradually it will make us more secure as a nation, it will shrink the price of oil—which is the best way to trigger political change in places like Saudi Arabia—and it will provide the alternative to Kyoto that Mr. Bush promised the world but never delivered.

He would tell the American people that we can no longer afford our selfish system of farm subsidies and textile protectionism. It is a system that tells developing nations they must open their borders to what we make, but we won't give them full access to our markets for what they make: farm goods and garments. If nations like Pakistan continue to live in poverty, if their people can only afford religious schools that teach only the Koran, then we will continue to live in fear. If our national security interests lie in their development, and their development requires access to our markets, we need to open our markets and live what we preach.

He would tell the Palestinians that the U.S. intends to cut off all assistance and diplomatic contacts until they get rid of their corrupt tyrant, Yasir Arafat, because no peace is possible with him. He would tell Ariel Sharon that unless he halts all settlement building—now—the U.S. will start cutting off Israel's economic aid. And he would tell both that he intends to put the Clinton peace plan back on the table as his plan.

He would also tell all Arabs that America has one purpose in Iraq, once it is disarmed of dangerous weapons: to help Iraqis implement the UN Arab Human Development Report, which states that the failing Arab world can only catch up if it embraces freedom, modern education, and women's empowerment.

Finally, he would tell Karl Rove to take a leave of absence until September 2004 so that nothing the president does in this war will be perceived as being done for political gain.

Friends, we are on the edge of a transforming moment for America in the world. If President Bush uses his enormous mandate to prepare for war—in a way that really deals with our political and economic vulnerabilities, increases our own staying power, and convinces the world that we have a positive vision and are responsible global citizens—there is a decent chance we can win at a reasonable cost. But if Mr. Bush simply uses his mandate to drive a hard-right agenda and indulge in more feel-good politics, the world will become an increasingly dangerous place for every American—no matter what war we fight, no matter what war we win.

December 8, 2002

BLAIR FOR PRESIDENT

With Al Gore now out of the presidential race, everyone is giving the Democrats advice on who their candidate should be. All I know is that whomever the Democrats choose needs to keep in mind a few basic rules that Democrats have forgotten in recent years.

Rule #1: People listen through their stomachs. The key to the success of any presidential candidate is to convey to voters—in a way they can feel in their gut—that you as a leader know what world they're living in. George Bush Sr. lost to Bill Clinton because he failed to convey to voters in their gut that he knew what world they were living in—a world of rising economic insecurity.

Mr. Clinton's campaign conveyed through one phrase, "It's the economy, stupid," that he knew exactly what world people were living in; and because of that, they were ready to overlook his foibles. Connect with people's gut concerns and they'll go anywhere with you—without asking for the details. Don't connect, and you'll never be able to show people enough details to get them to follow.

George W. Bush has conveyed to Americans in their gut that he understands exactly what world they're living in now—a world threatened by terrorism in which, as the former NSC adviser Sandy Berger put it, "national security is now personal security." In this new world, Mr. Bush has been a warrior without mercy. No Democratic leader has—yet—forged such a gut connection with the American people on this issue.

Rule #2: Never put yourself in a position where you succeed only if your country fails. The Democrats can't just wait for Mr. Bush to fail in Iraq or hope the economy collapses and assume they will benefit. People want to hear a positive alternative agenda. There can be a hard-nosed Democratic alternative. It is one that would say, "Yes, let's win the war on terrorism, but that requires a multipronged approach that addresses all our vulnerabilities and levels with the American people."

Right now the Bush bumper sticker reads, "You Can Have It All: Guns, Butter, War With Iraq, Tax Cuts, & Humvees." This is nonsense. America has never won a war without the public's being enlisted and summoned to sacrifice. Is there a Democrat ready to push for a crash oil conservation program and development of renewable energy alternatives—that would also respond to European anger over Kyoto? Is there a Democrat ready to take on our absurd farm subsidies and textile tariffs that help keep countries like Pakistan poor by keeping them hooked on aid, not trade? Is there a Democrat ready to take on the far-right Bush forces, which are now trying to undermine all U.S. support for global population controls? (Just what we need: more failed states with exploding populations.)

Is there a Democrat ready to say we don't need more long-term tax cuts, which will only produce chronic large deficits that will reduce resources for both homeland security and Head Start? And our economy doesn't need more short-term tax stimulus either—it needs a successful war on terrorism. The economy is recovering slowly on its own. What's holding it back now are fears about terrorism and war with Iraq, which keep oil prices high and investment low. The minute those are resolved, you will see consumers ready to spend and companies ready to invest.

Rule #3: Get a candidate people like. I don't know George Bush, and I do not like his domestic policies. But I find him hard to dislike. The "likability factor" is hugely underestimated in politics.

Rule #4: Get a candidate who can give a fireside chat. In these confusing times, people crave a leader who can explain why we're doing what we're doing and how it will lead to a better world. That is what the Democrats need. Mr. Bush conveys a lot of sincerity, but he lacks the emotional or intellectual depth to really reassure people. I'm convinced that one reason for his high poll ratings is projection: We desperately want to believe that he knows what he is doing and that he is always acting in the best interests of the nation—and not on naked political considerations—because if he isn't, we're all sunk.

Right now there is only one Democrat who could live up to all these rules: the British prime minister Tony Blair. Maybe the Democrats should give him a green card. He's tough on national security, he has an alternative global vision, people like him, and he is a beautiful, reassuring speaker. He's Bill Clinton without baggage. I'd say he's a natural.

December 18, 2002

AFTER THE STORM

CAIRO

Here's a prediction: In the end, 9/11 will have a much bigger impact on the Arab and Muslim worlds than it does on America. Lord knows, 9/11 has been a trauma for us, and our response has been to strike back and install better security. But 9/11 has been a trauma for Arabs and Muslims as well—a shock to their systems that ranks with Napoleon's invasion of Egypt, the creation of Israel, and the 1967 defeat.

For Arabs and Muslims, the shock has been that this act was perpetrated by nineteen of their sons in the name of their faith. As a result their religious texts, political systems, schoolbooks, chronic unemployment, media, and even their right to visit America have all been spotlighted and questioned—sometimes fairly and sometimes unfairly.

While the shock of 1967 was profound, it ultimately led to very little change in the Arab political or social order. Because the post-'67 shock was blunted by two factors: the existence of the Soviet Union, and Soviet aid, to cushion regimes from the need to reform; and the dramatic rise in oil wealth post-'67, which also bought off a lot of pressures for change.

Today there is no Soviet Union, and because of the huge population explosion in the Arab-Muslim world, there also is not enough oil wealth to buy off pressures anymore. At the same time, thanks to globalization, young Arabs and Muslims have a much better sense of where they stand vis-à-vis the world, and how far behind they are in many cases. Finally, because America was the target of 9/11, a refusal to face up to the local factors that produced the 9/11 hijackers runs the risk of a clash with the U.S.

Since 9/11 the Arab-Muslim world has passed through three basic stages: shock, denial, and finally, introspection. It is quite apparent here in Egypt, where, at least in part because of 9/11, issues that people did not feel empowered to discuss publicly are being tentatively aired.

"There was a strong collision on September 11 between East and West, between a car and a wall, and you can see the impact on both today," remarked the Egyptian playwright Ali Salem. "You have become more suspicious, and we will become more progressive. . . . Look at Iraq. People do not want to see any Iraqis killed. But few people will speak up for Saddam Hussein now. People are against Saddam, because they know there is no future for tyranny anymore."

Two weeks ago Egypt's most influential newspaper, *Al-Ahram*, ran a thoughtful series by President Hosni Mubarak's most important political adviser, Osama el-Baz, cautioning Egyptians against buying into European anti-Semitic conspiracy theories and Holocaust denial. His articles were triggered by intense criticism of Egypt for broadcasting, on its state-run TV, a docudrama, *Horseman Without a Horse*, that drew on the fraudulent anti-Semitic tract "The Protocols of the Elders of Zion."

"We must uphold the correct perspective on our relationship with the Jews, as embodied in the legacy of Arab civilization and in our holy scriptures," wrote Mr. Baz. "This legacy holds that ours is not a tradition of racism and intolerance, that the Jews are our cousins through common descent from Abraham and that our only enemies are those who attack us. . . . It is also important, in this regard, that we refrain from succumbing to such myths as 'The Protocols of the Elders of Zion' and the use of Christian blood in Jewish rituals."

In part as a reaction to the religious intolerance unleashed by 9/11, President Mubarak surprised his country last month by announcing that henceforth January 7 would be a national holiday. January 7 is the Coptic (Egyptian Christian) Christmas, and it has now been elevated to equal status with the Prophet Muhammad's birthday. For the first time the president's son, Gamal, attended midnight mass, a visit carried live on Egyptian TV.

After the prominent Egyptian journalist Mohammed Heikal raised the question, in a recent TV interview, of who will succeed President Mubarak, everyone has started talking in public about it, and several Egyptians expressed to me their hope that whenever the transition happens it will be the start of a more formal democratization process.

Will it? Will introspection around the region actually lead to a Stage 4—fundamental political and economic reform? I suspect that the leaders understand that this is a storm they can't ride out. But they don't know how to change without losing the control they've enjoyed. This tension will be the drama of Arab-Muslim politics for the next decade.

January 8, 2003

SEALING THE WELL

—

I attended Friday's noon prayers at Cairo's Al Azhar, the most important mosque in Islam. Thousands of Egyptian faithful went through their traditional prostrations and listened to the sermon by the sheik of Al Azhar, who spoke in measured tones about how God deals with "oppressors." At the end, he appealed to God to rescue the Palestinians. It was all very solemn and understated. And then the excitement started.

A split second after he finished, someone tossed in the air hundreds of political leaflets, and a young man was lifted onto the shoulders of the crowd and began denouncing "American tyranny." Hundreds of the faithful then marched around the mosque chanting behind him, while the silent majority shuffled out. It was as if you were seeing two services: first the state-run service and then the street-run service, where the real steam was let off. But here's what struck me most: While America came in for a lashing, no one in this crowd was chanting in support of Saddam Hussein.

This was in keeping with everything I heard in dozens of interviews in Cairo. The good news is that Saddam is no longer viewed as any kind of folk hero, and most people, it seems, would welcome his demise. The bad news is that George Bush and U.S. policy are disliked even more. What gives?

By steamrolling Kuwait in 1990, Saddam looked strong. Today, he appears to be weak, on the defensive and surrendering to everything the UN and U.S. are demanding. In the early 1990s Saddam was still benefiting from years of having bought off Arab journalists, who sang his praises. That chorus seems to have dried up now that he is no longer passing out so many Mercedes-Benzes. In the early 1990s Saddam was still viewed as the Sunni Muslim sword standing up to the Iranian Shiites, and most Arabs cared little about how he had abused his people. Now it gets written about. Finally, the 9/11 attack, which emanated from this region, has strengthened people who want to talk about Arab misgovernance.

Raymond Stock, a literary researcher here, told me that an Arab friend of his summed up the mood this way: "Iraq is like a plane that has been hijacked. If the American commandos can free the plane without harming the passengers, then most people will be relieved."

Then why is George Bush so intensely disliked? In part, it's because people feel the president and his team have stopped talking to the world. They only growl at it now. But the biggest factor remains the Bush team's seeming indifference to making any serious effort to solve the Israeli-Palestinian conflict when so much killing is going on. The administration's refusal to apply any creative imagination to defusing this conflict, and even belittling it while calling Ariel Sharon "a man of peace," has embittered the Arab public. This now clouds everything we do here: Invading Iraq is cast as a war to protect Israel. Democratization is cast as a way to punish the Arabs.

Yes, official Arab newspapers and TV have nourished Arab anger toward America and Israel for decades—and still do. And one regime after another has exploited this conflict for political purposes. But when you sit in a room at the U.S. ambassador's house with thirty bright young Egyptian entrepreneurs, mostly U.S.-educated, and this issue is practically all they want to talk about—or you meet with American studies students at Cairo University and they tell you that many students in their class refused to play a simulation game of the U.S. Congress for fear of being tainted—you feel that there has to be something authentic in their anger about this open wound.

Until it is sealed, it will remain a well for the "thoughts of mass destruction" that will energize every radical anti-American group out here. I am convinced that much of the anger over U.S. policy is really a cry for help from people who know what they have to do—to democratize, liberalize their economies—and who know that they will be lost for another fifty years if they don't, but can't do it because these ideas are promoted by a power they feel is indifferent to their deepest hurt.

I am not talking about what is right, or what is fair, or even what is rational. I am talking about what is. And if we ignore it, if we dismiss it all as a fraud, we will never fully harvest the positive changes that could come from regime change in Iraq. The Egyptian playwright Ali Salem says: "We have an Egyptian proverb: 'The drunk is in the care of the sober.' You are the sober. Don't forget that."

January 12, 2003

THE NEW MATH

You can understand everything you need to know about the Israeli-Palestinian conflict today through a simple math equation offered by Danny Rubinstein, the *Haaretz* newspaper's Palestinian affairs expert. The equation goes like this: Suppose Israel discovers that ten Palestinians from Nablus are planning suicide attacks. Israel says: If we can kill at least two, that will be progress, because only eight will be left. The Palestinians, by contrast, say: If you kill two, four more will volunteer to take their places, and you will be left with twelve. So for Israel ten minus two is eight, and for the Palestinians ten minus two is twelve.

And that explains why Ariel Sharon's all-stick-no-carrot crackdown over the past two years has failed to improve security for Israelis. When Mr. Sharon succeeded Ehud Barak, roughly fifty Israelis had been killed in the Palestinian uprising; today the number is more than seven hundred Israelis dead, and over two thousand Palestinians. When I asked an Israeli defense official why all the killings and arrests of Palestinians had had so little effect, the official said: "It's like we're mowing the grass. You mow the lawn one day and the next day the grass just grows right back."

Then why is Mr. Sharon still likely to win the upcoming Israeli election? Two reasons.

First, because as futile as the Sharon strategy has been, the Palestinian strategy has been even worse. The Palestinians still act as if they believe they can get more out of Israel by making Israelis feel insecure rather than by making them feel secure. After a while, you can't call this a mistake. After a while, you have to ask whether it reflects a conviction that a thriving Jewish presence in the middle of the Islamic world is simply not acceptable to them. Sure, the only thing Mr. Sharon knows how to do is cut the grass. But the only thing Yasir Arafat knows how to do is grow the grass—to sacrifice one generation of Palestinians after another to the fantasy of a return to all of Palestine.

The second is the failure of Israel's Labor party to develop an alternative to the Sharon policy. The problem for the Labor candidate, Amram Mitzna, an enormously decent former West Bank commander, is not that he is advocating what seventy percent of Israelis want—separation from the Palestinians and giving up most of the settlements. Rather it is that he has not persuaded Israelis, on a gut level, that he and his party are tough enough to bring this about in a safe way.

As a *Haaretz* essayist, Ari Shavit, explained: "I compare it to open-heart surgery. Israelis know that if we don't do it, if we don't separate, we will die. But if we do it in a rushed or messy way, we will also die. So when Mitzna calls for separation, 70 percent of Israel agrees. But when he says he is ready to do it unilaterally, if necessary, or to negotiate with Arafat, or even to negotiate under fire while the Intifada goes on, most people refuse to go along. It feels wrong to them in their guts. So they want a left-wing surgery to be carried out by a right-wing doctor. The problem is, Sharon won't carry out that surgery. He is so committed to the settlements that he built, he appears to be paralyzed."

Indeed, Mr. Sharon benefits from the people's desire to see him implement the Mitzna separation. But instead of really trying to do that, Mr. Sharon manipulates the public's fears to stay in power and maintain the settlements—while winking to the Americans that one day he will really make a deal.

As a result of all this, the conflict is entering a terrible new phase: the beginning of the end of the two-state solution. Under Mr. Sharon, the Jewish settlers have expanded existing settlements in the West Bank and also set up scores of illegal ones. The settlers want to ensure either the de facto or de jure Israeli annexation of the West Bank, Gaza, and East Jerusalem. And with no credible Arab or Palestinian peace initiative to challenge them, and no pressure from the Bush team, and no Israeli party to implement separation, the settlers are winning by default and inertia. Winning means they are making separation impossible.

But if there is no separation, by 2010 there will be more Palestinians than Jews living in Israel and the occupied territories. Then Israel will have three options: The Israelis will control this whole area by apartheid, or they will control it by expelling Palestinians, or they will grant Palestinians the right to vote and it will no longer be a Jewish state. Whichever way it goes, it will mean the end of Israel as a Jewish democracy.

January 15, 2003

THINKING ABOUT IRAQ (I)

As the decision on Iraq approaches, I, like so many Americans, have had to ask myself: What do you really think? Today I explain why I think liberals underappreciate the value of removing Saddam Hussein. And on Sunday I will explain why conservatives underappreciate the risks of doing so—and how we should balance the two.

What liberals fail to recognize is that regime change in Iraq is not some distraction from the war on Al Qaeda. That is a bogus argument. And simply because oil is also at stake in Iraq doesn't make it illegitimate either. Some things are right to do, even if Big Oil benefits.

Although President Bush has cast the war in Iraq as being about disarmament—and that is legitimate—disarmament is not the most important prize there. Regime change is the prize. Regime transformation in Iraq could make a valuable contribution to the war on terrorism, whether Saddam is ousted or enticed into exile.

Why? Because what really threatens open, Western, liberal societies today is not Saddam and his weapons per se. He is a twisted dictator who is deterrable through conventional means, because Saddam loves life more than he hates us. What threatens Western societies today are not the deterrables, like Saddam, but the undeterrables—the boys who did 9/11, who hate us more than they love life. It's these human missiles of mass destruction that could really destroy our open society.

So then the question is: What is the cement mixer that is churning out these undeterrables—these angry, humiliated, and often unemployed Muslim youth? That cement mixer is a collection of faltering Arab states, which, as the UN's Arab Human Development Report noted, have fallen so far behind the world that their combined GDP does not equal that of Spain. And the reason they have fallen behind can be traced to their lack of three things: freedom, modern education, and women's empowerment.

It we don't help transform these Arab states—which are also experiencing population explosions—to create better governance, to build more open and productive economies, to empower their women, and to develop responsible media that won't blame all their ills on others, we will never begin to see the political, educational, and religious reformations they need to shrink their output of undeterrables.

We have partners. Trust me, there is a part of every young Arab today that recoils at the idea of a U.S. invasion of Iraq, because of its colonial overtones. But there is a part of many young Arabs today that prays the U.S. will not only oust Saddam but all other Arab leaders as well.

It is not unreasonable to believe that if the U.S. removed Saddam and helped Iraqis build not an overnight democracy but a more accountable, progressive, and democratizing regime, it would have a positive, transforming effect on the entire Arab world—a region desperately in need of a progressive model that works.

And liberals need to take heed. Just by mobilizing for war against Iraq, the U.S. has sent this region a powerful message: We will not leave you alone anymore to play with matches, because the last time you did, we got burned. Just the threat of a U.S. attack has already prompted Hezbollah to be on its best behavior in Lebanon (for fear of being next). And it has spurred Saudi Arabia's Crown Prince Abdullah to introduce a proposal to his fellow Arab leaders for an "Arab Charter" of political and economic reform.

Let me sum up my argument with two of my favorite sayings. The first is by Harvard's president, Lawrence Summers, who says: "In the history of the world, no one has ever washed a rented car." It is true of countries as well. Until the Arab peoples are given a real ownership stake in their countries—a real voice in how they are run—they will never wash them, never improve them as they should.

The second is an American Indian saying: "If we don't turn around now, we just may get where we're going." The Arab world has been digging itself into a hole for a long time. If our generation simply helps it stop digging, possibly our grandchildren and its own will reap the benefits. But if we don't help the Arabs turn around now, they just may get where they're going—a dead end where they will produce more and more undeterrables.

This is something liberals should care about—because liberating the captive peoples of the Mideast is a virtue in itself and because in today's globalized world, if you don't visit a bad neighborhood, it will visit you.

January 22, 2003

THINKING ABOUT IRAQ (II)

In my column on Wednesday I laid out why I believe that liberals under-estimate how ousting Saddam Hussein could help spur positive political change in the Arab world. Today's column explores why conservative advocates of ousting Saddam underestimate the risks, and where we should strike the balance.

Let's start with one simple fact: Iraq is a black box that has been sealed shut since Saddam came to dominate Iraqi politics in the late 1960s. Therefore, one needs to have a great deal of humility when it comes to predicting what sorts of bats and demons may fly out if the U.S. and its allies remove the lid. Think of it this way: If and when we take the lid off Iraq, we will find an envelope inside. It will tell us what we have won and it will say one of two things.

It could say, "Congratulations! You've just won the Arab Germany—a country with enormous human talent, enormous natural resources, but with an evil dictator, whom you've just removed. Now, just add a little water, a spoonful of democracy and stir, and this will be a normal nation very soon."

Or the envelope could say, "You've just won the Arab Yugoslavia—an artificial country congenitally divided among Kurds, Shiites, Sunnis, Nasserites, leftists, and a host of tribes and clans that can only be held together with a Saddam-like iron fist. Congratulations, you're the new Saddam."

In the first scenario, Iraq is the way it is today because Saddam is the way he is. In the second scenario, Saddam is the way he is because Iraq is what it is. Those are two very different problems. And we will know which we've won only when we take off the lid. The conservatives and neo-cons, who have been pounding the table for war, should be a lot more humble about this question, because they don't know either.

Does that mean we should rule out war? No. But it does mean that we must do it right. To begin with, the president must level with the American people that we may indeed be buying the Arab Yugoslavia, which will take a great deal of time and effort to heal into a self-sustaining, progressive, accountable Arab government. And, therefore, any nation-building in Iraq will be a multiyear marathon, not a multiweek sprint.

Because it will be a marathon, we must undertake this war with the *maximum* amount of international legitimacy and UN backing we can possibly muster. Otherwise we will not have an American public willing to run this marathon, and we will not have allies ready to help us once we're inside (look at all the local police and administrators Europeans now contribute in Bosnia and Kosovo). We'll also become a huge target if we're the sole occupiers of Iraq.

In short, we can oust Saddam Hussein all by ourselves. But we cannot successfully rebuild Iraq all by ourselves. And the real prize here is a new Iraq that would be a progressive model for the whole region. That, for me, is the only morally and strategically justifiable reason to support this war. The Bush team dare not invade Iraq simply to install a more friendly dictator to pump us oil. And it dare not simply disarm Iraq and then walk away from the nation-building task.

Unfortunately, when it comes to enlisting allies, the Bush team is its own worst enemy. It has sneered at many issues the world cares about: the Kyoto accords, the World Court, arms control treaties. The Bush team had legitimate arguments on some of these issues, but the gratuitous way it dismissed them has fueled anti-Americanism. No, I have no illusions that if the Bush team had only embraced Kyoto the French wouldn't still be trying to obstruct America in Iraq. The French are the French. But unfortunately, now the Germans are the French, the Koreans are the French, and many Brits are becoming French.

Things could be better, but here is where we are—so here is where I am: My gut tells me we should continue the troop buildup, continue the inspections, and do everything we can for as long as we can to produce either a coup or the sort of evidence that will give us the broadest coalition possible, so we can do the best nation-building job possible.

But if war turns out to be the only option, then war it will have to be—because I believe that our kids will have a better chance of growing up in a safer world if we help put Iraq on a more progressive path and stimulate some real change in an Arab world that is badly in need of reform. Such a war would indeed be a shock to this region, but, if we do it right, there is a decent chance that it would be shock therapy.

January 26, 2003

THINKING ABOUT IRAQ (III)

Memo to: President Bush
From: A pro-American Arab leader

Dear Mr. President, I and my colleagues from the Arab world and Turkey share your view that Saddam Hussein is lying, has not complied with the UN, and must go. But is an American invasion the only way to remove him? Would you consider a deal for his exile?

I ask because we have been getting mixed signals. Your defense secretary seemed to endorse the idea, but others suggest to us that we shouldn't even bother. I admit, we and the Turks have not exactly been profiles in courage. The meeting that our foreign ministers held in Istanbul last week was a P.R. event staged by the Turks to show their public that they were looking for some alternative to war. But to tell you the truth, in all our discussions no one even brought up a deal for getting Saddam out.

Let me explain why. First, we're all uneasy about appearing to our publics as an extension of your military policy. Saddam is not popular in our region, Mr. President, but you are even less popular. Second, each of us is looking to the other guy to present the deal to Saddam, but none of us wants to be the one to do it for fear of being rebuffed. But the most important reason is that we have nothing concrete to offer. We need a hard offer, and neither we nor you are putting that together—even though we both believe that this could save a lot of pain if done right.

So, Mr. President, I am proposing that you give me a letter on your stationery authorizing a joint mission from the Arab League and the Islamic Conference to offer Saddam the following:

> 1. A U.S. commitment not to interfere with safe passage out of Iraq for Saddam and his whole entourage. (I assume they will want to go somewhere in the former Soviet Union.)
> 2. We understand that as a legal matter, the U.S. could never and would never forswear the right to hunt or prosecute Saddam for war crimes. But we need a public commitment from you that America's "priority" once Saddam leaves Iraq would be to focus on the rebuilding of that country and not on hunting Saddam or

any Iraqis who were once part of his regime. This last point is critical, because Iraqi Army officers who want to stay behind—and whose help you will need in holding Iraq together—have to know that they will not be prosecuted. If they know that, there is a much better chance they will pressure Saddam to go and cooperate with you later.

3. A commitment by you to give whichever Iraqi general succeeds Saddam a chance to work with you and the UN to complete the disarmament in good faith and begin political liberalization—before you opt for any military action. Iraq is a highly tribalized society, Mr. President, and it can be held together for now only by the Iraqi Army. We know, though, there are Iraqi generals eager to put Iraq onto a more normal path. It is true that if you occupy Iraq, you could have more control over its transformation. You also could find yourself in a hornet's nest.

This proposal has several virtues: By engineering Saddam's exile we make the moral, legal, and strategic point that no one can get away with defying the UN and flouting international norms forever. But we do it in a way that avoids a U.S. occupation of Iraq, with all the risks and dangers that could entail. It will be a big political win for you: Your tough line will have been vindicated, your public will be enormously relieved, uncertainty will be removed from your markets, and the image of the U.S. bully will be softened. Most of all, the Germans and French, who deep down would like to see you step into a mess in Iraq, will be left looking silly.

It would be a big win for us Arabs, too—because if we could actually broker a deal to avoid a war in Iraq, it would be the first time that we really assumed responsibility for our region.

The chances are very slim that we could persuade Saddam to accept such a deal. But we will know only if you keep your gun loaded and pointed right at his head—and if you accompany that with a firm offer. And the mere fact of your and our offering such a deal will strengthen your hand, by demonstrating to the world that we are going the extra-extra mile to avoid a war. But we need a firm offer from you. Without it, Saddam's argument that America will not be satisfied with anything but war will stand.

Mr. President, it would be a travesty if we all wanted an alternative to war for removing Saddam, but couldn't overcome our respective inhibitions to give it one real honest try.

January 29, 2003

AH, THOSE PRINCIPLED EUROPEANS

Last week I went to lunch at the Hotel Schweizerhof in Davos, Switzerland, and discovered why America and Europe are at odds. At the bottom of the lunch menu was a list of the countries that the lamb, beef, and chicken came from. But next to the meat imported from the U.S. was a tiny asterisk, which warned that it might contain genetically modified organisms—GMOs.

My initial patriotic instinct was to order the U.S. beef and ask for it "tartare," just for spite. But then I and my lunch guest just looked at each other and had a good laugh. How quaint! we said. Europeans, out of some romantic rebellion against America and high technology, were shunning U.S.-grown food containing GMOs—even though there is no scientific evidence that these are harmful. But practically everywhere we went in Davos, Europeans were smoking cigarettes—with their meals, coffee, or conversation—even though there is indisputable scientific evidence that smoking can kill you. In fact, I got enough secondhand smoke just dining in Europe last week to make me want to have a chest X ray.

So pardon me if I don't take seriously all the Euro-whining about the Bush policies toward Iraq—for one very simple reason: It strikes me as deeply unserious. It's not that there are no serious arguments to be made against war in Iraq. There are plenty. It's just that so much of what one hears coming from German Chancellor Gerhard Schröder and French President Jacques Chirac are not serious arguments. They are station identification.

They are not the arguments of people who have really gotten beyond the distorted Arab press and tapped into what young Arabs are saying about their aspirations for democracy and how much they blame Saddam Hussein and his ilk for the poor state of their region. Rather, they are the diplomatic equivalent of smoking cancerous cigarettes while rejecting harmless GMOs—an assertion of identity by trying to be whatever the Americans are not, regardless of the real interests or stakes.

And where this comes from, alas, is weakness. Being weak after being powerful is a terrible thing. It can make you stupid. It can make you reject U.S. policies simply to differentiate yourself from the world's only superpower. Or, in the case of Mr. Chirac, it can even prompt you to invite Zimbabwean President Robert Mugabe—a terrible tyrant—to visit Paris just to spite Tony Blair. Ah, those principled French.

"Power corrupts, but so does weakness," said Josef Joffe, editor of Germany's *Die Zeit* newspaper. "And absolute weakness corrupts absolutely. We are now living through the most critical watershed of the postwar period, with enormous moral and strategic issues at stake, and the only answer many Europeans offer is to constrain and contain American power. So by default they end up on the side of Saddam, in an intellectually corrupt position."

The more one sees of this, the more one is convinced that the historian Robert Kagan, in his very smart new book *Of Paradise and Power*, is right: "Americans are from Mars and Europeans are from Venus." There is now a structural gap between America and Europe, which derives from the yawning power gap, and this produces all sorts of resentments, insecurities, and diverging attitudes as to what constitutes the legitimate exercise of force.

I can live with this difference. But Europe's cynicism and insecurity, masquerading as moral superiority, is insufferable. Each year at the Davos economic forum protesters are allowed to march through the north end of town, where last year they broke shop windows. So this year, on demonstration day, all the shopkeepers on that end of town closed. But when I walked by their shops in the morning, I noticed that three of them had put up signs in their windows that read, "U.S.A. No War in Iraq."

I wondered to myself: Why did the shopkeepers at the lingerie store suddenly decide to express their antiwar sentiments? Well, the demonstrators came and left without getting near these shops. And guess what? As soon as they were gone, the antiwar signs disappeared. They had been put up simply as window insurance—to placate the demonstrators so they wouldn't throw stones at them.

As I said, there are serious arguments against the war in Iraq, but they have weight only if they are made out of conviction, not out of expedience or petulance—and if they are made by people with real beliefs, not identity crises.

February 2, 2003

VOTE FRANCE OFF THE ISLAND

Sometimes I wish that the five permanent members of the UN Security Council could be chosen like the starting five for the NBA All-Star team—with a vote by the fans. If so, I would certainly vote France off the Council and replace it with India. Then the perm-five would be Russia, China, India, Britain, and the United States. That's more like it.

Why replace France with India? Because India is the world's biggest democracy, the world's largest Hindu nation, and the world's second-largest Muslim nation, and, quite frankly, India is just so much more serious than France these days. France is so caught up with its need to differentiate itself from America to feel important, it's become silly. India has grown out of that game. India may be ambivalent about war in Iraq, but it comes to its ambivalence honestly. Also, France can't see how the world has changed since the end of the cold war. India can.

Throughout the cold war, France sought to differentiate itself by playing between the Soviet and American blocs. France could get away with this entertaining little game for two reasons: First, it knew that Uncle Sam, in the end, would always protect it from the Soviet bear. So France could tweak America's beak, do business with Iraq, and enjoy America's military protection. And second, the cold war world was, we now realize, a much more stable place. Although it was divided between two nuclear superpowers, both were status quo powers in their own way. They represented different orders, but they both represented order.

That is now gone. Today's world is also divided, but it is increasingly divided between the "World of Order"—anchored by America, the EU, Russia, India, China, and Japan, and joined by scores of smaller nations—and the "World of Disorder." The World of Disorder is dominated by rogue regimes like Iraq's and North Korea's and the various global terrorist networks that feed off the troubled string of states stretching from the Middle East to Indonesia.

How the World of Order deals with the World of Disorder is the key question of the day. There is room for disagreement. There is no room for a lack of seriousness. And the whole French game on Iraq, spearheaded by its diplomacy-lite foreign minister, Dominique de Villepin, lacks seriousness. Most of France's energy is devoted to holding America back from acting alone, not holding Saddam Hussein's feet to the fire to comply with the UN.

The French position is utterly incoherent. The inspections have not worked yet, says Mr. de Villepin, because Saddam has not fully cooperated, and, therefore, we should triple the number of inspectors. But the inspections have failed not because of a shortage of inspectors. They have failed because of a shortage of compliance on Saddam's part, as the French know. The way you get that compliance out of a thug like Saddam is not by tripling the inspectors, but by tripling the threat that if he does not comply he will be faced with a UN-approved war.

Mr. de Villepin also suggested that Saddam's government pass "legislation to prohibit the manufacture of weapons of mass destruction." (I am not making this up.) That proposal alone is a reminder of why, if America didn't exist and Europe had to rely on France, most Europeans today would be speaking either German or Russian.

I also want to avoid a war—but not by letting Saddam off the hook, which would undermine the UN, set back the winds of change in the Arab world, and strengthen the World of Disorder. The only possible way to coerce Saddam into compliance—without a war—is for the whole world to line up shoulder-to-shoulder against his misbehavior, without any gaps. But France, as they say in kindergarten, does not play well with others. If you line up against Saddam you're just one of the gang. If you hold out against America, you're unique. "France, it seems, would rather be more important in a world of chaos than less important in a world of order," says the foreign policy expert Michael Mandelbaum, author of *The Ideas That Conquered the World*.

If France were serious about its own position, it would join the U.S. in setting a deadline for Iraq to comply and backing it up with a second UN resolution authorizing force if Iraq does not. And France would send its prime minister to Iraq to tell that directly to Saddam. Oh, France's prime minister was on the road last week. He was out drumming up business for French companies in the world's biggest emerging computer society. He was in India.

February 9, 2003

PRESENT AT ... WHAT?

The tension that is now rising within the Western alliance, NATO, and the UN over how to deal with Iraq is deeply disturbing. It raises fears that the postwar security system, which stabilized the world for fifty years, could come unglued if America intervenes alone in Iraq. At the birth of this security system, Secretary of State Dean Acheson wrote a memoir titled *Present at the Creation.* Can we deal with Iraq and still ensure that Secretary of State Colin Powell's memoir is not titled *Present at the Destruction?*

Yes, we can—if we, the Russians, the Chinese, and the French all take a deep breath, understand our common interests, and pursue them with a little more common sense and a little less bluster.

That means the Bush hawks need to realize they cannot achieve their ultimate aim of disarming and transforming Iraq without maximum international legitimacy. And the Euro-doves need to realize they cannot achieve their aims of a peaceful solution in Iraq and preserving the UN and the whole multilateral order without a credible threat of force against Saddam Hussein.

Let's start with the Bush hawks. The first rule of any Iraq invasion is the pottery store rule: You break it, you own it. We break Iraq, we own Iraq—and we own the primary responsibility for rebuilding a country of 23 million people that has more in common with Yugoslavia than with any other Arab nation. I am among those who believe this is a job worth doing, both for what it could do to liberate Iraqis from a terrible tyranny and to stimulate reform elsewhere in the Arab world. But it is worth doing only if we can do it right. And the only way we can do it right is if we can see it through, which will take years. And the only way we can see it through is if we have the maximum allies and UN legitimacy.

We don't need a broad coalition to break Iraq. We can do that ourselves. But we do need a broad coalition to rebuild Iraq, so that the American taxpayer and Army do not have to bear that full burden or be exposed alone at the heart of the Arab-Muslim world. President Bush, if he alienates the allies from going to war—the part we can do alone—is depriving himself of allies for the peace—the part where we'll need all the friends we can get.

No question—Saddam never would have let the UN inspectors back in had President Bush not unilaterally threatened force. But if Mr. Bush keeps conveying to China, France, and Russia that he really doesn't care what they think and will go to war anyway, their impulse will be to never come along and just remain free riders.

The allies also have a willful blind spot. There is no way their preferred outcome, a peaceful solution, can come about unless Saddam is faced with a credible, unified threat of force. The French and others know that, and therefore their refusal to present Saddam with a threat only guarantees U.S. unilateralism and undermines the very UN structure that is the best vehicle for their managing U.S. power.

We need a compromise. We need to say to the French, Russians, and Chinese that we'll stand down for a few more weeks and give Saddam one last chance to comply with the UN disarmament demands—provided they agree now that if Saddam does not fully comply they will have the UN authorize the use of force.

If war proves inevitable, it must be seen as the product of an international decision, not an American whim. The timing cannot be determined by the weather or the need to use troops just because they are there. You cannot launch a war this important now simply because it's going to be hot later. I would gladly trade a four-week delay today for four years of allied support after a war. I would much prefer a hot, legitimate, UN-approved war with the world on our side to a cool, less legitimate war that leaves us owning Iraq by ourselves.

France, China, and Russia have to get serious, but so do we. The Bush talk that we can fight this war with just a "coalition of the willing"—meaning Latvia, Lithuania, and Estonia—is dangerous nonsense. There is only one coalition that matters to the average American and average world citizen. It is one approved by the UN and NATO. We may not be able to garner it, but we need to be doing everything we can—everything—to try before we go to war.

Why? Because there is no war we can't win by ourselves, but there is no nation we can rebuild by ourselves—especially Iraq.

February 12, 2003

PEKING DUCT TAPE

After a recent UN session on the Iraq crisis, I asked a Bush aide how China was behaving. "The Chinese?" the official said. "They don't think they have a dog in this fight."

That certainly is how China is behaving—as if this whole issue were for America to resolve. That is a deeply mistaken view, and it shows how little China (not to mention France and Russia) understands about the new world order. If I were explaining it to China's leaders, here's what I would say:

Friends, with every great world war has come a new security system. World War I gave birth to the League of Nations and an attempt to re-create a balance of power in Europe, which proved unstable. World War II gave birth to the UN, NATO, the IMF, and the bipolar American-Soviet power structure, which proved to be quite stable until the end of the cold war. Now, 9/11 has set off World War III, and it, too, is defining a new international order.

The new world system is also bipolar, but instead of being divided between East and West, it is divided between the World of Order and the World of Disorder. The World of Order is built on four pillars: the U.S., EU-Russia, India, and China, along with all the smaller powers around them. The World of Disorder comprises failed states (such as Liberia), rogue states (Iraq and North Korea), messy states—states that are too big to fail but too messy to work (Pakistan, Colombia, Indonesia, many Arab and African states)—and finally the terrorist and mafia networks that feed off the World of Disorder.

There has always been a World of Disorder, but what makes it more dangerous today is that in a networked universe, with widely diffused technologies, open borders, and a highly integrated global financial and Internet system, very small groups of people can amass huge amounts of power to disrupt the World of Order. Individuals can become super-empowered. In many ways, 9/11 marked the first full-scale battle between a superpower and a small band of super-empowered angry men from the World of Disorder.

The job of the four pillars of the World of Order is to work together to help stabilize and lift up the World of Disorder. Unfortunately, China doesn't seem to realize that. You (like some Bushies) still have a lot of cold war reflexes. Indeed, some Chinese intellectuals, not to mention French and Russian, actually believe you all have more to fear from American power than from Osama, Kim, or Saddam. That's nuts. If America has to manage the World of Disorder alone, the American people will quickly tire. And as Michael Mandelbaum, the Johns Hopkins foreign policy expert, notes, "The real threat to world stability is not too much American power. It is too little American power." Too little American power will only lead to the World of Disorder expanding.

China has to think clearly. If there is just one more 9/11, or if North Korea lobs just one missile our way, it will lead to the end of the open society in America, as we know it, and also constrict globalization. Because we will tighten our borders, triple-check every ship that comes into port, and restrict civil liberties as never before, and this will slow the whole global economy.

Now the last time I checked, China had decided to base its growth on manufacturing for the global market and in particular for the U.S. market, where you now send 40 percent of your exports—40 percent!—and where you just racked up a $100 billion trade surplus. One more 9/11 and your growth strategy will be in real trouble (unless you plan on only exporting duct tape), which means the Chinese leadership will be in real trouble.

So, you still think you don't have a dog in this fight? You still think you can be free riders on an Iraq war? You still think you can leave us to carry the burden of North Korea? Well, guess again. You need to get serious. It is quite legitimate for China to oppose war in Iraq or North Korea. But why isn't China's foreign minister going to Baghdad and Pyongyang, slamming his fist on tables and demanding that their leaders start complying with the UN to avoid war? I understand you don't want us to be impulsive, but why are you so passive?

One more 9/11, one bad Iraq war that ties America down alone in the Middle East and saps its strength, well, that may go over well with the cold warriors in the People's Liberation Army, but in the real world—in the world where your real threat is not American troops crossing your borders but American dollars fleeing from them—you will be out of business.

Now which part of that sentence don't you understand?

February 16, 2003

TELL THE TRUTH

As I was listening to the French foreign minister make his case at the UN for giving Saddam Hussein more time to comply, I was struck by the number of people in the Security Council chamber who applauded. I wish there were someone I could applaud for.

Sorry, I can't applaud the French foreign minister, because I don't believe that France, which sold Saddam his first nuclear reactor, the one Israel blew up, comes to this story with the lofty principles it claims. The French foreign minister, after basking in the applause at the UN, might ask himself who was clapping for his speech back in Baghdad and who was crying. Saddam was clapping, and all his political prisoners—i.e., most Iraqis—were crying.

But I don't have much applause in me for China, Russia—or the Bush team either. I feel lately as if there are no adults in this room (except Tony Blair). No, this is not a plague-on-all-your-houses column. I side with those who believe we need to confront Saddam—but we have to do it right, with allies and staying power, and the Bush team has bungled that.

The Bush folks are big on attitude, weak on strategy, and terrible at diplomacy. I covered the first gulf war, in 1990–91. What I remember most are the seven trips I took with Secretary of State James A. Baker III around the world to watch him build—face-to-face—the coalition and public support for that war, before a shot was fired. Going to someone else's country is a sign you respect his opinion. This Bush team has done no such hands-on spade work. Its members think diplomacy is a phone call.

They don't like to travel. Seeing senior Bush officials abroad for any length of time has become like rare-bird sightings. It's probably because they spend so much time infighting in Washington over policy, they're each afraid that if they leave town their opponents will change the locks on their office doors.

Also, you would think that if Iraq were the focus of your whole foreign policy, maybe you would have handled North Korea with a little less attitude, so as not to trigger two wars at once. Maybe you would have come up with that alternative—which President Bush promised—to the Kyoto treaty, a treaty he trashed to the great anger of Europe. You're not going to get much support in Europe telling people, "You are either with us or against us in a war on terrorism, but in the war you care about—for a greener planet—America will do whatever it wants."

I am also very troubled by the way Bush officials have tried to justify this war on the grounds that Saddam is allied with Osama bin Laden or will be soon. There is simply no proof of that, and every time I hear them repeat it I think of the Gulf of Tonkin resolution. You don't take the country to war on the wings of a lie.

Tell people the truth. Saddam does not threaten us today. He can be deterred. Taking him out is a war of choice—but it's *a legitimate choice*. It's because he is undermining the UN, it's because if left alone he will seek weapons that will threaten all his neighbors, it's because you believe the people of Iraq deserve to be liberated from his tyranny, and it's because you intend to help Iraqis create a progressive state that could stimulate reform in the Arab-Muslim world, so that this region won't keep churning out angry young people who are attracted to radical Islam and are the real weapons of mass destruction.

That's the case for war—and it will require years of occupying Iraq and a simultaneous effort to defuse the Israeli-Palestinian conflict to create a regional context for success. If done right, such a war could shrink Al Qaeda's influence—but Al Qaeda is a separate enemy that will have to be fought separately, and will remain a threat even if Saddam is ousted.

It is legitimate for Europeans to oppose such a war, but not simply by sticking a thumb in our eye and their heads in the sand. It's also legitimate for the Bush folks to focus the world on Saddam, but two years of their gratuitous bullying has made many people deaf to America's arguments. Too many people today no longer accept America's strength as a good thing. That is a bad thing.

Some of this we can't control. But some we can, which is why it's time for the Bush team to shape up—dial down the attitude, start selling this war on the truth, give us a budget that prepares the nation for a war abroad, not a party at home, and start doing everything possible to create a global context where we can confront Saddam without the world applauding for him.

February 19, 2003

MY SURVIVAL KIT

In the past few weeks I've started to have a heretical thought: Are we overreacting to 9/11? Are we going to drive ourselves crazy long before Osama bin Laden ever does?

Having argued that 9/11 was the start of World War III, I would never diminish its significance. And I do not have an ounce of criticism for the FBI, CIA, or Department of Homeland Security for issuing terrorism warnings at the hint of a threat. They are doing their job. But increasingly I wonder whether we're doing ours—which is learning to live with these dangers, instead of going to excesses that provide no additional security but a ton of additional anxiety.

This little voice first started creeping into my head as I watched the layers of airport security mount. It started with just pushing your bag through the X-ray machine and walking through the metal detector. Then it went to taking your computer out. Then it went to taking the tweezers out of your overnight kit. Then it went to taking off your shoes. Now it's your belt. Sometimes I look around me at airport security and I feel as if I'm at some weird adult pajama party. I now fear that a tongue-in-cheek column I wrote fourteen months ago, called "Naked Air," about how we should all just fly naked and save the hassle, is going to come true in my lifetime.

Then there was Code Orange. Again, I have no problem with the warnings. But do CNN and MSNBC really have to add the terror alert status to the bottom right corner of their screens, just above the stock market reports: "Nasdaq down, terror up—have a nice day." What do these networks expect their viewers to do when they see those warnings—other than get worried? The *Daily News* in New York quoted a local radio executive as saying what a relief the recent East Coast blizzard was because it drove out all the terrorism stories: "It was . . . a Saddam-free day—just the break we needed."

When a colleague asked me what was my family's emergency exit plan—in case Washington was attacked—I told her I didn't have one. I later felt pangs of parental guilt. But then I thought: How is anyone going to get out of this town in a panic? The Beltway is gridlock on normal days.

Another friend asked me, half seriously, about a counterterrorism etiquette joke making the rounds. Say you're driving home and, on your way, there is a terror alert that someone has released poison into the air. Your wife is home and has sealed herself into your family's "safe room" with duct tape and plastic wrap. When you arrive home, does your wife unseal the room to let you in or not? Hmmmmm. I suggested he ask Miss Manners—or a marriage counselor.

But what finally put me over the top was the report that Turkey initially demanded $32 billion in return for U.S. troops' using Turkish bases in an Iraqi invasion. I want to help the Turks, but you could almost hear them laughing at us, saying, "These Americans are so obsessed with Saddam and Osama, let's shake them down a little."

And then there is the new layer of pseudo-security, like when you go to Washington Wizards basketball games and they demand you open your purse or bag—as if any serious terrorist couldn't just hide his gun or bomb under a jacket. I wouldn't mind if this were actually making people feel more secure, but it's actually having the opposite effect—making people feel more insecure by making them feel as if they are living in a national security state.

In an open society, there are simply too many threats, too many openings, and too many interactions that are built on trust. You can't even begin to secure them all without also choking that open society. Which is why the right response, after a point, is not to demand more and more security—but to learn to live with more and more anxiety.

Because the question is not whether there will be more attacks. There will be. The question is whether we can survive them and still maintain an open society. What good is it to have Osama trapped in a basement somewhere if, by just whispering a few threats on Al Jazeera TV, he can trap us in self-sealed rooms?

No good at all, which is why the only survival purchase I've made since Code Orange is a new set of Ben Hogan Apex irons, and why my all-American survival kit would include a movie guide, a concert schedule, Rollerblades, a bicycle—plus a reminder to attend your local PTA meetings, Little League games, neighborhood block parties, and your book club and to get plenty of tickets for your favorite sports team.

Leave the cave-dwelling to Osama.

February 23, 2003

THE LONG BOMB

Watching this Iraq story unfold, all I can say is this: If this were not about my own country, my own kids, and my own planet, I'd pop some popcorn, pull up a chair, and pay good money just to see how this drama unfolds. Because what you are about to see is the greatest shake of the dice any president has voluntarily engaged in since Harry Truman dropped the bomb on Japan. Vietnam was a huge risk, but it evolved incrementally. And threatening a nuclear war with the Soviets over the Cuban missile crisis was a huge shake of the dice by President John Kennedy, but it was a gamble that was imposed on him, not one he initiated.

A U.S. invasion to disarm Iraq, oust Saddam Hussein, and rebuild a decent state would be the mother of all presidential gambles. Any one who thinks President Bush is doing this for political reasons is nuts. You could do this only if you really believed in it, because Mr. Bush is betting his whole presidency on this war of choice.

And don't believe the polls. I've been to nearly twenty states recently, and I've found that 95 percent of the country wants to see Iraq dealt with without a war. But President Bush is a man on a mission. He has been convinced by a tiny group of advisers that throwing "The Long Bomb" — attempting to transform the most dangerous Arab state — is a geopolitical game-changer. It could help to nudge the whole Arab-Muslim world onto a more progressive track, something that coaxing simply will not do anymore. It's something that can only be accomplished by building a different model in the heart of the Arab-Muslim world. No, you don't see this every day. This is really bold.

And that leads to my dilemma. I have a mixed marriage. My wife opposes this war, but something in Mr. Bush's audacious shake of the dice appeals to me. He summed it up well in his speech last week: "A liberated Iraq can show the power of freedom to transform that vital region by bringing hope and progress into the lives of millions. America's interest in security and America's belief in liberty both lead in the same direction — to a free and peaceful Iraq."

My dilemma is that while I believe in such a bold project, I fear that Mr. Bush has failed to create a context for his boldness to succeed, a context that could maximize support for his vision—support vital to seeing it through. He and his team are the only people who would ever have conceived this project, but they may be the worst people to implement it. The only place they've been bold is in their military preparations (which have at least gotten Saddam to begin disarming).

What do I mean? I mean that if taking out Saddam and rebuilding Iraq had been my goal from the minute I took office (as it was for the Bush team), I would not have angered all of Europe by trashing the Kyoto global warming treaty without offering an alternative. I would not have alienated the entire Russian national security elite by telling the Russians that we were ripping up the ABM treaty and that they would just have to get used to it. (You're now seeing their revenge.) I would not have proposed one radical tax cut on top of another on the eve of a huge, costly nation-building marathon abroad.

I would, though, have rallied the nation for real energy conservation and initiated a Manhattan Project for alternative energies so I would not find myself with $2.25-per-gallon gasoline on the eve of this war—because OPEC capacity is nearly tapped out. I would have told the Palestinians that until they stop suicide bombing and get a more serious leadership, we're not dealing with them, but I would also have told the Israelis that every new or expanded settlement they built would cost them $100 million in U.S. aid. And I would have told the Arabs: "While we'll deal with the Iraqi threat, we have no imperial designs on your countries. We are not on a crusade—but we will not sit idle if you tolerate extremists in your midst who imperil our democracy."

No, had Mr. Bush done all these things it would not have changed everything with France, Russia, and the Arabs—or my wife. But I am convinced that it would have helped generate more support to increase our staying power in Iraq and the odds that we could pull this off.

So here's how I feel: I feel as if the president is presenting us with a beautiful carved mahogany table—a big, bold, gutsy vision. But if you look underneath, you discover that this table has only one leg. His bold vision on Iraq is not supported by boldness in other areas. And so I am terribly worried that Mr. Bush has told us the right thing to do, but won't be able to do it right.

March 2, 2003

FIRE, READY, AIM

I went to President Bush's White House news conference on Thursday to see how he was wrestling with the momentous issue of Iraq. One line he uttered captured all the things that are troubling me about his approach. It was when he said, "When it comes to our security, we really don't need anybody's permission."

The first thing that bothered me was the phrase, "When it comes to our security." Fact: The invasion of Iraq today is not vital to American security. Saddam Hussein has neither the intention nor the capability to threaten America, and is easily deterrable if he did.

This is not a war of necessity. That was Afghanistan. Iraq is a war of choice—a legitimate choice to preserve the credibility of the UN, which Saddam has defied for twelve years, and to destroy his tyranny and replace it with a decent regime that could drive reform in the Arab-Muslim world. That's the real case.

The problem that Mr. Bush is having with the legitimate critics of this war stems from his consistent exaggeration on this point. When Mr. Bush takes a war of choice and turns it into a war of necessity, people naturally ask, "Hey, what's going on here? We're being hustled. The real reason must be his father, or oil, or some right-wing ideology."

And that brings us to the second phrase: "We really don't need anybody's permission." Again, for a war of no choice against the 9/11 terrorists in Kabul, we didn't need anyone's permission. But for a war of choice in Iraq, we need the world's permission—because of what it would take to rebuild Iraq.

Mr. Bush talks only about why it's right to dismantle the bad Iraq, not what it will take to rebuild a decent Iraq—a distant land, the size of California, divided like Yugoslavia. I believe we can help build a decent Iraq, but not alone. If we're alone, it will turn into a U.S. occupation and make us the target for everyone's frustration. And alone, Americans will not have the patience, manpower, and energy for nation-building, which is not a sprint but a marathon.

Mr. Bush growls that the world is demanding that America play "Captain, May I" when it comes to Iraq—and he's not going to ask anybody's permission. But with Iraq, the relevant question is not "Captain, May I?" It's "Captain, Can I?"—can I do it right without allies? No.

So here's where we are. Regime change in Iraq *is* the right choice for Iraq, for the Middle East, and for the world. Mr. Bush is right about that. But for now, this choice may be just too hard to sell. If the president can't make his war of choice the world's war of choice right now, we need to reconsider our options and our tactics. Because if Mr. Bush acts unilaterally, I fear America will not only lose the chance of building a decent Iraq, but something more important—America's efficacy as the strategic and moral leader of the free world.

A story. In 1945 King Abdul Aziz Ibn Saud of Saudi Arabia met President Franklin D. Roosevelt on a ship in the Suez Canal. Before agreeing to meet with Roosevelt, King Abdul Aziz, a Bedouin at heart, asked his advisers two questions about the U.S. president: "Tell me, does he believe in God and do they [the Americans] have any colonies?"

The real question the Saudi king was asking was: How do these Americans use their vast power? Like the Europeans, in pursuit of colonies, self-interest, and imperium, or on behalf of higher values?

That's still the most important question for U.S. national security. The world does not want to be led by transparent cynics like the French foreign minister and his boss. But it also does not want to be led by an America whose Congress is so traumatized by 9/11 that it can't think straight and by a president ideologically committed to war in Iraq no matter what the costs, the support, or the prospects for a decent aftermath. But, France aside, the world is still ready to be led by an America that's a little more humble, a little better listener, and a little more ready to say to its allies: How can we work this out? How much time do we need to give you to see if inspections can work for you to endorse the use of force if they don't?

Think about FDR He had just won World War II. America was at the apex of its power. It didn't need anyone's permission for anything. Yet, on his way home from Yalta, confined to a wheelchair, FDR traveled to the Mideast to meet and show respect for the leaders of Ethiopia, Egypt, and Saudi Arabia. Why? Because he knew he needed them not to win the war, but to win the peace.

March 9, 2003

GRAPES OF WRATH

I have a confession to make. Right after 9/11, I was given a CD by the Mormon Tabernacle Choir that included its rendition of "The Battle Hymn of the Republic." I put it in my car's CD player and played that song over and over, often singing along as I drove. It wasn't only the patriotism it evoked that stirred me, but the sense of national unity. That song was what the choir sang at the close of the memorial service at the National Cathedral right after 9/11. Even though that was such a wrenching moment for our nation, I look back on it now with a certain longing and nostalgia. For it was such a moment of American solidarity, with people rallying to people and everyone rallying to the president.

And that is what makes me so sad about this moment. It appears we are on the verge of going to war in a way that will burst all the national solidarity and goodwill that followed 9/11, within our own country and the world.

This war is so unprecedented that it has always been a gut call—and my gut has told me four things. First, this is a war of choice. Saddam Hussein poses no direct threat to us today. But confronting him is a legitimate choice—much more legitimate than knee-jerk liberals and pacifists think. Removing Saddam—with his obsession to obtain weapons of mass destruction—ending his tyranny and helping to nurture a more progressive Iraq that could spur reform across the Arab-Muslim world are the best long-term responses to bin Ladenism. Some things are true even if George Bush believes them.

The second thing my gut says, though, is that building a decent peace in Iraq will be so much more difficult than the Bush hawks think. Iraq is the Arab Yugoslavia. It is a country, congenitally divided among Kurds, Shiites, and Sunnis, that was forged by British power and has never been held together by anything other than an iron fist. Transforming Iraq into a state with an accountable, consensual, and decent government would be the biggest, most audacious war of choice any U.S. president has ever made—because it doesn't just involve getting rid of Saddam, but also building an integrated Iraq *for the first time.*

Which explains my third gut feeling—that to succeed in such an undertaking, in a country with so many wounds and pent-up resentments, will require an unrushed process that is viewed as legitimate in Iraq, the region, and the world. It cannot be done if we are looking over our shoulders every day, which is why UN approval and allied support are so important.

My main criticism of President Bush is that he has failed to acknowledge how unusual this war of choice is—for both Americans and the world—and therefore hasn't offered the bold policies that have to go with it. Instead, the president has hyped the threat and asserted that this is a war of no choice, then combined it all with his worst pre-9/11 business as usual: budget-busting tax cuts, indifference to global environmental concerns, a gas-guzzling energy policy, neglect of the Arab-Israeli peace process, and bullying diplomacy.

And this brings me to my last gut feeling: Despite all the noise, a majority of decent people in the world still hunger for a compromise that forces Saddam to comply, or be exposed, and does not weaken America.

So, Mr. President, before you shake the dice on a legitimate but audacious war, please, shake the dice just once on some courageous diplomacy. Pick up where Woodrow Wilson left off: Fly to Paris, bring the leaders of France, Russia, China, and Britain together, along with the chairman of the Arab League summit, and offer them any reasonable amount of time for more inspections—if they will agree on specific disarmament benchmarks Saddam has to meet and support an automatic UN authorization of force if he doesn't. If France still snubs you, the world will see that you are the one trying to preserve collective security, while France only wants to make mischief. That will be very important to the legitimacy of any war.

Mr. President, I never felt more traumatized as an American than in the days after 9/11. But despite the very real threats, I also never felt more optimistic—because of the national unity we had, and you had, to face those threats. If whatever is left of that post-9/11 solidarity is exploded by a divisive, unilateral war in Iraq, we will not only be sacrificing good feelings, but also the key to managing this complex, dangerous world. That is our ability to stand united and with others—our ability to sing, together, "The Battle Hymn of the Republic" and have the world at least hum along.

March 12, 2003

REPAIRING THE WORLD

Some days, you pick up the newspaper and you don't know whether to laugh or cry. Let's see, the prime minister of Serbia just got shot, and if that doesn't seem like a bad omen then you missed the class on World War I. Our strongest ally for war in Iraq is Bulgaria—a country I've always had a soft spot for, because it protected its Jews during World War II, but a country that's been on the losing side of every war in the last one hundred years. Congress is renaming French fries "freedom fries." George Bush has managed to lose a global popularity contest to Saddam Hussein, and he's looking to build diplomatic support in Europe by flying to the Azores, a remote archipelago in the Atlantic, to persuade the persuaded leaders of Britain and Spain to stand firm with him. I guess the North Pole wasn't available. I've been to the Azores. It was with Secretary of State James Baker on, as I recall, one of his seven trips around the world to build support for Gulf War I. Mr. Baker used the Azores to refuel.

Having said all that, I am glad Mr. Bush is meeting with Tony Blair. In fact, I wish he would turn over leadership on the whole Iraq crisis to him. Mr. Blair has an international vision that Mr. Bush sorely needs. "President Bush should be in charge of marshaling the power for this war," says the Middle East expert Stephen P. Cohen, "and Tony Blair should be in charge of the vision for which that power should be applied."

Why? What does Tony Blair get that George Bush doesn't? The only way I can explain it is by a concept from the Kabbalah called "tikkun olam." It means, "to repair the world." If you listened to Tony Blair's speeches in recent weeks they contain something so strikingly absent from Mr. Bush's. Tony Blair constantly puts the struggle for a better Iraq within a broader context of moral concerns. Tony Blair always leaves you with the impression that for him the Iraq war is just one hammer and one nail in an effort to do tikkun olam, to repair the world.

Did you see Mr. Blair's recent speech about the environment? He called for a new "international consensus to protect our environment and combat the devastating impacts of climate change." "Kyoto is not radical enough," he said. "Ultimately this is about our world as a global community. . . . What we lack at present is a common agenda that is broad and just. . . . That is the real task of statesmanship today."

Did you hear Mr. Blair talk Friday about the Middle East conflict? "We are right to focus on Saddam Hussein and his weapons of mass destruction," he said, "but we must put equal focus on the plight of the people whose lives are being devastated by lack of progress in the peace process, Israeli civilians and Palestinians."

Contrast that with Mr. Bush. His White House declaration about resuming the peace process was delivered with all the enthusiasm of someone about to have his teeth drilled. On the environment, the president has never appreciated how damaging it was for him to scrap the Kyoto treaty, which *was* unimplementable, without offering an alternative. Nothing has hurt America's image more than the impression Mr. Bush has left that when it comes to terrorism—our war—there must be a universal crusade, but on the environment—the universal concern of others—we'll do whatever we want.

Yes, some people and nations are just jealous of America's power and that's why they oppose us on Iraq. But there is something more to the opposition. I deeply identify with the president's vision of ending Saddam Hussein's tyranny and building a more decent, progressive Iraq. If done right, it could be so important to the future of the Arab-Muslim world, which is why I won't give up on this war. But can this Bush team be counted on to do it right? Mr. Bush's greatest weakness is that too many people, at home and abroad, smell that he's not really interested in repairing the world. Everything is about the war on terrorism.

Lord knows, I don't diminish the threats we face, but for eighteen months all we've been doing is exporting our fears to the world. Virtually all of Mr. Bush's speeches are about how we're going to protect ourselves and whom we're going to hit next. America as a beacon of optimism— America as the world's chief carpenter, not just cop—is gone. We need a little less John Wayne and a little more JFK. Once we get this Iraq crisis behind us, we need to get back to exporting our hopes, not just our fears.

March 16, 2003

D-DAY

President Bush is fond of cowboy imagery, so here's an image that comes to mind about our pending war with Iraq. In most cowboy movies the good guys round up a posse before they ride into town and take on the black hats. We're doing just the opposite. We're riding into Baghdad pretty much alone and hoping to round up a posse after we get there. I hope we do, because it may be the only way we can get out with ourselves, and the town, in one piece.

This column has argued throughout this debate that removing Saddam Hussein and helping Iraq replace his regime with a decent, accountable government that can serve as a model in the Middle East is worth doing—not because Iraq threatens us with its weapons but because we are threatened by a collection of failing Arab-Muslim states that churn out way too many young people who feel humiliated, voiceless, and left behind. We have a real interest in partnering with them for change.

This column has also argued, though, that such a preventive war is so unprecedented and mammoth a task—taking over an entire country from a standing start and rebuilding it—that it has to be done with maximum UN legitimacy and with as many allies as possible.

President Bush has failed to build that framework before going to war. Though the Bush team came to office with this Iraq project in mind, it has pursued a narrow, ideological, and bullying foreign policy that has alienated so many people that by the time it wanted to rustle up a posse for an Iraq war, too many nations were suspicious of its motives.

The president says he went the extra mile to find a diplomatic solution. That is not true. On the eve of the first Gulf War, Secretary of State James Baker met face-to-face in Geneva with the Iraqi foreign minister—a last-ditch peace effort that left most of the world feeling it was Iraq that refused to avoid war. This time the whole world saw President Bush make one trip, which didn't quite make it across the Atlantic, to sell the war to the only two allies we had. This is not to excuse France, let alone Saddam. France's role in blocking a credible UN disarmament program was shameful.

But here we are, going to war, basically alone, in the face of opposition, not so much from "the Arab Street," but from "the World Street." Everyone wishes it were different, but it's too late—which is why this column will henceforth focus on how to turn these lemons into lemonade. Our children's future hinges on doing this right, even if we got here wrong.

The president's view is that in the absence of a UN endorsement, this war will become "self-legitimating" when the world sees most Iraqis greet U.S. troops as liberators. I think there is a good chance that will play out.

But wars are fought for political ends. Defeating Saddam is necessary but not sufficient to achieve those ends, which are a more progressive Iraq and a world with fewer terrorists and terrorist suppliers dedicated to destroying the U.S., so Americans will feel safer at home and abroad. We cannot achieve the latter without the former. Which means we must bear any burden and pay any price to make Iraq into the sort of state that fair-minded people across the world will see and say: "You did good. You lived up to America's promise."

To maximize our chances of doing that, we need to patch things up with the world. Because having more allied support in rebuilding Iraq will increase the odds that we do it right, and because if the breach that has been opened between us and our traditional friends hardens into hostility, we will find it much tougher to manage both Iraq and all the other threats down the road. That means the Bush team needs an "attitude lobotomy"—it needs to get off its high horse and start engaging people on the World Street, listening to what's bothering them, and also telling them what's bothering us.

Some thirty-five years ago Israel won a war in Six Days. It saw its victory as self-legitimating. Its neighbors saw it otherwise, and Israel has been trapped in the Seventh Day ever since—never quite able to transform its dramatic victory into a peace that would make Israelis feel more secure.

More than fifty years ago America won a war against European fascism, which it followed up with a Marshall Plan and nation-building, both a handout and a hand up—in a way that made Americans welcome across the world. Today is a D-Day for our generation. May our leaders have the wisdom of their predecessors from the Greatest Generation.

March 19, 2003

THE WESTERN FRONT

PARIS

There are three fronts in this Iraq war: one in Iraq, one between America and its Western allies, and one between America and the Arab world. They are all being affected by this unilateral exercise of U.S. power. For now, I've embedded myself on the Western front, where, I can report, all is quiet. France is shocked and awed.

No, there is no massive retreat here from the position staked out by the French government and public opinion against the war in Iraq. But the angry chasm this has opened between Paris and both London and Washington has shocked many people here and prompted some to ask whether France went too far. The title of the latest cover story in the French newsmagazine *Le Point* said it all: "Have They Gone Overboard?" The "they" are President Jacques Chirac and his foreign minister, Dominique de Villepin.

Messrs. Chirac and de Villepin continue to insist that theirs was a principled opposition that will be vindicated. But some voices within the French foreign policy elite and the business community—which depends heavily on the U.S. for trade and investment—are now saying that Messrs. Chirac and de Villepin did indeed go too far. The term you hear most often is "intoxicated." These two became so intoxicated by how popular their anti-U.S., antiwar stand became across Europe, and in the whole world, that they went from legitimately demanding UN endorsement for any use of force in Iraq to blocking any UN-approved use of force—effectively making France Saddam's lawyer and protector.

"People here are a little lost now," said Alain Frachon, the senior editor of *Le Monde*. "They like that their country stood up for a principle, but they don't like the rift with the U.S. They are embarrassed by it."

French officials insist that their dispute with the U.S. was about means, not ends, but that is not true. It was about the huge disparity in power that has emerged between the U.S. and Europe since the end of the cold war, thanks to the vast infusion of technology and money into the U.S. military. That disparity was disguised for a decade by the softer touch of the Clinton team and by the cooperation over second-order issues, such as Kosovo and Bosnia.

But 9/11 posed a first-order threat to America. That, combined with the unilateralist instincts of the Bush team, eventually led to America deploying its expanded power in Iraq, with full force, without asking anyone. Hence the current shock and awe in Europe. As Robert Kagan, whose book *Of Paradise and Power* details this power gap, noted: "We and the Europeans today are like a couple who woke up one day, looked at each other and said, 'You're not the person I married!'"

Yes, we have changed. "What Chirac failed to understand was that between the fall of the Berlin Wall and the fall of the twin towers, a new world was created," said Dominique Moisi, a French foreign policy expert. "In the past, the Americans needed us against the Soviets and would never go so far as to punish France for straying. But that changed after 9/11. You have been at war since then, and we have not, and we have not integrated that reality into our thinking [and what that means] in terms of America's willingness to go it alone. We have fewer common interests now and more divided emotions."

Indeed, the French argue that only bad things will come from this war—more terrorism, a dangerous precedent for preventive war, civilian casualties. The Bush team argues that this war will be a game-changer—that it will spark reform throughout the Arab world and intimidate other tyrants who support terrorists.

Can this war produce more of what the Bush team expects than the Europeans predict? Yes, it can. Can the breach between Europe and America be healed? Yes, it can. But both depend on one thing—how we rebuild Iraq. If we turn Iraq into a mess, the whole world will become even more terrified of unshackled U.S. power. If we rebuild Iraq into a decent, democratizing society—about which fair-minded people would say, "America, you did good"—the power gap between America and Europe will be manageable.

For now, though, Europeans are too stunned by this massive exercise of unilateral U.S. power to think clearly what it's about. I can't quite put my finger on it, but people here seem to feel that a certain contract between America and the world has been broken. Which is why so much is riding, far beyond Iraq, on what the Bush team builds in Iraq. If we build it, they will come around—I hope.

March 23, 2003

MILESTONES FOR THE WAR

I was in a restaurant at Chicago's O'Hare Airport on Sunday, and it had an NCAA basketball game playing on the TV at one end of the bar and the Iraq war on the other. Most people were watching the basketball game—probably because it's so much easier to keep score. How will we know if we are winning in Iraq? Here are six things I am watching for:

1. Have we occupied Baghdad—without leveling the whole city? This war is not being fought simply to disarm the regime of Saddam Hussein. It is being fought to replace that regime with a decent, accountable Iraqi government. That is the real prize here, because only such a government can stabilize Iraq and ensure that another Saddam-like general does not emerge. That can't even begin to happen until the capital has been taken by U.S. and British forces.

2. Have we killed, captured, or expelled Saddam? President Bush keeps saying that this war is not against one man. Nonsense. We have been chasing one man in Iraq for twelve years, and it is essential that he be eliminated because until and unless he is, Iraqis will never express what they really think and feel. Indeed, average Iraqis will not even know what they really feel until the dictator who has run their lives with an iron fist for more than thirty years is removed and they are certain that he is not coming back. (Do not rule out, even now, an Arab-brokered deal for Saddam to leave peacefully.)

3. Have we been able to explain why some Iraqi forces are putting up such a fierce fight? Are these the most elite, pampered Special Republican Guard units, who have benefited most from Saddam's rule and are therefore willing to fight to preserve it? Or are these primarily Sunni Muslim units, terrified that with the fall of Saddam the long reign of the Sunnis of Iraq will end and they will be replaced by the Shiite majority? Or is this happening because even Iraqis who detest Saddam love their homeland and hate the idea of a U.S. occupation—and these Iraqis are ready to resist a foreign occupier, even one that claims to be a liberator?

Knowing the answer is critical for how we reconstruct Iraq. It is not at all unusual for Arabs to detest both their own dictator and a foreign occupier. (See encyclopedia for Israel, invasion of Lebanon, 1982.)

4. Have we won this war and preserved the territorial integrity of Iraq? We can't rebuild Iraq if we can't hold it together. Both the Kurds and the Turks would like to bite off part of northern Iraq. The Bush team claims to be committed to preserving Iraq's unity, in which case it had better tell both the Turks and the Kurds: "Which part of 'no' don't you understand? You Turks are not coming in, and you Kurds are not breaking away."

5. Has an authentic Iraqi liberal nationalist emerged from the U.S. occupation to lead the country? Some pundits are already nominating their favorite Iraqi opposition figures to be Iraq's next leader. My gut tells me the only person who is going to be able to rule Iraq effectively is someone who has lived through Saddam's reign, not sat it out in London or Washington, and who is ready to say no to both tyranny and foreign control in Iraq. But even if he is an Iraqi exile, the next leader of Iraq has to emerge through some sort of consensual process from within Iraq. If the Bush team intends to force Iraq's next leader to quickly embrace Israel, if it intends to impose someone who has been dining with Richard Perle, such a leader will never take root.

6. Is the Iraqi state that emerges from this war accepted as legitimate by Iraq's Arab and Muslim neighbors? That is very important, both for the viability of whatever Iraqi leadership follows Saddam and for the liberalizing effect it may have on others in the neighborhood. In the absence of any UN endorsement for this war, the successor regime to Saddam will have to legitimize itself by becoming something that Arabs and Muslims will point to and say, "We don't like how this was done, but we have to admit America helped build something better in our neighborhood." This outcome is crucial.

If you see these things happening, you'll know that the political ends for which this war was launched are being achieved. If you don't, you'll know we're lost in a sandstorm.

March 26, 2003

NATO'S NEW FRONT

In this time of war, I find it helpful to step back a little. So I went last week to NATO headquarters in Brussels, and, I must say, the view from there was illuminating. What I think I saw were some huge tectonic plates of history moving. Here's how I would describe it: 9/11 was the start of World War III, à la Pearl Harbor; the U.S. invasion of Afghanistan was the initial response, à la the North Africa campaign; the invasion of Iraq was akin to D-Day (I hope it ends as well); and now we are present at the creation of some kind of new global power structure.

At this new historical pivot point, we're still dealing with a bipolar world, only the divide this time is no longer East versus West, but the World of Order versus the World of Disorder. But here's the surprise: the key instrument through which the World of Order will try to deal with threats from the World of Disorder will still be NATO. Only in this new, expanded NATO, Russia will gradually replace France, and the region where the new NATO will direct its peacekeeping energies will shift from the East to the South. Yes, NATO will continue to be based in Europe, but its primary theaters of operation will be the Balkans, Afghanistan, Iraq, and possibly the Arab-Israel frontier.

No, I haven't lost my marbles. Here's what's going on: Ever since the U.S. invasion of Afghanistan, individual countries—first Britain, then Turkey, then the Netherlands and Germany—have taken responsibility for providing the 5,700-man peacekeeping force in Kabul. It is a very expensive job for one country and it is very inefficient to be changing brigades every six months, but that was how the Bush team wanted it. It didn't want NATO getting in the way of its combat troops or nation-building.

But in February, President Bush quietly told NATO's chief, Lord Robertson, that beginning in August, when the current Dutch-German force is supposed to leave Afghanistan, the U.S. would like to see NATO permanently take over peacekeeping duties there and work alongside U.S. combat troops. If this is approved by NATO, for the first time the North Atlantic Treaty Organization will be operating outside Europe, in the heart of the Muslim world.

France is fighting this idea, because it wants to see NATO, the anchor of America's military presence in Europe, wither away. But many key NATO members favor the idea, and what's really interesting is that the Russians have said they would consider sending a platoon as well, under the NATO-Russian partnership. Even the Chinese have winked their approval. Both of these big powers feel threatened by the disorder coming from parts of Central Asia and the Middle East. If France stands in the way, NATO officials say they will just work around it.

What the U.S. is doing in Afghanistan is "internationalizing" the nation-building process there, because we found we simply could not pull it off alone. Eventually, we will have to do the same in Iraq. That is what Prime Minister Tony Blair of Britain came over to tell President Bush this past week. The Bush team keeps arguing that this silly alliance it cobbled together to fight the war in Iraq is multilateral and therefore the moral equivalent of the UN nonsense. Other than Britain, we bought this alliance. Almost every government in it is operating without the support of its people. Fighting this war without international legitimacy is hard enough, but trying to do nation-building without it could be even harder.

Yet the Bush team is right about one thing: Nation-building in Iraq can't be done by the UN. It can't be done by a committee. So what we will eventually need in Iraq is a credible peacekeeping force that is multilateral, legitimate, and still led by the U.S. That will bring us back to NATO, possibly in partnership with some Arab and Muslim armies. This is not your grandfather's NATO anymore. That NATO patrolled the German-Soviet frontier. This one will be patrolling Kabul and Baghdad.

And while NATO is changing, it may just go all the way. NATO's chief, Lord Robertson, is retiring this year (a real loss). A favorite to succeed him is the Norwegian defense minister, Kristin Krohn Devold, a woman. So get ready for this CNN headline: "The NATO alliance, for the first time led by a woman and including a Russian platoon, took over peacekeeping operations in Afghanistan today, as a prelude to taking over peacekeeping in Iraq. France refused to participate."

Yea, we may be present at the creation of a very new world, and no, I have not lost my marbles.

March 30, 2003

COME THE REVOLUTION

CAIRO

To read the Arab press is to think that the entire Arab world is enraged with the U.S. invasion of Iraq, and to some extent that's true. But here's what you don't read: Underneath the rage, there is also a grudging, skeptical curiosity—a curiosity about whether the Americans will actually do what they claim and build a new, more liberal Iraq.

While they may not be able to describe it, many Arabs intuit that this U.S. invasion of Iraq is something they've never seen before—the revolutionary side of U.S. power. Let me explain: For Arabs, American culture has always been revolutionary—from blue jeans to *Baywatch*—but American power, since the cold war, has only been used to preserve the status quo here, keeping friendly Arab kings and autocrats in place.

Even after the cold war ended and America supported—and celebrated—the flowering of democracy from Eastern Europe to Latin America, the Arab world was excluded. In this neighborhood, because of America's desire for steady oil supplies and a safe Israel, America continued to support the status quo and any Arab government that preserved it. Indeed, Gulf War I simply sought to drive Saddam Hussein out of Kuwait to restore the Kuwaiti monarchy and the flow of oil. Once that was done, Saddam was left alone.

And that is why Gulf War II is such a shock to the Arab system, on a par with Napoleon's invasion of Egypt or the Six-Day War. But different people are shocked in different ways.

To begin with, there is the shock of Arab liberals, still a tiny minority, who can't believe that America has finally used its revolutionary power in the Arab world. They are desperate for America to succeed because they think Iraq is too big to ignore, and therefore a real election there would shake the whole Arab region.

Second is the shock of those Arabs in the silent majority. They recognize this is the revolutionary side of U.S. power, but they see it through their own narrative, which says the U.S. is upsetting the status quo not to lift the Arab world up, but rather to put it down so it will submit to whatever America and Israel demand. That's the dominant theme in the Arab media: This war is simply another version of colonialism and imperialism. Al Jazeera uses the same terms for U.S. actions in Iraq as it does for Israeli actions in the West Bank—Iraq is under U.S. "occupation," and Iraqis killed are "martyrs."

As Raymond Stock, a longtime Cairo resident and the biographer of the novelist Naguib Mahfouz, remarked, "People here, particularly the chattering classes who watch the Arab satellite channels, are so much better misinformed than you think. The Arab media generally tells them what they want to hear and shows them what they want to see. There is a narrative that is deeply embedded, and no amount of embedded reporting from the other side will change it. Only a different Iraq can do that."

But there is a third school: Egyptian officials, who are instinctively pro-American but are shocked that the Bush team would use its revolutionary power to try to remake Iraq. Egyptian officials view this as a fool's errand because they view Iraq as a congenitally divided, tribal country that can be ruled only by an iron fist.

Whose view will be redeemed depends on how Iraq plays out, but, trust me, everyone's watching. I spent this afternoon with the American studies class at Cairo University. The professor, Mohamed Kamel, summed up the mood: "In 1975, Richard Nixon came to Egypt and the government turned out huge crowds. Some Americans made fun of Nixon for this, and Nixon defended himself by saying, 'You can force people to go out and welcome a foreign leader, but you can't force them to smile.' Maybe the Iraqis will eventually stop resisting you. But that will not make this war legitimate. What the U.S. needs to do is make the Iraqis smile. If you do that, people will consider this a success."

There is a lot riding on that smile, Mr. Kamel added, because this is the first "Arab-American war." This is not about Arabs and Israelis. This is about America getting inside the Arab world—not just with its power or culture, but with its ideals. It is a war for what America stands for. "If it backfires," Mr. Kamel concluded, "if you don't deliver, it will really have a big impact. People will not just say your policies are bad, but that your ideas are a fake, you don't really believe them, or you don't know how to implement them."

In short, we need to finish the peace better than we started the war.

April 2, 2003

WATCH OUT FOR HIJACKERS

The State Department has been upset about how the Arab media have been portraying the U.S. invasion of Iraq. Personally, I don't see what the problem is. As far as I can tell from watching the Arab satellite networks there's only a one-word—actually just a one-letter—difference in how they report the war and how U.S. networks report it. CNN calls it "America's war in Iraq," and Arab television calls it "America's war on Iraq."

What a difference a letter makes. As I have traveled around the Arab world watching this war, I've been thinking a lot about that one letter. It contains an important message for President Bush: Beware of hijackers.

Saddam Hussein's regime will soon be finished, and the moment for building the peace will be upon us. As soon as it arrives, there will be people who will try to hijack this peace and turn it to their own ends. Mr. Bush must be ready to fend off these hijackers, who will come in two varieties.

One group will emerge from the surrounding Arab states—all the old-guard Arab intellectuals and Nasserites who dominate the Arab media, along with many of the regimes and stale institutions, like the Arab League, that feel threatened by even a whiff of democracy coming from Iraq. These groups will be merciless in delegitimizing and denouncing any Iraqis who come to power after the war—if it appears that they were installed by the U.S.

That means the U.S. has to move quickly to create a process through which moderate, but legitimate, Iraqi nationalists can emerge to start running their country and U.S. forces can recede into the background. We have only one chance to make a first impression in how we intend to reshape Iraq, and we must make a good one. America somewhat underestimated the resistance it would meet when it invaded Iraq; it should not now overestimate how much time it has to rule Iraq with U.S. generals before meeting political resistance.

The Egyptian playwright Ali Salem, a courageous Arab liberal, told me in Cairo the other day: "To my fellow Arab pen carriers, I say, 'Do not hasten to denounce them,'" meaning Iraqis who will work with the U.S. to rebuild their country. "'Do not resort to these ready-made accusations that such Iraqis are 'agents' of the Americans because it will take us nowhere. It will only blind our eyes to our real problems and diseases, which is the need for development and human rights. Don't stick your pens in the Iraqi wheel.'"

But to the Americans, Mr. Salem said, "'Please defend America the idea—defend it—because we are working to embody this idea—to make it stretch across the whole planet. Do not occupy our land under any slogan. It's hard, I know it's hard. [But] if there will be an American general presiding over Iraq [for long], it will be bad for us Arab liberals and for you.'"

The other hijackers are the ideologues within the Bush team who have been dealing with the Iraqi exile leaders and will try to install one of them, like Ahmad Chalabi, to run Iraq. I don't know any of these exiles, and I have nothing against them. But anyone who thinks they can simply be installed by America and take root in Iraqi soil is out of his mind.

Mr. Bush should visit the West Bank. It is a cautionary tale of an occupation gone wrong. It is a miserable landscape of settlements, bypass roads, barbed wire, and cement walls. Why? Because the Israeli and Palestinian mainstreams have spent the last thirty-six years, since Israel's victory in 1967, avoiding any clear decision on how to govern this land. So those extremists who had a clear idea, like the settlers and Hamas, hijacked the situation and drove the agenda.

Mr. Bush needs to approach the Iraq peace with the same single-minded focus with which he approached the war. I went to Ramallah to visit the Palestinian pollster Khalil Shikaki, a man steeped in what it takes to produce legitimacy in an Arab milieu, and I asked him what Mr. Bush should focus upon. "Focus on the process," he said, "not on a specific person. Iraqis must have confidence in the process. It must be seen as legitimate and fair."

Israel has been trying to get rid of Yasir Arafat for years, but it was a legitimate process, managed by the Palestinian legislature, that last month produced the first legitimate alternative: the first Palestinian prime minister, Mahmoud Abbas.

No, this is not going to be easy. Because the ideal Iraqi we are looking for is one who will say no to Saddam Hussein, no to Nasserism, no to tyranny, and no to any permanent U.S. presence in Iraq.

April 6, 2003

HOLD YOUR APPLAUSE

———

UMM QASR, IRAQ

It's hard to smile when there's no water. It's hard to applaud when you're frightened. It's hard to say, "Thank you for liberating me" when liberation has meant that looters have ransacked everything from the grain silos to the local school, where they even took away the blackboard.

That was what I found when spending the day in Umm Qasr and its hospital in southern Iraq. Umm Qasr was the first town liberated by coalition forces. But twenty days into the war, it is without running water, security, or adequate food supplies. I went in with a Kuwaiti relief team, who, taking pity on the Iraqis, tossed out extra food from a bus window as we left. The Umm Qasr townsfolk scrambled after that food like pigeons jostling for bread crumbs in a park.

This was a scene of humiliation, not liberation. We must do better.

I am sure we will, as more relief crews arrive. But this scene explained to me why, even here in the anti-Saddam Shia heartland of southern Iraq, no one is giving U.S. troops a standing ovation. Applause? When I asked Lt. Col. Richard Murphy, part of the U.S. relief operation, how Iraqis were greeting his men, he answered bluntly and honestly: "I have not detected any overt hostility."

Overt hostility? We've gone from expecting applause to being relieved that there is no overt hostility. And we've been here only twenty days. As I said, I'm certain things will improve with time. But for now, America has broken the old order—Saddam's regime—but it has yet to put in place a new order, and the vacuum is being filled in way too many places by looters, thugs, chaos, thirst, hunger, and insecurity. A particular problem here in the south is the fact that British troops still have not totally secured Basra, the regional center. Without free access to Basra, the whole southern economy is stalled.

It would be idiotic even to ask Iraqis here how they felt about politics. They are in a pre-political, primordial state of nature. For the moment, Saddam has been replaced by Hobbes, not Bush. When I asked Dr. Safaa Khalaf at Umm Qasr Hospital why the reception for U.S. forces had been so muted, he answered: "Many people here have sons who were soldiers. They were forced to join the army. Many people lost their sons. They are angry from the war. Since the war, no water, no food, no electricity. . . . We have not had water for washing or drinking for five days. . . . There is no law, no policeman to arrest people. I don't see yet the American reign of running the country."

The scene at Umm Qasr Hospital is tragic. A woman who delivered a baby an hour earlier is limping home, and her mother has the baby tucked under her black robe. An old orange Dodge speeds up and a malnourished teenage boy moans on the backseat. A little kid is playing with an X-ray film of someone's limb. In the hospital lab, the sink is piled with bloody test tubes, waiting to be washed when the water comes back on.

What is striking, though, is that after people get through complaining to you about their situation, they each seem to have a story about a family member or cousin who was arbitrarily jailed or killed by Saddam's thugs. They are truly glad to be rid of him. America did good in doing that, so now we must build a peace we can be equally proud of.

But this is such a broken land. Its spirit was broken by Saddam long before we arrived, and now, because of this war, its major cities and iron-fisted order are being broken as well. Killing Saddam alone will not bring America the thank-yous it expects because Iraqis are not yet feeling free. Only replacing Saddam's order with a better order will do that. "There is no freedom because there is no security," said Dr. Mohammed al-Mansuri, the hospital's director.

We are so caught up with our own story of "America's liberation of Iraq," and the Arab TV networks are so caught up with their own story of "America's occupation of Iraq" that everyone seems to have lost sight of the real lives of Iraqis.

"We are lost," said Zakiya Jassim, a hospital maintenance worker. "The situation is getting worse. I don't care about Saddam. He is far away. I want my country to be normal."

America broke Iraq; now America owns Iraq, and it owns the primary responsibility for normalizing it. If the water doesn't flow, if the food doesn't arrive, if the rains don't come and if the sun doesn't shine, it's now America's fault. We'd better get used to it, we'd better make things right, we'd better do it soon, and we'd better get all the help we can get.

April 9, 2003

THE SAND WALL

UMM QASR, IRAQ

As Berlin Walls go, the twenty-foot-high dirt berm around Iraq's southern port of Umm Qasr—the first wall to fall in the liberation of Iraq—
isn't much to look at, but it's a fitting symbol for this war. It is a sand wall,
easily breached by American power, exposing a rotten dictatorship with
little popular support on the other side. This area is full of regimes protected by such sand walls.

But unlike the Berlin Wall, whose fall unleashed a flowering of freedom all across Eastern Europe, the fall of the Sand Wall alone will not
do that. There are still two other walls holding back the explosion of freedom in the Arab East—much harder walls—that will also have to fall.

The first is the wall in the Arab mind. I hit my head against that wall
two weeks ago in Cairo, while discussing the war with Egyptian opposition journalists in Feshawi's teahouse, the writing hangout of Naguib
Mahfouz. These journalists could see nothing good coming from the
U.S. "occupation" of Iraq, which they insisted was being done only to
put Arabs down, strengthen Israel, and extract oil.

Such encounters made clear to me that America was not just at war
with Saddam, but with Saddamism: an entrenched Arab mind-set, born
of years of colonialism and humiliation, that insists that upholding Arab
dignity and nationalism by defying the West is more important than freedom, democracy, and modernization.

Throughout this war, Saddamism was peddled by Al Jazeera television, Arab intellectuals, and the Arab League. You cannot imagine how
much distress there is among certain Arab elites that the people of Iraq
preferred liberation by America to more defiance under Saddam. The
morning after Baghdad was liberated, Abdul Hamid Ahmad, editor of
The Gulf News, wrote, like so many of his colleagues: "This is a heartbreaking moment for any Arab, seeing marines roaming the streets of
Baghdad."

The wall of Saddamism, which helped bad leaders stay in power and
young Arabs remain backward and angry, was as dangerous as Saddam.
"The social, political, cultural, and economic malaise in this part of the
world had become a threat to American security—it produced 9/11,"

said Shafeeq Ghabra, president of the American University of Kuwait. "This war was a challenge to the entire Arab system, which is why so many Arabs opposed it. The war to liberate Kuwait from Iraq [in 1991] was outpatient surgery. This war was open-heart surgery."

But this open-heart surgery will succeed in toppling both Saddam and Saddamism only if we are successful in creating a healthy Iraq—an Arab state where people can find dignity, not just by saying no to the West but by building a decent, tolerant, modernizing society that they can be proud of, an Arab state where people can speak the truth and that other Arabs would want to emulate. The widespread looting that has followed the fall of Saddam tells me just how hard that will be. So far, all that we have unleashed in Iraq is chaos, not freedom. There is no civil society here. We are starting from scratch.

And then we must also take down the third wall—the wall of cement, fear, and barbed wire being erected between Israelis and Palestinians. We must defuse this conflict. If we let this Israeli-Palestinian wall stand, it will reinforce the wall of Saddamism. Arab dictators will hide behind this conflict as an excuse not to change, Arab intellectuals will use it to delegitimize U.S. power out here, and the enemies of the new leaders in Iraq will use it to embarrass them for working with us.

When one of the Egyptian journalists at Feshawi's insisted that we were out to "occupy Iraq," I quoted to him a line from Colin Powell: "America is as powerful as any empire in history, but when it has invaded other countries the only piece of land it has ever asked for was a tiny plot to bury its soldiers who would not be returning home." He actually smiled at that.

The moment reminded me of something the Arab columnist Rami Khouri liked to say, that Arabs for too long have seen the strength of America, but not the "goodness" of America. Partly that's because their media willfully distorted what we did, and partly it's because America has used its power out here more to defend oil and Israel than democracy. This war in Iraq was meant to bring the idealistic side of U.S. power into the Arab world.

Our task now is to apply that idealism to rebuilding Iraq and resolving the Palestine question. If we do it right, I am certain the other walls in this region will be taken down by the people themselves—and never again will we have to ask for even the tiniest plot of land to bury our soldiers here.

April 13, 2003

ROTO-ROOTER

I was chatting with an Egyptian friend in Cairo two weeks ago when she got a joke e-mailed to her cell phone, which she immediately shared with me. It read: "President Bush: Take Syria—get Lebanon for free."

Now that it's become apparent that the Syrians have given military help to Saddam Hussein's army and are alleged to be providing sanctuary for members of his despised clique, the question of whether the Bush team might take out Syria's regime next has been raised. After all, when the Roto-Rooter truck's in the neighborhood, why not take advantage?

My short answer is this: There are many good reasons for the U.S. to promote reform or regime change in Syria, but we have no legal basis to do it now by military means and are not likely to try. Yet Syria, and countries like it, will be a problem, and we need a new strategic doctrine in the post-Saddam era to deal with them.

Let's explore this in detail. For me, the best argument for pressuring Syria is that France's foreign minister, Dominique de Villepin, said on Sunday that this was not the time to be pressuring Syria. Ever since he blocked any UN military action against Saddam, Mr. de Villepin has become my moral compass: Whatever he is for, I am against. And whatever he is against, I am for.

Yes, Mr. de Villepin did say, while actually visiting Lebanon, that the world should focus not on Syria, but on rebuilding Iraq and advancing the Arab-Israeli peace process. But what he neglected to mention is something I am also for, and which France should be for and the world should be for: the end of Syria's occupation of Lebanon, which has been going on since 1976.

And that leads to the second-best reason for regime change in Syria: It could set Lebanon free. Lebanon is the only Arab country to have had a functioning democracy. It is also the Arab country that is most hard-wired for globalization. Trading and entrepreneurship are in Lebanon's DNA. Lebanon should be leading the Arab world into globalization, but it has not been able to play its natural Hong Kong role because Syria has choked the life out of the place.

Iraq is the only Arab country that combines oil, water, brains, and secularism. Lebanon has water, brains, secularism, and a liberal tradition.

The Palestinians have a similar potential, which is why I favor "triple self-determination." If Lebanon, Iraq, and a Palestinian state could all be made into functioning, decent, free-market, self-governing societies, it would be enough to tilt the entire Arab world onto a modernizing track.

The third reason for taking on the Syrian regime is the fact that next to Saddam's regime, Syria's is the most repressive in the region and the one most deeply implicated in protecting terrorists. Syria must get out of Lebanon, and Israel also needs to get out of Syria (the Golan), but that is going to happen only if there is a reformed Syrian government that no longer needs the conflict with Israel to justify its militarization of Syrian society.

But as I said, we're not going to invade Syria to change Syria. So what to do? The Middle East expert Stephen Cohen offers a useful concept. He calls it "aggressive engagement—something between outright military engagement and useless constructive engagement."

Bush-style military engagement with Syria is not in the cards right now. But French-style constructive engagement, which is just a cover for dancing with dictators, is a fraud. The natural third way is "aggressive engagement." That means getting in Syria's face every day. Reminding the world of its twenty-seven-year occupation of Lebanon and how much it has held that country back, and reminding the Syrian people of how much they've been deprived of a better future by their own thuggish regime.

Aggressive engagement of Syria also feels right to me because a U.S. attack on Syria right now would make many Iraqis feel very uncomfortable about working openly with America. Iraq may be liberated from Saddam, but never forget that it is still an Arab country, dominated by an Arab narrative. Iraqis are not watching Fox TV.

Which is why I would also apply "aggressive engagement"—in different ways—to Yasir Arafat and Ariel Sharon. The Arabs need to force Mr. Arafat to retire, and the Americans need to test Mr. Sharon's professed willingness for a fair deal with a reformed Palestinian Authority.

Aggressive engagement in support of triple self-determination—for Lebanon, Iraq, and the Palestinians—would be a great way to follow up and help consolidate the liberation of Iraq.

April 16, 2003

THE THIRD BUBBLE

Wars are always clarifying, and what this war clarified most was the degree to which there were actually three bubbles that burst at the beginning of the twenty-first century: a stock market bubble, a corporate ethics bubble, and a terrorism bubble.

The stock market bubble we're all too familiar with. When it burst three years ago, millions of people all over the world were made more sober investors. The second bubble was the corporate governance bubble — a buildup of ethical lapses by management that burst with Enron and Arthur Andersen, producing a revolution in boardroom practices.

But there was a third bubble that had built up over the 1990s — the terrorism bubble. It started with the suicide bombings against U.S. troops in Saudi Arabia, was followed by attacks on the U.S. embassies in East Africa and on the U.S.S. *Cole*, then ballooned with the rise of Palestinian suicide terrorism in Israel, and finally peaked with Al Qaeda's attack of 9/11.

Like the stock market and corporate bubbles, the terrorism bubble was the product of a kind of temporary insanity, in which basic norms were ignored and excessive behavior was justified by new theories. In the case of the terrorism bubble, we were told that suicide bombing was the work of desperate people who had no other way to get America's or Israel's attention.

People across Europe and the Arab-Muslim world bought such theories. Some Muslim religious leaders even came up with rulings justifying the suicide bombing of civilians in pizza parlors. Arab media called the terrorists "martyrs." It was moral creative accounting: If you are weak, there is no limit to what you can do, and if you are strong — like America and Israel — you have no moral right to defend yourself. Worse, after 9/11, some in the Arab-Muslim world actually believed they had found a new balance of power with America — through the suicide bomber.

And we in America believed them, so we blew up the bubbles more. We contorted our whole open society and imprisoned ourselves. My daughter's high school symphony orchestra trip to New Orleans was canceled because of the recent terrorism alerts. Insane.

Yes, this Iraq war was about Saddam. For George Bush and Tony Blair, though, I think it was about something larger but unstated. They were implicitly saying: "This terrorism bubble has come to threaten open societies and all they value, so we're going to use Iraq—because we can—to demonstrate to you that we'll come right into the heart of your world to burst this bubble. Take note."

We and the Arab-Muslim world must now draw the right conclusions. One hopes Americans will now stop overreacting to 9/11. Al Qaeda is not the Soviet Union. Saddam was not Stalin. And terrorism is not communism. America sliced right through Iraq. It did so because we are a free-market democracy that is capable of amassing huge amounts of technical power. And it did so because our soldiers so cherish what they have that they were ready to fight house to house from Basra to Baghdad. That was the real shock and awe for Iraqis—because the terrorism bubble said Nasdaq-obsessed Americans were so caught up with the frivolity of modern life, they had lost the will to fight. Wrong.

We are strong because of who we are. Iraq was weak because of what it was. So yes, let's add a metal detector or two at the airports, but let's stop thinking we have to remake our whole society, constrict all civil liberties, ban all Arab students, and throw out all our foreign policy doctrines that have served us so well—from deterrence to collective security to the usefulness of the UN—to meet this new terrorism threat. We do not, and we must not.

The message to Arabs who are depressed at how quickly Saddam folded is this: You can't take on America without building something of substance of your own. You thought rogues like Saddam would bring you dignity. They have only distracted you from doing what it takes to build your own societies.

We are all now in a post-bubble world. We need to calm down and get back to nurturing the sort of open society that is the real source of our strength. The Arab-Muslim states need to understand that if they build up this terrorism bubble again—and it may well happen—America will burst it again. But they also need to know that if they want to rebuild their societies—starting with Iraq—on a real foundation of decency, tolerance, and rule of law, we will pay any price and bear any burden to help them—if they want us.

April 20, 2003

DIARY

———◆———

Travels in a World Without Walls:

September 11, 2001–July 3, 2002

September 11, 2001, was such a supremely American moment, I wish I could have gone through it with my own family. But random violence often bonds us with the most unlikely people—the passengers in an airplane, the nameless seatmate on a bus, or the faceless crowd in an elevator. September 11 found me in Israel, far from home, with a cabdriver I barely knew and secretaries I had never met.

Ironically, September 11 was a Tuesday, and my column had appeared that morning from Israel. I had begun with a story about my daughter Natalie. Because I travel a lot, my girls tend not to focus on where I'm off to next until I'm about to disappear. The day before I was leaving for Israel, Natalie asked me where I was going and I told her "Israel," and she asked me, with a worried frown: "Why do you have to go there?" So I began my column from Jerusalem, which appeared on the morning of September 11, with that anecdote—"Why do you have to go there?"—to illustrate the point that one kind of fallout from the collapse of the Oslo peace process was that Israel in my daughter's eyes had become just another dangerous place to be avoided—even though she had been born there. The column was headlined "Walls," because I was trying to make the point that Israelis and Palestinians were each trying to protect themselves from the other by building walls, either on the ground or in their heads.

Just as *New York Times* readers were finishing their breakfasts that morning, some of them probably reading my column about how perilous Israel had become, four hijacked airliners were slamming into the World Trade Center, a field in Pennsylvania, and the Pentagon, just a few miles from my own house. My family thought I was at Ground Zero by being in Jerusalem, and it turned out to be the other way around.

At the time, I was just finishing an interview with Tel Aviv University president Itamar Rabinovich and had a gap in my schedule before my next interview at 6 p.m. So I left Itamar's office in the suburbs of Tel Aviv, walked down to my cab, and put my hand on the rear door to reach in and get my bathing suit off the backseat. I was going to take a swim in the Mediterranean. But before I could open the door, my driver, Yoram, with a look of horror painted on his face, said half in English, half in Hebrew that Israel Radio had just reported that two planes had hit the World Trade Center (the first at 8:48 a.m. EDT). Maybe because I had done a lot of research about the first attempt to blow up the Twin Towers, on February 26, 1993, for my book *The Lexus and the Olive Tree*, I did not waste even a second, not a split second, wondering whether this was an accident.

I ran back to Itamar's office, where the university's director of public relations and her staff were already watching, gape-mouthed, the instant replay on CNN of the second plane slamming into one of the towers. In a single phrase, one of the secretaries summed up the entire Israeli reaction to September 11: "Now the world will finally understand what we've been facing," she declared. Then, with barely a pause, she added: "Oh my God, they're going to blame us."

She was right on both counts.

As I grappled to understand what I was seeing on the TV, my mind kept flashing back to an unlikely scene a decade earlier. It was the press conference that Secretary of State James A. Baker III gave after his meeting with Iraqi deputy prime minister Tariq Aziz in Geneva on January 9, 1991. Baker had met with Aziz all day in the Geneva Intercontinental Hotel in an effort to persuade Iraq to back down and leave Kuwait peacefully; otherwise, he warned, a U.S.-led coalition would invade Kuwait and drive the Iraqi army out by force. As the Baker-Aziz meeting dragged on, we, the press, sat around interviewing each other. (For some reason, I remember that the staff at the Intercontinental had put a huge, life-size stuffed camel in the hotel newsroom, a bizarre nod to the Middle East origins of this story.) After hours of meetings between Baker and Aziz, all the reporters were finally summoned to the hotel ballroom for the press conference to learn whether Baker had been successful in talking Iraq out of Kuwait.

Baker spoke for several minutes, laying out in detail every argument he had made to Aziz to persuade the Iraqis to withdraw peacefully. I was sitting in the front row. I had my computer on my lap, and was typing notes as Baker spoke. Finally, after a long prologue about all the different ways he had tried to talk Iraq out of Kuwait, Secretary Baker said, "But regrettably, ladies and gentlemen, in over six hours of talks, I heard nothing today that suggested to me any Iraqi flexibility whatsoever. . . ."

As soon as he said those words my hands started to quiver and I couldn't quite move my fingers, because I knew that out of that simple sentence—"Regrettably, ladies and gentlemen . . ."—a major war would be born and history, whichever way it had been flowing that morning, would take a sharp right turn, making the world a different place. I always thought if I would have written a book about the Gulf War, I would have called it *Regrettably, Ladies and Gentlemen*.

And so, as I watched live on CNN as the Twin Towers imploded and collapsed onto the streets of Manhattan, it was equally obvious to me that history, wherever it had been heading before the morning of September 11, had just taken another sharp right turn, and a whole new history would flow from this towering inferno. And that is why, quite involuntarily, I just kept thinking to myself: "Regrettably, ladies and gentlemen . . ."

I stayed with those Israeli women for several hours, watching CNN on their office TV. Phone calls started coming. The Israeli newspaper *Yediot Ahronot* wanted to know if I would write an instant essay. No, I wouldn't. I shot off an e-mail to my wife and girls to let them know I was OK and to ask how they were doing. I watched more TV. The women kept asking what it would mean for Israel. "I don't know," I snapped. "It's World War III," I thought to myself. "It's much bigger than Israel."

I started to feel suffocated there. I wanted to be alone. So my taxi driver and I drove toward Jerusalem, but the highway was temporarily closed around the airport and there was a five-mile-long traffic jam. So we headed into Tel Aviv and I got a room at the Hilton, on the beach. I watched more TV. I ran into friends in the lobby of the Hilton, who asked if I would like to join them for dinner. I didn't. I wanted to be alone. I watched more TV. And then finally, around 10 p.m., I went out for a walk alone on the seafront.

It was there, massaged by the Mediterranean breeze, that my head started to clear and I finally gave birth to the thought that had been bothering me most: "What kind of world are my two girls going to grow up in?" And it was there that I first completed the sentence: "Regrettably, ladies and gentlemen . . . Regrettably, ladies and gentlemen, my girls and yours will not grow up in the same world that we did. History just took a right turn into a blind alley and something very dear has just been taken away from us."

And that was when I first started to get angry.

I didn't notice that anger at first. But sometime in October, about six weeks after the attack, several friends and readers remarked to me, "Your columns are really angry." I honestly hadn't thought about it, but once they pointed it out I said, "You know, I *am* angry." I was angry that my country had been violated in this way, angry at the senseless deaths of so many innocent people, angry at the megalomaniacal arrogance of Osama bin Laden and his men, who so blithely assumed that their grievance, whatever it was, justified this mass murder. I was angry that my stockbroker, Mark Madden, lost his brother in one of the Trade Center towers, and angry about all the analyses of why people around the world hate America—when all I could think about was how much I hated these terrorists.

But most of all, of course, I was angry that the America I had grown up in would never quite be the same for my two daughters, ages thirteen and sixteen. It only took a couple of weeks after September 11 before my daughter Orly's county youth orchestra, which had been planning a tour to Italy over the summer—a tour which had motivated her to practice extra-hard all summer in order to retain her chair in the violin section— announced that the trip was canceled. It was too dangerous for an American orchestra to be traveling around Italy, the staff concluded. I thought this was an awful decision. In fact, I was outraged. But other parents were more worried, and there was no persuading them otherwise—although I wanted to. It was a new world knocking, and I didn't want to let it in.

Ditto at my daughter Natalie's junior high school. She was supposed to take a class trip to New York three weeks after September 11. We had a parents' meeting. The overwhelming sentiment was against going. Some of the teachers said their own kids would be afraid to see them go. I understood, but I didn't understand. It was a new world knocking, and I didn't want to let it in. So I refused to acknowledge that there was any reason to change any plans. I insisted on going to concerts and Baltimore Orioles baseball games; I chafed at the extra searches suddenly imposed at Camden Yards, and got enraged while standing in long security lines at Dulles Airport. It was a new world knocking—not the one I had grown up in, but the one my girls would now grow up in—and I didn't want to let it in.

To be honest, it wasn't only about my kids. Because, as a journalist, I often travel to war zones and other not particularly nice places, coming home to America has always had a special feel for me. Often I would come home from trips abroad—from Russia or Venezuela, the West Bank or Africa—and my wife would ask me how it was, and I would answer: "You know, honey, the wheels aren't on very tight out there." I would often come home and marvel at things like Camden Yards—the beautiful downtown stadium in Baltimore—or the sleek, clean subway system in Washington, and think to myself how much community, how many tax dollars, and how much sheer working together by different people, by different government agencies and the private sector, it took to build these public institutions. And I would think how great it was to live in a country that could come together to create the public goods and public spaces that make up the quilt and quality of American society. No matter how crazy the world was out there, America was my cocoon that I could always crawl back into, where my girls would always be safe.

That's what was violated on September 11, and it was violated by people who didn't even know us.

That's why the American in me was so angry. But the reporter in me was also very curious. Who exactly were these people? What historical forces produced them? So these two impulses—anger and curiosity—have been my emotional companions ever since September 11, wrestling for my head and heart, one winning one day and the other the next. They have been the hammer and anvil out of which every one of my columns was forged.

Late on the evening of September 11, I started to focus on what I should say in my first post-attack column from Israel. By happenstance, earlier in the week I had interviewed Major General Amos Malka, the head of the Israeli army's intelligence branch. I had always been impressed with General Malka's own intelligence, so late on September 11 I left him a message to see whether we could get together for a talk on the morning of September 12, since the world had just been turned upside down. He was already heading for Washington, but he set up a 7 a.m. session for me with some of the Israeli army's key terrorism experts. Obviously I was interested in what information or insight the Israelis might have about who was behind the attack on the United States. Already, Osama bin Laden had emerged as a suspect. But I was even more interested in what, if anything, the Israelis had learned from their own long experience with suicide bombers. How does an army deter people who want to kill themselves? This was a very new problem for America, because, as Israeli writer Ari Shavit pointed out to me, America's longtime enemy in the cold war—the Soviet Union—loved life more than it hated us. That's why, in the end, it backed away from mutual assured destruction during the Cuban missile crisis. But these suicide bombers were a very different kind of enemy—they hated us more than they loved life.

The Israeli army terrorism experts confided something that has stuck with me ever since: The only time Israel had really effectively curbed suicide attacks from Palestinians was when Yasir Arafat did it for them—when he had either the incentive, or the pressure on him, to restrain his own people and they had the incentive, or pressure, to restrain themselves. It was very simple, the Israelis explained: You can have the best intelligence network in the world, but there is no way that Israelis will ever be able to penetrate Palestinian society better than Palestinians. There is no way they will ever know Ahmed from Mohammed the way Ahmed and Mohammed do, because that knowledge is embedded in their family ties, culture, and DNA—things unspoken. Only the host society can penetrate itself enough to effectively restrain or delegitimize its own suicide bombers. Outsiders can't.

That insight has stayed with me ever since: We can only win this war on terrorism if we have local partners ready to take preemptive action (not just wait for us to call them) out of their own self-interest—whether it is closing down suspect charities or rounding up suspected terrorists or speaking out to denounce suicide bombing. Yes, sometimes we will get lucky, sometimes the terrorists will make mistakes. But to effectively deter them in a sustained way, we need partners within their own societies and partners in their own police who will expose them, and partners in their own governments and partners in their own media who will delegitimize them.

The other insight I remember from that session came from one of the Israeli army officers. I had mentioned in passing that there must have been an "intelligence agency" or government behind these hijackers. Bin Laden and his boys, or some ad hoc group like them, I argued, could not have done this alone, especially given the amazing skill it took to have flown those planes so accurately into the World Trade Center towers.

One of the Israeli experts demurred: "It's not that difficult to learn how to fly a plane once it's up in the air," he said. "And remember, they never had to learn how to land."

MR. HOBBES'S NEIGHBORHOOD

A couple of days later I decided to go to Jordan, since I still could not fly home. I wanted to soak up the fallout from September 11 from somewhere in the Arab-Muslim world. Within hours of the bombing I had received many e-mails from Arab and Muslim friends around the world, apologizing for what had happened in the name of Islam and checking on me and my family. I was heartened by every one of them. They were a reminder of how many good people there are in that part of the world, people desperate for a different future for their own countries—different from both bin Laden's religious totalitarianism and the military dictators and autocrats under whom they are trapped. But there was one e-mail that really disturbed me. It came from a close American friend living in Dubai. He told me that a rumor had spread throughout the Persian Gulf that four thousand Jews had stayed away from work in the World Trade Center on the morning of September 11 because they had been warned not to go there that day by Israeli intelligence. He asked me: "Is that true?" His message rattled me because, I thought, if such an intelligent person could even wonder aloud if that were true, the rumor must be pervasive, and it must mean that the masses, who would never check, were thoroughly predisposed to believe such a thing. This was the first time I would meet this outrageous fabrication, but unfortunately not the last. I would meet it over and over and over again in every Arab or Muslim country I visited after September 11, and if you took a poll—a real poll—today, you would find that the vast majority of Arabs and Muslims still believe this terrible lie. It was the beginning of an epidemic of denial that spread throughout the Arab-Muslim world, which refused to really face how this outrage could have come from its bosom.

My second night in Amman, a Jordanian friend organized a dinner with some young Jordanian techies and businesspeople. They were a smart and lively group and I found the discussion a balm, even though at times I could sense that they did not greet the events of September 11 with quite the horror I did, nor did they think America was as blameless as I did. It was also my first inkling of this attitude across the Arab and Muslim world, something else I would meet many times over—in much worse forms. These Jordanians did not hate America. To the contrary, they admired it. But precisely because they admired it, precisely because they wanted America on their side, they resented the fact that America seemed always to side with Israel and never with the Palestinians. So, like many in the Arab world, their view was that if America got humbled a little bit, got to taste a little Arab anger, it wouldn't be altogether bad—particularly for the Bush administration, which gave off the feeling that it really did not care what Arabs thought or felt.

An American diplomat in Saudi Arabia later explained the immediate post-9/11 mood in the Arab world to me thus: There are many Arabs, he said, who are "frustrated and feeling inferior." They "have a lot of pent-up emotions," he added. "Their attitude about September 11 was:

I am not celebrating your hurt, but I am happy something happened to you that you could not control, because I live in a world where I can't control my life."

This sense of having fallen behind in the quest for modernity, this sense of having failed to build the freedom and technological prowess of the West, is pervasive in the Arab-Muslim world today. And it expresses itself in various forms: denial of responsibility for bad things that come out of the Arab world, conspiracy theories that relieve them of any responsibility, and a constant love-hate relationship with America.

Those are the *pro*-American Arabs. The hardcore *anti*-American Arabs, whose numbers are not small, were not so ambivalent about September 11. That point was also first driven home to me in Jordan. One of the Jordanian entrepreneurs at the dinner ran a popular Arabic Internet site. His company had done on-line polling in the hours and days immediately after September 11. The results were so overwhelmingly in support of the attack, he told us that night, that "we decided to stop taking polls."

Where did the strongest support for the attack come from? I asked.

"From subscribers in Saudi Arabia and the United Arab Emirates," he answered without hesitation. He stressed that on his Web site you could not send this anti-American stuff in anonymously. You had to identify yourself, and people were proud to put their name with their rage. Hmmmm, I started to think, Houston, we may have a problem here that is much deeper than we originally thought.

The other early insight I got from visiting Jordan came from interviewing young King Abdullah. He and his wife, Queen Rania, invited me to their home one afternoon to talk about the events. In the king's private study he has a huge collection of handguns that covers an entire wall, floor to ceiling. All those guns struck me as out of sync with his gentle nature. But as I sat there contemplating them, it occurred to me that they explained another reason why Jordanians and Arabs were not as shocked by September 11 as Americans: They do not live in Mr. Rogers' neighborhood. They live in Mr. Hobbes's neighborhood.

So for them September 11 was something only slightly different in degree, slightly more outrageous and terrifying, than things that go on around them every day. If you've lived through the '48, '56, '67, '73, and '82 wars, if you've lived through Black September (when a Palestinian gunman assassinated a Jordanian prime minister outside the Cairo Sheraton and then knelt down to try to sip his blood) or the Gulf War, if you've lived through countless assassinations, hijackings, and car bombings, then September 11 is not the biggest or most frightening thing that has happened in your life. Not at all. For many Middle East residents, September 11 was just the second Tuesday in the ninth month of the year 2001.

King Abdullah was sincerely sympathetic, not only because he is instinctively pro-American but because Jordan and his throne also had been threatened by the bin Laden network. But the thing I learned most from him was very simple: "Follow the money." It was he who first explained to me that some Middle East charities and religious NGOs were not always what they appeared to be, particularly in the Gulf, and that Osama bin Laden had funded his operations in Afghanistan, Jordan, and other places by siphoning off charitable donations given by good, but unsuspecting, Muslims.

When it came time to leave Jordan, I took an early morning flight to London. As I was sitting in the departure lounge waiting to leave at 3 a.m., I took out my computer and began working on a column. A few minutes later a young Arab man in a well-tailored business suit walked up to me and asked, "Are you Thomas Friedman?"

"Yes, I am," I nodded.

"That's amazing," he said. "I'm reading your book right now—*From Beirut to Jerusalem*." He had it in his hand.

"Hey, that's great," I said. "Where are you from?"

He was an Egyptian, he said, working for a major Western oil company. He asked me what I was writing and I told him I was working on a column about whether people in the Arab-Muslim world were really upset or not with what bin Laden had done. In fact, I think I actually read him some of it. He told me he thought it was a little soft and didn't totally capture what people were feeling. He tried to explain it to me in a way I would understand—by throwing my own words back in my face.

As best I can recollect, he said: "You know how in your book you said about the terrorists in Beirut that they were not that different from everybody else—that they usually felt what other people around them felt, and the only difference was that they were ready to pull the trigger when others were not. You ought to think about that with this story. . . ."

His basic message, in other words, was that there are two kinds of terrorists: those who feel what everyone around them feels, only they decide to act on those feelings, and those who truly are extremists, who feel what no one around them feels, but act anyway. Bin Laden and his boys, he was telling me, were the former.

"I get it," I said, and thanked him for his time. I then returned to my column—rewriting the whole thing to make sure I made the point that anyone who thought bin Laden was some crazy outlier and wasn't surfing on some very deep grievances in the Arab-Muslim world was completely fooling himself.

The tip I got from the Jordanians to "follow the money" was reinforced about a week after I got home. I had raised this issue in a column, and the morning it came out I had to fly to Detroit to give a talk at the University of Michigan. I called my assistant, Maya Gorman, from Detroit Metro Airport after I arrived and asked her if there were any messages. She told me that a senior Kuwaiti government official had just called and wanted to speak to me. Standing in a phone booth at the Detroit airport, I had her patch me through to him in his office in Kuwait.

"Tom," he said, "I just read your column this morning [on the Internet]. It's true. We have not taken this issue of money seriously at all. We had a big fight in the Kuwaiti cabinet over cracking down on these Islamist charities. I told the others, 'We know where this money is being raised and we know where it is going. We know.' But everyone is afraid to stop it. They just want to ignore it. I gave your article to some Kuwaiti papers and told them they should translate it."

After hearing this, it didn't surprise me when, a few months later, on January 9, 2002, Treasury Secretary Paul O'Neill announced that the United States was blocking the assets of the "Revival of Islamic Heritage Society" (RIHS), a Kuwaiti NGO linked to bin Laden through Pakistan. O'Neill's statement said: "The RIHS is a Kuwaiti-based nongovernmental organization. . . . The Pakistan office [of RIHS] defrauded RIHS donors to fund terrorism. In order to obtain additional funds from the Kuwait RIHS headquarters, the RIHS office in Pakistan padded the number of orphans it claimed to care for by providing names of orphans that did not exist or who had died. Funds then sent for the purpose of caring for the nonexistent or dead orphans were instead diverted to Al Qaeda terrorists."

Thank you for your donation, and have a nice day.

The first tears I shed over September 11 were at my daughter Natalie's junior high school, Eastern Middle School in Silver Spring, Maryland. I finally got home from Jordan in time for Back to School Night, the annual meet-the-teacher evening at the start of every school year. Eastern is a public school in a middle-class neighborhood in suburban Washington. The student body is made up of forty different nationalities, with well over half the student body either black or Hispanic. Before the parents were sent off to visit their kids' classes, we all gathered in the school gym to be greeted by the principal. There was a big American flag up in the center of the leaky-roofed gym and the program began with the school chorus, a Noah's Ark of black, white, and Hispanic kids, singing "God Bless America" and the school orchestra plucking out the National Anthem. I just took in that scene, choked back the tears, and said to myself: Here is the whole story right here—E Pluribus Unum—Out of Many, One. It is both what we are fighting to protect and why we are strong—and it is what many foreigners just don't get about America, least of all bin Laden & Sons.

But Natalie's school and the World Trade Center actually have a lot in common—both are temples of America's civic religion. Our civic religion is built on the faith that anyone can aspire to come to our shores, become a member of this American nation, work hard, and make of him- or herself whatever he or she wants. The economic strength of America derives from millions of individuals doing just that, and the military might of America derives from the ability of all these different individuals to come together into a fist when these bedrock values are threatened.

The World Trade Center was a place where thousands of people were practicing this civic religion—kissing their spouses good-bye each morning, going off to work, and applying their individual energy in a way that added up to something much larger. It was just like Natalie's school—one of a million such temples of America's civic religion, only the World Trade Center was home to ninety different nationalities instead of just forty.

I was driving home from work one night after 9/11 and I heard the most remarkable report on National Public Radio. As part of its occasional feature "Lost and Found Sound," NPR asked listeners to contribute to a "sonic memorial" to the World Trade Center—a collection of recollections of the sounds and the acoustic environment that made the place unique. Listeners were invited to call in or play in their recollections to a special recorded phone line.

That evening NPR shared some of them. What touched me most was the recording of an unidentified Hispanic man who called in with a thick accent to say the following—but when he reached the last line he started to cry: "So [the World Trade Center] is an American building. The people that cleaned it were mostly illegal ladies, people from Mexico and Central America. And a lot of the music, a lot of the sounds this building had at nighttime, came from these people. Maybe in one of your little remembrances there, you could put in a little bit of that night music. And the Mexicans that came here and picked up your dirty work. They died with you guys. Help them out. Remember them. Thanks. . . ."

For bin Laden, the World Trade Center was some great white mansion on the hill that looked down with contempt on the whole world. But for most Americans, the World Trade Center was just two tall towers, embodiments of American ingenuity and energy to reach for the sky, which looked down on the Statue of Liberty. For bin Laden, there was no connection between the Statue of Liberty and the Twin Towers—America was rich in his view because it stole something from someone else, or because it had no values. But for those who worked in the World Trade Center, it was the embodiment of what the Statue of Liberty stood for—the ability to harness the daily work of millions of people, many of them recent immigrants, and transform it into skyscrapers and businesses, factories and universities.

I guess that's why I was struck by another caller to the NPR Sounds of the World Trade Center hot line. It was a young woman identified as Beverly Eckert, who lost her husband, Sean Rooney. She called to tell about the music CD she had made for his fiftieth birthday.

"There was another song that was on the tape [and it] was 'We Gotta Get Out of This Place' by the Animals," she said, "and it was something that Sean used to sing in high school with his friends, just not wanting to be in high school, I guess. . . . But the words right now have a very different meaning to me, considering he couldn't get out of the World Trade Center. . . . And then a song called 'You've Made Me So Very Happy' by Blood, Sweat & Tears. . . . It was our song, and the meaning it has for me now is that those were almost the exact words we used when saying goodbye to each other on September 11, because he did make me so very happy, and I got a chance to tell him that, so . . ." Then her voice cracked.

That was the World Trade Center. It was a place where thousands of Sean Rooneys and Hispanic workers and Wall Street bond traders and my broker Mark Madden's brother went to work each day, humming some tune that all of us knew. The reason their deaths touched so many Americans so deeply was because in some way we knew each of the victims. We all went to high school with someone just like each and every one of them.

As I said, for bin Laden, the Twin Towers were the symbol of a godless, corrupt, materialistic society—a society that got rich and powerful precisely because it had no values. Of course, what bin Laden never understood was that the truth was exactly the opposite: We are rich and powerful *because* of our values—freedom of thought, respect for the individual, the rule of law, entrepreneurship, women's equality, philanthropy, social mobility, self-criticism, experimentation, religious plural-ism—not despite them.

But for us to preserve our strength, our workplaces have to be secure, our institutions strong, and our society ever vigilant of these core values. And that is why one thing Americans have learned from September 11 is to treat our firemen and our policemen, our governing institutions and our regulators, with renewed respect. Because they protect and preserve the bedrock of our society—our workplaces and public schools. They are the guardians of the temples of our civic faith.

A couple of months after visiting Natalie's school, I was up in New York at the World Economic Forum, which was being held in Manhattan, not Davos, Switzerland, in 2002. I was standing by a computer terminal getting some e-mail when a French-speaking couple came up and introduced themselves. The husband, Alex J. Attal, is CEO of Adonix North America, a software company. He just stopped to say that he and his wife were regular readers of my column. But what most pleased me was that he said that his favorite column "was the one you did about your daughter's school."

Why, I asked?

"What I love about America is that there is a value of respecting all the individuals," said Attal, elaborating in an interview later. "America is an incredibly powerful integration system, and I have no way to explain this to my French family. You don't get it unless you live here. I am first-generation French. My father was from Tunisia and my mother from Eastern Europe. I am French by accident. I happen to have been born there. But even though I was born in France, you feel different [from those with French parents]. I wasn't even born here, but now that I am here, and working here, I don't feel different at all from people with American parents. Integration is in your genes, and it is impossible to replicate anywhere. In France you have some main profiles, and if you are not in those profiles, one day it is going to be a problem. Here nobody really cares, as long as you believe in the things in common. I am not an American, but as long as I respect how people are living here it is fine with everybody. Of course bin Laden has no clue, because this American thing is the result of a 250-year-old mechanism to integrate—and in his world there is no recipe for that."

POLITICAL CORRECTNESS 101

If a Frenchman could understand all this so well, why couldn't American college students and professors? I have a confession to make: Some of the most depressing conversations I had after September 11 happened on American college campuses, with American professors and students who just didn't seem to get it. What they didn't get was that bin Laden and his gang were not just motivated to change American policy in the Middle East. Did you ever hear bin Laden say, "Gee, I would have no trouble with America if it would just reduce its troop presence in Saudi Arabia or remove its McDonald's; I would have no trouble with Israel if it would just withdraw to the pre-1967 borders"? He was not looking for some new form of coexistence with us. He was looking to weaken, or destroy, our entire country. That's why the hijackers never left a note with a list of demands. They didn't need to. Their act was their note. And the act was an act of war. They were not mere terrorists out to gain attention for a cause or a list of grievances. They were warriors with a geopolitical agenda—to defeat America. Of course they didn't leave a note. Did we leave the Nazis a note on D-day?

That was also why the Pakistani Muslim fanatics who murdered *Wall Street Journal* reporter Danny Pearl—slitting his throat and chopping off his head, on camera, after first making him declare, "I am a Jew and my mother is a Jew"—also didn't leave a note. Their act was their note.

Let me be very clear about something. Not everything America has done or does now is right and perfect or cannot be improved. We have done some very stupid and bad things over the years in just about every corner of the world. We have supported some very ugly regimes and still continue to do so, particularly in the Middle East. We have not always been our best.

But in more places on more days in more years, America has done more to make this world a better, more livable place for more people than any other country in history. Some people don't like that. They detest the freedom, the pluralism, the religious toleration, the secularism, the gender equality, the democracy, the faith, the free markets, and the multiethnicity with which we have built our society, and which we urge others to emulate. There really are people who hate us for who we are, not just for what we do, because who we are is the refutation of all that they believe in. It is the opposite of the world they want to construct. There really are people who hate Christians, hate Jews, hate secularism, hate the equality of women. At some point you have to either kill those people or be killed by them. This is not a misunderstanding that can be cleared up by a few courses in multiculturalism.

While reflecting on all this I came across a thoughtful review of Peter L. Bergen's book about bin Laden, *Holy War, Inc.* The review was written by Bruce Hoffman in *The Atlantic Monthly* (January 2002), and it rightly pointed out that while many in the West refused to see this as a war of civilizations, that was precisely how bin Laden saw it: "His effective melding of religious fervor, Muslim piety, and a profound sense of grievance into a powerful ideological force—however invidious and repugnant—stands as an undeniably towering accomplishment. Bin Laden cast this struggle as precisely the 'clash of civilizations' that America and its coalition partners have labored so hard to avoid. 'This is a matter of religion and creed,' he declared in a videotaped speech broadcast over the Al Jazeera television network on November 3. 'There is no way to forget the hostility between us and the infidels. It is ideological, so Muslims have to ally themselves with Muslims.'"

When Zacarias Moussaoui, the alleged twentieth hijacker who was captured in Minnesota trying to learn how to fly a 747, appeared in court in April 2002, he was given a chance to make a fifty-minute statement. In it he said he prayed for "the destruction of the United States," "the destruction of the Jewish people and state," and "the return of Spain to Muslim rule."

Bin Laden and his men were not only unique in their cocktail of hatred for us, but in the audacity of their imagination—the lengths to which they would go in an attempt to destroy us. Hoffman related a stunning quote from T. E. Lawrence, the legendary Lawrence of Arabia, that perfectly captured bin Laden. Lawrence said: "All men dream: but not equally. Those who dream by night in the dusty recesses of their minds wake in the day to find that it was vanity: but the dreamers of the day are dangerous men, for they may act their dream with open eyes, to make it possible."

Osama bin Laden was a dreamer of the day, but such dreamers—men who tell us to our face that they hate us for who we are, men who slit the throat of an innocent journalist simply because he is a Jew and his mother is a Jew, people who want to blame others for all their troubles because they cannot face looking at themselves—are alien to many politically correct American college campuses. We don't teach Evil 101.

So I discovered when, shortly after September 11, I was speaking at a large Big Ten university in the Midwest. During a gathering with professors, donors, and students, a professor from the university's Middle East Studies department insisted on explaining bin Laden's rage, and that of his fellow hijackers, as a result of constantly seeing Israel brutalizing Palestinians on Arab television. Personally, I think Israel's colonial occupation and settlements on the West Bank and Gaza are an abomination. I have no doubt that they fuel a good deal of the Arab anger with Israel and its main backer, the United States. But the fact is that bin Laden never focused on this issue. He only started talking about "Palestine" after September 11, when he sensed that he might be losing the support of the Arab street. Moreover, the fact that Palestinians were as responsible for those horrific TV images as Israelis seemed of no matter to this professor.

This was my first taste of the intellectual hijacking that would become rampant after September 11. First there was the hijacking on 9/11, and then there was an endless series of hijackings of the hijackers by all sorts of people who wanted to use 9/11 to support their favorite cause, grievance, or worldview. They constantly wanted to write the note and list the grievances that the hijackers never did: "We did it for Palestine!" "We did it because we hate globalization!" "We did it to save Iraq from American brutality!"

The impulse to blame America first is a general disease on some American college campuses, not to mention in Europe. I was speaking to a faculty group at a small southern college, and after I made the point that the hijackers never left an explanatory note, because their act was their note, a professor present insisted: No, no, no—it was all a response to American policy. All bin Laden was trying to do, she said, was get U.S. troops out of Saudi Arabia. How could I not understand that? I was aghast at this comment. Did bin Laden's quest to get U.S. troops out of Saudi Arabia entitle him to kill nearly three thousand innocent civilians in New York City? Did he have no other recourse? And what gave him the right to make this demand in the name of all Saudis, whose country had been attacked by Iraq only a few years earlier and who may actually have desired American protection?

The idea that there are radical Muslims who hate us because they see us as "infidels" and blame us for all the ills that plague their own societies is simply not allowed to be said on most college campuses. Sorry, but this is true. Osama bin Laden's boys were not singing "We Are the World" when they slammed into the World Trade Center. After barely holding my temper during the above discussion, I excused myself early to prepare for my lecture. The college had provided a security guard for me while I was on campus. He was an off-duty fireman or policeman— I forget. Anyway, he was a wonderfully earthy guy, the sort of cop or fireman America is built on. He had been in the room during the above exchange, and when we got outside he could see I was really agitated. But it was he who spoke first: "I don't know what world those people are living in," he said to me, shaking his head. I was so heartened to know that I wasn't the only person in the room who thought that.

It was this political correctness that prompted me to write the column "Yes, but What?" about all the people who were saying "Yes, this September 11 attack was terrible, but somehow we deserved it." It was also these college visits that prompted me to turn to my daughters at the dinner table one evening and tell them, "Girls, you can have any view you want—left, right, or center. You can come home with someone black, white, or purple. But you will never come in this house and not love your country and not thank God every day that you were born an American."

I repeated this story at a NATO conference in Brussels in January 2002. A French academic attending the conference came up to me afterward and said, "I agreed with your analysis, but Tom, what you said to your daughters—that was too much." For some reason people are really uncomfortable with American academics, intellectuals, journalists, or commentators expressing any sort of patriotism or love of country. Since the end of the cold war, anti-Americanism has overtaken soccer as the world's most popular sport. And there is this general assumption in intellectual circles that America is to be blamed first for whatever happens, and a given that American intellectuals will play along and accept this role as the world's punching bag. And when you refuse to do this in mixed company, it's as if you unleashed a huge fart at a cocktail party—people look at you funny and just start to back away.

Not everyone, though. Just when I was feeling most despondent about all this, I wrote a column titled "We Are All Alone." The next morning I was at my office. The phone rang, and on the line was a housewife calling from Sydney, Australia. My column had just appeared in her newspaper that morning, and she called me all the way from Australia to complain that her husband was in the Australian special forces, in the SAS, and had just left to fight with American troops in Afghanistan. She already missed him terribly and therefore wanted to tell me that I had no right to say that we were all alone! I thanked her for her call, apologized for my mistake, and told her that she had made my day.

Let me end this particular diary entry with an excerpt from an essay that comedian and writer Larry Miller wrote for the January 14, 2002, issue of *The Weekly Standard*, which made me cheer. Miller had also become exasperated with the political correctness he was encountering on college campuses and elsewhere. In his essay, he offered a list of the stupidest clichés that people were mouthing about September 11. His number one idiotic cliché was: "We're not good, they're not evil, everything is relative."

Miller's response was this:

> Listen carefully: We're good, they're evil, nothing is relative. Say it with me now and free yourselves. You see, folks, saying "We're good" doesn't mean "We're perfect." Okay? The only perfect being is the bearded guy on the ceiling of the Sistine Chapel. The plain fact is that our country has, with all our mistakes and blunders, always been and always will be the greatest beacon of freedom, charity, opportunity, and affection in history. If you need proof, open all the borders on Earth and see what happens. In about half a day, the entire world would be a ghost town, and the United States would look like one giant line to see *The Producers*.

Miller concluded by adding: "So here's what I resolve for the new year: To never forget our murdered brothers and sisters. To never let the relativists get away with their immoral thinking. After all, no matter what your daughter's political science professor says, we didn't start this."

FOREIGN POLICY 101

I always felt before September 11 that I was writing for a relatively small foreign policy–concerned audience. But all that changed on September 12. I found myself being stopped by all kinds of people I never assumed were readers, who would comment on a column or ask what I thought might happen next. To me, this was all about one thing: our kids. People understood after September 11 that foreign policy was now a life-and-death matter, for them and their kids. And they really wanted to know. Parking attendants, waiters, elevator operators, limo drivers, secretaries, and dental hygienists—people I never imagined being interested in foreign affairs—all came up to me at one time or another after September 11 with questions about what was going on.

My friend Glenn Prickett, a senior executive at Conservation International, and I were having dinner a few months after September 11, and out of the blue I asked him how this huge event had affected his work trying to preserve biodiversity around the globe.

"It is so much easier now to tell people what I do," said Glenn. "People now are much less interested in the Nasdaq and much more interested in the world. They also now get what conservationists have been saying—that there are no real walls anymore and you can't protect yourself by trying to put them up now. It's one ecosystem out there and everything is connected with everything else, so every part of it needs to be tended. Before 9/11 my college friends would ask me what I'm doing and I would say 'conservation,' and there was this sense of, like, 'What are you doing that for?' [Conservation International's Web address, like other nonprofits', ends with "dot.org"—not "dot.com" like all the hot startups.] So I got this e-mail last year from a college friend from Yale, who said to me, 'Dot.org—what's up with that?' It was, like, 'You mean you're not working for a dot.com?'"

I don't know how long this seriousness will last. I don't know what will come next. But I do know that at 8:48 a.m. on the morning of September 11, 2001, the 1990s, and a lot of their silliness, officially ended.

THE CIRCLE OF BIN LADENISM

By early November 2001, with the war in Afghanistan under way, I wanted to get back out in the field, so I headed off to Pakistan. At the time, the Taliban had thrown most journalists out, so except for a few reporters traveling with the Northern Alliance, the Western press was largely covering the war from Islamabad, Peshawar, and other Pakistani border towns.

I flew into Pakistan via Qatar and Dubai. In Doha, Qatar, I had breakfast with a group of Qatari friends, all of whom were rather despondent about where things were going, and complaining to me around our breakfast table that without Islam being taken out of the hands of backward-looking imams, and without some separation between church and state, development in the Arab world would forever be retarded. One of the journalists present said his only hope was an "Arab Ataturk" who would forcibly secularize Arab society the way the founder of modern Turkey had done in his own country. When you are with modern, progressive Arabs like this who really let down their hair, you start to realize the simmering frustration that boils in them every day— having to live in a world so full of lies, so full of religious leaders they don't respect, so full of newspapers they can't believe, so full of political leaders they've never elected.

But what I remember most from that breakfast was how one of my Qatari friends who was present, someone whose home I had been to for dinner, quietly confided: "I have a real problem. My eleven-year-old son thinks bin Laden is a good man."

He was in obvious agony over this. This was a man of the Arab middle class, with not a hint of anti-Americanism in him. Where did his son get this? At school? Watching TV? Unfortunately, this attitude wasn't hard to come by, since it was all over the Arab street. Someone even told me that in Saudi Arabia, as in Cairo, they have a tradition each season of selling date fruit according to its quality, often using the different classes of Mercedes-Benz cars. It would be like a fruit vendor in America calling his best apples Cadillacs, his second-best ones Chryslers, and so on. This season some Saudi and Egyptian vendors, I was told, were calling their best dates Osamas, after you-know-who. So why shouldn't young boys pick up on this?

I don't think it was that they approved of his mass killings of Americans. I don't think they really even understood that. But they did approve of bin Laden as the thumb that every young Arab wanted to stick in his ruler's eye, and in America's eye for supporting Israel. Bin Laden was the closest thing they had to an Arab Robin Hood—an authentic figure who challenges the power structure. And it is always worth remembering that bin Laden, much as we may detest him, was an authentic person in his own way. That is, he gave up the life of a multimillionaire in Saudi Arabia to go off to Afghanistan to live in a cave and fight the Soviets and then the Americans. He was more authentic in that sense than any Arab leader of his generation.

The tragedy is that he used his authenticity to preach and promote hate and exclusion. The only way to defeat him ideologically, therefore, is via another authentic message—a modern-looking, progressive, inclusive vision, but one rooted in Arab culture and reinforced by a modernist interpretation of Islam. That is precisely what Arab leaders have failed to offer for fifty years. They want to arrest their bin Ladens and evict them, but never really challenge them ideologically by laying down a progressive countervision. Instead, they either leave an ideological vacuum or they let it be filled by local religious leaders who are actually as extreme and hostile to modernity as bin Laden, but just slightly less violent. These domesticated religious leaders, in return for being anointed by the regimes as the "official" clerics and given state funds, then turn around and bless the unelected leader.

It's all part of what I call "the Circle of bin Ladenism," which is made up of three components: antidemocratic Arab leaders, who empower antimodernist Muslim religious educators to gain legitimacy, who then produce a generation of young people who have not been educated in ways that enable them to flourish in the modern world and who end up wallowing in poverty. The antidemocracy reinforces the antimodernism and the antimodernism reinforces the poverty and the poverty reinforces the antidemocracy, and the wheel just goes round and round and round. . . .

WELCOME TO THE *TITANIC*

From Doha I flew to Dubai to transit onto Emirates Air for my flight to Pakistan. As I was standing in line to board Emirates Air, I noticed that the Pakistani gentleman in front of me was wearing what we would have called a high school letterman's jacket in the States, only across the back was emblazoned one word: TITANIC.

It seemed like an omen.

When I arrived in Islamabad, I headed straight to the Marriott Hotel, which at the time was News Central. My first evening at the Marriott I ran into a Lebanese TV journalist. She recognized me and engaged me in conversation which, as best I can recall, went like this:

"You have been very tough on the Arabs and Muslims, and very unfair," she said, somewhat surprised that I would even dare show up in Pakistan.

"Well," I answered, "I think some things just needed to be said." I was very jet-lagged at the time, and not in a particularly good mood, so her next comment really lit my fuse.

"Do you know how much the world hates you?" she said, referring not to me but to America. "I was in Paris on September 11 and you should have seen how many French people were celebrating."

At that point I nearly lost it. I snapped back: "Do you know how much we hate *your* lack of democracy, do you know how much we hate *your* lack of transparency, *your* lack of economic development, the way you treat *your* women? Do you think you're the only ones who get to judge people?"

This put her back on her heels, and before we could continue, her producer literally pulled her away to do her evening broadcast from the roof of the hotel.

What saddened me even more in Pakistan, though, was the story a close Pakistani friend told me about his kids a few days later. They came home from their Islamabad private school shortly after September 11 and told him that they had heard from their classmates about the four thousand Jews who were supposedly warned not to go to work at the World Trade Center on September 11.

My Pakistani friend, a thoughtful and decent man, told me he sat his kids down and explained to them why this could not possibly have been true. Who would have a master list of all the employees from hundreds of different companies located in the World Trade Center? And how would you identify who was Jewish on such short notice and then get all their home phone numbers and call them all on the night before September 11 and not have one of them call the police or wonder that something suspicious was going on? And how could you warn four thousand people not to go to work and have not one of them, not one, be identified afterward by name? It didn't make any sense.

My Pakistani friend told me his kids listened and seemed to understand and went back to school with that message. A week later, though, he got word from the school that the views of his children were out of step with those of the rest of their classmates and that he needed to tell them to stop challenging the story that four thousand Jews were warned not to go to work; otherwise his kids would be ostracized.

One afternoon I drove to Peshawar, the teeming market town on the border with Afghanistan, and along the way we stopped at the Darul Uloom Haqqania, the biggest madrasa, or Islamic boys' school, in Pakistan, with 2,800 live-in students. This madrasa is particularly renowned because Mullah Muhammad Omar, the Taliban leader, attended it, but without graduating. When I and the Pakistani journalist I was traveling with arrived, the madrasa's headmaster was outside, giving an interview to an Iranian film crew, so one of his aides took us on a tour. There were two memorable stops. One was the library, where we asked to see the shelf of science books. We were shown one paltry metal rack with about thirty books, none of which seemed to have been published after 1932.

The other was the Koran class. It was a small room with a blackboard in the front, next to which stood the teacher. About twenty-five boys, ages eight to fifteen, were sitting on the floor, with Korans in front of them on little wooden bookholders. We talked to the boys. All of them thought America was evil and that Osama bin Laden was a hero. When I looked around that room, I had no doubt that there was not a single young man there who would not have signed up for this 9/11 or the next. I asked Rahim Kunduz, age twelve, one of the boys in the class, for his view of Americans. He said, "They are unbelievers and do not like to befriend Muslims, and they want to dominate the world with their power."

Nobody seemed to have told Rahim that America fought to liberate or rescue the Muslims of Bosnia, Kosovo, Somalia, Kuwait, and now Afghanistan, at a time when no other country in the world, including any Muslim country, was prepared to lift a finger. Too bad that never made it into the madrasa curriculum. But this is partly our fault. We used the Pakistanis to fight off the Russians in Afghanistan and then walked away, leaving their country crumbling and under military dictatorship—so much so that the Pakistani public school system virtually collapsed. For many young Pakistani boys, the only way to get an education and three meals a day was by going to one of these madrasas. In

1978 there were 3,000 madrasas in Pakistan and now there are 39,000 — the vast majority of them factories churning out young men who are unprepared for modernity, have little exposure to women, and are hostile to everything the West stands for.

On my way home from Pakistan I stopped off in Abu Dhabi, in the United Arab Emirates, which is always a good source of uncensored information on neighboring Saudi Arabia. At lunch at an American friend's home there, a senior executive at one of the top schools in the UAE told me that he had just been to a conference in Saudi Arabia. He said a Saudi colleague took him aside while he was there and told him: "Don't believe what you hear. Bin Laden is in every home [in Saudi Arabia]."

From Abu Dhabi I flew to New Delhi for what I hoped would be a break from all the anger and angst in the Arab world. Despite its ever-present flare-ups between Hindus and Muslims, India is still a multicultural democracy that works. It's messy, but it works. Talking to Indian officials about Pakistan, though, my head started to spin: They sounded exactly like Israelis talking about Palestinians.

"You can never trust these people," Indian officials and academics would tell me. "You don't really believe Musharraf is telling the truth, do you? He is a terrorist." I was struck by the intense insecurity among Indians that somehow America was going to embrace Pakistan just as India was forging its first close relationship with the United States. I just kept telling my Indian friends and interlocutors who assaulted me with this view to calm down. India has an enormous amount going for it. As a multicultural democracy, even one in which simmering tensions between Hindus and Muslims occasionally explode to the surface, India has a natural bond with America that few countries enjoy, and it's a bond that will not be easily broken. So calm down. They would nod their heads for a moment, take in what I was saying, and then go off again on Musharraf, warning me: "Never turn your back on these people."

I wanted to fly off to a snow-capped mountain in Colorado, find a nice cabin, and put on earmuffs.

THE C-WORD

Instead I went to Moscow.

Just before Christmas, I decided to visit Russia. I needed to get a better read on the new president, Vladimir Putin. Putin was so quick to join the American war against bin Laden, and he seemed so shockingly willing to accept the Bush administration's decision to scrap the ABM treaty and to station U.S. troops in former Soviet republics on Russia's southern border, and even to accept more NATO expansion under the right conditions, that it had taken me by surprise. What was up?

Part of the answer you could find at the original McDonald's in central Moscow. The last time I had been there, three years earlier, young Russians had been milling around outside trying to bum money for a bag of french fries. Not this time. McDonald's was packed, but not with the fur-coated yuppies and privatization rip-off artists found there in the early 1990s. It was crowded with lower-middle-class Russian families who could now afford this luxury and were partaking of it in droves. Sure, this is just in the capital, while the countryside is still lagging. But in virtually every country, things start in the capital and radiate outward—and in Moscow, a messy capitalism is finally taking root.

I have never believed in the Henry Kissinger–Zbigniew Brzezinski line about Russia—that it is immutably destined to be aggressive, expansionist, and America's enemy. Islam in the context of democracy—whether it is in Turkey or India—is a different Islam from Islam in the context of dictatorship. And a Russia that for the first time in its history is governed by an elected president answerable to a parliament, with a limited free press and an unlimited free market, is simply a different Russia.

Yes, the roots of this different Russia are still shallow. But Putin is for real. Far from yanking his countrymen into a more pro-Western camp against their will and instincts, he is following and reflecting their aspirations. As my Russian friend Leon Aron, the premier biographer of Boris Yeltsin, put it: "The significance of Russia's post–September 11 behavior goes far beyond short-term relations with the United States. Russia's steps have indicated a profound and continuous shift in national priorities brought about by the revolutionary changes of the past decade: demilitarization and the end of the Soviet empire; the emergence of competitive politics and public opinion as key factors in policymaking; the slow but inexorable erosion of the nationalist anti-Western left; acceptance of a private economy and a free market by a majority of the political class; the diffusion of the first significant benefits from the new economic system; and the growing perception of the necessity of integration into the world economic system by the elite and general public alike." Russia, Leon concluded, has finally come close "to what Lord Byron in *Don Juan* called 'a sort of post-house, where the Fates change horses, making history change its tune.'"

As I lay awake at night in my hotel next to the Bolshoi Theater, just outside the Kremlin walls, I thought about Russia and the Arab world.

There is a lesson here: Change the context in which people live and you change the way people look at themselves, the world, and their own government. Change some of the worst Arab and Muslim regimes around the world, and you might change the behavior patterns of these countries as well. Not everything is mandated by history and geography. How people are governed, what voice they have in their own lives, what opportunities their kids have to live a better life than their parents, determine a lot about how they treat each other and the rest of the world.

For far too long we have been in bed with Arab and Muslim dictators who, we told ourselves, are more liberal than their own people. Therefore, we also told ourselves, better to have pro-American dictators than prodemocratic societies that might be anti-American. This has been very shortsighted, because these pro-American Arab and Muslim regimes have bought their stability by giving their people free rein to hate us and Israel, in their press and on the street. One reason politics moves into mosques and co-opts the language of the Koran in so many of these countries is that it's the only place for people to gather outside the control of the regime. There is no true parliament building where real freedom can be exercised.

September 11 was a by-product of that. I would much prefer democratically elected Arab and Muslim leaders we can live with, even if they don't particularly like us, than dictators, autocrats, and kings who profess to like us, but whose people detest us because they view us as sustaining their unjust regimes. As Middle East historian Bernard Lewis has pointed out, the 9/11 hijackers basically came from Egypt and Saudi Arabia—the two most pro-American regimes in the region, who happen to have the most anti-American populations. The reason: Egyptians and Saudis blame us for their autocracies. Iran, the most anti-American regime in the region, probably has the most pro-American population, because one thing Iranians do not do is blame us for propping up their unjust government.

"To think that Russia is an exception is wrong," Mikhail M. Fridman, the chairman of Alfa Group, a big energy conglomerate, told me over breakfast at a new Moscow bistro in a refurbished library. "It is the same as any country—all that is different is size and the history. First we had McDonald's, and it was cheap and easy to accept, and now more sophisticated things are coming. People have the salaries and are able to travel, so they try different things. . . . Putin is quite pro-Western. He deeply believes in the Western approach. . . . We are a product and part of European culture. The elite are completely committed to a European way of life."

This explains why, for the first time, I heard Russians using the C-word—"civilization." The point they were making was that we, America and Russia, were in the same civilization and we needed to stick together. That's not to say that Putin, or average Russians, are prepared to roll over for everything the Americans ask, or that many Russians in the older generation don't still pine away for the long-lost power of the Soviet Union or resent the West's predominance. But on the whole, most Russians will tell you, "We resent you, we resent your bullying, we will occasionally oppose you and even look for opportunities to stick it to you. But on the big, big thing—whose side do we want to be on?—we want to be with you."

"It is not East versus West anymore," Otto Latsis, deputy editor of the journal *New Isvestia*, remarked to me over tea in his cramped Moscow rooftop office. "It is the stable versus unstable worlds, and we have to pull or push China into this stable world. That is very difficult. Another zone of instability is the Islamic world. Some of our leaders thought it was better that Arafat was a dictator. Democracy is a difficult and uncomfortable way to control people. But [to do otherwise turns out] to be a very bad mistake. Democracy is not comfortable, but dictatorship can do nothing good. Some of the people around Putin think democracy is interfering with what they are doing. It is important for the civilized countries to understand that only democracy can ensure stability."

CRACKS IN THE RUBBLE

By January the war in Afghanistan was largely over; the Taliban had been routed and Osama bin Laden forced underground, if not six feet under. I wanted to see Kabul the first chance I got. Senator Joseph R. Biden of Delaware, the Democratic chairman of the Senate Foreign Relations Committee, wanted to go there at the same time, and we decided to go together to keep each other company and share impressions. We flew to Islamabad and then grabbed a UN relief flight into Bagram Air Base, fifty miles from Kabul. Joe stayed at the newly reopened U.S. Embassy, with no flush toilets or running water, and I stayed at the house being rented by *The New York Times*, which had only slightly better plumbing but a friendly group of Afghan drivers and cooks who kept the fireplace roaring and the raisin pilaf and warm Afghan bread on the table.

My first impression of Kabul? It was Ground Zero East.

That's what I kept telling my wife when she asked what the Afghan capital looked like. I could have said Dresden or the Green Line in Beirut or Hiroshima. But the phrase that kept coming to mind was that about half of downtown Kabul, including the university district, neighborhood apartment blocks, many former ministry buildings, and the massive old Soviet Embassy compound, looked exactly like Ground Zero at the former World Trade Center—like a piece of cake smashed by a large fist. This was not the result of American bombing but of twenty-three years of Afghan civil wars (for which we provided a lot of the guns and ammo). I described it to myself as "Liberia with snow and ice." Everything seemed broken by a nation too long at war—walls, windows, and spirits.

One morning Biden and I went over to the old Soviet Embassy, where thousands of refugees were packed into a beehive of makeshift one-room apartments, heated only by wood stoves and sheltered from the wet cold by plastic sheets. Everyone seemed to be shuffling around in sandals, with blankets for overcoats. Open sewers and mud were their front yards; hollow cheeks and wide eyes marked their faces.

I found myself conflicted throughout my stay in Kabul. My heart told me to write that America must remain here, for however long it takes, with however many troops it takes, to repair this country, and provide a minimum level of security so it can get on its feet again. It was the least we owed the place, having already abandoned it once after the Soviet withdrawal. We didn't have to make it Switzerland, just a little better, a little freer, and a little more stable than it was under the Taliban. But even this would require a major investment of men, money, and energy. The notion that we could just pour in money and stir and the Afghanistan of old would reemerge was ludicrous. For the money to have any effect, you needed a glass, a governing structure, and that had been utterly shattered in Afghanistan.

But while my heart kept pulling me in one direction, my head, and my eyes, kept encountering things that were deeply troubling. It started when I went along with Biden to meet the Minister of the Interior for the Interim Government, Yunus Qanooni, who is a Tajik. Behind his desk, where a minister should be hanging the picture of his president (Hamid Karzai, an ethnic Pashtun), he had a picture of Ahmed Shah Massoud (an ethnic Tajik), the leader of the Northern Alliance who was assassinated just before September 11.

Tom Friedman's first rule of politics: Never trust a country where a new minister has the picture of his favorite dead militia leader, not the country's (interim) president, over his desk. It seemed to me that the tribal warrior culture ran so deep in this place, it would be hard for any neutral central government to sink real roots. As I contemplated that militia leader's picture, I wondered to myself: "When were the good old days for government in Afghanistan? Before Genghis Khan? Before gun-powder?"

My wife collects postcards and asked me before I left if I would bring her some from Kabul. I said to her, "Honey, where am I going to get postcards in Kabul?" They don't do postcards in Dante's Inferno. Well, sure enough, the Inter-Continental Hotel's bookstore had some. So I grabbed a fistful, paid a few dollars, stuffed the postcards in my jacket, and brought them home. When I got home, I started handing them out to Ann.

"Here's Kabul by day. . . . Here's Kabul by night. . . ." Then, suddenly, I got to one postcard that stumped me. It was a two-part picture; one part was of a shell-ravaged building, and the other part of a damaged hallway, with the roof collapsed and rubble strewn all over the floor.

"What the heck is this?" I said. I flipped the postcard over, and on the back, in the upper left-hand corner, it said: "Afghanistan, the looted and destroyed Kabul Museum. Photos: J. Leslie & M. Anderson." It was a postcard of the destroyed national museum. I thought: How do you know when your country has been too long at war? When they start making postcards of the rubble!

My other worrying indicator about Afghanistan came from reading James Michener's novel *Caravans*. It was one of his first big best-sellers, about an American girl in Afghanistan. Like most of Michener's books, it is a historical novel. I used to read it at night by flashlight in my room at *The New York Times* house in Kabul (in between having to go out on the balcony in subzero temperatures, point my satellite phone up at the stars at just the right angle, and call in my column or speak to my editor). As I was reading one night, under a pile of blankets because the electricity (and the electric heater) went out at around 10 p.m., I came across a troubling Michener passage: "In Afghanistan almost every building bears jagged testimony to some outrage. Some, like the walled fortress now owned by Shah Khan, were built to withstand sieges, and did so many times. Others were the scenes of horrible murder and retaliation. In distant areas, scars still remained of Alexander the Great or Genghis Khan or Tamerlane or Nadir Shah, of Persia. Was there ever a land so overrun by terror and devastation as Afghanistan?"

After reading that paragraph, I flipped to the inside cover to see when Michener wrote *Caravans*: it was 1963. That was during one of Afghanistan's peaceful, faintly pro-Western progressive phases. Those were the "good" years! Oh, boy. So yes, my heart told me that America had to stay behind and help Afghanistan get on its feet. But my head said, "Be careful, this is a country where the favorite sport is goat polo, known as *buzkashi,* where whip-wielding horsemen gallop around, bump, and tussle with one another for control of the carcass of a headless goat instead of a ball, and try to carry it across their goal line. If we stay, we need to make sure we're not that goat."

The day Biden and his staff were supposed to fly out, with me tagging along, bad weather descended on Bagram Air Base and the UN canceled its flight. This was a problem. The Delta Shuttle doesn't serve Kabul. No UN flight, no exit.

One of Biden's security detail managed to get him and the rest of us seats on a U.S. military transport that was supposed to come in late that evening and fly right out, first to Pakistan and then to Bahrain. As a result, we had to sit around Bagram all day with the U.S. Special Forces, who were headquartered there. It gave me a chance to talk to many of them casually, which was interesting for a couple of reasons. To begin with, Bagram was also the site of a makeshift prison for Al Qaeda POWs, who were being held in an airplane hangar. What interested me was not them but their guards, several of whom were female blond U.S. Army MPs. And they were not dressed in burkas but in U.S. Army camouflage khakis. I asked one MP what it was like guarding her Arab prisoners. She told me that at first most of them would not even acknowledge the women guards, and often would make faces at them. But, as one of the MPs told me, "they get over it." Think what a mind-bending experience it must be to go from being in Al Qaeda, living, as James Michener put it, "in this cruel land of recurring ugliness, where only men were seen," and then suddenly being guarded by a woman with blond locks spilling out from under her helmet and an M16 hanging from her side. Actually, it was the best introduction to America, and what makes us strong, that we could offer—the fact that we have empowered our whole society, not just half of it.

A few weeks later I was in Oxford, giving a talk on globalization at Rhodes House, when an Afghan student there got up and harangued me about the fact that all the troubles in Afghanistan were the result of "outsiders meddling in Afghanistan's internal affairs." I answered back that his analysis reminded me of what the Lebanese always used to say—that theirs would be a nice peaceful country if only the "outsiders" didn't meddle there. Of course this was nonsense, in Lebanon and in Afghanistan. These countries became the battleground for outsiders precisely because the insiders were not united enough to make a fist.

The other revealing thing about sitting around Bagram hit me when I went to dinner in the mess tent. I suddenly had a flash of déjà vu. I felt like I was back at Natalie's Eastern Middle School. I looked around the room at the Special Forces A-teams that were there and could see America's strength hiding in plain sight. It wasn't smart missiles or night-fighting equipment. It was the fact that these Special Forces teams each seemed to be made up of a collection of black, Asian, Hispanic, and white Americans. It is our ability to blend those many into one hard fist that is the real source of our power. This is precisely what Afghans have not been able to do in recent decades, and it has left them weak, divided, and prey to outsiders.

Getting out of Afghanistan turned out to be harder than getting in (which I hope will not be a metaphor for U.S. operations there generally). When the U.S. military transport that Joe Biden and friends were supposed to fly out on arrived at Bagram, the U.S. Army captain running the control tower informed the senator that orders had come down from the Pentagon that no civilians were to be allowed on military aircraft. Throughout Biden's trip, the Pentagon, presumably under orders from Secretary of Defense Donald Rumsfeld, had denied Biden any help, even though he chaired the Senate Foreign Relations Committee. No planes, no military tours, no nothing. This seemed to be the last straw. Biden was very cool, didn't throw a tantrum, but was quietly pissed. I was just depressed, as I had visions of being stuck in Kabul for days. I confess that I suggested that Biden try to contact Secretary of State Colin Powell. Biden didn't know how. I had a satellite phone in my pocket and the number of the State Department's operations room in my head. I dialed it for Biden and handed him the phone. It was early Sunday morning, Washington, D.C., time.

"This is Joe Biden, could you connect me with Colin Powell?" Biden asked the State Department operator. A few minutes passed. "Colin? Hey, it's Joe Biden. . . . Yeah, I'm standing here on the runway at Bagram Air Base in Afghanistan, trying to get out on a military transport, and they're telling me that the Pentagon has ordered that no civilians be let on the plane. I'm sorry to trouble you, Colin, but could you give us a hand here?"

Powell told Biden to hold on for a minute while he tried to get Rumsfeld. Rumsfeld was in church, so Powell tracked down his deputy, Paul Wolfowitz. There were a few more minutes of phone calls to Centcom headquarters in Florida before Powell came back on the phone with Biden.

"Joe," said the Secretary of State, "let me talk to the air traffic controller there."

Biden then handed the satellite phone to the air traffic controller with the following words: "Captain, the Secretary of State would like to talk to you."

It was pitch-dark, but I was sure I saw that captain's face turn completely white with shock that he was talking to the Secretary of State, a former Chairman of the Joint Chiefs, no less. All I heard him saying to Powell was, "Yessir, yessir, yessir." When he was done, he handed back the phone and told Biden, "You're welcome to board, sir."

As we strapped into the back of the C-130, the crew shouted that someone was firing tracer bullets at the other end of the runway, "so we are gettin' the fuck out of here right now." With this big cargo plane empty except for us, it felt like we took off straight up, like a rocket, which was fine with me, since Bagram is almost surrounded by tall mountains that had already claimed two U.S. transports. Three hours later, we landed in Jacobabad, Pakistan, somewhere in the middle of the country, at a Pakistani base being used by the U.S. Air Force. We had a few hours to kill before we hopped a C-17 to Bahrain.

Talking to the U.S. airmen at Jacobabad was an eye-opener. One of them told us, "We don't have a flight to Afghanistan that doesn't get shot at by small-arms fire *from inside Pakistan* somewhere near the border."

But Pakistan is our ally in this war, we said. Tell that to the Pakistanis who live along the Afghan border, he shrugged.

It was one of those moments when you realize as a journalist that there are a million stories going on in and around this larger war story that you have no clue about. It was one of those moments when you get an inkling that you are standing on a story with a false bottom. But when *Wall Street Journal* reporter Danny Pearl tragically got his throat slit a few weeks later by anti-American Pakistani terrorists, I remembered that conversation at Jacobabad, and suddenly the senseless murder of an American in Pakistan didn't seem so out of context anymore.

THE MOSQUES OF EUROPE

From the moment 9/11 happened, one issue has gnawed at me more than any other: Who were the hijackers? That is, we know who Osama bin Laden is. He is a unique combination—part cult figure, part megalomaniac with the geopolitical agenda of a nation-state, and part corporate leader with the organizational skills of Jack Welch. We also know who the bin Ladenites are—all those people who passively supported bin Laden out of anger with their own leaders, America, Israel, or all of the above.

But who were the hijackers? I would divide them into two groups. One group were the key terrorists who piloted the plot and the airplanes and who clearly knew exactly what they were doing. I call them, for reasons which will soon become clear, "the Europeans." The other group were the terrorists who were the muscle. Their job was to keep the passengers away from the pilots once the planes were hijacked. According to bin Laden's home videotape captured in Afghanistan, all these musclemen were told when they were recruited was that it was for "[a] martyrdom operation and we asked each of them to go to America, but they didn't know anything about the operation, not even one letter. We did not reveal [it] until just before they boarded the planes." I call them "the Saudis."

Where did these two groups come from? It seemed to me that as long as we could not answer that question, we were still unsafe and had not even begun to deter the next 9/11. In part, this question was difficult to answer because all the hijackers were killed. In part, this question was hard to answer because fifteen of the nineteen had Saudi nationality, and the Saudis were uncooperative in helping us determine who they were. In part, we just contented ourselves with calling them all "suicide hijackers" and moved on to what the Bush administration considered a bigger threat: Iraq. But this seemed to me a mistake, so I devoted my next two trips to my own personal investigation, and they took me to two very different places: Belgium and Saudi Arabia.

I decided to go to Belgium after reading an article, one of the most original written about 9/11, that appeared in the November 5, 2001, issue of *National Review*, the conservative journal. It was written by Adrian Karatnycky, the president of Freedom House. The article was titled "Under Our Very Noses," and basically tried to answer the question that was bothering me: Who were these guys?

Karatnycky made the following argument: "The key hijackers were well-educated children of privilege. None of them suffered firsthand economic privation or political oppression." Indeed, the top 9/11 operatives and pilots, like Mohamed Atta and Marwan al-Shehhi, who shared an apartment in Hamburg, where Atta was attending the Technical University of Hamburg-Harburg, all seem to have been first radicalized while studying in Europe (home now to 15 million Muslims), where they formed their Islamist terrorist cell. The same is true of the top Al Qaeda operatives who surrounded this 9/11 story. These include Richard Reid, the shoe bomber, whose paternal grandfather was a Jamaican immigrant to England. Reid grew up in London and, like his father, converted to radical Islam while doing time in a British prison. As *Time* magazine noted (February 25, 2002):

> Since the early 1980s, Bangladeshi and Pakistani imams, often associated with evangelist Islamic groups, have targeted young black inmates of British prisons. "Islam is a sort of natural religion for underdogs," says Ziauddin Sardar, a British scholar of Islam, "and that's one reason why Afro-Caribbean people have found its message very attractive." Prison authorities have allowed imams to bring literature into the jails — everything from copies of the Koran to anti-American leaflets highlighting the importance of jihad.

Zacarias Moussaoui, the Frenchman whose single mother was a Moroccan immigrant to France, first embraced a conservative brand of Islam at age nineteen in southern France. Moussaoui was reportedly radicalized a few years later in a London mosque while attending business school in England. He was eventually arrested in Minnesota, shortly before 9/11 — after drawing the attention of the FBI for insisting at his flight school that he be taught how to fly a Boeing 747 before he could even handle a little propeller plane.

The same pattern of conversion to radical Islam was true of Ahmed Omar Saeed Sheikh, the London-born Pakistani terrorist who oversaw the abduction and murder of *Wall Street Journal* reporter Danny Pearl. Ditto for Tunisian-born Abedessatar Daham, who was radicalized by an Islamist cell after immigrating to Belgium. As *Time* magazine also reported (December 17, 2001), Dahman and his friends were not "particularly religious at first. [But] they soon were influenced by fellow Tunisians espousing Islamic extremism," and they eventually joined a radical Islamist group in Belgium that played a major role in ferrying new recruits to Al Qaeda camps in Afghanistan. And it was there that Dahman, and a still unidentified accomplice who also carried a Belgian passport, were persuaded to blow themselves up while standing next to Ahmed Shah Massoud, the leader of the Northern Alliance in Afghanistan. Dahman and his accomplice were masquerading as TV journalists interviewing Massoud. Massoud was murdered on September 9, in what is now believed to have been a prelude to September 11, as bin Laden and the Taliban tried to eliminate the leadership of the Northern Alliance, whom they apparently feared would be used by the United States to get at them in Afghanistan.

None of these plotters were recruited in the Middle East and planted within Europe years in advance by bin Laden, notes Karatnycky. To the contrary, virtually all of them were living in Europe on their own, grew alienated from the European society around them, gravitated to a local prayer group or mosque to find warmth and solidarity, got radicalized there by Islamist elements, went off for training in Afghanistan, and presto, a terrorist was born. These "Europeans" were born-again Muslims; they are young men who rediscovered their faith, or had it rekindled in them, by their encounter with Europe. And like born-again Christians or Jews, they brought to their religion a special intensity and fervor and, in their case, fanaticism.

"To understand the September 11 terrorists, we should have in mind the classic revolutionary: deracinated, middle-class, shaped in part by exile. In other words, the image of Lenin in Zurich; or of Pol Pot or Ho Chi Minh in Paris," wrote Karatnycky. "Like the leaders of America's Weather Underground, Germany's Baader-Meinhof Gang, Italy's Red Brigades, and Japan's Red Army Faction, the Islamic terrorists were university-educated converts to an all-encompassing neo-totalitarian ideology. . . . For them Islamism is the new universal revolutionary creed, and bin Laden is Sheikh Guevara."

In search of how all this worked, I went to Brussels. I chose Brussels because several of the key Al Qaeda figures passed through there and because Belgium, unbeknownst to most people, has three hundred mosques today. While in Belgium, I sought insight from two people in particular. The first was Nordin Maloujahmoum, president of the Muslim Executive Council of Belgium, who told me in his tightly guarded Brussels office that "our problem in Belgium is that there is Islamophobia. Some 54 percent of the population here say they don't believe non-Belgian ethnic groups could ever be real Belgians. A woman wearing a veil here finds it impossible to get a job." The same day, I had lunch at the Belgian Parliament with Fauzaya Talhaoui, the only Muslim woman in the Belgian legislature. A lovely, energetic young woman of Moroccan descent, she told me her parents' generation came from North Africa and just wanted to assimilate, but many in her generation, after being frozen out, have turned to Islam. "They took the view, If you want to treat us differently, we will act differently," she said.

I think the personal encounter between the young Muslim hijackers and Europe is the key to understanding where the main plotters and pilots in this story came from. Europe is not a melting pot for Muslims. In America, Muslims can enjoy a reasonably rapid transition to citizenship, but in Europe the melting pot often doesn't get warm enough to melt, and Muslim immigrants are often left permanently out in the cold.

North African and Turkish Muslims are to Europe what Mexicans are to America, the source of cheap labor who come in as guest workers but never leave, but also never get fully absorbed (5 million in France, 3.2 million in Germany, 2 million in Britain). This breeds young, angry Muslim men (and women) who feel permanently frozen out, if not in employment terms, then in psychological ones. Richard Reid's father, Robin, told *Time* magazine (February 25, 2002) about his son: "He was born here in Britain, like I was. It was distressing to be told things like 'Go home, nigger.'"

All this produces poverty of dignity, not poverty of money. It is the poverty of dignity that can really drive people to do extreme things—much more than the poverty of money. There are pools of such dignity-deprived people all over the Muslim diaspora in Europe. They are young men who are full of pride as Muslims, who are taught from youth in the mosque that theirs is the most complete and advanced form of the three monotheistic faiths—superior to both Christianity and Judaism—yet who become aware that the Islamic world has fallen behind both the Christian West and the Jewish state in education, science, democracy, and development. This produces a cognitive dissonance in these young men—a cognitive dissonance that is the original spark for all their rage. They must be saying to themselves: If Islam is God 3.0 and Christianity is God 2.0 and Judaism is God 1.0, how could it be that those living in countries dominated by God 2.0 and God 1.0 are, on average, doing so much better—politically, economically, and educationally—than those living in countries practicing God 3.0?

Young Islamists reconcile this by concluding that the Islamic world has fallen behind the rest of the world either because the Europeans, Americans, and Israelis stole something from the Muslims, or because the Europeans, Americans, and Israelis are deliberately retarding the progress of Muslims, or because those who are leading the Muslim world have drifted away from the true faith and are behaving in un-Islamic ways, but are being kept in power by America. What they are unwilling to acknowledge is that much of Christianity is really God 2.0.1—it is the updated version that has gone through the Enlightenment. The same goes for much of Judaism, which is actually God 1.0.1. Islam would benefit so much from a reformation of its own, a version of God 3.0.1, that would separate mosque from state, secular territorial law from religious law, and find within Islam and its sacred teachings all the interpretations necessary to embrace modernity. Some modern Muslim scholars have attempted such a reinterpretation-reformation, but they have often been censored or attacked for their efforts.

It is not hard to understand why, given the deep dissonance between how Muslims look at the world, their faith, the law, and the state and how Western societies—whether in Europe or North America—look at these things. This contrast is going to become an increasing source of tension as more and more Muslims immigrate to the West. British philosopher Roger Scruton summarized the problem well in an essay in *National Review* (June 17, 2002):

Public anxiety concerning the ability of Muslims to assimilate [in Western societies] is not entirely ill-founded. It may be exaggerated to talk of a clash of civilizations; but it is not exaggerated to refer to a clash of jurisdictions. A religious jurisdiction can coexist with a territorial jurisdiction, when each is careful to relinquish the space required by the other. In effect, this coexistence was what the Enlightenment set out to achieve, and it achieved it so effectively that religion has all but vanished from the public and political life of Western nations. But the Enlightenment was an episode within Judeo-Christian civilization, and has had no parallel in the Islamic world. This does not mean that Muslims cannot be loyal citizens of Western states—of course they can. But in becoming loyal citizens they must exchange tribal and [religious] loyalties for loyalties of a very different kind, founded on common territory and secular rule of law. Many have done this. But some find the jettisoning of their rival loyalties to be either difficult or impossible. Some do not even understand that this is what might be required of them, in exchange for the privileges afforded by their new abode. . . . Islamist terrorism is founded on a holy law that does not exist in order to resolve conflicts peacefully [as secular Western law does], still less to offer terms to the unbeliever. Nor is it defined over territory. Islamic law is strictly speaking an extra-territorial, indeed, an extra-terrestrial law, which marshals human society with a loud voice from the heavens. Islam means "submission," and peace comes only when all opposition to Divine command is vanquished. . . . It is hardly surprising, therefore, that people who have internalized the Islamic conception of law find it difficult to integrate into Western societies. For integration is only possible by becoming a citizen, and citizens must see themselves as such. In other words, they must confine their religious and ethnic loyalties to the private sphere, and be fellow citizens with people from other families, other tribes, and other faiths. . . . While our native institutions—including the churches—are constantly extending the messages of peace and conciliation to the Islamic newcomers, the newcomers themselves for the most part remain silent, comprehending neither the gesture nor the culture that extends it. . . . How we in the West are to deal with this, I do not know. But one thing is certain, which is that we must learn to confront the new realities, and not censor those who draw attention to them.

In addition to this theological dissonance between Western and Islamic values, there is also the sheer daily reality of it—the fact that when these young Muslim men in Europe turn to religion, and to Islam, it becomes the sole source of meaning in their lives, and they see it, and feel it, as being under attack every day all around them. They see it as being besieged by the liberation of women, who no longer obey any of the traditional social rules; by the general secularization of European society; and by the promotion of consumerism and materialism—all of which they believe is driven primarily by America. They see America as the most powerful lethal weapon destroying their religious universe, or at least the universe they would like to build. And that is why they transform America into the ultimate evil, even more than Western Europe, an evil that needs to be weakened and, if possible, destroyed. Even by suicide? Why not? If America is destroying the source of meaning in their lives, then it needs to be destroyed back.

(There is also something about the fact that virtually none of these young men were married, or had their religious fervor tempered in any way through a relationship with a woman, that must have contributed to their rage and extremism. It is just not normal, but I would need Dr. Freud to help me sort all that out.)

While it was this chemical reaction with the West that bred the rage and motives in these alienated young men, someone needed to light their fuses and direct their rage at America as the source of all evil. Here too, Europe played a role as a haven for radical Muslim preachers who were evicted from Arab countries, like Egypt, and permitted to stay in Europe under the guise of political asylum. Rather than really keeping a close eye and ear on these radical preachers, the Europeans often turned a blind eye and deaf ear to them. As one senior U.S. military officer at NATO headquarters in Brussels told me, "The Belgian attitude toward terrorists was: Do whatever you want, just don't do it here. . . . We won't bother you if you won't bother us."

Put young Muslim males suffering from a poverty of dignity together with radical Muslim preachers and a lax security environment in

Europe (and America) and you have all the basic ingredients that went into producing Mohamed Atta and his fellow key pilots and plotters. (I'll talk about the muscle guys, the Saudis, later.)

"All this makes clear that many of the terrorists we are now confronting are a Western phenomenon, existing inside the Islamic diaspora that is an established fact of life in the U.S. and Europe," concludes Karatnycky. "And this means that the war against terrorism will require relentless efforts within the borders of the West, even as it is prosecuted in the far-flung outposts of the Islamic world. It means that networks of terrorists may well be found among the students and scholars who today walk the halls of Western universities and congregate after hours in sundry political and 'religious' groups, not as 'sleepers' ready to act under orders, but as Islamic radicals minted right here."

THE MAGIC KINGDOM

Before I left for Saudi Arabia, I got an e-mail from a Bahraini friend in which she wryly wished me well on my visit to "the Magic Kingdom." She was warning me that this country was otherworldly, and she was right. My trip to Saudi Arabia turned out to be one of the most unusual of my career. As readers of this book will note from my columns, I pointed the finger early and harshly at the Saudis as being partly responsible for September 11. It was not just because fifteen Saudi young men were among the hijackers, or because Osama bin Laden was a Saudi, or because Saudi Arabia had supported and funded the Taliban. It was also because Saudi charities, either deliberately or unknowingly, had helped to fund Al Qaeda and ultraconservative Islamic schools around the world and because the Saudi education system itself used textbooks that, in part, promoted intolerance against non-Muslims.

What angered me above all, though, was the fact that Saudi Arabia never even apologized for the fact that fifteen of its sons took part in the biggest mass murder in American history. I did not expect them to take responsibility, but I did expect Saudi Arabia's government to say, "These young men were out to destroy the U.S.-Saudi relationship and to undermine our own country. They do not reflect the will or the interests of the Saudi people. But we must nevertheless acknowledge that they came from our breast, and for that reason we say to the American people that we are sorry and we will do our part to ensure that nothing like this happens again."

Just a short statement like that would have bought the Saudis a great deal of goodwill in America. Instead, the word from Riyadh was first silence and then denial—the hijackers couldn't have been Saudis; and even if they were, they were deviants, so Saudi Arabia was not responsible for them; and even if Saudi Arabia was responsible for them, the real blame belonged to Israel for making so many young Arabs angry by the way Israel treated the Palestinians.

I found this flight from responsibility both enraging and dangerous, and it eventually led me to conclude that Saudi Arabia could be to the war on terrorism what the Soviet Union was to the cold war—the source of the money, the ideology, and the people who were now threatening us.

But that also made Saudi Arabia essential to the solution. We could not even begin to resolve this problem of Islam-and-modernity-and-the-West without the resources and Islamic credibility of Saudi Arabia. And that was why in January of 2002 I asked the Saudi Embassy in Washington for a visa, so I could try to answer for myself a simple question: Does Saudi Arabia want to be part of the solution? And even if it wants to be, can it be—will the system there allow it to promote a more tolerant version of Islam?

I was surprised by the fact that as soon as I requested a visa from the Saudis, through Adel al-Jubeir, the young foreign policy adviser to Crown Prince Abdullah bin Abdulaziz, it was granted. This was early January of 2002. It was part of a general charm offensive the Saudis had decided to mount to let more reporters visit the country—on the assumption that they would come away with a more textured picture than the one they had without visiting. I definitely did get a more textured view of the place. Indeed, I met many Saudis, many more than I expected, whom I really liked. But I also saw and heard things that disturbed me very deeply.

Before describing the high points, I need to backtrack just a moment to relate something I wrote before leaving for Saudi Arabia that would prove important for how the trip unfolded.

After I returned from Afghanistan and Brussels in late January, I went up to New York for a day to attend the World Economic Forum. Soon after I arrived at the Waldorf-Astoria, the event site, I ran into an old friend of mine, the wise Moroccan statesman André Azouli. André, a Moroccan Jew and longtime trusted adviser to the royal family of Morocco, has been involved in the peace process with Israel for many years. The two of us spent fifteen minutes talking in the lobby about how bad the situation had become since the start of the latest intifada. In our back-and-forth, we often finished each other's sentences, and one idea that emerged from our discussion was the need for the Arabs to take some initiative to break the deadlock. There had been an Israeli peace plan put forward by Ehud Barak, there had been an American peace plan put forward by Bill Clinton, but there was no Arab peace plan — one that stipulated not just what the Arabs wanted from Israel but also what they were ready to give Israel, particularly in terms of normal trade, tourism, and diplomatic relations. The more André and I talked, the more I thought I should write a column saying as much.

"I think what I'll do," I told André, "is write a letter from Bush to the Arab League suggesting that they propose a peace plan at their next summit." He liked the idea and encouraged me to do so.

A short while later, I went into the bar and ran into Amr Moussa, the former Egyptian foreign minister and current head of the Arab League. I have known Moussa for a long time, and while we have had our disagreements, we've always been able to talk to each other frankly. We sat down at a table together with my friend Shafik Gabr, an enlightened Egyptian businessman, along with the Arab League ambassador to the UN. As best I can recollect, I asked Moussa the following: "Amr, what are you going to do with the Arab League? The organization is going nowhere. Are you just going to preside over its decline?"

We then talked about all sorts of things, among them what might make the Arab League relevant. I mentioned the idea that had come out of my conversation with André, and my intention to write it up as a column. Smoking a big cigar, Moussa rolled the idea over in his mind and the cigar in his fingers. Then he said, "You should write that column."

Hmmm, I thought, maybe there *is* an Arab constituency for this idea. Before I left New York, I tried the idea out on several other Arab diplomats there, and it met with approval from all of them. Later in the day, I ran into Moussa again, and he asked me, "Are you going to write that column?" I assured him I would.

The column ran less than a week later, on February 7, 2002. It was a mock letter from President Bush to the top Arab leaders proposing that the March 2002 Arab League summit in Beirut come out with a simple declaration offering Israel full normalization of relations — trade, tourism, embassies — in return for full Israeli withdrawal from all the territories occupied in the 1967 war. A few days after that, a friend of mine in the Jordanian government told me that Jordan's King Abdullah had sent President Bush a letter making a very similar proposal on September 8, 2001, and a few days later the Jordanians sent me a copy of that letter from Amman. But the Jordanians asked that it not be published.

They told me that if the idea did not originate with one of the "big boys," that is, Egypt or Saudi Arabia, it would never be able to garner a majority in the Arab League.

All this was in the back of my mind when, two days after arriving in Saudi Arabia, I was offered an interview with Crown Prince Abdullah, who is the effective ruler, since King Fahd has suffered a debilitating stroke. On Wednesday afternoon, February 13, Adel al-Jubeir picked me up at my hotel to drive me out to the crown prince's ranch on the outskirts of Riyadh, just across from the main track where Abdullah races some of his Arabians. After we arrived, Adel and I sat for an hour or so outside Abdullah's tent, eating candy and waiting for him to finish his meetings. (Abdullah works from the late afternoon until about 5 a.m.— a tradition dating back to Bedouin times, when it was too hot to work outside during the day.)

When I was finally ushered into his long tent, I found myself in a room with chairs all around the walls, on which were seated various members of the royal family and the cabinet. Abdullah was sitting at the far end in a larger chair, angled so it could face a wall of TV screens. I counted over twenty small TV screens surrounding a single huge big-screen TV. Abdullah had a tray in front of him on which was the TV remote so he could shift anything from the small screen to the big screen, three tall glasses with three different kinds of juice, and a small bowl of popcorn.

He asked me to introduce myself to everyone in the room, so I went around and shook hands with each person there, a collection of royals and senior officials, all in Saudi national dress. I had this overwhelming sense of being somewhere I had never been before—not only in this life, but in all previous lives. As an American Jew from Minnesota, and as *The New York Times* columnist who had been most critical of Saudi Arabia, I felt like a total alien as all eyes were on me. There were only men present. They seemed to be just sitting around, schmoozing and smoking water pipes, known in Saudi Arabia as "hubbly-bubbly."

Abdullah does not speak English, so we made small talk, with Adel translating. I broke the ice by presenting the crown prince with an Arabic version of my book *The Lexus and the Olive Tree*. I asked him about his farm and his horses, and he responded with one eye on me and one eye looking back and forth at all the TV screens. He was obviously watching news from the Middle East, in particular, Israel and Palestine, broadcast from Arab TV stations and CNN all day long. The Arab broadcasts, the only ones whose commentary he understood, made no attempt to be balanced or objective. I'm sure he had other sources of information, but he clearly relied heavily on Arab television for his window on the world.

Having said that, Abdullah, who is in his seventies—I don't think they had birth certificates around in the desert when he was born—struck me as something of a fox. He was not worldly, but he had the savvy of a tribal elder whose family has had to survive by its wits.

After about forty-five minutes of small talk (I was really hungry and helped myself to a few handfuls of his popcorn), we went into another long tent, where a mile-long buffet had been set up. Abdullah led the way, sampling each of the dishes that struck his fancy, using a tasting spoon. Anything he liked, a servant following behind him heaped onto a plate. There were Arab, Italian, French, Asian, and American dishes. It was a Roman feast, but I think it went on every night he was home, and members of the royal family seemed to just float in and out. Abdullah was seated at the head of the long, rectangular table, and directly in front of him, pretty well blocking his view of everyone else there, was—you guessed it—another huge big-screen TV. We ate and talked and watched TV. After dinner we went back into the first tent and had more coffee.

I started to wonder whether anything was going to happen. Finally, at around 10 p.m., Abdullah signaled that he wanted to have a serious talk and we should adjourn to his house, which was about a hundred yards away. We walked over there, and he and Adel and I closeted ourselves in one of his sitting rooms.

That's when the fun started.

I took out my notepad and we began the interview, with me focusing in on who the fifteen Saudi hijackers were and why Saudi Arabia never apologized for its citizens' role in 9/11. His response was because it was obvious to them that bin Laden and his boys were out to destroy the U.S.-Saudi relationship, among other things; they thought this surely would be obvious to the Americans too. "We never thought for a second that the Americans would doubt the kingdom's friendship," said Abdullah, as I scribbled notes. "We misunderstood the American psyche. We thought they thought like us. If you have a genuine friendship, you don't doubt your friends."

This was typical of the whole Saudi response to 9/11: Bin Laden and his boys were bad apples and working against the interests of Saudi Arabia—therefore Saudi Arabia has no responsibility for them and, anyway, some "foreign intelligence service" was actually behind them. There was no acknowledgment, and indeed no willingness even to consider publicly, whether the plotters were who they were because of things they had learned in Saudi schools, or because of the failure of the Saudi system to provide jobs and opportunities for its young people, or because the Saudi government had turned a blind eye to radical preachers in their own backyard who, the government knew, were preaching messages of anti-American hate from mosques or in private prayer groups. To the extent that Saudis were prepared to examine what produced the suicidal rage of these hijackers, their explanations started and stopped with one thing: Israel and the Israeli occupation. That, they told me over and over, is the only reason young Arabs are angry and why they focus their anger on America.

In fairness to Abdullah, immediately after 9/11 he spoke publicly and forcefully about the need for "self-examination" by Saudis and other Arabs, but it's hard to point to any credible initiative taken by any Arab state in this regard. Only one Saudi newspaper did any serious investigation into who the fifteen Saudi hijackers were. Nobody else either wanted to know or was allowed to ask.

It was probably an hour or so into the interview before I raised the question of the Arab League summit, saying basically the following:

"Your Highness, the Arab League will be meeting soon in Beirut. I wrote a column before I came here suggesting that if the Arab League really wanted to do something productive, really wanted to foster a breakthrough, it would have to put an Arab peace plan on the table. Let's be honest. There is an Israeli peace plan that was put forward by Prime Minister Barak. There is an American peace plan that was put forward by President Clinton. But there is no Arab peace plan—one that says not only what the Arabs want but what they are ready to give. So isn't it time the whole Arab League put something of its own on the table—like offering full normalization of relations, trade, and tourism with Israel, in return for a full Israeli withdrawal from all the territories occupied in the 1967 war?"

At that point Abdullah looked at me with mock astonishment and said, "Have you broken into my desk? Have you entered my office?" Then, turning to Adel, he said, "Adel, did you take him into my office? The reason I ask is because this is exactly my idea, and only two people have seen it. I have been working on this idea for three months. My plan was to put it before the Arab League summit. But now that Sharon has gone on a rampage I have decided it would be difficult to get support for it, so I am not going to deliver it now. But if I were to pick up the phone now and tell my assistant to read you the speech I was thinking of delivering, it would be identical to the idea you proposed . . . [Now,] if I give it as a speech, people will think I got the idea from you, but it was my idea."

As I took all this in, I was trying to think fast. On the one hand, it seemed like his statement had real potential news value, even if he wasn't ready to give the speech yet. On the other hand, our conversation was off the record, so it only had value if I could get his quotes on the record. And the bit about his being ready to give the speech, but then putting it back in the drawer because of Sharon's actions, was an obvious cop-out.

"Frankly, Your Highness, I've heard that before," I said to him. "So many times in the past, Arab leaders have said, 'Oh, if only Netanyahu had not done this, I was just about to make peace with Israel. Oh, if only Sharon had not done that, I would have visited Israel.' After a while, sir, it's a little hard to take seriously. If you are serious about it, you have to put it on the record."

Abdullah then asked me what I would quote him as saying. I suggested the main idea about normalization of relations with Israel in return for full withdrawal. He mulled it over for a while and then said, "I have to think about it."

We then went on to other subjects, talking for another hour and a half. As I got up to leave, I made one last appeal for putting his quotes on the record. I said to him, "There is no way that President Bush is going to take a political risk to break the Israeli-Palestinian deadlock if you aren't ready to take a risk as well."

Abdullah, who was also standing, thought about that for a second and said, "Why didn't President Bush ever say that to me?"

"I don't know," I said. "I think the Arabs have not done a very good job of understanding this administration. The first thing you have to understand is that this is not 'Bush II.' This is 'Reagan III.' This is not the continuation of President Bush, the father's administration. This is the continuation of the neo-conservative Reagan administration. This administration is Reagan squared."

Abdullah's eyes lit up at that. He immediately knew what that meant. He seemed eager to learn more about Washington. So I continued, as best I can recall, with the following: "The other thing you guys have gotten completely wrong, Your Highness, is that you thought that with Clinton gone, all the Jews were gone from Middle East policymaking—no more Dennis Ross, no more Sandy Berger, no more Madeleine Albright, no more Aaron Miller—no more Jews. And you all thought that was a great thing. Well, you're right, the Jews of the Clinton administration are gone, and they aren't making Middle East policy anymore."

But now you have the WASPs, I added, and they are very capable and experienced, but "they couldn't care less about the Israeli-Palestinian conflict. It is not an issue that resonates with them at all. They have no emotional connection to it." The Jews of the Clinton administration may not have succeeded at making peace, I concluded, "but their mistake was that they cared too much, not too little."

Abdullah drank all this in and asked more questions about Washington. This was not the sort of information he was getting from watching all those Arab TV broadcasts. I left his house around 2 a.m. and went back to my hotel. It had been a fun evening in a touristy sort of way, but I did not have high hopes that Abdullah would put his remarks on the record. When I got up the next morning, I started working on a totally different column.

The next afternoon, though, Adel called and asked me to type up the exact quotes I would want to use and fax them over, which I did. He would check again with Abdullah. A couple hours later he called back to say, "Go with it. It's all yours."

"Adel," I said, "I don't mean to be insulting, but does he know what he said? Does he know what 'normalization' means? Did you give him the right translation in Arabic? I don't want to publish this and then have him deny it."

Adel said, "Let me double-check all the language."

He called back later and said: "He said exactly what he means. He understands perfectly that 'peace' means peace, 'normalization' normal relations—embassies, trade, the whole business."

"OK," I said, "then I'm going with it."

This was now late Thursday afternoon, February 14. I still had thirty-six hours before I would send this column to New York (my Sunday column is filed by midnight Friday), and I was certain that at any moment I was going to get a phone call asking me to tone down the crown prince's remarks. So, just in case, I finished my alternative column so I wouldn't be left high and dry right on deadline.

In the meantime I went about my business, seeing many other Saudi ministers, including some members of the royal family, over the next three days. It quickly became apparent to me that Abdullah had not told anyone else in his family or his government that he was making this statement. He also did not notify his embassy in Washington. I know, because at one point on Saturday night Abdullah's aide asked me for the State Department and White House phone numbers for several senior U.S. officials. When I asked why they didn't go through their Washington embassy, it was apparent to me that they were working around it.

By Saturday night, I was exhausted from the whole business and was out for a late dinner at a Saudi journalist's house. When I got back to my hotel, the Jidda Sheraton, the desk clerk stopped me and said, "President Clinton is trying to reach you. He left his number," and he handed me the message. I could not imagine what this was about. I called back. It was the former President's New York home, and Mrs. Clinton answered. We exchanged pleasantries and then she put her husband on the line. Clinton had been in discussions with Shimon Peres and his longtime aide, Uri Savir, about a back-channel negotiation that Peres and Arafat aide Abu Ala'a had been conducting. They had drafted a general outline of a land-for-peace deal that Mr. Clinton said Arafat had even initialed. He suggested I write it up. I couldn't help but be impressed by Clinton's desire to try to resurrect the peace deal that had eluded him, but I told him that because I was in Saudi Arabia I was not in a position to sort out how solid it all was, and I would have to wait until I got back home and could make some phone calls to Israel. I tipped him off about the Abdullah statement that would be coming out the next morning, and he immediately recognized that it was important and said he would try to be supportive. By the time we were done, it was 3 a.m. I was exhausted from the week. I craved sleep.

When the column came out in the *Times* on Sunday morning, February 17, and hit the Saudi newspapers on Monday—where it was translated word for word into Arabic with no shenanigans—everyone in Saudi Arabia was taken by surprise. What made the moment even more meaningful was the fact that the hajj, the annual Muslim pilgrimage to Mecca, was set to begin the next day. So there were an extra 2 million Muslims from all around the Muslim world in Saudi Arabia at the time—2 million extra Muslims and one extra Jew.

In retrospect, what do I think Abdullah was up to? Unquestionably, one of his objectives was to improve his country's badly damaged image in America, as a result of the involvement of so many Saudis in 9/11—by changing the subject. But that was not the only thing on his mind. His declaration was in many ways a coup d'état at home. He spoke for the al-Saud family on the most sensitive issue, making a whole new departure toward Israel, and did so without really consulting the family. I think that in some ways Abdullah finally became king with this statement. I don't think all of his brothers and half brothers necessarily approved of that. But by this statement he made himself a bigger player in Arab and world politics than he had ever been before. And he leveraged his increased status abroad to increase his power back home and really establish himself as the man in charge.

Last, Abdullah understood that if the Arab summit happened and all the Arab leaders did was throw a rock at Ariel Sharon and wrap their arms protectively around Iraq, they were headed for a collision with the United States of America. He had to begin a different narrative and demonstrate to the United States that attacking Iraq was not the only game in the Middle East. On one level, the Saudi ruling family uses the Palestinian issue to deflect attention from its own corruption and misgovernance, but on another level Saudi rulers have to worry about the genuine feelings on their street about this issue. If it remains unresolved, those feelings, which are constantly stoked up by the Arab media and melded with rage against America for supporting Israel, could create a mood among young Saudis that would make it impossible for Saudi Arabia to maintain any public cooperation with the United States. That is a threat to the ruling family. On a personal level, Abdullah was clearly obsessed with reasserting Muslim control over the two sacred mosques in Jerusalem. From what I could tell, when we discussed Jerusalem, the whole city for him consisted of the two holy mosques on the Temple Mount. He did not seem particularly aware of Jewish Jerusalem or its geography.

It took a couple of days for the Abdullah statement to garner attention, but once it did, it took over the Arab debate. A few days after I returned from Saudi Arabia, a very senior Lebanese political figure called me at home in Bethesda from Paris. He said the following: "Tom, I can call you from here, because here in France only the Americans and French tap my phone [not the Syrians]." He suggested that I call Syrian foreign minister Farouk al-Sharaa and see if I could get him to do an interview and endorse the Saudi peace plan. The Lebanese were desperate to see it go forward, but the Syrians were holding back from embracing it in full. I told him it would not be appropriate for me to make such a call, and anyway, Sharaa would never take it. He offered to try to help facilitate it, but I passed. I also got a call from a member of the Israeli cabinet, who wanted to know how real the Saudi initiative was, as well as from the emir of one of the Arab Persian Gulf states, who wanted to know the same. Both were friends, so I told them each the story I am telling here. It also gave me a chance to catch up on Israeli and inter-Arab gossip.

In the end, Abdullah was true to his word and brought his ideas to the Arab summit in Beirut at the end of March. Under pressure from the Syrians, Abdullah watered down his offer to Israel from "normalization" of relations—trade, tourism, embassies—to a more vague "normal" relations, but he did in the end give the basic speech that he said was in his drawer. Was it really in his drawer? Or had he gotten the idea from my column and then decided, with the help of Adel and their P.R. firm, that by appropriating it and then repackaging it through an interview with me, he could help transform Saudi Arabia from terrorist factory to peace-maker—without any cost, because he knew Ariel Sharon would reject it? I have no idea. I would not rule anything out.

But my own bottom line was very simple: If in any way I helped get the leader of Saudi Arabia, the world's most important Muslim country, to put on the record for the first time his willingness to normalize rela-tions with the Jewish state in return for an Israeli withdrawal, and if in any way that helped break the deadlock with Israel or change the lan-guage of the debate over the long haul, it was a good thing. It would be the first real counteroffer the Arabs had made since President Clinton summoned Arafat to Camp David.

But as exciting as all this was, I also had no intention of letting it divert me from the main reason I had come to Saudi Arabia.

MR. TOM

I had come to better understand the forces that produced those fifteen Saudi hijackers. The day after I arrived in Riyadh, I flew down to the Empty Quarter of Saudi Arabia—the world's largest sand desert—in the southeastern part of the country. I was invited to join the Saudi Minister of Petroleum and Mines, Ali al-Naimi, who was giving a tour to his Nor-wegian counterpart and his accompanying press delegation from Nor-way. Our plane landed on a short airstrip sandwiched between two three-hundred-foot-high reddish-brown sand dunes, in a place called Shaybah, one of Saudi Arabia's newest oil fields. Soon after we arrived, Naimi, a shortish, intense man with a very sharp mind, insisted we all follow him for a walk onto the dunes. So we all took off our shoes, rolled up our pants, and started trudging up and down the dunes, feet sinking deep into the sand with every step, until we were about a mile into the desert. The sun was setting, turning the dunes into an ocean of sandy waves, which were all you could see for 360 degrees. It was like a *National Geographic* centerfold, one of the most spectacular sights to which I've ever been treated.

Sitting alone atop one of those dunes, I got two insights into Saudi Arabia. One was what an isolated place it was, insulated from the world first by geography and later by oil wealth, which allowed it to be very selective about whom it let in. Because of this isolation, both geographic and self-created, Saudi Arabia is a country that has been talking to itself for a long time without really being challenged, or jolted, by outsiders or outside ideas. That's why September 11 would turn out to be such a shock to the Saudi system. The world crashed right through Saudi Arabia's isolation, arriving without a visa and demanding answers about who those fifteen Saudi hijackers were. The post-9/11 world was just like Jack Nicholson in the famous bathroom scene in the movie *The Shining* where he hacks through the bathroom door with an ax, peers in, and shouts: *"Heeeeere's Johnny!"* It shocked Saudi Arabia as much as it terrified Shelley Duvall in that movie.

The second thing that hit me, sitting atop that dune, was how natural it was that a puritanical, austere version of Islam would have taken root in this landscape. I thought to myself: "If you can't believe in one God out here, you never will, because out here there's nothing between you and heaven. There isn't even a tree or rock to pray to. Buddhism never could have emerged here."

Because many of my columns had been translated into Arabic and run in Saudi newspapers or read there on nytimes.com over the Internet, everywhere I went I found people who were keenly aware of what I had written about Saudi Arabia. My average conversation with a Saudi intellectual, official, or businessman who had not been prepped to meet me (and therefore to be nice) went like this:

"Hi," I would say, "I'm Tom Friedman."

"The one who writes about us?" they would answer.

"Yes," I would say. "That one."

"You're here?" they would ask.

"Yes," I would say, "I'm here."

"Someone gave you a visa?" they would ask.

"Yes, I came on a visa. I'm not here illegally."

"I have to tell you I hate everything you've written about Saudi Arabia—I think you are really biased," they would then say. But then the conversation would end like this: "Would you come to my house for dinner? I would really like to get some people together to talk to you."

Everywhere I went, people really wanted to talk—they wanted to tell me why I was wrong about Saudi Arabia and why it was not a factory for Islamist terrorists. Most of my time there was spent in group meetings, with me debating five, ten, and even thirty people at a time. It was exhausting, exhilarating, frustrating, and often depressing, because of the profound cultural, moral, religious, and political gaps between us.

Most of the people I was talking to were educated Saudis who were deeply upset that their country and faith were being criticized and denigrated in the world's press. Typical was a meeting I held with about twenty-five doctors and nurses at King Fahd National Guard Hospital in Riyadh. Seated next to me at the lunch was an American-trained Saudi doctor who, as she sat down, handed me the printout of an e-mail she had written to me a month earlier but never sent because she couldn't find an address. It said at the top of the page:

From: Hiba Fatani
To: Thomas Friedman . . . Lay off the Muslims and look at your own teachings.

The rest of the memo consisted of quotes from the Old Testament that suggested either the racial or religious supremacy of Jews or justified Jewish violence against others. It concluded by saying, "The Talmud's unashamed and frequent references to non-Jews as animals and 'supernal refuse,' as well as accounts of boiling their enemies in semen and excrement, *might have even made Hitler blush.*" Everything was supposedly footnoted with biblical citations. The subtext was not hard to discern: The Koran is not the only holy book with bloodcurdling pronouncements in it, and if you want to take ours out of context to judge us, we will take yours that way.

Of course she was right that the Old Testament, like the New Testament and the Koran, is full of violent and intolerant references. And I could understand how it looked from her point of view. But there was just one difference: There was no Christian or Jewish terrorist leader I knew of who was citing those references as justification for going out and killing non-Jews or non-Christians, while in Saudi Arabia there were preachers, albeit a minority, who were issuing religious rulings, precisely on the basis of Koranic verses, to justify September 11. And not only were they doing it, but before September 11 no one within their community seemed to be censuring them for it. In today's world, this is dangerous stuff. In the Middle Ages, those who wanted to use religion for political or destructive ends had to mobilize or excite thousands or millions of people to march to Jerusalem or somewhere else. Not today. Today you just need to motivate nineteen young men to hijack four modern passenger jets and fly them into tall buildings. Today scripture plus technology plus acolytes can be a weapon of mass destruction.

Another doctor stood up at our lunch and told me that his father was the author of one of the most important and widely used Islamic textbooks in the Saudi education system, and he and his five brothers and sisters were all doctors. His point, he said, was that if the Saudi Islamic education system was so perverse and violence-inducing, how did they end up all serving mankind as doctors?

I heard their anguish at feeling miscast. And I have to say I was quite impressed by how many of them had been educated in the United States at their government's expense, and had fulfilled their obligation to come back and repay their debt to Saudi society. While some were legally bound to do so, many, nevertheless, seemed to sincerely want to be back and help build their country.

All that aside, the point I tried to make over and over again was that, while the Western media were by no means perfect, Islam was not being perverted by us, but by Muslims who, claiming to be speaking in the name of Islam, were committing suicide against American buildings or murdering journalists like Danny Pearl. And while our own President kept giving speeches about how Islam was a peaceful faith, only a few Arab or Muslim leaders gave similar speeches after September 11 taking on their own radical Islamists or denouncing suicide bombing. The reason these leaders, including the Saudi ones, did not do so was because they are unelected, and actually alienated in many ways from their faith or ignorant of its real teachings, and therefore loath to ideologically challenge extreme religious authorities, upon whom they depend for legitimacy.

Iranian historians (and sisters) Ladan and Roya Boroumand wrote an essay in the April 2002 issue of the *Journal of Democracy* titled "Terror, Islam, and Democracy," which I happened to read soon after I got home from Saudi Arabia. I regretted that I hadn't had it with me when I was there. In their essay they demonstrate how violent Islamists have basically appropriated the symbols and language of Islam in ways that pose a modern totalitarian challenge to both authentic Islam and democracy—and the mainstream Islamic leaders and theologians have done little to really challenge them.

"The Islamists see themselves as bold warriors against modernity and the West," they wrote,

> but in fact it is they who have imported and then dressed up in Islamic-sounding verbiage some of the most dubious ideas that ever came out of the modern West [such as Fascism and Leninist totalitarianism], ideas which now—after much death and suffering—the West itself has generally rejected. Had we not become so alien to our own cultural heritage, our theologians and intellectuals might have done a better job of exposing the antinomy

between what Islamists say and what Islam actually teaches. They might have more effectively undercut the terrorists' claim to be the exclusive and immediate representatives of God on earth, even while they preach a doctrine that does nothing but restore human sacrifice, as if God had never sent the angel to stop Abraham from slaying his son.

So while I listened to the anguish of Saudis who felt miscast, and acknowledged their pain, I also made sure every Saudi I spoke with understood that to this day Saudi Arabia had never explained to Americans what produced their fifteen hijackers. Often I was told, "Hey, we have our nuts and you have yours. Look at Timothy McVeigh or the Unabomber." Yes, I would answer, look at them. First of all, they didn't fly three thousand miles to kill people of a different country and blame them for all their ills. They were Americans who killed Americans. Second, virtually no one in America stood up and applauded Timothy McVeigh. There was no movement behind him. He was a lone, deranged man. Ditto the Unabomber. Yet in Saudi Arabia, many, many people quietly or not so quietly applauded what bin Laden and his boys did. And Saudis needed to face that, because if they couldn't tell me what produced that sort of hatred—and not just what we have done to produce it by supporting Israel, but what they have allowed to grow in the dark corners of their own society—then many Americans would continue to be frightened of them.

I spent one evening at the offices of the *Okaz* newspaper in Jidda, the largest in Saudi Arabia. When I got there at 9 p.m. expecting to just sit around and chat with a few journalists, I found myself in a large room with a rectangular table in the middle, around which were seated some twenty-five journalists, academics, and businesspeople, both men and women. There was a computer next to me where people in *Okaz* bureaus outside Riyadh were e-mailing or phoning in questions. On the wall was a large banner that read: OKAZ WELCOMES THOMAS FRIEDMAN. I was overwhelmed by the intensity of their hospitality, and then by the intensity of their grilling. At times it was touching, particularly when the Saudi women present talked about the pain they felt at having their religion denounced around the world in the wake of 9/11. I could feel the depth of their anguish, and one of them almost brought me to tears talking about how important Islam was for her identity and how upset she was by seeing and hearing it tarnished. And at times, the conversation got very heated, but they treated me respectfully and I tried to do the same. Typical of our exchanges was one that went like this:

Okaz reporter: "Why don't you call Ariel Sharon a terrorist? By your definition of terrorism, he is murdering innocent civilians."

"OK," I said. "Let's make a deal." I then took out a blank piece of white paper. "Let's have a contract. I promise that in the future I will always call Ariel Sharon a terrorist in my columns—on the condition that in the future you will always call Palestinians who blow up Israeli kids in pizza parlors terrorists. Do we have a deal?"

I got no takers.

They could very clearly see what was being done to Palestinians, but they refused to acknowledge, even one iota, what Palestinians were doing to Jews. Because Saudi Arabia does not allow the open practice of any other religions on its soil, and because there was no such thing as a Christian or Jewish Studies department (let alone an American Studies department) in any of its universities—where Saudis might learn about other faiths firsthand—it was clear to me that the standard myths, straight out of *The Protocols of the Elders of Zion*, about Jews controlling America, the world, and global finance were widely and deeply held there.

I interviewed, off the record, one of the most senior Saudi ministers, a top member of the royal family. We spoke for two hours, mostly about who the Saudi hijackers were. At the close of the interview, he said to me through his interpreter: "Now I have a question for you."

I knew what was coming.

"Is it true that the Jews in America control all the banks and media?" he asked. It was asked with such sincere curiosity—since I may have been the first authentic Jew this man had ever met—that I was almost tempted to whisper back to him: "How did you know? We thought we had kept it a secret!"

I did my best to try to explain that our biggest media companies and banks and corporations were all public companies, and not under the control of a Jewish cabal or, in many cases, even Jewish executives, but I'm sure it did little to change his mind. And this was a very senior minister.

I did have some fun, though, when this same senior minister told me over and over again that he was certain that the fifteen Saudi hijackers must have been directed by a "foreign intelligence agency" (read either the CIA or Mossad) because they simply were incapable of pulling off an operation like this on their own. Translation: Arabs are not that clever or organized.

At that point I said to him, "You know, Your Highness, I have to tell you a story: I was in Israel on September 11, and on the morning of September 12 I went to the Israeli Ministry of Defense to talk to Israeli army terrorism experts about who they thought might have perpetrated this mass murder. I said to one of them: 'There is no way a group of Arab individuals could have done such a sophisticated operation on their own. There must have been a state intelligence agency behind them.' And do you know how the Israelis responded to me, Your Highness? They told me, 'You're wrong, Friedman.' First of all, they said, it was not all that hard to fly planes once they were up in the air. But more important, they said, look at the way Hezbollah organized itself to drive the mighty Israeli army out of Lebanon, and look at all the successful suicide operations that Palestinians have organized against Israeli targets. They have plenty of sophistication."

"So," I said, "you know, Your Highness, it strikes me as funny that the only people in the Middle East who believe Arabs are smart enough to pull off September 11 are the Jews."

At least he laughed when it was translated for him.

So who were the Saudi hijackers? As I said earlier, the hijackers, in my view, fell into two broad groups—the key plotters ("the Europeans") and the muscle men, most of whom were from Saudi Arabia. I could not interview any of the musclemen, but I think I know who they were: They were like a million young Saudi men today who finish high school or even college and have no jobs waiting for them—not with the government and not in the private sector, since unemployment in Saudi Arabia is roughly 30 percent of the available workforce (largely because most Saudis still refuse to do menial labor, so they have a huge imported labor force *and* Saudi unemployment). Many of them are the first in their families to get a higher education, and their parents are naturally proud of them. But when they can't find jobs and end up sitting around the coffeehouses, their parents no longer hold them in such high esteem. Go out any evening in Jidda and you can see these young men all over, in malls or cruising in cars, ogling veiled women or surfing the Internet in search of some cyber-contact with females. Some 40 percent of the population of Saudi Arabia are under fourteen, and they are all marching toward a workplace where there are not enough jobs to go around.

Some of these young men naturally drift into a mosque or a prayer group. Many of these prayer groups are now led by unofficial preachers outside the Saudi state religious system. They preach hatred toward the infidels and intolerance toward the non-Muslim world. It seems likely that some of the Saudi hijackers first came in contact with Al Qaeda and went through Terrorism 101 when they signed up for the jihad in Afghanistan against the Soviets. Then they returned to Saudi Arabia and drifted some more. And one day someone from Al Qaeda probably showed up again at one of their mosques and whispered to these young men that they had another special mission for them, one that could be dangerous, but one that was big and important, something that would elevate how they think of themselves and how their families would think of them. And so they signed up. And on 9/11 they found themselves hijacking an airplane with box cutters.

Regrettably, ladies and gentlemen . . .

Ali Sa'ad al-Mussa, a Saudi columnist from the newspaper *Al-Watan*, published an article on December 24, 2001, about some of the Saudi hijackers, who came from his own home region—the mountainous southwestern Asir province of Saudi Arabia, near the border with Yemen.

"Most of the perpetrators were from families that had been favored by fortune," he wrote. "In most cases, they weren't even middle class, but higher. If poverty was a cause of terrorism, we wouldn't hear about a single Saudi in this affair." So what was it? Al-Mussa argues essentially that the young Saudi men caught up in this affair were dupes of those who knew how to use religion "as a cover beneath which venom is disseminated. . . . The southerners, primarily the mountain dwellers, are trustworthy and natural people, who believed in the Prophet [Muhammad], whose [Islam] reached them without conquest or warfare. But their problem is that since then they believe everything they are told. . . . Some of them did what they did because they listened even more attentively than they should have, regardless of who stands in the preacher's pulpit."

Qenan al-Ghamdi, the editor of *Al-Watan*, the only Saudi newspaper to do a serious investigation on who the hijackers were, was quoted by *The Boston Globe* (in a report from Saudi Arabia dated March 3, 2002) as saying that the Saudi hijackers were mostly "middle-class adventurers." They came from small towns located along the southwestern Highway 15—in the Asir region, which is known for its lack of strong governmental control. It was a relatively easy place for Al Qaeda agents and preachers to operate. This beautiful, mountainous southwestern region, the *Globe* also noted, is the center of Saudi tourism today: "The development of five-star hotels, amusement parks and concert venues, accompanied by a cool breeze in the high elevations of Asir, have drawn the wealthy royal and merchant families from other parts of the kingdom, and only served to increase the sense of resentment and frustration among the more middle-class locals."

Somewhere in these reports is the real story—Saudi young men, from middle-class families, unemployed or underemployed, sitting around, easy prey for radical imams and Al Qaeda. And that's why the top U.S. government experts on Saudi Arabia are worried. Because when they look at Saudi Arabia, what they see is a country getting younger, poorer, more religious, and more anti-American every day. I got an insight into this as I was driving around Jidda one afternoon. While I was in Saudi Arabia, I had two government escorts to keep an eye on me. (Frankly, with Danny Pearl having been abducted at the same time, I did not mind.) They were nice guys. Curious guys. And over our eight days together we got to know each other, and talked to each other quite personally about our families.

One day, one of them said to me in passing, "You know, Mr. Tom, the problem here is not Islam. The problem is too many young men with no job and no university and nowhere to go except to the mosque, where some [radical preachers] fill their heads with anger for America. Every home now has two or three not working. This the real problem, Mr. Tom."

When I flew into Saudi Arabia on British Airways, I was seated for the trip from London next to an attractive raven-haired Saudi woman, who was wearing blue jeans. We didn't exchange a word the whole way from London to Riyadh, but as we got closer to landing, I could see her getting increasingly agitated. As we pulled into the gate and I got up to leave, she explained to me her problem.

"I forgot my [veil] in my apartment in London," she said sheepishly. "I can't get off the plane without it. I called my husband before I left the airport in London and told him to send someone with it to meet the plane. I hope they're here."

She then went about furiously dialing her cell phone to call her house in Riyadh and see if the veil was on the way. All I could think was, What a waste! What a waste that such a lovely woman had to be covered, what a waste of her time and energy that she had to go through all this stress just to veil herself.

I met a lot of people in Saudi Arabia, many of whom I respected, even if we harshly disagreed. But I must say the people who impressed me the most were the women. Obviously, the only women I really talked to were educated and, for the most part, middle-class or wealthier. But I was struck by how much more they than the men really got in my face and told me what they thought. I think one of the hidden frustrations of

Saudi Arabia is not that it has kept its women barefoot, pregnant, and barred from driving. No, it's that all these Saudi fathers have educated their daughters but that Saudi society has provided few real outlets to satisfy them in the workplace.

The trend toward greater liberation for Saudi women was well on its way by the mid-1970s, but then came the Islamic revolution in Iran—a revolution which spurred a global competition between Iran and Saudi Arabia over who was the more authentic representative of Islam. That competition had a big impact globally, because Iran and Saudi Arabia started competitively funding fundamentalist schools all over the Muslim world. It also had a big impact inside Saudi Arabia. The Iranian revolution coincided with an attempted takeover of the Holy Mosque in Mecca by a group of Saudi fundamentalists who charged the Saudi ruling family with not being sufficiently pious. This, plus the Iranian revolution, terrified the Saudi rulers, and instead of challenging the religious hard-liners, they bowed to them, imposing even more severe religious practices on the society, like forcing malls to close their shops during daily prayers. As one Saudi minister put it to me: "If the Iranian revolution had not happened, women would be driving today in Saudi Arabia."

Yet, having said that, I was struck by how many Saudi women, even progressive ones, accepted the veil, and even not being allowed to drive, as part of their own unique culture—every bit as much as the red-checked headdresses that their husbands and sons wore. I am not suggesting that if tomorrow the Saudi religious police declared that women no longer had to wear the veil in public, all of them would continue doing so anyway. But I think a lot of them would, particularly women age thirty and older. It is not an Islamic thing—there is nothing in the Koran that dictates that women have to be veiled—it is a cultural thing, a conservative desert Bedouin thing.

It goes very deep. I toured one of the most modern hospitals in Riyadh as a guest of the director, and he insisted on showing me the intensive care unit. As we walked through, he pulled back the curtain on one patient—an elderly woman who had just suffered a heart attack. She was being given oxygen. She had the oxygen mask covering her mouth and then had put her black face veil over the oxygen mask. It was scary even to look at, and struck me as almost medieval. It was not mandated by the hospital at all, the doctor insisted. It was her desire, a deeply rooted cultural norm.

One evening in Jidda I was sitting in a seaside restaurant with Khalid al-Maeenah, the editor of *Arab News*, the main English-language Saudi newspaper, and his wife. Khalid's wife was wearing a black robe and head scarf as she unloaded on me with great passion her resentment that the United States never raised the issues of civil rights, human rights, and political reform in its discussions with Saudi Arabia. A well-educated and articulate woman, speaking in English, she made a strong case. We were then interrupted as the waiter came and laid out dinner. Khalid was smoking a big hubbly-bubbly water pipe, and I was thinking about what his wife had said.

Apropos of nothing, Khalid, a delightful rabble-rouser whom the Saudi regime tolerates, launched into a denunciation of the religious police for having confiscated all the red roses from the flower shops in Jidda on the day before Valentine's Day so that young, amorous Saudi boys and girls would not be able to exchange flowers. I was sitting there, eating my hummus and nodding my head, when Khalid's wife burst back into the conversation.

She told her husband he was completely wrong, that it was totally appropriate for the religious police to do this because "Valentine's Day is not our holiday—it is a Western holiday. We need to protect our Saudi culture from these foreign influences."

So there you have it. Over the first course, this modern Saudi woman was criticizing America for not being more aggressive in pressing a reform agenda on her country, and over the main course the same modern Saudi woman was defending the right of the religious police to confiscate all the roses on Valentine's Day.

The more time I spent in Saudi Arabia, the more I realized it was totally normal to find both views being held by the same person.

Not every conversation, though, left me in such a reflective mood. I had one particularly unpleasant session at the newspaper *Al-Medina*, a conservative Saudi daily. While meeting with a group of editors and columnists there, one of them, Abdul Mohsen Musalam, launched in on me that the whole problem in the Middle East was that America was "controlled by the Jews," and he knew this to be true, he said, because a few years ago some American congressman came through Saudi Arabia and told them that. I just got up and walked out, and not only because it was insulting. As I said to a Saudi friend later, how would he feel if he came to America and visited *The New York Times* editorial board and someone there piped up that the whole problem in the world was that Muslims and Arab oil money controlled everything—and we knew this to be true because a Lebanese parliamentarian once came through and told us that it was so? It was just so stupid and foolish that I didn't want to waste a second talking to someone who believed such nonsense. The Minister of Information called me a couple of hours later to apologize for this jerk. "You have your rednecks and we have ours," he said. Two months after I left Saudi Arabia, this same Saudi writer was thrown in jail for writing a poem suggesting that all Saudi judges were corrupt.

This sort of the-Jews-control-the-world conspiratorial thinking is deeply embedded in Saudi Arabia—more deeply, in fact, than in any country I have ever visited. As I noted earlier, this conspiratorial view of history is one of the great debilitating factors in Arab political life today, the notion that the future is always being shaped by forces or groups outside the Arabs' control, so they are never at fault for anything that befalls them. The idea that many Americans might identify with Israel not because the Israel lobby ordered them to do so, but for the same reason that they identify with Taiwan or South Korea or modern Germany—because they are free-market democracies that share our basic values and outlook on life—is a completely alien notion. Somebody, they insist, must have rigged this for Israel from behind the scenes.

Maybe my hardest conversation was my last one. It started in the home of a Saudi newspaper friend and included some male and female members of the royal family who had wanted to see me to express their outrage at what I had been writing about Saudi Arabia. I know they were sincere in their defense of their country and faith, but what drove me around the bend was their total unwillingness, at least in my presence, to acknowledge that they, their society, or their education system had played any role in producing the 9/11 hijackers. Every time you got to that issue, they had only one explanation: Israel. It was all Israel's fault. Young Arab men were angry because of the brutality they saw Israel meting out to Palestinians on their TV screens. Forget the fact that their own governments had shown enormous indifference to the plight of the Palestinians over the years. Forget the fact that Osama bin Laden never mentioned the Palestinian cause as motivating his actions until he felt he was losing support in the Arab world. Forget the fact that all kinds of people around the world are angry today but don't go hijacking planes and driving them into skyscrapers in New York. It was all Israel's fault.

At the end of this conversation, which coincided with my last day in Saudi Arabia, I turned to them and said, "I fear that the cultural, political, and religious gulf between us may just be unbridgeable." They did not disagree. Afterward, when I got back to my hotel room, I called a Saudi friend and told him I felt deeply, deeply depressed, and asked him: "Do you know where I can get a drink—moonshine, firewater, bootleg, anything?" He just chuckled. Even though alcohol was banned in Saudi Arabia, he said that just four blocks from my Jidda hotel it could all be arranged.

Just when I was feeling that there was no one in the whole country who really understood what I was saying, one of the participants at this lunch got in contact with me later in the afternoon. He gave me an eye-opening explanation of what I had been through.

"I was so frustrated listening to the conversation," he said to me. "They [the Saudi royals] know what the problem is, but they just were not going to say it in front of you, because what you are writing hits a nerve. I keep telling people: 'What this guy is writing are true things. Forget about his way of presenting things. Look at the facts.' It is true we have a problem with our educational system. . . . The tribal mentality here is very strong, and in the desert, when the tribe is attacked, you'd better stick together or you're dead. People know there are problems with our [Islamic] education system, and part of them is glad you're raising it. But they feel under attack, so they won't talk frankly to you [or want to be seen as making] changes because you demand them. The problem is not the books, but the preachers who use their Friday sermons to tell [young] people that America wants to destroy Islam. King Abdul Aziz created these [Wahhabi] religious leaders to unite the Arabian tribes. And then these religious leaders went against him, and then he had to control them. Since then there has been a kind of balance. The [al-Saud ruling family] let them operate where they won't destabilize the government, in education and in the mosque. But now [after 9/11] these extreme religious people went across a red line, and the government will pull them back. That is why 9/11 is a good thing . . . [Because] these people need to be controlled. But always it has to be in secret—never tell the outsiders you have a problem. No, I say—let's fix the problem and tell people we've fixed it, and they should fix theirs. Until we get over this tribal outlook, we will never develop."

I told this person that he had really salvaged my trip. He left me feeling that there are more than just a handful of people in Saudi Arabia who can be America's partners. The question is, How many of them are there, and will they ever have the power, and the courage, to reform the Magic Kingdom before it's too late?

THE ARAB AND MUSLIM LIBERALS

In April 2002 I went back to Jordan and Israel (and to Dubai and Indonesia) to measure how things had changed since I was there on September 11 and to close this diary where it began. Let me first discuss Jordan. In contrast to my visit in September, when the only subject in the air was bin Laden, this time around the only subject in the air was Ariel Sharon. My Arab friends—almost all of whom I would describe as Arab liberals who wanted to see their countries democratizing, liberalizing, and globalizing rather than stagnating—were all somewhat frustrated with me. The Arab liberals had been excited in some way about the post-9/11 events. They were hoping that they would, in the end, result in more American pressure on Arab autocratic regimes to open up, empower reformers, deal with some of their own domestic problems that had contributed to bin Ladenism, and pave the way for a breakthrough on the Palestine question.

But by the spring of 2002, all those hopes were on hold. My Arab liberal friends bombarded me with questions and e-mail messages: "Why can't you see what Ariel Sharon is doing to us? He's inflaming the whole Arab world by his actions, and he's destroying the liberal agenda." And my message back was: "We never would have had Sharon, we never would have been in this place, had Yasir Arafat chosen to negotiate a deal on the basis of the Clinton peace proposals. And I will not pretend that those proposals were not out there, and I will not forget that Arafat walked away from them."

I understood why they were frustrated. The Oslo decade had been good for many of them, and at least hopeful for many others (including me). They dreamed of a different future, at least for their kids—and not just a future without war, but one with better government and more opportunity for Arabs to realize their full potential, after being held back for so long by bad regimes. When the Oslo process, for all its problems, was moving forward in the mid-1990s, these reformers were empowered and on the rise. Never forget: The peace process in the Middle East has always been about so much more than just peace between Arabs and Israelis. It's also always been a cover, an engine, and a platform for all the progressive forces in the Arab world who want to integrate with the rest of the world, who want to trade, who want to open their economies, because they recognize that their societies are lagging far behind.

The peace process is precisely what gave Arab and Muslim liberals the first real political space to get beyond the one question that has dominated their politics for nearly a century—Who rules Palestine?—and into the questions that must dominate their politics if they are ever going to catch up with the rest of the world and thrive: How are we going to educate our kids? What kind of economy are we going to develop? What kind of constitutionalism and rule of law are we going to build?

It's not that Arab and Muslim liberals don't care about the Palestine problem, or care about it less than others in their society. It resonates with them just as deeply. The difference is that they really want to see it resolved so that they can address the other issues, in contrast to the nationalists, the worn-out intellectuals, and the dictators, who don't really want to see it resolved because they don't want to address the other issues.

I could smell the foul wind from the rotting of the Oslo peace process as soon as I sat down for breakfast in Amman with a group of young reformers from the business community and the circle of King Abdullah. The Israeli-Palestinian violence had so inflamed the Arab street— thanks in large part to Arab satellite TV stations that were competing to see who could show the most Israeli brutality in the most pro-Palestinian manner—that it had become almost impossible for Jordan to keep its public focused on King Abdullah's liberal agenda, which involved revamping Jordan's education system, putting computers in every school, wiring every school to the Internet, and investing in rural development.

As Jordan's Queen Rania put it to me when I went to interview her and her husband in their home in Aqaba: "It is like we were running this race and we were really starting to sprint, and suddenly this new situation came and put these weights on our ankles. We're still running, but it is a lot harder now."

With the collapse of the peace process, on top of 9/11, it was also becoming difficult to interest foreign investors, or even tourists, in coming to the Middle East. (While I was walking through the Old City of Jerusalem a couple of days before I came to Amman, one Palestinian shopkeeper said to me, when I went into his store to browse, "I swear, you are the first person to cross that door in five days." It was just about closing time, 6:30 p.m., and another shopkeeper nearby said to me, "Please, come into my store and be my first and last customer of the day.")

Jordan at least was trying to run the race. Egypt, Syria, and Saudi Arabia were all drifting aimlessly, and, if anything, the upsurge in Israeli-Palestinian fighting gave their retrograde regimes another excuse not to focus on modernization, which might require them to loosen their grip on power or reduce their opportunities for corruption. The ongoing struggle with Israel is such a valuable resource for failed Arab leaders, such a perfect diversion, such an all-encompassing excuse for not democratizing or modernizing their states, as the East Asians did, that they will not give it up easily. Nevertheless, there are many liberals in these countries as well, and if we are ever going to heal the deep wound bin Laden inflicted on relations between the Arab-Muslim world and the West, they will be our necessary partners. The question is how to empower and encourage them.

To me there is only one answer: We have to get that one big question—Who rules Palestine?—out of the way, or at least on track to resolution. There is this illusion in the Bush administration that somehow getting rid of Saddam Hussein in Iraq and installing a democratic regime there will do the trick and magically prompt the whole region to get on the democratization-modernization train. I disagree. Even if that is done and done properly, if the Palestine issue has not been neutralized it will continue to be a ball and chain on Arab and Muslim political development. It will continue to slow down the real reformers and continue to provide an excuse for the phony ones.

But the real reformers are out there, and from the moment 9/11 happened I heard from them—many of them women—by letter, by e-mail, or in conversations. Their voices told me that they feel trapped in countries or communities where they simply cannot break through, but they know what needs to be done, and it is killing them. They know their controlled press is full of lies, their leaders are running from the truth, and their religious authorities are out of touch with the times. Some probably should have been more courageous; others went amazingly far at times, given the dangers of imprisonment or isolation that they face if they openly challenge authority. They wrote me not because they always agreed with me, but because, I think, they sensed that I actually cared about them, or wanted to see them succeed, and they were right. I share with you here just a few of their messages.

One, from a young American Muslim woman, which arrived in my e-mail on September 27, began like this:

I'm very sorry to bother you, but on the chance that you read that letter we've been circulating, I was wondering if you had any comments. . . . I am not an activist—the only flyers I've ever circulated advertised 40 cents per pound of laundry for my college job. Nonetheless, I need to at least try to get Muslims to speak out, which I believe is absolutely necessary, if we're ever to be safe again.

She then signed her name and attached a flyer, addressed to the elders in her Muslim community, that began like this:

We are your youth, the next generation of Islam, your sisters and brothers, and your peers. Many of you are our elders, those who have planted our cherished faith in this country, and as such we respect your thoughts and wish to share with you our own concerns. . . . During the terrorist bombings of the World Trade Center and the Pentagon, we watched helplessly as our friends, families, children, and compatriots were brutally slaughtered. . . . These terrorists are, regrettably, our loudest voice in America as Muslims. When our families came to this country seeking liberty, justice, peace, and a new life they could not have imagined this would be their children's inheritance.

Therefore, let the voice of terrorism not be the strongest voice of Islam, but a voice that we as Muslims have a duty to smother swiftly and justly. . . . We request firmly that the Islamic community denounce these terrorists as "enemies of Islam" regardless of their faith or cause.

Another moving and articulate e-mail came in on May 11, 2002, in the middle of the worst Israeli-Palestinian fighting. It was sent by an Arab liberal friend, who commutes between Beirut and Amman, in response to a query from me about how he was feeling. It began as follows:

Dear Tom: The Arab liberal has become an endangered species. He/she has either opted for a new nationality or has been silenced and rendered irrelevant by decrepit Arab leadership and [Muslim] fundamentalist alternatives. It is self-evident that the relentless decades-long onslaught on Arab liberal traditions has practically erased them from our social fabric and political culture. The vacuum in which Islamic fundamentalist currents have been thriving for close to two decades now is one of the saddest accomplishments of repressive Arab polities. Truth be told, today there is no organized liberal opposition to official oppression. There is only organized, sometimes "well-oiled" Islamic opposition. It fights for people's rights; it fights for liberation; it educates our penniless youth; it helps the destitute cope with poverty; it alone offers an alternative. Meanwhile, we liberals lumber on in our near silence, co-opted by our fears that the alternative to the bankruptcy of our regimes is a brand of political sadism even worse than that from which we have been suffering for the better part of the twentieth century.

Our role, as Arabs, in contributing to this heartbreaking state of affairs is undeniable. But to suggest that our predicament is only of our own making is a gross distortion of history that is no less offensive in its ignorance than Arab claims of helpless victimhood. . . . What has always been most disturbing to Arab liberals is that in fighting reactionary politics, they have found themselves, more often than not, at odds with the U.S. itself. . . .

The U.S., almost without fail, has supported repressive, retrograde political systems and, yes, has actively encouraged and sponsored the growth of Islamic fundamentalism to fight the supposed Soviet menace, illusory though it clearly was. . . . Even the most idealistic amongst us understand that international diplomacy is not the stuff of altruistic human intentions. But what has gnawed at us liberals is that your interests, not only ours, could have been far better served if you had not opted for immediate gratification from unquestioning and subservient clientele, and instead pursued the more creative, if slightly more demanding, "constructive engagement" with the rest of us. . . .

I got an equally profound and thought-provoking e-mail on March 10, 2002, from a young woman from Saudi Arabia. I can only assume that it was authentic, since she signed her name and sent it to me two weeks after I returned from visiting her country. Again, it was the kind of e-mail that reminds you how many good people are out there and that, under the right conditions, America would have partners for change in that part of the world.

I will share just three paragraphs:

Dear Mr. Friedman, I thought of writing you this letter to thank you first as a moderate Saudi for your efforts to expose what's going on in Saudi Arabia. . . . We want the whole world to know that we are suffering as human beings from the religious control that is applied over our minds and our souls. We cannot write anything in the newspapers or publish any book that holds a different theme than what they are used to. Mr. Friedman, our schools teach religious intolerance, most of our mosques preach hate against any non-Muslims, our media is exclusively controlled by the government and religious people. Our moderate ideas have no place to be presented. . . . The Saudi youth are exclusively supplied by only one stream of thinking and any other is banned and labeled as sinful and wrong. This is our problem. . . . The Internet in Saudi Arabia is controlled by the King Abdulaziz City for Science and

Technology and [it] decides for us what to see and what not to see. . . .

Mr. Friedman, we need help. We have been suffering for too long. I am a Saudi female. I have a lot of skills and interests as well as dreams and hopes like any other person in the world, but the difference is that sometimes I cannot do what I want because I am a Saudi female! The kind of Islam Saudi Arabia has teaches people to underestimate women. I cannot apply to any job I want. I cannot go to some colleges I may have an interest in. Also, when I work I should know that I will be harassed and treated differently than my male colleagues. . . . The religious police even decide for me what to wear and also how to behave. . . . I dream of the day when I become independent and have my own car. I dream of having all my rights as a human being. Saudi women need your pen, Mr. Friedman.

. . . I wish. I really wish that you can publish this letter without my real name. I will be so thankful. Yours truly.

And then she signed her name.

My favorite example of this line of thinking from within the Arab-Muslim world was a courageous essay written by the Egyptian satirist and playwright Ali Salem. It was published in the London-based Arabic daily *Al-Hayat* on November 5, 2001. In it, Salem openly mocks the way so many Arab satellite TV stations, newspapers, and intellectuals spend all their time shaking their fists at the world and inciting the Arabs to more self-destructive rage. The article was titled "A New Curriculum of Extremism for Children."

"I am looking for sponsors for the establishment of a modern kindergarten for extremism," wrote Salem.

Thus, I would guarantee that when they reach high school and university, these children will remain extremists; no creature nor any scientific curriculum could undermine their extremism or tame them. We will make the clever ones our journalists and intellectuals, our editors-in-chief, our radio broadcasters, and our officials in all areas of life. Give me your children, and I promise you that they will become bona fide extremists. . . .

I will say to them: "Kids, don't believe that others worship the same God as we; they are infidels who worship other deities. . . . Don't believe the story that they stick to about freedom, democracy, human rights, progress, and civilization; they are liars and deceivers. They hate us because we are better, greater, and stronger than they. You will easily notice that they love life, and that is the weak point that we will exploit. We, in contrast, love death and protect it. Do not believe that Allah created life for us to live, build, and enjoy. [No,] Allah created us to test our ability to rebel against life, to despise it, and to get rid of it at the earliest opportunity. . . .

"Dear children: Hate the beaches. Hate the flowers and the roses. Hate the wheat fields. Hate the trees. Hate music. Hate all manner of artistic, literary, or scientific endeavor. Hate tenderness. Hate reason and intellect. Hate your families and your country-men. Hate others—all others. Hate yourselves. Hate your teach-ers. Hate me. Hate this school. Hate life and everything in it. Go on, get to class."

IT MAKES A VILLAGE

Looking back over the period covered in these columns and this diary, it seems to me I owe the reader the answer to one last question: What is the real meaning of September 11—what did it tell us?

Some historic events turn out to be smaller than they first seem. September 11 is just the opposite. It is, I am convinced, one of those rare major historic events that will turn out to be even larger, even more important, than it first seemed. And we are not at the beginning of the end of understanding it or its implications. We are not even at the end of the beginning. We are still at the beginning of the beginning.

As I write these words I am sitting in the David Citadel Hotel in Jeru-salem looking out at the lit walls of the Old City of Jerusalem. It is late on the evening of April 25, 2002, and I'm back in the country where I accidentally started this journey on September 11. The Old City walls are exactly the right backdrop for what I am about to say, because for me September 11 was all about walls.

What do I mean? I mean that what made 9/11 so profoundly shock-ing to most Americans and civilized people around the world was the fact that it breached such a fundamental wall of civilization. If it is pos-sible to recruit nineteen educated young men to hijack four planes and commit suicide by flying them into the Pentagon and the World Trade Center, and thereby kill close to three thousand totally innocent people who kissed their spouses good-bye that morning and a few hours later were phoning home to their loved ones (if they were lucky) and telling them they were about to die, then anything is possible. Whatever civilizational restraints on human behavior you thought existed before are no longer there. An important wall has been blown away.

Not only has the wall of civilized behavior been breached, but it happened at a time when, thanks to globalization, the walls between countries and people were increasingly being lowered or erased by rapid advances in telecommunications. So the whole world got to watch live as the Twin Towers went down. And they got to tell each other exactly what they felt and thought as they went down. What I'm saying is that 9/11 released some very intense feelings, but it did so in a world in which—thanks to independent satellite TV stations, fiber optics, the Internet, cell phones, beepers, and Palm Pilots—those feelings could be multiplied, amplified, and circulated around the globe faster than ever. It is as if your crazy aunt did something absolutely outrageous and the whole family was now together around the dinner table arguing about it, shouting about it, occasionally exchanging blows over it—and no matter where you went in the house, you couldn't get away from the conversation.

During one of my forays into and out of Pakistan immediately after September 11, I flew via Doha, Qatar. I arrived late on a Monday, filed my column with a Qatar dateline, and the next morning had breakfast with my friend Howaida Nadim from the U.S. Embassy. While Howaida and I were eating breakfast at the Sheraton, and she was filling me in on the latest Arab press reaction to 9/11, her cell phone rang. It was a mutual friend of ours, a top official from Qatar University. She said to Howaida, "I was reading Tom Friedman's column on the Internet and I see he's in Doha. Do you know where he is?"

"He's right here," said Howaida, and she handed me the phone. After I hung up, though, I couldn't help but marvel at just how small a village the world had become: I file my column from Doha, bounce it back to New York, the *Times* bounces it back around the world via nytimes.com, a friend reads it in Qatar on the Internet, discovers I'm there, and then tracks me down via her cell phone—with one call.

The New York Times on the Web has amassed more regular daily readers—over 1.5 million—than *The New York Times* printed on paper. On top of those regulars, nytimes.com now has some 15 million occasional, but registered, users. The effect of this has been to extend the reach of the paper farther and wider than ever before. As a result, even before 9/11 it was rare that I wrote a column that did not elicit some e-mail feedback or letter from some far-flung corner of the world. But this was magnified tenfold after 9/11. The combination of the intensity of this event with the intensity of global integration and with the passion and curiosity that both readers and writers brought to this subject—because they all felt it was about their future and the future of their kids—made this by far the most emotional experience I have ever had as a journalist.

Shortly after my interview with Crown Prince Abdullah, I received an e-mail from a Jordanian friend. A far-right Israeli columnist had written a rabid column in *The Jerusalem Post* that day criticizing me for even quoting Abdullah. My Jordanian friend said this to me in his e-mail:

> Dear Tom, You stirred quite a few feathers in our part of the world: (1) Your articles are reprinted by *The Jordan Times* the minute they get out, and translated into *Al-Raya*, the Arabic newspaper. (2) Your columns are transmitted and discussed in the local NETS—some with, some against (the usual Zionist-Jewish conspiracy theory). . . . Have you seen [the] article in *The Jerusalem Post* today by [so-and-so] attacking you? What a schmuck.

So here was an e-mail from Jordan telling me about how my column was being discussed in the local Internet chat rooms and then commenting on an article in that morning's *Jerusalem Post* which we had both just read over the Web, and then adding that, by the way, he thought the author was a "schmuck"!

After 9/11, I was spending almost an hour a day reading and answering e-mails from all over the world. Thanks to translation services like those of MEMRI or *Middle East Mirror*, you now get instant feedback on what commentators in Arab newspapers are saying about what you are saying, and vice versa. The Saudi ambassador to London publishes a small poem in praise of a Palestinian suicide bomber in an Arabic paper in London, and I've got a translated copy in my e-mail the next morning.

We are all right up in each other's face now, with no walls from behind which we can refine our messages at home, or scream to ourselves in private and then communicate calmly with each other. Instead, I write something in a white-hot rage and it gets right into someone's face in the Middle East or Europe, and then they write back in a white-hot rage, and we both end up angrier than we might have been had we not been so easily connected. It's making the whole world's blood pressure rise in a very dangerous and unhealthy manner.

And this leads to the deeper point that 9/11 is trying to tell us: that while the world is being globalized, shrunk, and tied together ever more closely in technological terms, this has not been accompanied by a better mutual understanding between cultures, countries, and civilizations. There is a mismatch. We are technologically closer—and culturally and politically as far apart as ever, at least among certain communities. Maybe the Internet, fiber optics, and satellites really are, together, like a high-tech Tower of Babel. It's as though God suddenly gave us all the tools to communicate and none of the tools to understand.

In some ways, in fact, technology is actually making understanding more difficult. In part this is because, thanks to the Internet and satellite TV stations, everyone now can watch the news that is perfectly tailored to their own views—and not be exposed to the other guy's point of view at all. As a result, all your own stereotypes get reconfirmed and rein-forced. I was sitting in the Dubai airport watching Arab News Network, ANN—one of the most popular Arab satellite TV stations. It was late at night, and all it was showing was a video stream of Israelis beating, kick-ing, and shooting Palestinians. Not only was there no context, no men-tion of Palestinian suicide bombers, there were no words at all. It was just film footage and martial music. As I was watching, I said to myself, "No wonder Crown Prince Abdullah got enraged by the Israeli crackdown against Palestinians—if this is what he is watching on all those TVs!" American Jews, though, who only get their news about Israel from the right-wing *Jerusalem Post Online*, would also be using a lens that caters totally to their bias. The Internet works the same way. No one has to wait now for CNN or the BBC to pull together a balanced summary of the news. The Internet not only allows you to very selectively choose your news from only those sources you already agree with, it also connects you with other people who hold your views, in chat rooms and on Web sites, so you can feel part of a community—no matter how loony your views are. Now young Arabs can exchange vivid e-mail photographs of what happened in Jenin or somewhere else in the West Bank before they ever hit the newspapers. I was showered with such photos. How accurate were they? Who took them and when? Who knows?

What's even more dangerous is that the Internet, because it has the aura of technology around it, also has a totally undeserved aura of instant credibility. People now say, "It must be true—I read it on the Internet." The fact that it was conveyed in this high-tech manner somehow adds authority to what is conveyed, when in fact the Internet is a global con-veyer of unfiltered, unedited, untreated information. It is not only the greatest tool we have for making people smarter quicker. It's also the great-est tool we have for making people dumber faster. Rumors published on the Internet now have a way of immediately becoming facts. This is particularly true among less-educated people, who might not them-selves have access to the Internet but hear a piece of news or gossip from one of the elites around them who do have access. There is no greater example of this than the canard about the four thousand Jews who were warned not to go to work in the World Trade Center on the morning of September 11.

"In the 1930s, when photography really started to be popularized, people would say, 'The camera never lies,'" said Israeli political theorist Yaron Ezrahi. "Then people slowly discovered that in the right hands the camera was a great tool for distorting reality. The same is true with the Internet. People assume that because it is so much based on technology, the information it carries must be the same. But like the camera, the Internet lies. Many people just don't understand that yet."

The New York Times Magazine (April 21, 2002) happened to run a thoughtful essay by the writer George Packer on exactly this theme just as I was experiencing it most vividly out in the field. He wrote: "In some ways, global satellite TV and Internet access have actually made the world a less understanding, less tolerant place. What the media provide is superficial familiarity—images without context, indignation without remedy. The problem isn't just the content of the media, but the fact that while images become international, people's lives remain parochial—in the Arab world and everywhere else, including here."

Precisely because our ability to integrate technologically has run so far ahead of our ability to understand each other better culturally, politically, and religiously, added Packer, we are at a kind of "halfway point between mutual ignorance and true understanding, [in which] the 'global village' actually resembles a real one . . . a parochial place of manifold suspicions, rumors, resentments, and half-truths."

That is certainly the conclusion I have drawn from my travels since 9/11, and because things are not getting better, many people's natural instinct is to try to protect themselves by rebuilding walls against the craziness going on out there. And that's why the whole bin Laden phenomenon presents a profound challenge to the globalized, integrated world that was being born at the dawn of the new millennium. When Americans, or others, hear all the hate and anger boiling out there against them, even if they don't experience it firsthand, the natural instinct is to want to build walls against it. But walls just aren't what they used to be. In the short term, maybe they can help, but technology is erasing them too quickly.

In the long term, the only answer is to figure out ways to change the attitudes and intentions of the people on the other side of the wall, or at least narrow the gap between differing cultures and political traditions so we can share this shrinking planet. You can't do this on-line. You can't download understanding. You have to upload it, the old-fashioned way—with exchange programs, outreach, diplomacy, real communication, and one-on-one education. As an old friend of mine, Richard Day, a former psychology professor at the American University of Beirut now living with his family in Dubai, remarked to me while I was on a stopover, if we are going to survive globalization "we have to get to know each other, and understand each other better—because now our lives depend on it. It didn't seem that way before. We could live in blissful ignorance. That's over."

After I raised this issue in a column, Allan E. Goodman, who heads the Institute of International Education, sent me a short essay he wrote that made this point so well. It went like this:

> About a year ago . . . I paid a call to the Minister of Education in Indonesia. The minister's first contact with American society was as a high school student in the AFS exchange program. He was assigned to a family in Iowa, where he was "about the only Muslim within five hundred miles." His host mom, he said, got up with him each morning so that he would be sure to say his prayers. The minister never forgot that act of kindness: "It taught me that even Americans who might never visit my country respect other religions and cultures." And I doubt the mom ever forgot the experience either, since it turned out that the call-to-prayer schedule was based on Eastern Standard Time and often meant rising between three and four in the morning Iowa time. . . . Without international education, the Internet, CNN, and all that technology and the media have done to transcend borders are not necessarily changing the way people think, or even assuring that they have accurate information. And the people who bring us the news and keep the Internet running do not get up way before dawn on cold mornings in Iowa so that a young person named Mohammed might be able to say his prayers and then have a hot breakfast.

After 9/11, a lot of people intuitively understood this need for greater understanding in this more intimate world, which is why practically overnight most of the top one hundred best-selling books on Amazon.com were suddenly about Islam, the Arab world, or the Koran. I only wish there were an Arabic Amazon.com and the top one hundred books there after 9/11 were about American civilization. A desire to understand the other has to go both ways, and it is a battle that has to be fought both within and without. That's also why Stephen P. Cohen, the Middle East analyst, is so right when he says, "Either we have wars within civilizations"—wars between those in each civilization who want to embrace modernity, integration, and coexistence with other cultures, faiths, and peoples and those who oppose all that—"or we will end up with wars between civilizations."

And no wall will ever be high enough or thick enough in this age of technology to spare us this challenge.

WALLS

I guess it's appropriate to close this diary where it all really began—at Ground Zero.

I was attending a party in April 2002 when a tall reporter walked up and introduced himself. His name was James Glanz, and he was one of *The New York Times*'s top science writers. About two months after 9/11, James was with the first group of reporters who were taken six stories down beneath the site of the World Trade Center to the PATH train station, part of which was still intact. But that wasn't what he came over to tell me. He came to tell me about something he found there that belonged to me.

"We entered under the ruins through what was the freight entrance of the World Trade Center," said James, who, after piquing my interest, told me the full story two days later. "There was no light, so you had to take a flashlight. It takes a while for your mind to adjust to what it's seeing—because it looks like a place that has been bombed. There's duct-work hanging crazily from the ceiling, beams dangling down like threads, cars at crazy angles that had been smashed in the implosion. We saw one car that had literally been melted into a puddle because of the incredible heat. You could see twenty floors that were compressed to six inches apart. One steel beam had melted into a stalagmite about three feet high, like a drip candle. It was like going down into a prehistoric dig. It was so alien that you needed someone with you to convince you of what you were seeing. A few more levels down was the PATH station and tracks. There was something called the Commuter's Cafe there, and there were still liquor bottles on the shelf behind the bar. There were even glasses still hanging neatly on a rack. A few feet from there, you could see the turnstiles for the trains, and some were still intact. But if you took just one step in the wrong direction, you'd find a black hole.

"Once past the turnstiles, you went down the escalator to the actual train platform. There were three or four intact PATH cars there. I saw one train car, half of which was intact and half of which had been smashed flat, right down to the tracks, by something that had fallen through the ceiling. I walked along, reading some of the advertisements inside the train. The juxtaposition of normal things and total destruction started to get to me. I was taking all this in when I turned around, and behind me I saw this bench. I think it must have been wooden, and there was a little can of unopened iced tea on it. And I asked the person who was with me to shine his flashlight on the iced tea and read me the label.

"Then I looked just a foot away from it, and spread out right there, on the other end of the bench, was *The New York Times*, opened to the Op-Ed page. You couldn't read it in the dark. It had this fine white dust on the top, so I got closer and looked at the open page, and there was your column in the upper-right-hand corner, and there was just a one-word headline, and it said 'Walls.' At that point my hand started shaking. I was trying to see what the column was about, but I just kept coming back to the headline: 'Walls.' I started thinking about it. How does that Robert Frost poem go? 'Something there is that doesn't love a wall, / That sends the frozen-ground-swell under it, / And spills the upper boulders in the sun; . . . / Something there is that doesn't love a wall, / That wants it down.'

"On one level, it is such a civilized thing to build a wall, and especially in the center of lower Manhattan. But it wasn't a force of nature that brought down these walls, it was the forces of anti-civilization. It was forces that you never thought were there before, but they had come into the middle of the most civilized and advanced city, a place that is the most sterling example of our ability to build walls, and therefore civilization. I am not really claustrophobic, but down there you felt all these walls were coming in on you, and then, when I saw that headline on your column—it just really hit me that this is what it was all about."

So what happened to that newspaper?

"It was a little like being in Pompeii," said James. "I didn't feel like I should pick it up and move it. I left it there and just described it in my story the next day. So that's my story about your column. That's where I found it. I don't know where it is now."

James's instinct was exactly right. So much of this story of 9/11 is about walls and how they have been breached: the walls of distance that always seemed to protect America from the world, but can't any longer be counted on to do so after 9/11; the walls that defined permissible civilized behavior that were so violated on that day; the walls that held up one of the great temples of America's civic religion, the World Trade Center; and the walls of that temple which came tumbling down to entomb so many of its workers.

How we learn to live in a world where technology every day is erasing more and more walls—making it so much easier to communicate, trade, and integrate, but also so much easier for small groups to reach around the world and wreak great havoc thousands of miles away—is the great challenge of the new century.

Which is why my final entry into this diary goes like this: I have always wanted to live a long and healthy life—to dance at my daughters' weddings and to shoot my age in golf at seventy-two. But I've never felt that more strongly than now. For one reason: I really want to see how this story ends. I really do.

ACKNOWLEDGMENTS

This book, like virtually my whole journalistic career, has been a collaboration between myself and *The New York Times*. I will be forever indebted to Arthur Sulzberger, Jr., not only for the opportunity he gave me to be the foreign affairs columnist for *The New York Times*, but for the way he constructed the job—with the resources to go anywhere, anytime, and to write whatever I wanted. There is only one newspaper in the world that would have such a job, with such a commitment to foreign news, and it is one led by the Sulzberger family.

Howell Raines, currently the executive editor of the *Times*, was my Washington Bureau Chief and first editorial page editor, and helped nurture me to the point where, when 9/11 happened, I was ready to take it on. He has been a hugely important friend and mentor to me. Gail Collins took over for Howell as editorial page editor in September 2001. The first time Gail and I spoke was on September 11, when I called her from Israel. It was Gail who oversaw most of the columns that went into this book. She could not have been more supportive during the stressful months when these columns were being written and could not have been more helpful in seeing this book project come to fruition. For both those things, I am deeply grateful. The same applies to Gail's deputy and my longtime friend, Phil Taubman.

Tom Carley and Mike Levitas, who oversee all book publications of *New York Times* material, graciously handled all the complicated business and editorial negotiations around this project, and they and my longtime literary agent, confidante, and friend, Esther Newberg, are still talking to one another! For the third time, let me say that Esther is the best. And for the third time, let me say the same about my other friend and most talented editor, Jonathan Galassi, who runs Farrar, Straus and Giroux, and his assistant, James Wilson, who couldn't have been more professional in helping to put this book together. I have had the same agent and book editor for fifteen years and for all three of my books. What could be better?

All the columns in this book first appeared in *The New York Times*. Every one of them was edited for publication in the *Times* by Steve Pickering, Karen Freeman, or Sue Kirby. They not only made each one better, they made each one fit! Many thanks to all of them. As always, my enormously talented and supportive assistant, Maya Gorman, provided her energetic help in making every one of these columns and this book happen. I so enjoy working with her.

And then there is my brain trust—the intellectual partners with whom I discussed virtually every one of these columns. They include Stephen P. Cohen, who simply understands the Middle East, Arabs, and Jews, better than any human being I know. He is such a good soul, who always forces me to dig deeper and helps me get there. I benefited equally from my nearly daily conversations with Michael Mandelbaum, the foreign policy expert at the Johns Hopkins School of Advanced International Studies. Michael's original mind, and his deep knowledge of history and ability to listen to my stories from the field and help me put them in context, were absolutely invaluable. Larry Diamond, the democracy expert at the Hoover Institution, was always generous with his time when I needed help sorting out some of the internal politics surrounding countries involved in this story, especially as it related to developing countries like Pakistan. Hebrew University political theorist Yaron Ezrahi once again brought his creative mind to each one of our many conversations. His voice and his insights enriched many of these columns and the diary. My old friends Rabbi David Hartman and Rabbi Tzvi Marx were, as always, my tutors on things religious. Former Pakistani diplomat and writer Hussein Haqqani, now at the Carnegie Endowment, educated me on Pakistan and made anything I said from there smarter. Finally, to my many e-mail pen pals around the Arab world—Nadia, Howaida, Serene, Lamees, Fadi, Samir—who sometimes agreed with these columns and were sometimes troubled by them, but always gave me the benefit of their honest commentary—thanks.

A special thanks also to my regular golf partners—Joel Finkelstein, Jonathan and Leslie Plutzik, Alan Kotz, Dan Honig, Jack Murphy, Frank Laznovsky, Steve Woolf, George Stevens, Jr., and Vernon Jordan—for keeping me sane since 9/11 by continuing to try to beat my brains out, and to take my money, on the golf course.

Last, my wife, Ann, was my primary and toughest editor. She always brings out the best in me and never tolerates anything less. I am so, so lucky to have her as my wife, friend, and inspiration. And we are both so lucky to have my mom, Margaret Friedman, and Ann's parents, Matt and Kay Bucksbaum, standing behind the two of us. And then there are

Orly and Natalie, my girls. They had to hear many of these columns first recited at the dinner table or in the form of a rant from their father. They also had to put up with my long absences after 9/11 to countries where they don't sell souvenirs.

For all that, and for so much more, I dedicate this book to them.